Business English

Seventh Edition

Mary Ellen Guffey

Professor of Business Emeritus, Los Angeles Pierce College

SOUTH-WESTERN

THOMSON LEARNING

Australia · Canada · Mexico · Singapore · Spain · United Kingdom · United States

Business English, 7e by Mary Ellen Guffey

Publisher: Dave Shaut
Acquisitions Editor: Pamela M. Person
Developmental Editor: Mary Draper
Media Developmental Editor: Sally Nieman
Marketing Manager: Mark Callahan
Production Editor: Kelly Keeler
Media Production Editor: Robin Browning
Manufacturing Coordinator: Sandee Milewski
Production House: WordCrafters Editorial Services
Printer: Transcontinental

Printed in Canada
   3 4 5 03

For more information contact South-Western, 5101 Madison Road, Cincinnati, Ohio, 45227 or find us on the Internet at http://www.swcollege.com

For permission to use material from this text or product, contact us by
• **telephone: 1-800-730-2214**
• **fax: 1-800-730-2215**
• **web: http://www.thomsonrights.com**

Library of Congress Cataloging-in-Publication Data

Guffey, Mary Ellen.
   Business English / Mary Ellen Guffey.—7th ed.
      p. cm.
   Includes index.
   ISBN 0-324-05854-3 (pbk.)
      1. English language—Business English. I. Title.

PE1115.G83 2002
428.2′088′65—dc21

                                    2001020402

Student Edition with Electronic Study Guide ISBN 0-324-05854-3
Annotated Instructor's Edition with Electronic Study Guide ISBN 0-324-05855-1
Student Edition (only) ISBN 0-324-12154-7
Annotated Instructor's Edition (only) ISBN 0-324-14495-4
Electronic Study Guide (only) ISBN 0-324-12155-5

Business English

Contents

Preface for Students

Dear Student:

Dr. Mary Ellen Guffey

For over two decades *Business English* has helped hundreds of thousands of students improve their language skills. It was written to assist you in reviewing English grammar, punctuation, style, and usage. By improving your control of these language principles, you'll feel more confident about yourself. You'll also have a strong foundation for becoming an effective business communicator. In addition, this book will help you improve your awareness of and ability to use digital tools in this Internet age.

How to Use This Book

You can get the most out of this book by following this three-step plan:

1. **Before you read a chapter,** set aside a quiet time and place where you can study without interruption. First, examine the chapter objectives to preview what will be covered. Then, take the pretest to assess your knowledge. Next, check your answers (given at the bottom of the page).
2. **As you read a chapter,** use a marking pencil to highlight important concepts and examples. If you don't understand a principle or if you have a question, write your question in the margin so that you can ask about it in class. Because the chapters are fairly short, you'll probably read them quickly. Remember, this is one book that you should write in. Don't be afraid to mark it up!
3. **After reading a chapter,** review the passages you highlighted. Ask yourself whether you understand the concepts presented. Then, take the posttest and compare it with your pretest performance. Next, complete Exercise A and immediately check your answers (at the bottom of the page). If you have more than three incorrect responses (out of ten), reread the chapter before continuing with the other reinforcement exercises. Complete all the assigned exercises before going to class.

Some students try to fill in answers for the reinforcement exercises without first reading a chapter. This is like trying to program a VCR without reading the instruction manual. You'll be much more successful if you read the chapter first!

Features to Make You Successful

The following features and supplements for *Business English* will help you understand and remember the language concepts presented.

- **Three-Level Approach.** Beginning with Chapter 4, language concepts appear in levels. These levels progress from fundamental, frequently used concepts in Level I to more complex concepts in Level III. Each level has its own trial exercises as well as numerous reinforcement exercises. Dividing a chapter into three levels provides you with small, easily mastered learning segments.

- **Hotline Queries.** One of the most popular features of *Business English* has been its questions and answers from grammar hotline services across the country. These authentic questions—and the author's suggested answers to them—illustrate everyday communication problems just like the ones you will meet on the job. As you read the questions, imagine how you would answer them.

- **Pretests and Posttests.** Each chapter includes a brief pretest to preview concepts, stimulate interest, and help you recognize your strengths and weaknesses. The posttests enable you to judge your achievement and improvement.

- **Supplementary Self-Help Exercises.** Most students ask for additional try-out exercises to test their learning. *Business English* has hundreds of extra exercises at the back of the book. The answers are also provided so that you receive immediate feedback.

- **Learning Web Ways.** New to this edition are short exercises that help you improve your Internet skills. You'll learn about browsers, URLs, hot links, and many exciting tips for using the Web effectively.

- **Writer's Workshops.** At the end of each unit, special tips and exercises introduce basic writing principles. Workshop activities teach you how to write sentences, paragraphs, e-mail messages, memos, letters, and short reports.

- **Editor's Challenge**. Cumulative proofreading activities show you realistic business documents while at the same time testing your skills at applying the grammar principles you are learning.

- **Marginal Annotations.** The following icons identify helpful, interesting marginal notes giving you study advice and extra information:

 Study Tip

Memory devices and learning suggestions appear as study tips. They help you understand and retain the many language principles you will be reviewing.

 Career Tip

These tips suggest applications and practical career advice that relate language concepts you are learning to your needs on the job.

 Spot the Blooper

To provide humorous relief from the sometimes heavy load of grammar and mechanics, these bloopers demonstrate common language errors.

Did You Know?

These inquisitive tidbits relate interesting trivia to *Business English* concepts.

 Hot Link

Recommended Web sites help you learn more about the chapter.

Unparalleled Digital Study Aids to Reinforce Your Learning

In addition to a free CD-ROM Study Guide, we provide you with the most comprehensive student learning Web site on the Internet. The unmatched digital study aids that support *Business English* will help you develop language skills while at the same time strengthening your computer skills.

- **FREE CD-ROM Study Guide**. Additional reinforcement exercises for each chapter are provided on a special CE-ROM disk written just for *Business English*. This CD is free with every new book.

- **Web Interactive Chapter Reviews**. You can test your comprehension and retention of chapter concepts by taking a chapter review quiz at the Guffey Web site (see the URLs below).

- **Web Editor's Challenge**. At the Guffey Web site you will find for each chapter a business document badly in need of editing. These documents are a terrific learning tool, and no rekeying is needed. You can focus totally on proofreading and revising.

- **Web PowerPoint™ Slides.** At the Guffey site these interactive slides provide a colorful, quick summary of chapter concepts. You can spend as long as you like reviewing at your own pace.

- **Web Crossword Puzzles**. Challenging and entertaining crossword puzzles strengthen your grasp of chapter concepts and vocabulary.

- **WebCheck Reinforcement Exercises**. These matching, fill-in, multiple-choice, and sentence revision exercises progress from simple to complex and help you understand and remember the language concepts you are learning.

Premier Student Web Site

No other author provides such a comprehensive Web site to partner with a textbook. With this edition, we've added many new interactive online exercises just for *Business English* students. Because nearly all of these exercises provide instant feedback, it's like having your own personal tutor. In addition to all of the *Business English* learning tools, the Guffey Student Web site provides a constantly updated list of employment, intern, résumé, and job links. And when you need a break from studying, you can click on "Fun Time." Be sure to check us out at **<http://www.westwords.com/guffey/students.html>** or its mirror site **<http://www.meguffey.com>**.

My Personal Guarantee

When you finish reading and studying this book, I personally guarantee that your language skills will be much better than when you started. However, your mind is not a computer and can't record everything for instant recall. Like most professionals, you will occasionally need reference books to find answers. That's why you'll probably want to keep this book, along with a good dictionary and an office manual, for review and reference after you leave this class.

If you have any comments about this book or suggestions for improvement, please let me know. I wish you well in your studies!

Dr. Mary Ellen Guffey
Professor of Business

E-mail: meguffey@westwords.com
Web: http://www.westwords.com/guffey/students.html
Mirror Web Site: http://meguffey.com

Pretest

In the following sentences, faulty grammar, punctuation, capitalization, or number expression may appear. For each sentence underline any inappropriate form(s). Then write a corrected form in the space provided. Hint: one sentence at each level is correct. In this case, write C.

Example: The inheritance will be given to my brother and <u>myself</u> on our twenty-first birthdays.   **me** _____

L e v e l   I

1. Mr. Cortez paid into the system for thirty years, then he retired and began to draw benefits.   _____

2. A tax seminar in Boulder, Colorado in the spring sounds as if it will be worthwhile.   _____

3. The announcement from our Human Resources Department surprised the secretaries as much as I.   _____

4. Bill and I certainly appreciate you answering the telephone when he and I are away from the office.   _____

5. A list of restaurants with dinners costing less than $6 were given to her and her friends.   _____

6. Every classified employee, as well as every management and certified employee, is eligible for sales discounts.   _____

7. For you Mrs. Alison, we have a one-year subscription to your favorite magazine.   _____

8. Under the circumstances, we can give you only 90 days time in which to sell the house and its contents.   _____

9. We normally hire only experienced operators; but on occasion we consider well-trained individuals who lack experience.   _____

10. During the fall Lisa took courses in history, spanish, and accounting.   _____

11. All our customers names and addresses have been transferred to our computer database.   _____

12. Either Mr. Harris or his assistant will be working at the shop on the next two Sunday's.   _____

13. Of the 500 letters mailed, Mr. Turner's secretary reported that only five were returned.   _____

14. If you want a three-week vacation, you must speak to the Manager immediately.   _____

15. The warehouse has been moved from 5th Street to 39th Street.   _____

16. Chapter 15, which is entitled "Credit Buying," is one of the best chapters in *Today's Consumer*.   _____

17. Before her trip to the East last summer, my mother purchased a Kodak Camera.   _____

18. We need only 20 34-cent postage stamps to finish the mailing.   _____

19. Your account is now 90 days overdue, therefore, we are submitting it to an agency for collection.   _____

20. I feel badly about your missing the deadline, but the application has been lying on your desk for 15 days.   _____

21. The award will be made to whomever has the best record.   _____

22. All letter styles must comply to those shown in the company style manual.   _____

23. Iris Products is larger than any food processing plant on the West Coast.   _____

24. The number of employees interested in attending the seminar are surprising.   _____

25. Our school's alumni are certainly different than its currently enrolled students.   _____

26. She is one of those efficient, competent managers who is able to give sincere praise for work done well.   _____

27. Because she looks like her sister, Kendra is often taken to be her.   _____

28. If I was him, I would call the Morrises' attorney at once.   _____

29. Three employees were given merit raises, namely, Carol Chang, Tom Nelson, and Toni Simpson.   _____

30. Surely it was he who left the package on the boss's desk.   _____

Business English

unit 1 Laying a Foundation

chapter 1
Reference Skills

Objectives

When you have completed the materials in this chapter, you will be able to do the following:

- Describe three types of dictionaries.
- Use a dictionary confidently to determine spelling, meaning, pronunciation, syllabication, accent, word usage, and word history.
- Select a dictionary to suit your needs.
- Anticipate what information is included in dictionaries and what information is not.
- Understand the value of reference manuals.
- Use an electronic dictionary with confidence.

Each chapter begins with a brief pretest. Answer the questions in the pretest to assess your prior knowledge of the chapter content and also to give yourself a preview of what you will learn. Compare your answers with those at the bottom of the page. When you complete the chapter, take the posttest to measure your improvement.

Write *T* (true) or *F* (false) after the following statements.

1. College students need a current unabridged dictionary for daily use.   _____

2. Dictionary guide words help readers pronounce words correctly.   _____

3. The usage label *archaic* means that a word is very old.   _____

4. All dictionaries present word definitions in the same order.   _____

5. A reader should not expect to find the spelling of the plural form of *branch* in most dictionaries.   _____

1. F   2. F   3. T   4. F   5. T

2

Business English is the study of language fundamentals. These basics include grammar, usage, punctuation, capitalization, and number style. Because businesspeople must express their ideas clearly and correctly, such language basics are critical. In today's workplace, you can expect to be doing more communicating than ever before. You will be participating in meetings, writing reports, and sending many e-mail messages. Suddenly, business English skills are becoming very important. Businesspeople who never expected to be doing much writing on the job are finding that the Internet is forcing everyone to exchange written messages. As a result, businesspeople are increasingly aware of their communication skills. Misspelled words, incorrect grammar, sloppy punctuation—all these faults stand out glaringly when printed. Not only are people writing more, but their messages are traveling farther and being seen by larger audiences than ever before.

Because of the growing emphasis on exchanging information, business English is increasingly relevant. As a businessperson, you will want to feel confident about your writing skills. This textbook and this course can help you sharpen your skills and greatly increase the confidence you have in expressing your ideas. Improving your communication skills is the first step toward success in your education, your career, and your life.

When Jennifer S. enrolled in business English, she did not plan to become an expert in the subject. When she finished the course, she didn't think of herself as an expert, although she had done well enough in the class. But when she started to work, she discovered that many of her fellow workers considered her an English expert. Most of them had no training in grammar or they had studied it long ago, and their skills were rusty. Jennifer found that even her boss asked her questions such as "What are they doing now about letter salutations?" or "Where do you think we should put that apostrophe?" Everyone seemed to think that because she had just finished school, she would know all the answers. Jennifer didn't know all the answers. But she knew where to find them.

One of the goals of your education is to know where to find answers, as well as how to interpret the information you find. Experts do not know *all* the answers. Attorneys refer to casebooks. Doctors consult their medical libraries. And you, as a student of the language, must develop skill and confidence in using reference materials. You will become a business English expert not only by learning from this textbook but also by learning where to find additional data when you need it.

Using references should become second nature to you. You'll use dictionaries and online resources to verify word spellings and meanings, punctuation style, and usage. You can find information quickly and efficiently by having your own personal library of reference materials. At the minimum a current desk or college dictionary and a good reference manual are needed. Another helpful reference book is a thesaurus, which is a collection of *synonyms* (words with similar meanings) and *antonyms* (words with opposite meanings). Many helpful resources are now available digitally, whether online or in a software program such as MS Word.

Dictionaries

Businesspeople today make use of both print dictionaries and online dictionaries. First, you'll learn about print dictionaries, including how to select one and how to use it. Then, you'll learn about using an online dictionary, such as the one that comes with your word processing software.

Career Tip

The lifetime earnings of a person with a college degree are about three times those of a person without a college degree.

Spot the Blooper

On résumés that crossed the desk of personnel expert Robert Half: "I am a rabid typist." "Here are my qualifications for you to overlook." "Hope to hear from you shorty."

Selecting a Print Dictionary

Not all dictionaries are the same, as you will doubtless notice when you shop for one. To make a wise selection, you should know how to distinguish among three kinds of print dictionaries: pocket, desk, and unabridged. You should also know when your dictionary was published (the copyright date), and you should examine its special features.

- **Pocket dictionary.** As its name suggests, a pocket dictionary is small. Generally, it contains no more than 75,000 entries, making it handy to carry to class and efficient to use. However, a pocket dictionary doesn't contain enough entries to be adequate for postsecondary or college reference homework.

- **Desk or college-level dictionary.** A desk or college-level dictionary generally contains over 170,000 entries plus extra features. For college work you should own a current desk dictionary. The following list shows some of the best-known desk dictionaries. Notice that the titles of three dictionaries contain the name *Webster*. Because names cannot be copyrighted, any publisher may use the word *Webster* on its dictionary. Definitions and usage in this textbook are based on *Merriam-Webster's Collegiate Dictionary*, Tenth Edition. Many publishers rely on this dictionary as their standard. Some readers, however, prefer *The American Heritage College Dictionary*. It provides more plural spellings, more usage labels, and more opinions about appropriate usage than other dictionaries. Any of the following dictionaries is a good choice for postsecondary and college students:

  The American Heritage College Dictionary
  Random House Webster's College Dictionary
  Merriam-Webster's Collegiate Dictionary, Tenth Edition*
  Webster's New World Dictionary

  *The standard dictionary for definitions and usage in this book.

Study Tip

To *abridge* means to "shorten"; a bridge shortens the distance between points. An "unabridged" book has not been shortened.

- **Unabridged dictionary.** An unabridged dictionary is a complete dictionary. (Abridged dictionaries, such as pocket and desk dictionaries, are shortened or condensed.) Because unabridged dictionaries contain nearly all English words, they are large, heavy volumes. Schools, libraries, newspaper offices, and business offices concerned with editing or publishing use unabridged dictionaries. One of the best-known unabridged dictionaries is *Merriam-Webster's New International Dictionary*. It includes over 450,000 entries. Another famous unabridged dictionary is the *Oxford English Dictionary (OED)*. This 20-volume set shows the historical development of all English words; it is often used by professional writers, scholars of the language, and academics. CD-ROM versions are available for easy computer searching.

- **Copyright date.** If the copyright date of your current dictionary shows that it was published ten or more years ago, consider investing in a more recent edition. English is a responsive, dynamic language that admits new words and recognizes changes in meaning, spelling, and usage of familiar words. These changes are reflected in an up-to-date dictionary.

- **Features.** In selecting a dictionary, check the features it offers in addition to vocabulary definitions. Many editions contain biographical and geographical data, abbreviations, standard measurements, signs, symbols, foreign words and phrases, lists of colleges and universities, and information about the language.

Using a Print Dictionary

Whether you purchased a new one or you are using a family dictionary, take a few moments to become familiar with it so that you can use it wisely.

- **Introduction.** Before using your dictionary, take a look at the instructions located in the pages just before the beginning of the vocabulary entries. Pay particular attention to the order of definitions. Some dictionaries show the most common definitions first. Other dictionaries develop meanings historically; that is, the first known meaning of the word is shown first.

- **Guide words.** In boldface type at the top of each dictionary page are two words that indicate the first and last entries on the page. When searching for a word, look *only* at these guide words until you locate the desired page.

- **Syllabication.** Most dictionaries show syllable breaks with a centered dot, as you see in Figure 1.1 for the word *signify*. Compound words are sometimes troublesome to dictionary users. If a compound word is shown with a centered dot, it is one word, as in *work•out* (workout). If a compound word is shown with a hyphen, it is hyphenated, as in *old-fashioned*. If two words appear without a centered dot or a hyphen, they should be written as two words, as in *work up*. If you find no entry for a word or phrase in a college-level dictionary, you may usually assume that the words are written separately, for example, *ball field*. For newer terms, such as *home page* or *firewall*, you should check an online dictionary.

- **Pronunciation.** Special symbols (diacritical marks) are used to help you pronounce words correctly. A detailed explanation of pronunciation symbols is found in the front pages of a dictionary; a summary of these symbols may appear at the bottom of each set of pages. If two pronunciations are possible, the preferred one is usually shown first.

- **Accent.** Most dictionaries show accents with a raised stress mark immediately following the accented syllable, as shown for the syllable *sig* in our example. Other dictionaries use a raised stress mark immediately *preceding* the accented syllable (*'sig ni'fi*). Secondary stress may be shown in lighter print (as illustrated on the syllable *fi* from our example), or it may be shown with a *lowered* accent mark (*'sig ni,fi*).

- **Etymology.** College-level dictionaries provide in square brackets [ ] the brief history or etymology of the word. For example, the word *signify* has its roots in Middle English, Old French, and Latin. Keys to etymological abbreviations may be found in the introductory notes in your dictionary. Do not confuse the etymological definition shown in brackets with the actual word definition(s).

Hot Link

Merriam-Webster maintains an award-winning Web site <http://www.m-w.com>. At this site you can play word games as well as look up definitions, pronunciation, etymology, spelling, and usage.

Hot Link

For word lovers with online connections, check out Merriam-Webster's Word of the Day feature <http://www.m-w.com>. Each day editors define a new word, use it creatively, and, best of all, include a "Did You Know" section offering bits of fascinating word lore.

Figure 1.1
Dictionary Entry

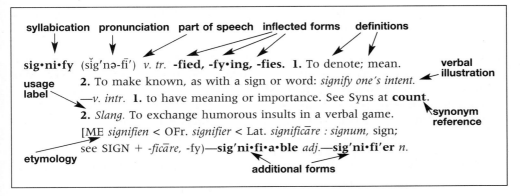

© Houghton Mifflin Company. Reproduced by permission from *The American Heritage Dictionary of the English Language. Third College Edition.*

Career Tip

Businesspeople are judged by the words they use. Knowing the part of speech for a word helps you use it correctly. For example, if you discover that a word is a verb, you won't try to use it to describe a noun.

- **Part of speech.** Following the phonetic pronunciation of an entry word is an italicized or boldfaced label indicating what part of speech the entry word represents. The most common labels are the following:

adj	(adjective)	*prep*	(preposition)
adv	(adverb)	*pron*	(pronoun)
conj	(conjunction)	*v* or *vb*	(verb)
interj	(interjection)	*vt* or *v tr*	(verb transitive)
n	(noun)	*vi* or *v int*	(verb intransitive)

Spelling, pronunciation, and meaning may differ for a given word when that word functions as different parts of speech. Therefore, check its grammatical label carefully. If the parts of speech seem foreign to you at this time, do not despair. Chapter 2 and successive chapters will help you learn more about the parts of speech.

- **Labels.** Not all words listed in dictionaries are acceptable in business or other writing. Usage labels are given to warn readers about the use of certain words. In the dictionary entry shown in Figure 1.1, notice that one meaning for the word *signify* is labeled *slang*. The following list defines *slang* and other usage labels:

Label	Example
archaic: words surviving from a previous period	*knave* (meaning *male servant*)
obsolete: no longer in use	*miss* (meaning *a loss*)
colloquial or *informal**: used in casual writing or conversation	*shindig* (*festive party*)
slang: very informal but may be sparingly used for effect	*boonies* (*rural area*)
nonstandard and *substandard*: not conforming to usage among educated speakers	*hisself* (*himself*)
dialect, *Brit.*, *South*, *Scot*, etc.: used in certain regions	*bogle* (used in Britain to mean *goblin*)

*Some dictionaries no longer use the labels *colloquial* or *informal*.

If no usage label appears, a word is considered standard; that is, it is acceptable for all uses. However, it should be noted that many lexicographers have substantially reduced the number of usage labels in current editions. Lexicographers, by the way, are those who make dictionaries.

- **Inflected forms.** When nouns, verbs, adverbs, or adjectives change form grammatically, they are said to be *inflected*, as when *child* becomes *children*. Because of limited space, dictionaries usually show only irregular inflected forms. Thus, nouns with irregular or unusual plurals (*wife*, *wives*) will be shown. Verbs with irregular tenses or difficult spelling (*gratified*, *gratifying*) will be shown. Adverbs or adjectives with irregular comparatives or superlatives (*good*, *better*, *best*) will also be shown. But regular noun plurals, verb tenses, and comparatives generally will *not* be shown in dictionaries. Succeeding chapters will elucidate regular and irregular parts of speech.

- **Synonyms and antonyms.** *Synonyms*, words having similar meanings, are often provided after word definitions. For example, a synonym for *elucidate* is *explain*.

Spot the Blooper

In a Chinese fortune cookie: "You will gain admiration from your pears."

Synonyms are helpful as word substitutes. *Antonyms*, words having opposite meanings, appear less frequently in dictionaries; when included, they usually follow synonyms. One antonym for *elucidate* is *confuse*. The best place to find synonyms and antonyms is in a thesaurus.

Plugging in to Electronic Dictionaries

An increasing number of electronic resources are available both on the Internet and on CD-ROMs. As shown in Figure 1.2, various kinds of dictionaries can be used at Web sites. By accessing Merriam-Webster Online, for example, you can search for word definitions at no cost. The site for OneLook Dictionaries provides over 600 different dictionaries in various fields. And all of these are searchable electronically. This means you can find words quickly and easily. You can also look for unusual words in a wide range of areas without owning a specialized dictionary and without traveling to a library. Electronic dictionaries are especially useful because, unlike print dictionaries, they can be updated immediately when new words enter the language.

Some people, however, don't want to be bothered with firing up a computer and using a Web browser to access online dictionaries. But they do want access to a large database of words, and they prefer the ease of electronic searching. For these people, a CD-ROM dictionary, such as the Microsoft Encarta World English Dictionary or the Random House Compact Unabridged Dictionary, is the answer. By the way, many new electronic dictionaries not only provide definitions but also offer *pronunciations*. Of course, your computer must be equipped with a sound card.

Figure 1.2
Notable Electronic Dictionaries

- **Merriam-Webster Online <http://www.m-w.com>.** Indicates the pronunciations, etymologies, and authoritative definitions of a vast number of words. Site also provides essays on the history of English and the processes involved in the making of dictionaries. *Word of the Day* feature defines an infrequently used word.

- **OneLook Dictionaries <http://www.onelook.com>.** Features an index of over 350,000 words contained in more than 600 different dictionaries. Site accesses computer/Internet, science, medical, technological, business, sports, religion, and general dictionaries.

- **Management and Technology Dictionary <http://www.euro.net>.** Claims to be the largest Internet dictionary on management and technology.

- **Microsoft Encarta World English Dictionary (CD-ROM).** Features more than 3 million words with contributions from 250 lexicographers working in ten countries. Purports to be the world's first English dictionary. Also available in print version that is updated on the Web.

- **Random House Compact Unabridged Dictionary (CD-ROM).** Comprehensive resource with definitions for over 315,000 entries. Includes over 2,000 line drawings and offers spoken pronunciation of 120,000 words.

- **Oxford English Dictionary, 2nd ed. (CD-ROM).** Claims to be the most authoritative English dictionary. Traces use of each word through the centuries. Provides easy access to more than 2.5 million illustrative quotations. Continually updated Web version available by subscription **<www.oed.com>.**

For links to dozens of online dictionaries and other electronic reference tools, visit the Guffey Web site **<http://meguffey.com/reftools.html>.**

Using Electronic Dictionary Programs

Most high-end word processing programs today come with a dictionary/thesaurus feature that helps you locate misspelled words as well as search for synonyms and antonyms.

- **Locating misspelled words.** An electronic dictionary (also called a *spell checker*) compares your typed words with those in the computer's memory. MS Word uses a wavy red line to underline misspelled words caught "on the fly" as you key. If you immediately recognize the error, you can quickly key in the correction. If you see the red wavy line and don't know what's wrong, you can click *Tools* and *Spelling and Grammar*. This opens a dialog box, as shown in Figure 1.3. The box generally shows a variety of options to solve your spelling problem. If one of the suggested spellings appears helpful, you can click it and the misspelled word is replaced. If none of the suggestions is useful, you can type in the correct version in the "Not in Dictionary" box.

  Although some writers dismiss dictionary spell checkers as an annoyance, most of us are only too happy to have our typos and misspelled words detected. The real problem is that spell checkers can't always distinguish between similar words, such as *too* and *two* and many other confusions. That's why you're wise to print out every message and proofread it word by word.

- *Searching for synonyms and antonyms.* Electronic dictionary programs can also help you find alternative word choices. Let's say you are writing a message and you find yourself repeating the same word. With MS Word you can highlight the overused word and click on *Tools, Language,* and *Thesaurus*. A number of synonyms appear in a dialog box, as illustrated in Figure 1.4. If none of the suggested words seems right, you can change the search term by using a closely related word from the *Replace with Synonym* column. From the new *Meanings* list,

Figure 1.3
Locating Spelling Errors with MS Word

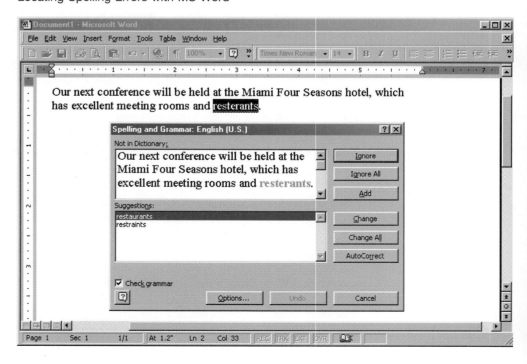

Words not found in the computer's dictionary are highlighted. You can edit the word or select a word in the "Suggestions" box.

MS Word lists synonyms based on the meaning that is highlighted in the "Meanings" box.

Figure 1.4
Searching for Synonyms and Antonyms

you can also change the word or phrase to help you find the most precise word for your meaning.

You can use an electronic thesaurus feature to look up words and phrases even if you haven't selected any words in your document. Just type in the word and click the *Tools, Language*, and *Thesaurus* options. A good online thesaurus can be a terrific aid to writers who want to increase their vocabularies and are seeking precise language.

Reference Manuals

In addition to one or more printed dictionaries, every writer and business communicator should have a good reference manual or handbook readily available.

Reference Manual Versus Dictionary

A reference manual generally contains helpful information not available in a dictionary. Most reference manuals provide information such as the following:

- **Punctuation.** Detailed explanations of punctuation rules are presented logically. A well-written manual will also provide ample illustrations of punctuation usage so that the reader can readily find solutions to punctuation dilemmas.

- **Hyphenation.** Dictionaries provide syllable breaks. Words, however, cannot be divided at all syllable breaks. A reference manual will supply rules for, and examples of, word division. Moreover, a good reference manual will explain when compound adjectives such as *up-to-the-minute* should be hyphenated.

- **Capitalization.** Complete rules with precise examples illustrating capitalization style will be shown.

- *Number style.* Deciding whether to write a number as a figure or as a word can be very confusing. A reference manual will provide both instruction and numerous examples illustrating number and word styles.

Other topics covered in reference manuals are confusing words (such as *effect* and *affect*), abbreviations, contractions, literary and artistic titles, forms of address, and letter and report formats. In addition, some manuals contain sections devoted to English grammar and office procedures. This textbook is correlated with the widely used *Handbook for Office Workers* (South-Western College Publishing) by Clark and Clark.

Reference Manual Versus Textbook

You may be wondering how a reference manual differs from a business English textbook such as the one you are now reading. Although their content is similar, the primary difference is one of purpose. A textbook is developed *pedagogically*—that is, for teaching—so that the student understands and learns concepts. A reference manual is organized *functionally*, so that the reader finds accurate information efficiently. A well-written reference manual is complete, coherent, and concise.

Most of the language and style questions that perplex businesspeople and students could be answered quickly by a trained person using a reliable dictionary and a well-written reference manual.

Now complete the reinforcement exercises on the following pages.

Name _____

Note: At the beginning of every set of reinforcement exercises, a self-check exercise is provided so that you will know immediately if you understand the concepts presented in the chapter. Do not look at the answers until you have completed the exercise. Then compare your responses with the answers shown at the bottom of the page. If you have more than three incorrect responses, reread the chapter before continuing with the other reinforcement exercises.

A. (Self-check) Write *T* (true) or *F* (false) after the following statements.

1. Students and office workers would find an unabridged dictionary handy to carry with them. _____

2. Guide words help a dictionary user to pronounce a word. _____

3. The label *colloquial* means that a word is informal and may be used in casual writing and conversation. _____

4. Most dictionaries use centered dots to indicate syllables. _____

5. Dictionaries usually show noun plurals only if they are irregular. _____

6. Synonyms are words that are spelled alike or sound alike. _____

7. Rules for hyphenating compound adjectives may be found in a reference manual. _____

8. All dictionaries show definitions in historical order. _____

9. Internet dictionaries are generally more up-to-date than print dictionaries. _____

10. Internet dictionaries may be fast and current, but they are also expensive to use. _____

Check your answers at the bottom of the page.

Use a desk, college-level, or electronic dictionary to complete the following exercises. If you do not have a dictionary, use one at a library. The definitions, pronunciations, and usage in this book come from *Merriam-Webster's Collegiate Dictionary*, Tenth Edition.

B. Select the letter that provides the best definition or synonym for each word shown.

1. imminent (adj)   (a) famous, (b) impending, (c) infamous, (d) emphatic _____

2. entomology (n)   (a) study of words, (b) study of fossils, (c) study of insects, (d) love of outdoors _____

3. oblivious (adj)   (a) unmindful, (b) old, (c) fixed, (d) stubborn _____

4. plethora (n)   (a) abundance, (b) shortage, (c) infectious disease, (d) deciduous shrub _____

5. superficial (adj)   (a) managerial, (b) attractive, (c) elevated, (d) shallow _____

C. Write the correct form of the following words. Use a current dictionary to determine whether they should be written as one or two words or should be hyphenated.

Example: print out (n)   <u>printout</u>

1. double space (v) _____   4. out of date _____

2. key board _____   5. street smart _____

3. in as much as _____   6. sweat suit _____

1. F 2. F 3. T 4. T 5. T 6. F 7. T 8. F 9. T 10. F

D. For each of the following words, write the syllable that receives the primary accent. Then give a brief definition or synonym of the word.

Word	Syllable	Definition or Synonym
Example: judicious	di _____	prudent, exhibiting sound judgment
1. comparable	_____	_____
2. desert (n)	_____	_____
3. desert (v)	_____	_____
4. indefatigable	_____	_____
5. irrevocable	_____	_____
6. posthumous	_____	_____

E. If your dictionary shows usage labels for the following words, write them in the spaces provided. If no label appears for a word, which of the following labels would you consider giving it if you were a lexicographer? Put your initials next to the labels you suggest.

Labels: archaic   nonstandard   colloquial or informal   dialect   slang

Example: goober   dialect _____

1. dork _____   4. bonnet (meaning car hood) _____

2. dinkum _____   5. irregardless _____

3. grizzle (gray hair) _____   6. sawbones _____

F. Select the letter that most accurately completes the sentence.

1. The word *chauvinism* derives from Nicholas *Chauvin*, a Frenchman known as a(n) _____

    a. fanatical bomb thrower   **b.** extreme misogynist (woman hater)
    c. excessive patriot   **d.** radical critic of Napoleon

2. If you *encrypt* an e-mail message, you are _____ it. _____

    a. preserving   **b.** encoding (scrambling)   **c.** erasing
    d. decoding (unscrambling)

3. An office desk and chair that were *ergonomically* designed would _____

    a. reduce fatigue and discomfort   **b.** improve office decor   **c.** save money
    d. eliminate depreciation

4. The abbreviation* for the Occupational Safety and Health Administration is _____

    a. O.S.H.A.   **b.** Osha   **c.** OSHA   **d.** OS&HA

5. Which of the following is correctly written? _____

    a. Monarch butterfly   **b.** monarch butterfly   **c.** Monarch Butterfly
    d. monarch Butterfly

6. The film star's sequined jumpsuit was somewhat *ostentatious* for the opening of a juice bar; thus the outfit was considered too _____

    a. expensive   **b.** showy   **c.** revealing   **d.** dated

7. If an expression is *redundant,* it is _____

    a. repetitive   **b.** obsolete   **c.** clever   **d.** awkward

Does your dictionary list abbreviations after the main entries?

8. The word *harass*, which means "to annoy persistently," may be pronounced _____

   a. ha-RASS   **b.** HAR-ass   **c.** either a or b   **d.** neither a nor b

G. Writing Exercise. All employers seek workers with good writing skills. In *Business English*, you will find unit workshops devoted to developing your writing skills. In addition, each chapter will include a short writing exercise. Let's say that a friend asks you to explain what an electronic dictionary is and why it might be useful. Write about three sentences with your explanation.

_____

_____

_____

_____

Editor's Challenge

The following e-mail message contains 15 misspelled or misused words, some of which you looked up in earlier exercises. Underline any error and write a correction above it. Note: The Editor's Challenge documents that you see in this book are double-spaced so that you can write in corrections. Actual business documents would be single-spaced.

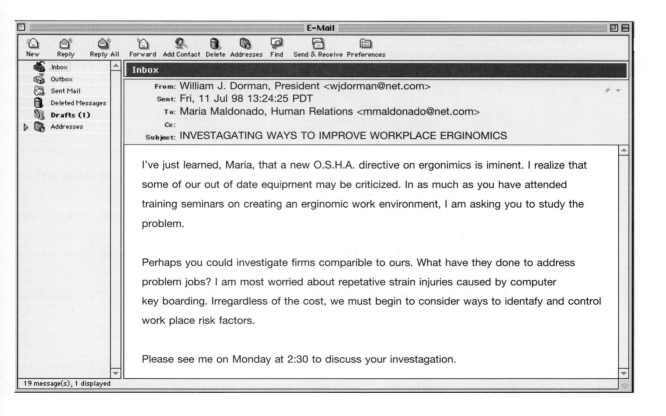

E-Mail

New   Reply   Reply All   Forward   Add Contact   Delete   Addresses   Find   Send & Receive   Preferences

Inbox
Outbox
Sent Mail
Deleted Messages
Drafts (1)
Addresses

Inbox

From: William J. Dorman, President <wjdorman@net.com>
Sent: Fri, 11 Jul 98 13:24:25 PDT
To: Maria Maldonado, Human Relations <mmaldonado@net.com>
Cc:
Subject: INVESTAGATING WAYS TO IMPROVE WORKPLACE ERGINOMICS

I've just learned, Maria, that a new O.S.H.A. directive on ergonimics is iminent. I realize that some of our out of date equipment may be criticized. In as much as you have attended training seminars on creating an erginomic work environment, I am asking you to study the problem.

Perhaps you could investigate firms comparible to ours. What have they done to address problem jobs? I am most worried about repetative strain injuries caused by computer key boarding. Irregardless of the cost, we must begin to consider ways to identafy and control work place risk factors.

Please see me on Monday at 2:30 to discuss your investagation.

19 message(s), 1 displayed

To make sure you enter the work world with good Internet skills, *Business English* provides a short Web exercise in each chapter. If your instructor assigns this exercise, you will need access to a computer with an Internet connection. Additionally, your computer must have a Web browser, such as Microsoft Explorer or Netscape. These programs enable you to see and use Web pages.

All Web pages have addresses called URLs (Uniform Resource Locators). URLs must be typed exactly as they are shown, including periods (.), hyphens (-), underscores (_), slashes (/), tildes (~), and upper- or lowercase letters. URLs are often enclosed in angle brackets < >. You do not need to include the angle brackets when typing a URL.

The following exercise introduces you to an electronic dictionary. A major advantage of an online dictionary is that it presents the latest information. For example, you will look up two terms that are so new they are not currently listed in the print version of *Merriam-Webster's Collegiate Dictionary*.

Goal: To gain confidence in using an electronic dictionary.

1. With your Web browser on the screen, key the following URL in the location box: **<http://www.m-w.com>. (Don't include the angle brackets.) Press Enter.**

2. Look over the **Merriam-Webster Online** home page. Move up and down the page by using the scroll bar at the right.

3. Scroll to the top and move your cursor to the **Collegiate Dictionary** box.

4. Key the word **spam**. Click **Look it up**.

5. Scroll down to see the definition for **spam—noun**.

6. Print a copy of the page by clicking on **File** (upper left corner of your browser). Click **Print** and **OK**. Save all printouts to turn in.

7. Click **Back** (upper left corner of browser) to return to the search page.

8. In the **Collegiate Dictionary** box, delete **spam**. Key the word **firewall** and click **Look it up**. Read the definition and print a copy.

9. Click **Back**. Using either the **Dictionary** or **Thesaurus** feature, look up one word from Exercise F. Print the definition or synonym.

10. Click **Word of the Day** (left navigation panel). Read about the word. Print a copy.

11. End your session by clicking the **X** box (upper right corner of browser). Turn in all printed copies.

POSTTEST

Write *T* (true) or *F* (false) after the following statements. Compare your answers with those at the bottom of the page.

1. The best dictionary for a college student's assignments is a pocket dictionary.   _____

2. When searching for a word in a dictionary, look only at the guide words until you locate the desired page.   _____

3. The etymology of a word is usually contained within square brackets.   _____

4. The usage label *colloquial* means that the word may be used in certain regions only.   _____

5. A dictionary user could expect to find the spelling of the past tense of an irregular verb such as *build*.   _____

CHECKLIST OF BONUS LEARNING RESOURCES

See the inside cover for a complete description of these activities. Your instructor will tell you which of the following to complete. To access any of the Web activities, go to Guffey Student Web site **<http://www.westwords.com/guffey/students.html>** or **<http://www.meguffey.com>**. Click on **Book Support**, click on your book cover, and click on the appropriate activity.

Web Editor's Challenge Exercise. Provides a business document to be revised.

Web Interactive Chapter Review. Tests knowledge of chapter concepts.

Web PowerPoint Slides. Summarize chapter principles; include checkups.

Web Crossword Puzzle. Reviews vocabulary and chapter concepts.

WebCheck Reinforcement Exercises 1.1, 1.2. Provide dictionary practice; strengthen vocabulary.

Self-Help Exercises. Offer worksheets with additional chapter exercises.

Electronic Study Guide. Reinforces chapter concepts.

1. F 2. T 3. T 4. F 5. T

chapter 2
Parts of Speech

Objectives

When you have completed the materials in this chapter, you will be able to do the following:

- Define the eight parts of speech.
- Recognize how parts of speech function in sentences.
- Compose sentences showing words playing more than one grammatical role.

Study the following sentence and identify selected parts of speech. For each word listed underline the correct part of speech. Compare your answers with those at the bottom of the page.

Dustin **and** I **carefully completed** our **tax** forms **before** April 15.

1. and	(a) prep	(b) conj	(c) verb	(d) adverb
2. carefully	(a) prep	(b) conj	(c) verb	(d) adverb
3. completed	(a) prep	(b) conj	(c) verb	(d) adverb
4. tax	(a) adj	(b) pronoun	(c) noun	(d) adverb
5. before	(a) prep	(b) conj	(c) noun	(d) adverb

Career Tip

"Whatever your program in college, be sure to include courses in writing and speaking. Managers must constantly write instructions, reports, memos, letters, and survey conclusions. If this comes hard to you, it will hold you back."
—James A. Newman and Alexander Roy in *Climbing the Corporate Matterhorn*

1. b 2. d 3. c 4. a 5. a

As you learned in Chapter 1, business English is the study of the fundamentals of grammar, current usage, and appropriate business style. Such a study logically begins with the eight parts of speech, the building blocks of our language. This chapter provides a brief overview of the parts of speech; the following chapters will deal with these topics more thoroughly.

The Eight Parts of Speech

Learning the eight parts of speech helps you develop the working vocabulary necessary to discuss and study the language. You especially need to recognize the parts of speech in the context of sentences. That's because many words function in more than one role. Only by analyzing the sentence at hand can you see how a given word functions.

Nouns

In elementary school you probably learned that *nouns* are the names given to persons, places, and things. In addition, though, nouns name qualities, concepts, and activities.

Persons:	Victoria, Mr.Takimoto, president, Scott
Places:	Toledo, island, Canada, college
Things:	computer, billboard, motorcycle, chair
Qualities:	dependability, honesty, initiative
Concepts:	knowledge, freedom, friendship, happiness
Activities:	skiing, surfing, management, eating

Nouns are important words in our language. Sentences revolve around nouns since these words function both as subjects and as objects of verbs. To determine if a word is really a noun, try using it with the verb *is* or *are*. Notice that all the nouns listed here would make sense if used in this way: *Victoria is young, Toledo is in Ohio, computers are fun,* and so on. In Chapter 4 you will learn four classes of nouns and rules for making nouns plural.

Pronouns

As substitutes for nouns, *pronouns* are used in our language for variety and efficiency. Compare these two versions of the same sentence:

Without pronouns:	Elizabeth gave the book to Matt so that Matt could use the book to study.
With pronouns:	Elizabeth gave the book to Matt so that *he* could use *it* to study.

In sentences pronouns may function as subjects of verbs (for example, *I, we, they*) or as objects of verbs (*me, us, them*). They may show possession (*mine, ours, his*), and they may act as connectors (*that, which, who*). Only a few examples are given here. More examples along with functions and classifications of pronouns will be presented in Chapters 6 and 7.

Verbs

Verbs express an action, an occurrence, or a state of being.

Spot the Blooper

From *The Wall Street Journal* comes a report that Marshall Field's, the big Chicago retailer, announced it would serve hot chocolate to "tiresome" shoppers. (The store later blamed this misused adjective on a computer spell checker. Did the computer get a bum rap?)

Jason *built* an excellent Web site. (Action)

It *has* many links. (Occurrence)

He *is* proud of it. (State of being)

Action verbs show the action of a sentence. Some action verbs are *runs*, *studies*, *works*, and *fixes*. Verbs that express a state of being generally link to the subject words that describe it. Some linking verbs are *am*, *is*, *are*, *was*, *were*, *be*, *being*, and *been*. Other linking verbs express the senses: *feels*, *appears*, *tastes*, *sounds*, *seems*, *looks*.

Verbs will be discussed more fully in Chapters 8–11. At this point it is important that you be able to recognize verbs so that you can determine whether sentences are complete. All sentences have at least one verb; many sentences will have more than one verb. Verbs may appear singly or in phrases.

Stacy <u>submitted</u> her application to become a management trainee. (Action verb.)

Her résumé <u>is</u> just one page long. (Linking verb.)

She <u>has been training</u> to become a manager. (Verb phrase.)

Stacy <u>feels</u> bad that she <u>will be leaving</u> her old friends. (Linking verb and verb phrase.)

Adjectives

Words that describe nouns or pronouns are called *adjectives*. They often answer the questions *What kind? How many?* and *Which one?* The adjectives in the following sentences are italicized. Observe that the adjectives all answer questions about the nouns they describe.

Small, *independent* businesses are becoming *numerous*. (What kind of businesses?)

We have *six* franchises in *four* states. (How many franchises? How many states?)

That chain of hotels started as a *small* operation. (Which chain? What kind of operation?)

He is *energetic* and *forceful*, while she is *personable* and *deliberate*. (What pronouns do these adjectives describe?)

Adjectives usually precede nouns. They may, however, follow the words they describe, especially when used with linking verbs, as shown in the first and last examples above. Here is a brief list of words often used as adjectives:

successful	sensitive	effective
terrific	bright	small
helpless	long	wet

Three words (*a*, *an*, and *the*) form a special group of adjectives called *articles*.

Adverbs

Words that modify (describe or limit) verbs, adjectives, or other adverbs are *adverbs*. Adverbs often answer the questions *When? How? Where?* and *To what extent?*

Today we must begin work. (Must begin when?)

James proceeded *rapidly* with the orders. (Proceeded how?)

He seemed *exceedingly* happy. (How happy?)

Did you see the schedule *there*? (Where?)

The prosecutor did not question him *further*. (Questioned him to what extent?)

Here are additional examples of common adverbs:

now	evenly	commercially
very	only	really
rather	carefully	greatly

Many, but not all, words ending in *ly* are adverbs. Some exceptions are *friendly*, *costly*, and *ugly*, all of which are adjectives.

Prepositions

Prepositions join nouns and pronouns to other words in a sentence. As the word itself suggests (*pre* meaning "before"), a preposition is a word in a position *before* its object (a noun or pronoun). Prepositions are used in phrases to show a relationship between the object of the preposition and another word in the sentence. In the following sentence notice how the preposition changes the relation of the object (*Mr. Lee*) to the verb (*talked*):

Kent often talked *with* Mr. Lee.

Kent often talked *about* Mr. Lee.

Kent often talked *to* Mr. Lee.

The most frequently used prepositions are *to*, *by*, *for*, *at*, *from*, *with*, and *of*. A more complete list of prepositions can be found in Chapter 13. Learn to recognize objects of prepositions so that you won't confuse them with sentence subjects.

Conjunctions

Words that connect other words or groups of words are *conjunctions*. The most common conjunctions are *and*, *or*, *but*, and *nor*. These are called *coordinating conjunctions* because they join equal (coordinate) parts of sentences. Other kinds of conjunctions will be presented in Chapter 15. Study the examples of coordinating conjunctions shown here:

Koshi, Bill, *and* Amber are all looking for jobs. (Joins equal words.)

You may be interviewed by a personnel officer *or* by a supervising manager. (Joins equal groups of words.)

Interjections

Words expressing strong feelings are *interjections*. Interjections standing alone are followed by exclamation marks. When woven into a sentence, they are usually followed by commas.

Wow! Did you see the total of our bill?

Gosh, I hope I have my credit card.

Study Tip

To remember more easily what an *adverb* does, think of its two syllables: *ad* suggests that you will be adding to or amplifying the meaning of a *verb*. Hence, adverbs often modify verbs.

Spot the Blooper

The menu of a restaurant in Columbia, South Carolina, offers "A humongous baked potato, slightly hallowed and stuffed."

Career Tip

To sound businesslike, credible, and objective, most writers avoid interjections and exclamation marks in business messages.

Summary

The sentence below illustrates all eight parts of speech.

Inter   Adverb   Preposition   Conjunction   Noun
  Pronoun   Verb   Noun   Adjective

Oh, I certainly will send for literature and free samples!

Did You Know?

The vocabulary of American English is constantly growing, and some Britishers criticize our eagerness to accept new words and meanings. Prince Charles pronounced American English "very corrupting" and to be avoided at all costs. He told the British Council that Americans tend to "invent all sorts of new nouns and verbs and make words that shouldn't be."

You need to know the functions of these eight parts of speech in order to understand the rest of this textbook and profit from your study of business English. The explanation of the parts of speech has been kept simple so far. This chapter is meant to serve as an introduction to later, more fully developed chapters. At this stage you should not expect to be able to identify the functions of *all* words in *all* sentences.

A word of caution: English is a wonderfully flexible language. As noted earlier, many words in our language serve as more than one part of speech. Notice how flexible the word *mail* is in these sentences:

Our *mail* is late today. (Noun—serves as subject of sentence.)

The knight's suit of *mail* protected him. (Noun—serves as object of preposition.)

Mail the letter today. (Verb—serves as action word in sentence.)

Your voice *mail* box is full. (Adjective—used with *voice* to describe *box*, which is the subject of sentence.)

Now complete the reinforcement exercises for this chapter.

HOTLINE QUERIES

Businesspeople are very concerned about appropriate English usage, grammar, and style. This concern is evident in the number and kinds of questions called in to grammar hotline services across the country. Among the callers are business supervisors, managers, executives, secretaries, clerks, administrative assistants, and word processing specialists. Writers, teachers, librarians, students, and other community members also seek answers to language questions.

Selected questions and appropriate answers to them will be presented in the following chapters. In this way you, as a student of the language, will understand the kinds of everyday communication problems encountered in the work world.

The original questions in our Hotline Queries came from the Los Angeles Pierce College Business English Hotline, which is no longer in service. More recently, questions have come from grammar hotline services across the country. To receive a list of these Hotline services, send a self-addressed, stamped envelope to **Grammar Hotline Director, Writing Center, Humanities Division, Tidewater Community College, Virginia Beach, VA 23456.** For immediate access, this list of currently operating hotlines is also maintained at a Web site **<http://www.tc.cc.va.us/writcent/gh/hotlinol.htm>**. If this URL (address) is not operative, use a search engine to look for "grammar hotline directory." Some of the listed grammar hotlines provide e-mail addresses to which you can send inquiries.

Q: We're having a big argument in our office. What's correct? *E-mail, e-mail, email,* or *Email?* And is it *on-line* or *online?*

A: Initially, most people capitalized *E-mail* and hyphenated *on-line*. With increased use, however, both of these forms have been simplified: *e-mail* and *online*, which I recommend. Although *Merriam-Webster's College Dictionary,* Tenth Edition (our standard reference) clings to *E-mail* when used as a noun, it does recognize the lowercase form for the verb form (*I will e-mail my response to you*). In my observation most publications today are moving toward *e-mail* for both noun and verb forms and *online* for both adjective and adverb functions. You might want to check with your company's in-house style manual for its preferred style for these words.

Q: What is the name of a group of initials that form a word? Is it an abbreviation?

A: A word formed from the initial letters of an expression is called an *acronym* (pronounced ACK-ro-nim). Examples: *snafu* from *situation normal, all fouled up*, and *PIN* from *personal identification number*. Acronyms are pronounced as single words and are different from abbreviations. Expressions such as *FBI* and *dept.* are abbreviations, not acronyms. Notice that an abbreviation is pronounced letter by letter (*F, B, I*) while an acronym is pronounced as a word (*MADD*, which stands for *Mothers Against Drunk Driving*).

Q: I saw this sentence recently in the newspaper: *At the movie premiere the crowd scanned the arriving limousines for glitterati.* Is *glitterati* a real word?

A: A recent arrival to our vocabulary, *glitterati* means "celebrities or beautiful people." New words are generally considered legitimate when their use is clear and when they are necessary (that is, when no other word says exactly what they do). If educated individuals begin to use such words, the words then appear in dictionaries, and *glitterati* has made it.

Q: Which word should I use in this sentence? *Our department will disburse or disperse the funds shortly.*

A: Use *disburse*. *Disperse* means "to scatter" (*Police dispersed the unruly crowd*) or "to distribute" (*Information will be dispersed to all divisions*). *Disburse* means "to pay out." Perhaps this memory device will help you keep them straight: associate the *b* in *disburse* with *bank* (*Banks disburse money*).

Q: How should I address a person who signed a letter *J. R. Henderson*?

A: Use *Dear J. R. Henderson*.

Q: What's the difference between *toward* and *towards*?

A: None. They are interchangeable in use. However, it's more efficient to use the shorter word *toward*.

Q: Is *every day* one word or two in this case? *We encounter these problems every day.*

A: In your sentence it is two words. When it means "ordinary," it is one word (*she wore everyday clothes*). If you can insert the word *single* between *every* and *day* without altering your meaning, you should be using two words.

Q: Should an e-mail message begin with a salutation or some kind of greeting?

A: When e-mail messages are sent to company insiders, a salutation may be omitted. However, when e-mail messages travel to outsiders, omitting a salutation seems curt and unfriendly. Because the message is more like a letter, a salutation is appropriate (such as *Dear Courtney, Hi Courtney, Greetings,* or just *Courtney*). Including a salutation is also a visual cue to where the message begins. Some writers prefer to incorporate the name of the recipient in the first sentence (*Thanks, Courtney, for responding so quickly.*)

Name _____

A. (Self-check) Complete these statements.

1. Used for variety and efficiency, pronouns substitute for _____

   a. interjections **b.** nouns **c.** verbs **d.** conjunctions

2. The part of speech that answers the question *What kind?* is a/an _____

   a. adverb **(b.)** adjective **c.** interjection **d.** conjunction

3. Names for persons, places, things, qualities, concepts, and activities are _____

   a. verbs **b.** adjectives **c.** nouns **d.** pronouns

4. Words that answer the questions *How?* and *To what extent?* are _____

   (a.) adverbs **b.** adjectives **c.** pronouns **d.** conjunctions

5. *I, we, you,* and *he* are examples of _____

   (a.) pronouns **b.** nouns **c.** verbs **d.** adverbs

6. *Beautifully, frankly,* and *smoothly* are examples of _____

   a. adjectives **b.** verbs **c.** interjections **(d.)** adverbs

7. *And, or, nor,* and *but* are _____

   a. conjunctions **b.** verbs **c.** interjections **d.** adverbs

8. Words that join noun or pronoun objects to other words in sentences are _____

   a. adverbs **(b.)** prepositions **c.** interjections **d.** adjectives

Check your answers below.

B. In each of the following groups of sentences, one word is used as an adjective, as a noun, and as a verb. For each sentence indicate the part of speech for the italicized word.

Example: We have little *time* in which to make a decision. **noun**

Officials will *time* the runners in the marathon. **verb**

Factory workers must punch a *time* clock. **adjective**

1. Put that desk in the *corner*. _____

2. Your new pickup truck *corners* well. verb

3. CEOs seem to prefer *corner* offices. _____

4. Travelers boarded the supersonic *jet* in Paris. noun

5. Tony complained of *jet* lag when he arrived in Los Angeles. _____

6. Can businesspeople *jet* from Hong Kong to Honolulu in four hours? verb

7. Advertisements promised instruction from a *master* teacher. _____

8. Few students can *master* Web design in a short course. verb

9. The pilot of a merchant ship is considered its *master*. _____

1. b 2. b 3. c 4. a 5. a 6. d 7. a 8. b

Write complete sentences using the word *work* as a noun, as an adjective, and as a verb.

10. (noun)   _____

11. (verb)   _____

12. (adjective)   _____

C. The italicized words in the following sentences are either prepositions or conjunctions. Write *C* for conjunction or *P* for preposition.

1. Technical skills are important *for* entry-level positions, *but* communication skills are necessary for promotion *into* management.

   for   _____
   but   _____
   into   _____

2. Writing good letters *and* e-mail messages *to* customers creates goodwill *for* business organizations.

   and   _____
   to   _____
   for   _____

D. Read the following sentences and, taking into account the function of each word within each sentence, identify the part of speech of each word shown. Use a dictionary if necessary.

Six job candidates applied, but only she was selected for the interview.

Six	_____	but	_____	selected	_____
job	_____	only	_____	for	_____
candidates	_____	she	_____	the	_____
applied	_____	was	_____	interview	_____

Hurriedly she parked the small sports car and quickly raced to class.

Hurriedly	_____	small	_____	quickly	_____
she	_____	sports	_____	raced	_____
parked	_____	car	_____	to	_____
the	_____	and	_____	class	_____

E. Selected verbs in the following sentences have been italicized. Use a check mark to indicate whether these verbs are linking or action.

	Linking Verb	Action Verb
Example: We *are* the chief suppliers of camera film.	✓	
1. An optimist *is* a person who thinks a housefly is looking for a way out.	✓	
2. Control Systems, Inc., *produces* components for computers.		✓
3. The hotel manager *selected* four trainees from many applicants.		✓
4. Jeffrey *was* our webmaster until recently.	✓	
5. Please *deliver* the computers and printers before April 4.		✓
6. The manager and the personnel director *studied* all job descriptions carefully.		✓
7. The first equipment proposal *was* quite adequate for our needs.	✓	
8. Sheila *felt* bad that too much month was left at the end of her money.	✓	~~✓~~

F. Writing Exercise. In a couple of complete sentences, explain why it is important to understand the parts of speech for this course and later on the job.

_____

_____

_____

Editor's Challenge

To develop your vocabulary skills, supply a single word for each blank in the following sentences. The word you supply should represent the part of speech shown.

⭐ **Atlantic Industries**
Interoffice Memo

TO: Allison Hever

FROM: Tran Nguyen

DATE: June 3, 200x

SUBJECT: JOB-SEARCH ADVICE

I'm sorry to learn that you have completed your internship with us and that you will be leaving, Allison. Since you (verb) _requested_ advice in finding a job, I'd like to share with you a few pointers that I've learned.

My experience suggests that serious candidates will devote as much (noun) _time_ to job hunting as they do (preposition) _to_ working at a full-time job. If possible, hand deliver your résumé (conjunction) _with and_ your cover letter to the (noun) _person_ in charge of hiring.

Be sure that your (adjective) _cover_ letter (verb) _describes_ the requirements of the position advertised. If you mailed your résumé, it's a (adjective) _good_ idea to follow up with a telephone call in a few days. A(n) (adverb) _very_ high number of résumés are never received, are lost, or are thrown out.

You'll find that an interviewer often asks why (pronoun) _you_ want this particular job. In addition to answering (noun) _them_, you should be prepared to ask (adjective) _some_ questions of your own. Try to remember that interviews are (adjective) _great_ learning experiences, whether (conjunction) _or_ not you get the job.

I hope this (noun) _letter_ is helpful to you, and I wish you well in your (adjective) _tiresome_ search.

---

learning.web.ways

Many colleges and universities offer online writing labs (OWLs). These Web sites provide helpful resources for students and businesspeople. You can read online or download handouts providing help with punctuation, spelling, sentence construction, parts of speech, and writing in the job search.

Goal: To learn to use an online writing lab.

1. With your Web browser on the screen, key the following URL in the location box: **<http://owl.english.purdue.edu>**. Press **Enter.**

2. Look at the **Purdue University Online Writing Lab** home page.

3. Scroll down to reveal the site's six areas. When you move your cursor over an underlined title, you see a hand. This indicates a hot link.

4. Click **Instructional Handouts.**

5. From the list of handouts, click on **Parts of Speech**.

6. Click **Using Pronouns Clearly**. Read the handout.

7. Print a copy. Circle three examples illustrating incorrect use of pronouns.

8. Click **Back** in the upper corner of your browser. Return to the **OWL Handouts Index**.

9. Select another topic to peruse.

10. End your session by clicking the X box in the upper right corner of your browser. Turn in your printout.

POSTTEST

Identify the parts of speech in this sentence by underlining the correct choice. Compare your answers with those at the bottom of the page.

Our **manager explained** the use **of** the **new** program **slowly.**

1. manager	<u>a. noun</u>	b. pronoun	c. prep	d. conj
2. explained	a. adverb	<u>b. verb</u>	c. prep	d. conj
3. of	a. noun	b. pronoun	<u>c. prep</u>	d. conj
4. new	a. verb	b. adverb	<u>c. adj</u>	d. prep
5. slowly	a. verb	<u>b. adverb</u>	c. prep	d. conj

CHECKLIST OF BONUS LEARNING RESOURCES

See the inside cover for a complete description of these activities. Your instructor will tell you which of the following to complete. To access any of the Web activities, go to Guffey Student Web site **<http://www. westwords.com/guffey/students.html>** or **<http://www.meguffey. com>**. Click on **Book Support**, click on your book cover, and click on the appropriate activity.

- Web Editor's Challenge Exercise

- Web Interactive Chapter Review

- Web PowerPoint Slides

- Web Crossword Puzzle

- WebCheck Reinforcement Exercises 2.1, 2.2

- Self-Help Exercises

- Electronic Study Guide

chapter 3 Sentences: Elements, Patterns, Types

Objectives

When you have completed the materials in this chapter, you will be able to do the following:

- Recognize subjects and predicates.
- Convert fragments into complete sentences.
- Recognize basic sentence faults such as comma splices and run-on sentences.
- Complete sentences in three basic sentence patterns.
- Punctuate statements, commands, questions, and exclamations.

Write the correct letter after each of the numbered groups of words below to identify it.

a = correctly punctuated sentence   c = comma splice
b = fragment   d = run-on sentence

1. Mark, completing the training course in less than four weeks. _B_

2. Troy works 30 hours this week, Lisa works 32. _AC_

3. Across the street are the copy store and a mini mart. _A B D_

4. Some employees use the company van however others rely on their own cars. _A D_

5. Although many employees start at 6 a.m., which explains the empty parking lot. _B_

Career Tip

You may be worth an additional $5,000 to your employer (and to yourself) if you have writing skills, says one communications expert. Because companies can no longer afford expensive on-site training, employees with already developed skills are much more valuable to employers.

Sentences are groups of words arranged to express complete thoughts. In this chapter you'll review the basic elements of every sentence. In addition, you'll learn to recognize sentence patterns and types. This knowledge will help you use and punctuate sentences correctly. This chapter also introduces proofreading marks, which are helpful in revising messages.

Sentence Elements

Sentences are composed of subjects and predicates. In addition, sentences must make sense. When any one of these elements is missing, readers or listeners are confused. To help you better understand the structure of sentences, you'll learn to distinguish between simple and complete subjects and predicates. You'll also learn to recognize and avoid fragments, comma splices, and run-on sentences.

Subjects and Predicates

The *subject* of a sentence is the person or thing being talked about, and the *predicate* tells what the subject is, what the subject is doing, or what is being done to the subject.

The new <u>manager</u> of the office   <u><u>received</u></u> our cooperation.

        complete subject   complete predicate

The *complete subject* of the preceding sentence includes the subject (in this case a noun) plus all the words that describe or limit the subject (its modifiers). The *complete predicate* includes the verb plus its modifiers.

The heart of the complete subject is the simple subject (*manager*), and the heart of the predicate is the simple predicate, or verb (*received*). The following sentences are divided into complete subjects and complete predicates. The simple subjects are underlined once, and simple predicates (verbs) are underlined twice.

Complete Subjects	Complete Predicates
All <u>branches</u> of the company	<u>are linked</u> by an intranet.
Our largest office supply <u>store</u>	<u>will be hiring</u> new employees.
A Florida pilot <u>program</u>	<u>will be launched</u> next month.
Fast-food restaurant <u>owners</u>	<u>conduct</u> traffic counts.

Notice in the previous sentences that the verbs may consist of one word or several. In a verb phrase the principal verb is the final one; the other verbs are *helping* or *auxiliary verbs*. The most frequently used helping verbs are *am, is, are, was, were, been, have, has, had, must, ought, can, might, could, would, should, will, do, does,* and *did*.

Sentence Sense

In addition to a subject and a predicate, a group of words must possess one additional element to qualify as a sentence: The group of words must make sense. Observe that the first two groups of words that follow express complete thoughts and make sense; the third does not.

Athletic shoe <u>makers</u> <u><u>convinced</u></u> us that we need $100 tennis shoes. (Subject plus predicate making sense = sentence.)

Did You Know?

The English language has about three times as many words as any other language on earth. English is estimated to include at least 450,000 words. German has 185,000, Russian 130,000, and French 100,000.

Study Tip

Many linking verbs also serve as helping verbs. Note that a verb phrase is *linking* only when the final verb is a linking verb, such as in the phrase *might have been*.

Anthony now <u>owns</u> different sneakers for every sport. (Subject plus predicate making sense = sentence.)

Although sports shoe <u>manufacturers</u> <u>promote</u> new versions with new features (Subject plus predicate but NOT making sense = no sentence.)

In the third case a reader or listener senses that the idea expressed is incomplete. We do not have a sentence; instead, we have a fragment.

Sentence Faults

Three typical sentence faults are fragments, comma splices, and run-on sentences. Good writers eliminate these sentence faults by applying the following advice.

Fragment

Fragments are groups of words that have been broken off from preceding or succeeding sentences. They cannot function as complete sentences. Avoid fragments by making certain that each sentence contains a subject and a verb and makes sense by itself. In the following examples the fragments are italicized. Notice how they can be revised to make complete sentences.

Fragment:	We're looking for a potential manager. *An individual who can accept responsibility and supervise other employees.*
Revision:	We're looking for a potential manager who can accept responsibility and supervise other employees.
Fragment:	My local vending machine dispenses microwavable popcorn. *Which contains a warning to remove the plastic outerwrap before heating.*
Revision:	My local vending machine dispenses microwavable popcorn, which contains a warning to remove the plastic outerwrap before heating.

Comma Splice

A *comma splice* results when two sentences are incorrectly joined or spliced together with a comma. The following sentences show how comma splices could be revised into acceptable sentences.

Comma Splice:	Let us help you develop your online résumé, visit us at Resume.org.
Revision:	Let us help you develop your online résumé. Visit us at Resume.org.
Comma Splice:	First, fill out an employment application, then submit your résumé and prepare for an interview.
Revision:	First, fill out an employment application. Then submit your résumé and prepare for an interview.
Comma Splice:	Many applicants responded to our advertisement, however only one had the proper computer training.
Revision:	Many applicants responded to our advertisement; however, only one had the proper computer training. (Semicolons will be discussed in Chapters 14 and 17.)

Hot Link

For more examples of sentence faults and sentence patterns, visit the Purdue University Online Writing Lab **<http://owl.english. purdue.edu>**. Click on *Instructional Handouts, Sentence Construction.*

Spot the Blooper

In a newspaper article: "He is recovering from a near-fatal accident that sent him into a comma."

Run-On Sentence

A *run-on sentence* joins two complete thoughts without proper punctuation. Notice how the following run-on sentences can be corrected by dividing the two thoughts into separate sentences.

Run-on Sentence:	The work ethic in America is not dead it is deeply ingrained in most people.
Revision:	The work ethic in America is not dead. It is deeply ingrained in most people.
Run-on Sentence:	Send an e-mail message to all members of the committee tell them our next meeting is planned for Friday.
Revision:	Send an e-mail message to all members of the committee. Tell them our next meeting is planned for Friday.

Sentence Patterns

Three basic word patterns are used to express thoughts in English sentences.

Pattern No. 1: Subject–Verb

In the most basic sentence pattern, the subject is followed by its verb. No additional words are needed for the sentence to make sense and be complete.

Subject	Verb
We	worked.
Everyone	is studying.
She	might have called.
All employees	are being informed.

Pattern No. 2: Subject–Action Verb–Object

In this kind of sentence, the subject is followed by an action verb and its direct object. The object usually answers the question *What?* or *Whom?*

Subject	Action Verb	Object
Most workers	carried	insurance.
The manager	praised	all employees.
Joy Haynes	supervised	them.

This basic sentence pattern may also employ an indirect object that usually answers the question *To whom?*

Subject	Action Verb	Indirect Object	Direct Object
Our company	offers	employees	excellent benefits.
Tiffany	gave	him	the book.

Career Tip

As a business writer, you'll most often use Patterns 1, 2, and 3 because readers want to know the subject first. For variety and emphasis, however, you can use introductory elements and inverted order.

Pattern No. 3: Subject–Linking Verb–Complement

In the third kind of sentence, the subject is followed by a linking verb and its complement. A *complement* is a noun, pronoun, or adjective that renames or describes the subject. A complement *completes* the meaning of the subject.

Subject	Linking Verb	Complement	
The instructor	was	Shirley Leung.	(Noun complements.)
Our customers	are	friends.	
Your supervisor	is	she.	(Pronoun complements.)
The callers	might have been	they.	
These data	are	accurate.	(Adjective complements.)
His report	is	excellent.	

The sentences shown here have been kept simple so that their patterns can be recognized easily. Although most speakers and writers expand these basic patterns with additional phrases and clauses, the basic sentence structure remains the same. Despite its length the following sentence follows the basic subject–verb–object order:

Many large *companies*, as well as small companies with sizable real estate holdings, *employ* specialized risk *managers* to handle their insurance problems. (The simple subject is *companies*, the verb is *employ*, and the object is *managers*.)

Inverted Order

In some sentences the elements appear in inverted order, with the verb preceding the subject.

Sitting in front is Megan.

Practicing daily was the swim team.

In questions the verb may precede the subject or may be interrupted by the subject.

What is their e-mail address?

Have the bills been sent?

In sentences beginning with *here* or *there*, the normal word order is also inverted.

Here are the applications.

There were three steps in the plan.

To locate the true subject in any inverted sentence, mentally rearrange the words. Place them in the normal subject–verb order.

Megan is sitting in front.

Their e-mail address is what?

The applications are here.

Three steps were [there] in the plan.

Punctuating Four Sentence Types

The end punctuation used in a sentence depends on whether it is a statement, question, command, or exclamation.

Statements

Statements make assertions and end with periods.

> <u>Laws</u> <u>require</u> truth in advertising.

> <u>Manufacturers</u> today <u>must</u> <u>label</u> the contents of packages.

Questions

Direct questions are followed by question marks.

> How many daily e-mail messages <u>do</u> <u>you</u> <u>receive</u>?

> What <u>are</u> your peak message <u>hours</u>?

Commands

Commands end with periods or, occasionally, with exclamation points. Note that the subject in all commands is understood to be *you*. The subject *you* is not normally stated in the command.

> <u>Shut</u> the door. ([<u>You</u>] <u>shut</u> the door.)

> <u>Insure</u> your home against fire loss. ([<u>You</u>] <u>insure</u> your home . . .)

Exclamations

Exclamations show surprise, disbelief, or strong feelings. They may or may not be expressed as complete thoughts. Both subject and predicate may be implied.

> Wow! Static <u>electricity</u> <u>gave</u> me a terrific shock!

> What a remarkable employee <u>she</u> <u>is</u>!

> How extraordinary [<u>that</u> <u>is</u>]!

Now complete the reinforcement exercises for this chapter.

HOTLINE QUERIES

Q: This sentence doesn't sound right to me, but I can't decide how to improve it: *The reason I'm applying is because I enjoy editing.*

A: The problem lies in this construction: *the reason . . . is because. . .* Only nouns or adjectives may act as complements following linking verbs. In your sentence an adverbial clause follows the linking verb and sounds awkward. One way to improve the sentence is to substitute a noun clause beginning with *that: The reason I'm applying is that I enjoy editing.* An even better way to improve the sentence would be to make it a direct statement: *I'm applying because I enjoy editing.*

Q: My colleague says that this sentence is correct: *Please complete this survey regarding your satisfaction at our dealership, then return it in the enclosed addressed envelope.* I think something is wrong, but I'm not sure what.

A: You're right. This sentence has two independent clauses, and some writers attempt to join them with a comma. But this construction produces a comma splice. The adverb *then* cannot function as a conjunction, such as *and*, to join these two clauses. Start a new sentence or use a semicolon between the clauses.

Q: My boss dictated a report with this sentence: *Saleswise, our staff is excellent.* Should I change it?

A: Never change wording without checking with the author. You might point out, however, that the practice of attaching *-wise* to nouns is frowned on by many language experts. Such combinations as *budgetwise*, *taxwise*, and *productionwise* are considered commercial jargon. Suggest this revision: *On the basis of sales, our staff is excellent.*

Q: At the end of a letter I wrote: *Thank you for attending to this matter immediately.* Should I hyphenate *thank you*?

A: Do not hyphenate *thank you* when using it as a verb (*thank you for writing*). Do use hyphens when using it as an adjective (*I sent a thank-you note*) or as a noun (*I sent four thank-yous*). Since *thank you* is used as a verb in your sentence, do not hyphenate it. Notice that *thank you* is never written as a single word.

Q: A fellow worker insists on saying, *I could care less.* Seems to me that it should be *I couldn't care less.* Who is right?

A: You are right. The phrase *I couldn't care less* has been in the language a long time. It means, of course, "I have little concern about the matter." Recently, though, people have begun to use *I could care less* with the same meaning. Most careful listeners realize that the latter phrase says just the opposite of its intent. Although both phrases are clichés, stick with *I couldn't care less* if you want to be clear.

Name _____

A. (Self-check) Indicate whether the following statements are true (*T*) or false (*F*).

1. The verbs *are*, *may*, and *have* are examples of auxiliary or helping verbs. **T**

2. A group of words with a subject and a predicate is automatically a complete sentence. _____

3. The complete subject of a sentence includes a noun or pronoun and all its modifiers. **~~F~~T**

4. Two complete sentences joined by a comma create a *comma splice*. _____

5. In questions the verb may appear before the subject. **T**

6. The complete predicate of a sentence tells what the subject is, what the subject is doing, or what is being done to the subject. _____

7. Sentences that show strong feeling are usually concluded with question marks. **F**

8. The verb phrase *could have been* is considered to be a linking verb. _____

Check your answers below.

B. Study the examples shown below. Then fill in the words necessary to complete the three sentence patterns.

PATTERN NO. 1: SUBJECT–VERB

Example: The boss called.

1. The telephone **sucks / rang**   4. Senators _____

2. Our computer _____   5. Our fax machine **sucks / died**

3. Students **complain**   6. E-mail messages _____

PATTERN NO. 2: SUBJECT–ACTION VERB–OBJECT

Example: Administrative assistants use **software.**

7. Kelly answered the **telephone**   10. Congress passes _____

8. UPS delivers _____   11. Stock pays **wett. dividends**

9. Salespeople sold **everything**   12. Students threw a _____

PATTERN NO. 3: SUBJECT–LINKING VERB–COMPLEMENT

Fill in noun or pronoun complements.

Example: The manager is **Bill.**

13. The applicant was **Jason**   15. The caller could have been **Jason**

14. Tina is the new _____   16. The president is _____

Fill in adjective complements.

Example: The salary is <u>**reasonable.**</u>

17. My investment was <u>*minimal.*</u>

18. New York is _____

19. Movies once were <u>*Cheap.*</u>

20. The report could have been _____

C. The following sentences do not follow normal word order. Revise each sentence so that the subject comes first. Then underline the simple subject once and the simple predicate twice.

Example: Here are some of the materials we need.
<u>Some</u> of the materials we need <u><u>are</u></u> here.

1. There are two telephone numbers listed for that organization.
<u>*That Organization has two numbers listed.*</u>

2. Here is the agenda for the Tuesday board meeting.
_____

3. Where is the Rendell contract?
<u>*The Rendell contract is where?*</u>

4. Across from our office is the subway station.
_____

5. Who is the leader in online shopping?
<u>*The leader in online shopping is who?*</u>

D. From the list below select the letter that accurately describes each of the following groups of words. If a group of words requires an end punctuation mark, add it.

a = fragment   c = command   e = exclamation
b = statement   d = question

Example: The resources of that country, although never fully developed   <u>a</u>

1. School and work holidays should always be scheduled on Mondays and Fridays   <u>*b*</u>

2. Do employers and workers contribute jointly to the retirement fund   _____

3. Since 95 percent of the world's population lives outside the United States   <u>*A*</u>

4. Analyze the gross domestic product for the past ten years   _____

5. Although Singapore flourishes as a center of banking, shipbuilding, offshore-oil technology, refining, aircraft maintenance, electronics manufacturing, and international trade   <u>*A*</u>

6. What a splendid view we have from the observatory on the tenth floor   _____

7. Do you know whether Tom Truong received the purchase order   <u>*D*</u>

8. Turn off the power, close the windows, and lock the doors before you leave   _____

E. Expand the following sentence fragments into complete sentences.

Example: If I had seen the red light at the intersection <u>**, I could have stopped in time.**</u>

1. Since I am looking for a position in hotel management _____
_____

2. The Internal Revenue Service, although I promised to make an appointment to meet with them soon _____

_____

3. If I had just won a lottery prize of $37 million _____

_____

4. All students, including those with over 40 credits _____

_____

5. Although we have no openings for a person with your skills _____

_____

F. For each of the following groups of words, write the correct letter to indicate whether it represents a fragment, a correctly punctuated sentence, a comma splice, or a run-on sentence.

a = fragment   c = comma splice
b = correctly punctuated sentence d = run-on sentence

Example: Because the world seems to be getting smaller. a

1. Anyone doing business in another country should learn what kinds of gifts are expected and when to give them. B

2. Gifts for the children of an Arab are welcome, however gifts for an Arab's wife are inappropriate. _____

3. In Latin America a knife is not a proper gift it signifies cutting off a relationship. D

4. Since one third of all U.S. corporate profits are now generated through international trade. _____

5. Making eye contact in America is a sign of confidence and sincerity. B

6. Although Arabs, Middle Easterners, and Latin Americans stand very close to each other when talking. _____

7. In Japan, Korea, and India, looking away is a sign of respect, however, in Arab countries long and intense eye contact among men is important. C

8. Being on time is important in North America in other countries time is less important. _____

9. Italians who are good friends embrace when they meet, they also embrace when they part. C

10. In many countries people do not address each other by given names unless they are family members or old friends. _____

For class discussion: In the preceding exercise, how could each of the incorrectly punctuated groups of words be made acceptable?

G. Writing Exercise. On a separate sheet write complete sentences illustrating each of the following forms: a statement, a question, a command, an exclamation, a sentence with a pronoun complement, and a sentence in inverted order. Identify each sentence.

Editor's Challenge

The following e-mail message contains errors in sentence structure, spelling, and proofreading. Make corrections. Your instructor may ask you to read about proofreading marks on page 45 and use those marks in noting your corrections.

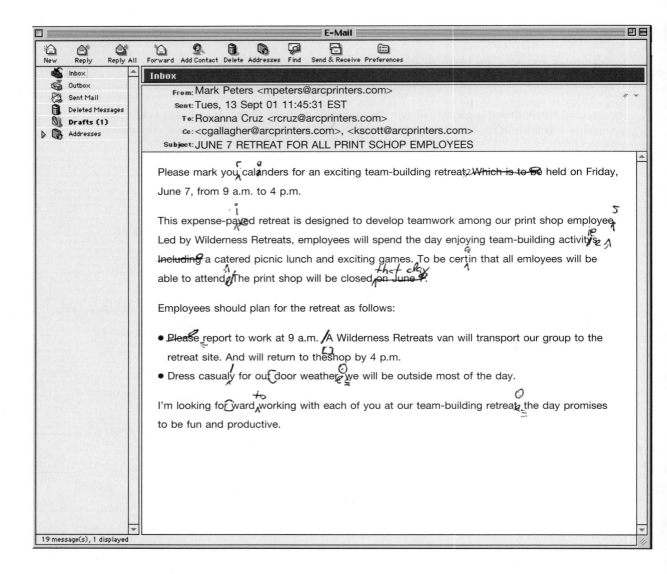

A number of search tools—such as AltaVista, Yahoo!, and Google—are available at specialized Web sites devoted to searching. These tools help you find Web pages related to the search term you enter. However, search tools cannot index all the pages on the Web. Using a search tool is like using a telephone book that lists only a third of all the numbers available. Even though search tools don't survey everything that's out there, they usually turn up more information than you want.

Goal: To become familiar with a search engine

1. With your Web browser on the screen, key the following URL: **<http://www.altavista.com>**. Press **Enter.**
2. Look over the AltaVista home page. Ignore the advertisements and locate the **Find this** box.
3. In this box, key "**English grammar**" as your search term. Enclosing an expression in quotation marks ensures that the two words will be searched as a unit. Click **Search** or press **Enter.**
4. Wait a moment for AltaVista to locate Web pages with your search term. Then scroll down to **Web pages found.** Notice that nearly 40,000 Web pages were located.
5. To refine your search, scroll back to the **Find this** box and replace the search term with "**Business English grammar.**"
6. Look over the listed pages. Click on one. Examine the page and print a copy (Click on **File, Print**, and **OK.)**
7. Return to the AltaVista home page. (It may be faster to key the URL in your browser **Location** box than to use the **Back** button.)
8. Choose another search item, such as **spam, netiquette,** or **intranets**. Select an interesting page. Examine it. Print one or two pages.
9. End your session by clicking the **X** in the upper right corner of your browser.
10. Turn in all printed copies.

POSTTEST

Write the correct letter after each of the numbered items below.

a = correctly punctuated sentence   c = comma splice
b = fragment   d = run-on sentence

1. The computer was installed Monday the printer is expected shortly.   *D*

2. Outside the front office is the receptionist's desk.   *A*

3. Since the contract was mailed Monday but not received until late Friday.   *B*

4. On Monday my e-mail box is overflowing, on Friday my box is empty.   *C*

5. Because Celeste, who is one of our best employees, was ill last week.   *B*

1. d 2. a 3. b 4. c 5. b

CHECKLIST OF BONUS LEARNING RESOURCES

- Web Editor's Challenge Exercise

- Web PowerPoint Slides

- Web Crossword Puzzle

- WebCheck Reinforcement Exercises 3.1, 3.2

- Self-Help Exercises

- Electronic Study Guide

Unit Review Chapters 1–3

Name _____

Begin your review by rereading Chapters 1–3. Then check your comprehension of those chapters by writing *T* (true) or *F* (false) in the blanks below. Compare your responses with the key at the end of the book.

1. All dictionaries use the same plan for showing the order of definitions. _____

2. Usage labels such as *obsolete*, *archaic*, and *informal* warn dictionary users about appropriate usage. _____

3. The etymology code helps you to pronounce a word correctly. _____

4. Because the English language changes very little, the publication date of a dictionary is unimportant. _____

5. Most dictionaries show noun plurals only if the plurals are irregular, such as the word *children*. _____

6. A thesaurus is a collection of words and their definitions. _____

7. Accent marks may appear before or after stressed syllables. _____

8. The usage label *nonstandard* means that a word is no longer in use. _____

9. The terms *desk* and *college-level* refer to the same kind of dictionary. _____

10. A summary of diacritical marks is often found at the bottom of dictionary pages. _____

Read the following sentence carefully. Identify the parts of speech for the words as they are used in this sentence.

He looked quickly at the page and then scribbled two answers.

11. He	a. noun	b. pronoun	c. adverb	d. adj	B
12. looked	a. conj	b. prep	c. verb	d. adverb	C
13. quickly	a. conj	b. prep	c. adj	d. adverb	D
14. at	a. conj	b. prep	c. adj	d. adverb	B
15. page	a. noun	b. pronoun	c. conj	d. adverb	A
16. and	a. noun	b. pronoun	c. conj	d. prep	C
17. then	a. noun	b. adverb	c. conj	d. prep	B
18. scribbled	a. verb	b. adverb	c. conj	d. prep	A
19. two	a. verb	b. adverb	c. adj	d. prep	C
20. answers	a. noun	b. pronoun	c. adj	d. prep	A

For each of the following statements, determine the word or phrase that correctly completes that statement and write its letter in the space provided.

21. In the sentence *Excellent communication skills are needed for this job*, the simple subject is _____

    a. Excellent b. communication c. skills d. job.

22. In the sentence *Here are the contracts*, the simple subject is _____

    a. Here b. are c. contracts d. you.

23. In the sentence *I feel bad*, the verb *feel* is considered a

    a. linking verb **b.** helping verb **c.** subject **d.** predicate.

24. The sentence *She sent many e-mail messages* represents what sentence pattern?   _____

    a. subject–verb **b.** subject–action verb–object **c.** subject–linking verb–complement
    d. subject–linking verb–object.

From the list below select the letter(s) to accurately describe each of the following groups of words.

    a = command   c = fragment   e = run-on sentence
    b = complete sentence   d = comma splice

25. I must call one more person, then I will be ready to evaluate his application.   ~~B~~ D

26. Whenever Mr. Jackson calls to confirm the shipping date.   C

27. Turn on your computer when you arrive and leave it on all day.   A

28. That company's products are excellent its service is slow, however.   E

29. Most of us would rather risk catastrophe than read directions.   ?? ~~X~~ B

30. Although you will be on vacation when your check is issued.   C

31. Complete the form and send it with your check.   A

32. This computer and its software are very powerful, I'm not sure I need that much power.   D

33. Your letter arrived today your package should be here next week.   E

34. Many companies today feature profit-sharing plans, but some employees are reluctant to participate.   B

35. After you read the contract, sign and return it.   A

Hotline Review

Write the letter of the word or phrase that correctly completes each statement.

36. _____ for providing me with the application.   C
    a. Thankyou **b.** Thank-you **c.** Thank you

37. We will _____ brochures at the beginning of our promotion.   ~~B~~ A
    a. disperse **b.** disburse

38. You may have deliveries _____ if you wish.   B
    a. everyday **b.** every day **c.** every-day

39. The reason I am late is _____ my car stalled.   B
    a. because **b.** that

40. Send me an _____ message as soon as you find out.   C
    a. email **b.** E-mail **c.** e-mail

Developing Proofreading Skills

As you complete a set of chapters (a unit), you will find a workshop exercise that introduces various techniques to help you improve your writing skills. This first workshop emphasizes proofreading skills. You will learn about proofreading marks, which are often used by business writers to edit printed material. Study the basic symbols shown here. See the inside front cover of your textbook for a more comprehensive list.

≡ Capitalize	⩗ Insert apostrophe	⨀ Insert period
℘ Delete	⩘ Insert comma	/ Lowercase
∧ Insert	⩠ Insert hyphen	⌒ Close up space

Example:

Proof reading marks are used by writers an editors too make corrections and revisions in printed copy they use these Standard Marks for clarity and consistency. If you are revising your own work, Youll probable use these mark only occasional. In many jobs today however you will be working in a team environment Where writing tasks are shared. Thats when its important to able to aply these well known marks correctly.

The preceding paragraph illustrates the use of proofreading marks. You'll also benefit from the following tips on how to look for errors.

- Be sure to check spelling. If you have composed at a computer, use its spell checker. But don't rely on it totally. It can't tell the difference between *it's* and *its* and many other confusing words.

- Look for grammar and punctuation errors. As you complete this book, you'll be more alert to problem areas, such as subject-verb agreement and comma placement.

- Double-check names and numbers. Compare all names and numbers with their sources because inaccuracies are not immediately visible. Especially verify the spelling of the names of individuals receiving the message. Most of us immediately dislike someone who misspells our name.

- For long or important documents, always print a copy (preferably double-spaced), set it aside for at least a day, and then proofread when you are fresh.

- Be prepared to find errors. One student confessed, "I can find other people's errors, but I can't seem to locate my own." Psychologically, we don't *expect* to find errors, and we don't *want* to find them. You can overcome this obstacle by anticipating errors and congratulating, not criticizing, yourself each time you find one.

Writing Application 1.1. After you read and edit the letter on the next page, your instructor may ask you to write a similar introductory personal business letter to her or him. On a separate sheet of paper, explain why you enrolled in this class, evaluate your present communication skills, name your major, describe the career you seek, and briefly tell about your current work (if you are employed) and your favorite activities. Your instructor may ask you to write a first draft quickly, print it, and then use proofreading marks to show corrections. Make a final copy. Double-space the rough draft; single-space the final copy. Turn in both copies. See Appendix C for a model personal business letter.

The following personal business letter contains intentional errors in typing, spelling, capitalization, and sentence punctuation. Use proofreading marks to edit this letter. You should mark 30 changes.

810 North Miller Road
Marion, IN 46952
September 8, 200x

Professor Margaret M. Sullivan
Department of Business Administration
Schoolcraft College
Marion, IN 46954

Dear Professor Sullivan:

I enrolled this class to help me improve the way I use language. I know that comunication skills are important, and I'm afraid that my pressent skills are below average. They're not good enough for me to get the kind of job I want I also enrolled in this class because its required in my major.

Accounting is my major I chose this majer because I like working with figures And because I know that many good jobs are available in accounting. Although I thought that accountants worked totaly with figures My advisor tells me that accountants also need to be able to explain their work to management, to fellow employees, and to clients. My language skills are not terrific, and I want to improve. When I finish my accounting program, I hope to get a job in the entertainment industry as a Junior/Accountant.

I have a parttime job at Pizza Bob's Where I deliver pizzas to campus dormitories, of to apartments an homes. I like my job because I get to meet people and because it helps me pay for my car and it's insurance.

When I'm not studing or working, I like to surf the internet. My favorite places to visit are World wide web sites devoted to unusual hobbys and businesses. Right now I'm interested in "CyberSlice," a site showing the menus of participating pizzerias in a neighborhood. May be I can get Pizza Bob to participate!

Sincerely,

unit 2 Knowing the Namers

chapter 4 Nouns

Objectives

When you have completed the materials in this chapter, you will be able to do the following:

Level I

• Recognize four kinds of nouns.

Level II

• Spell troublesome plural nouns ending in *y*, *o*, and *f*.
• Form the plurals of compound nouns, numerals, letters, degrees, and abbreviations.

Level III

• Recognize and use correctly foreign plural nouns and selected special nouns.
• Use plural personal titles appropriately.

Underline any incorrectly spelled noun in the following sentences. Write the correct spelling in the space provided.

1. Three children put their books on the bottom shelfs. *shelf*

2. At the market she purchased some tomatoes and potatos. *potatoes*

3. Several attornies requested tax write-offs for books. *attorneys*

4. Our two CPAs both asked for leave of absences in June. *absence*

5. Based on all the criterion, several diagnoses were given to all. *criteria*

PRETEST

As you will recall from Chapter 2, nouns *name* persons, places, things, qualities, and concepts. In this chapter you'll learn to distinguish concrete from abstract nouns and common from proper nouns. The principal emphasis, however, will be on forming and spelling plural nouns, an area of confusion for many business writers.

Beginning with this chapter, concepts are presented in levels, progressing from basic, frequently used concepts at Level I to more complex and less frequently used concepts at Level III. This unique separation of concepts has proved very effective in helping students understand, retain, and apply the information taught in *Business English*.

Level I

Kinds of Nouns

As the "namers" in our language, nouns perform an important function. They often serve as sentence subjects. To help you understand nouns better, we divide them into two categories: concrete and abstract.

Concrete and Abstract Nouns

Concrete nouns name specific objects that you can actually see, hear, feel, taste, or smell. Abstract nouns name qualities and concepts. Because concrete nouns are precise, they are more forceful in writing and talking than abstract nouns.

Concrete Nouns

jetliner	dentist	stapler
orchid	lemonade	dictionary
gorilla	refrigerator	bagel

Abstract Nouns

freedom	happiness	anger
accuracy	memory	personality
truth	love	success

Common and Proper Nouns

Common nouns name *generalized* persons, places, and things. Proper nouns, on the other hand, name *specific* persons, places, and things. They are always capitalized. Rules for capitalization are presented in Chapter 19.

Common Nouns

document	dog	organization
candy	student	radio
photocopier	company	magazine

Proper Nouns

Bill of Rights	Labrador retriever	United Nations
Snickers candy bar	Mark McKinley	Walkman radio
Xerox machine	Coca-Cola Company	*Forbes* magazine

Note: Common nouns following proper nouns are not capitalized.

Career Tip

Successful job applicants fill their résumés with concrete expressions and quantifiable data rather than abstractions. Instead of *Worked as lab assistant*, try *Assisted over 300 students and 25 faculty members using MS Word in computer lab.*

Hot Link

For more information about nouns, visit the Purdue University Online Writing Lab **<http://owl.english. purdue.edu>**. Click on *Instructional Handouts, Parts of Speech, Nouns.*

Basic Plurals

Singular nouns name *one* person, place, or thing. Plural nouns name *two* or more. At Level I you will learn basic rules for forming plurals. At Level II you will learn how to form the plurals of nouns that create spelling problems.

- **Most regular nouns** form the plural with the addition of *s*.

advantage, advantages	desk, desks	graphic, graphics
house, houses	issue, issues	merchant, merchants
passenger, passengers	Johnson, Johnsons	Juan, Juans

Note: Most proper nouns (*Johnson, Paul*) become plural the same way that common nouns do.

- **Nouns ending in s, x, z, ch, or sh** form the plural with the addition of *es*.

box, boxes	brush, brushes	business, businesses
bunch, bunches	dish, dishes	fax, faxes
quartz, quartzes	Sanchez, Sanchezes	BUT: quiz, quizzes

- *Irregular nouns* form the plural by changing the spelling of the word.

child, children	foot, feet	goose, geese
man, men	mouse, mice	ox, oxen, oxes

Because of space restrictions most dictionaries do *not* show plurals of *regular* nouns. Thus, if you look up the plural of *ranch*, you probably will not find it. Dictionaries *do* show the plurals of nouns that might be confusing or difficult to spell.

Be careful not to use apostrophes (') to form plural nouns. Reserve the apostrophe to show possession. (Chapter 5 discusses possessive nouns in detail.)

Incorrect: Many basketball and football star's earn big salary's.

Correct: Many basketball and football stars earn big salaries.

In using plural words, do not confuse nouns with verbs (*He saves* [verb] *his money in two safes* [noun]). Be especially mindful of the following words:

Nouns	Verbs
belief, beliefs	believe, believes
leaf, leaves (foliage)	leave, leaves (to depart)
loaf, loaves (of bread)	loaf, loafs (to be idle)
proof, proofs	prove, proves

Now complete the reinforcement exercises for Level I beginning on page 59.

Troublesome Noun Plurals

Your ability to spell certain troublesome nouns can be greatly improved by studying the following rules and examples.

- **Common nouns ending in *y*** form the plural in two ways.

  a. When the *y* is preceded by a vowel (*a, e, i, o, u*), the plural is formed with the addition of *s* only.

attorney, attorneys	journey, journeys	key, keys
turkey, turkeys	valley, valleys	Garvey, Garveys

  b. When the *y* is preceded by a consonant (all letters other than vowels), the plural is formed by changing the *y* to *ies*.

city, cities	country, countries	currency, currencies
luxury, luxuries	quality, qualities	secretary, secretaries

Note: This rule does *not* apply to the plural forms of proper nouns: Amy, Amys; Lowry, Lowrys; Kelly, Kellys.

- **Nouns ending in *f* or *fe*** follow no standard rules in the formation of plurals. Study the examples shown here, and use a dictionary when in doubt. When two forms are shown, the preferred appears first.

Add *s*	Change to *ves*	Both Forms Recognized
brief, briefs	half, halves	calves, calfs
cliff, cliffs	knife, knives	dwarfs, dwarves
safe, safes	leaf, leaves	wharves, wharfs
staff, staffs	shelf, shelves	scarves, scarfs
sheriff, sheriffs	wife, wives	
Wolf, Wolfs	wolf, wolves	

- **Nouns ending in *o*** may be made plural by adding *s* or *es*.

  a. When the *o* is preceded by a vowel, the plural is formed by adding *s* only.

studio, studios	curio, curios	radio, radios

  b. When the *o* is preceded by a consonant, the plural is formed by adding *s* or *es*. Study the following examples and again use your dictionary whenever in doubt. When two forms are shown, the preferred one appears first.

Add *s*	Add *es*	Both Forms Recognized
auto, autos	echo, echoes	cargoes, cargos
folio, folios	embargo, embargoes	commandos, commandoes
memo, memos	hero, heroes	mosquitoes, mosquitos
patio, patios	potato, potatoes	tornadoes, tornados
ratio, ratios	tomato, tomatoes	volcanos, volcanoes
Soto, Sotos	veto, vetoes	zeros, zeroes

c. Musical terms ending in *o* always form the plural with the addition of *s* only.

alto, altos	banjo, banjos	basso, bassos
cello, cellos	contralto, contraltos	piano, pianos

- **Compound nouns** may be written as single words, may be hyphenated, or may appear as two words.

  a. When written as single words, compound nouns form the plural by appropriate changes in the final element.

bookshelf, bookshelves	footnote, footnotes	payroll, payrolls
photocopy, photocopies	printout, printouts	walkway, walkways

  b. When written in hyphenated or open form, compound nouns form the plural by appropriate changes in the principal noun.

accounts payable	bills of lading	boards of directors
editors in chief	leaves of absence	lookers-on
mayors-elect	mothers-in-law	runners-up

  c. If the compound noun has no principal noun at all, the final element is made plural.

cure-alls	go-betweens	know-it-alls
no-shows	run-ins	show-offs
start-ups	trade-ins	write-ups

  d. Some compound noun plurals have two recognized forms. In the following list, the preferred form is shown first.

  attorneys general, attorney generals

  cupfuls, cupsful; teaspoonfuls, teaspoonsful

  courts-martial, court-martials; notaries public, notary publics

- **Numerals, alphabet letters, isolated words, and degrees** are made plural by adding *s, es,* or *'s.* The trend is to use the *'s* only when necessary for clarity.

  a. Numerals and uppercase letters (with the exception of *A, I, M,* and *U*) require only *s* in plural formation.

2000s	all Bs and Cs	three Rs
three Cs of credit	W-2s and 1040s	9s and 10s

  b. Isolated words used as nouns are made plural with the addition of *s* or *es,* as needed for pronunciation.

pros and cons	ands, ifs, or buts	yeses and noes
whys and wherefores	ins and outs	(*or* yeses and nos)

  c. Degrees are made plural with the addition of *s.*

A.A.s	B.S.s	Ph.D.s
R.N.s	M.B.A.s	M.D.s

  d. Isolated lowercase letters and the capital letters *A, I, M,* and *U* require *'s* for clarity.

p's and q's	M&M's	A's

- **Abbreviations** are usually made plural by adding *s* to the singular form.

bldg., bldgs.	VCR, VCRs	CPA, CPAs
dept., depts.	IOU, IOUs	mgr., mgrs.
No., Nos.	wk., wks.	yr., yrs.

The singular and plural forms of abbreviations for units of measurement are, however, often identical.

deg. (degree or degrees)	in. (inch or inches)
ft. (foot or feet)	oz. (ounce or ounces)

Some units of measurement have two plural forms.

lb. or lbs.	yd. or yds.	qt. or qts.

Now complete the reinforcement exercises for Level II.

L e v e l I I I

Special Plural Forms

Selected nouns borrowed from foreign languages and other special nouns require your attention because their plural forms can be confusing.

- **Nouns borrowed from foreign languages** may retain a foreign plural. A few, however, have an Americanized plural form, shown in parentheses below. Check your dictionary for the preferred form.

Singular	Plural
alumna (*feminine*)	alumnae (pronounced a-LUM-nee)
alumnus (*masculine*)	alumni (pronounced a-LUM-ni)
analysis	analyses
bacterium	bacteria
basis	bases
crisis	crises
criterion	criteria (or criterions)
curriculum	curricula (or curriculums)
datum	data*
diagnosis	diagnoses
erratum	errata
formula	formulae (or formulas)
hypothesis	hypotheses
memorandum	memoranda (or memorandums)
parenthesis	parentheses
phenomenon	phenomena
stimulus	stimuli
thesis	theses

*See discussion on p. 57.

Study Tip

Language purists contend that the word *data* can only be plural (*the data are*). However, see the Hotline Queries for another view.

Spot the Blooper

From *The Bath Country Journal* [Ohio] announcing honors for two female graduates: . . . the award goes "to an alumni who has made a significant contribution or given extraordinary service."

- **Personal titles** may have both formal and informal plural forms.

Singular	Formal Plurals	Informal Plurals
Miss	the Misses Smith	the Miss Smiths
Mr.	Messrs.* Kahn and Lee	Mr. Kahn and Mr. Lee
Mrs.	Mmes.† Davis and Klein	Mrs. Davis and Mrs. Klein
Ms.	Mses.‡ Dean and May	Ms. Dean and Ms. May

* Pronounced MES-erz (abbreviation of Messieurs).
† Pronounced May-DAHM (abbreviation of Mesdames).
‡ Pronounced MIZ-ez (Ms. is probably a blend of Miss and Mrs.).

- **Special nouns,** many of which end in *s*, may normally be *only* singular or plural in meaning. Other special nouns may be considered *either* singular *or* plural in meaning.

Study Tip

You can practice these special nouns by using them with the singular verb *is* or the plural verb *are*. For example, *Genetics is fascinating* (sing.); *scissors are useful* (plural).

Usually Singular	Usually Plural	May be Singular or Plural
genetics	clothes	corps
mathematics	goods	deer
measles	scissors	Vietnamese
economics	statistics	sheep
news	thanks	politics

- **Single-letter abbreviations** may be made plural by doubling the letter.

pp. (pages)	See pp. 18–21. (That is, pages 18 through 21)
(and following)	See pp. 18 ff. (That is, page 18 and following pages)

Now complete the reinforcement exercises for Level III.

HOTLINE QUERIES

Q: In e-mail messages is it acceptable to use abbreviations such as *IMHO (in my humble opinion), ROTFL (rolling on the floor laughing),* and *TIA (thanks in advance)*?

A: Among close friends who understand their meaning, such abbreviations are certainly acceptable. But in business messages, these abbreviations are too casual and too obscure. Many readers would have no idea what they mean. Smileys such as :-) are also too casual for business messages.

Q: It seems to me that the meaning of the word *impact* has changed. I thought it meant "an effect." But now I hear this use: *How does this policy impact on the Middle East?* What's happening to this word?

A: In our language, nouns often become verbs (to *bridge* the gap, to *corner* a market, to *telephone* a friend). Whether a noun-turned-verb is assimilated into the language seems to depend on its utility, its efficiency, and the status of the individuals who use it. Skilled writers, for example, avoid the word *prioritize* because it is inefficient and sounds bureaucratic. Transformation of the noun *impact* into a verb would appear to be unnecessary, since the word *affect* clearly suffices in most constructions (*How does this program affect the Middle East?*). Although we hear *impact* used frequently as a verb today, some language specialists find it offensive.

Q: Could you help me spell the plurals of *do* and *don't*?

A: In forming the plurals of isolated words, the trend today is to add *s* and no apostrophe. Thus, we have *dos* and *don'ts*. Formerly, apostrophes were used to make isolated words plural. However, if no confusion results, make plurals by adding *s* only. Because of capitalization, the lowercase *dos* would not be confused with the uppercase *DOS (disk operating system).*

Q: One member of our staff consistently corrects our use of the word *data*. He says the word is plural. Is it never singular?

A: The word *data* is indeed plural; the singular form is *datum*. Through frequent usage, however, *data* has recently become a collective noun. Collective nouns may be singular or plural depending on whether they are considered as one unit or as separate units. For example, *These data are much different from those findings.* Or, *This data is conclusive.*

Q: I don't have a dictionary handy. Can you tell me which word I should use in this sentence? *A [stationary/stationery] circuit board will be installed.*

A: In your sentence use *stationary*, which means "not moving" or "permanent" (*she exercises on a stationary bicycle*). *Stationery* means "writing paper" (*his stationery has his address printed on it*). You might be able to remember the word *stationery* by associating *envelopes* with the *e* in *stationery*.

Q: My mother is always correcting me when I say, *I hate when that happens.* What's wrong with this? I hear it on TV all the time.

A: Your mother wants you to speak standard English, the written and spoken language of educated people. Hearing an expression on TV is no assurance that it's acceptable. The problem with an expression like *I hate when that happens* is that an adverbial phrase (*when that happens*) is used as the object of a verb (*hate*). Only nouns, noun clauses, or pronouns may act as objects of verbs. Correction: *I hate it when that happens,* or *I hate this to happen.*

Q: As a sportswriter, I need to know the plural of *hole-in-one*.

A: Make the principal word plural, *holes-in-one.*

Q: In the sentence, *Please read our FAQs*, does the abbreviation need an apostrophe?

A: No. The abbreviation for *Frequently Asked Questions* is *FAQs*, as you wrote it. Avoid using an apostrophe for plural forms.

Name _____

Level I

Note: At the beginning of each level, a self-check exercise is provided so that you may immediately check your understanding of the concepts in this chapter. Do not look at the answers until you have finished the exercise. Then compare your responses with the answers shown at the bottom of the page. If more than three of your answers do not agree with those shown, reread the chapter before continuing with the other reinforcement exercises.

A. (Self-check) Write the plural forms of the singular nouns shown in parentheses.

Example: The (Cox) have purchased an office building on Grand Boulevard. **Coxes**

1. Our company cafeteria now offers low-fat (lunch). _____

2. The cafeteria uses over a dozen (loaf) of bread every day. *loaves*

3. Most toy manufacturers employ (child) to test their new products. _____

4. All (fax) in our office are printed on plain paper. *faxes*

5. Tracy made two (batch) of chocolate chip cookies after school. _____

6. The condition will not change unless Congress passes a law with (tooth) in it. *teeth*

7. One administrative assistant may serve six (boss). _____

8. Although the (Davis) can't attend, the Garcias will be at the wedding. *Davises*

Check your answers below.

B. Correct any errors in the use of plural nouns in the following sentences by underlining the incorrect form and writing the correct form in the space provided. If the sentence is correct as it stands, write *C*.

Example: The advertising agency submitted several <u>sketch</u> of the design. **sketches**

1. We left four boxs for UPS to deliver to other branches locally. _____

2. Ryan placed all the <u>dishs</u> on the kitchen shelves carefully. *dishes*

3. New dispatchs from Europe described four new tunnels through the Alps. _____

4. Each year the American Cancer Society sells <u>bunchs</u> of daffodils. *bunches*

5. Because three Jeffrey's are employed in that department, surnames are used. _____

6. Each employee received two free <u>pass's</u> to the exhibit. *passes*

7. Mona Jackson purchased two different lens for her new camera. _____

8. Last year the losses of Laser Industries exceeded its profits. *C*

1. lunches 2. loaves 3. children 4. faxes 5. batches 6. teeth 7. bosses 8. Davises

59

C. Write plural forms for the nouns listed.

1. employee   _____
2. watch   *Watches*
3. Lynch   _____
4. franchise   *Franchises*
5. quota   _____
6. rich   *riches*
7. foot   _____
8. glass   *glasses*

9. hunch   _____
10. goose   *goose*
11. bias   _____
12. Lohman   *Lohmans*
13. service   _____
14. gas   *gases*
15. Hernandez   _____
16. committee   *Committees*

Even

Level II

A. **(Self-check)** Provide the correct plural form of the words shown in parentheses.

1. Both (bill of lading) showed excessive shipping charges.   _____
2. Upper (shelf) contain infrequently used company files.   _____
3. Small businesses can afford few administrative (luxury).   _____
4. None of the (Kennedy) were running for election this year.   _____
5. Students had to show their (ID) before they were admitted.   _____
6. Neither of our (attorney) recommended settling out of court.   _____
7. Deciduous trees drop their (leaf) in the autumn.   _____
8. Our organization is prepared to deal in foreign (currency).   _____

Check your answers below.

B. Write the correct plural form of the singular expressions shown in parentheses.

1. All that remains standing are two blackened (chimney).   _____
2. Liquidity (ratio) of the two companies were compared.   _____
3. What percentage of (CEO) are women?   _____
4. President Sandra Rendell wanted a manager with conservative (belief).   _____
5. Both (Lisa) are outstanding customer service representatives.   _____
6. More graduates with (M.B.A.) are available than ever before.   _____
7. Do the (Wolf) subscribe to *Business Week*?   _____
8. Sales are increasing with all Pacific Rim (country).   _____
9. Both of our publications managers were former (editor in chief).   _____
10. Congress established the Small Business Administration in the (1950).   _____
11. Computer users must distinguish between zeros and (O).   _____

1. bills of lading   2. shelves   3. luxuries   4. Kennedys   5. IDs   6. attorneys   7. leaves   8. currencies

12. We will tabulate all (yes and no) before releasing the vote. _____

13. The two (board of directors) voted to begin merger negotiations. _____

14. President Lincoln had four (brother-in-law) serving in the Confederate Army. _____

15. At least two employees recently took (leave of absence). _____

C. Write plural forms for the nouns listed. Use a dictionary if you are unsure of the spelling.

1. balance of trade _____
2. half _____
3. bill of sale _____
4. IPO (initial public offering) _____
5. subsidiary _____
6. TV _____
7. Sunday _____
8. liability _____
9. Murray _____
10. valley _____

11. cure-all _____
12. L.V.N. _____
13. C _____
14. No. _____
15. governor-elect _____
16. if _____
17. avocado _____
18. RSVP _____
19. dept. _____
20. q _____

D. **Writing Exercise.** Write sentences using the plural form of the nouns shown in parentheses.

1. (get-together) _____

_____

2. (Cortez) _____

_____

3. (do and don't) _____

_____

4. (R.N.) _____

_____

5. (hero) _____

_____

6. (business) _____

_____

7. (attorney) _____

_____

8. (father-in-law) _____

_____

A. **(Self-check)** Write the correct plural form of the words shown in parentheses.

1. Moving lights and other (stimulus) affect the human eye. _____

2. Black holes are but one of the (phenomenon) of astronomy. _____

3. Numerous (crisis) within education will only be worsened by budget cuts. _____

4. Fund raisers contacted all (alumnus) of Colorado State University. _____

5. Formal invitations were sent to (Mrs.) Wagner, Phillips, and Wang. _____

6. You will find the index on (p.) 116–120. _____

7. Experts presented conflicting (analysis) of the problem. _____

8. The announcement reported that (Mr.) Clinton and Gore had formed a partnership. _____

Check your answers below.

B. Write the correct plural form of the words shown in parentheses.

1. Researchers collected substantial (datum) to support their hypothesis. _____

2. The girls' school will honor its illustrious (alumna). _____

3. References to LaserJet printers may be found on pp. 25 (and following pages). _____

4. Dr. Hsu revealed the two startling (hypothesis) in a press conference. _____

5. All variant spellings are shown in sets of (parenthesis). _____

6. Dr. Waters requested information about two related (curriculum). _____

7. Galileo's (hypothesis) about the solar system were rejected by his peers. _____

8. Our catalog shows accounting courses on (p.) 226–231. _____

9. Her disorder has resulted in several different (diagnosis). _____

10. Joan's master's and doctor's (thesis) were both in the library. _____

C. Complete the following sentences, selecting the proper singular or plural verb to agree with the nouns.

1. Economics (is, are) a dynamic field of study. _____

2. (Is, Are) the proceeds to be donated to charity? _____

3. If the scissors (is, are) sharp, we can cut the ballots. _____

4. Mathematics (is, are) feared by some female students. _____

5. The statistics on crime (is, are) staggering. _____

6. (Was, Were) proper thanks given you for your efforts? _____

7. Several Vietnamese (is, are) enrolled in this class. _____

1. stimuli 2. phenomena 3. crises 4. alumni 5. Mmes. 6. pp. 7. analyses 8. Messrs.

D. *Review of Levels I, II, and III.* In the following sentences underline any errors in nouns or noun-verb agreement. For each sentence write a corrected form in the space provided. If a sentence is correct, write *C* in the space.

1. In the 1990s many students earned all As in their classes. _____

2. When you first join an electronic news group, you'll want to read the FAQ's (frequently asked questions) before posting any messages. _____

3. The huge number of inquirys resulting from the news announcement overwhelmed their two Web sites. _____

4. Although many stimulus are being studied, scientists have not yet determined an exact cause of the bacterial mysteries. _____

5. Unless the IRS proves that the Kellys owe federal taxs, no penalty can be assessed. _____

6. Both woman asked for leaves of absence during the week of June 7. _____

7. Tomatoes are grown to perfection in the interior vallies. _____

8. Our directory lists R.N.'s and M.D.'s separately. _____

9. Because economics are the primary concern, be sure your proposal outlines a careful budget for the entire project. _____

10. After numerous brushs with the law, Mark became a consultant to a security company. _____

11. The Lopez's named three beneficiaries in their insurance policies. _____

12. Attorneys and judges were advised to place their heaviest books on the lower shelfs. _____

13. Because of many glitches in our software, e-mail messages arrived in irregular batchs. _____

14. Despite the new flexible hours for Mondays through Thursdays, all employees must put in a full workday on Fridays. _____

15. The Morrises discussed all the in's and out's of the transaction before signing the contract. _____

Editor's Challenge

The following letter contains 30 intentional errors in spelling, proofreading, noun plurals, and sentence structure. Use proofreading marks to correct them.

SHEARMAN BROTHERS
502 Fifth Avenue
New York, NY 10032

Phone: (212) 502-8694   Fax: (212) 502-7619   Web: http://www.shearmanbros.com

April 5, 200x

Ms. Judy Bender Bachman
The Miami News Examiner
4421 Second Street
Miami, FL 33157

Dear Ms. Bender:

Thanks for the opportunity to contribute to the magazine article that you are writting about fast-food promotions. As an analyst with Shearman Brothers, I specialize in the fast-food and beverage industrys.

You specifically wanted information about what sells fast food. Actually, competition among the fast-food giants has always been as much about appearances as reality. Its a lot like a three-ring circus, with new flashy showstoppers needed to keep men, woman, and children coming back. Some promotions by companys have been fiascos. I assume, however, that you are most interested in sucessful strateggs such as the following:

- **Giveaways**. Fast-food giants suchas McDonald's use movie tie-ins and toy promotions that appeal children, who then persuade their parents to come into the stores.

- **Advertising**. Companys spend million on ad campaigns promoting expressions that they hope will become part of everyone's speech, such as classics like "You deserve a break today."

- **Food**. Nothing else matters if the food doesn't taste good. McDonald's, for example, grows its own potatos and raises cattle to ensure that its french frys and sandwichs meet rigid specifications.

- **Price**. Cutting prices increases sale but usually for a short time only. In the end, price-cutting erodes profits. Another strategy is repackaging popular items in "value" combinations Which is an effort to boost sales.

- **Convenience**. People often go to a fastfood restaurant on impulse, the more restaurants that a company has, the likelier that it will make a sale.

I hope theseideas are helpful to you in prepareing your article. If you use any of this material, I must submit your article to our attornies for approval. Call me when you would like to talk further about this artical.

Sincerely,

Paul Lahijanian

Paul Lahijanian
Senior Analyst

learning.web.ways

Many Web sites provide summaries of information about well-known companies. Some sites, such as Hoovers.com, allow you to see a capsule of information at no charge. For more extensive information, you must subscribe. You can find information such as a company's addresses (Web and land), the names of its current officers, its subsidiary locations, its products, and its competition. You can even find out its annual revenue and other financial information. In this short exercise you will search for information about The Coca-Cola Company.

Goal: To learn to search for company data on the Web.

1. With your Web browser on the screen, key the following URL: **<http://www.hoovers.com>.** Press **Enter**.
2. Look over the Hoover's Online home page. Ignore the advertising clutter and click **Search Help.** A window opens. Scroll down to learn about search parameters (characteristics or boundaries). For how many companies does Hoovers provide data? Close the box by clicking the **X** is the right corner of window.
3. Run your cursor over **Site Search**. Click **Company**. In the **For** box, key **CocaCola**. Click **Go**.
4. Wait for the search results. When the **Search Results** page is fully loaded, scroll down to find a listing for The Coca-Cola Company. Click **Capsule** to see a summary of company information.
5. Read about Coca-Cola's main products. What percentage of its sales come from outside the U.S.?
6. Print one page from the capsule.
7. Use the **Back** button to return to the Search page.
8. Search a company of your choice. Print one page of its capsule.
9. If ever you get lost at a Web site or can't find what you want, look for the **Site Map**. It is usually found in a navigation bar at the top, bottom, or along the left side. Find the Hoover's **Site Map** at the top of the screen. Click to see its contents.
10. End your session by clicking the **X** in the upper right corner of your browser. Turn in all printed copies.

POSTTEST

Underline any incorrectly spelled nouns. Write the correct form.

1. The children were warned to be careful of the sharp knifes. *Knives*
2. Three bunches of red tomatos look ripe enough to eat. *tomstoes*
3. Gray wolves are reported to live in the two vallies. _____
4. In the 1980s many companys were searching for M.B.A.s. *e*
5. After several business crises, we hired two attornies. *ettorneys*

1. knives 2. tomatoes 3. valleys 4. companies 5. attorneys

CHECKLIST OF BONUS LEARNING RESOURCES

The following additional learning resources are available to you. Your instructor will tell you which to complete.

- Web Editor's Challenge Exercise

- Web Interactive Chapter Review

- Web PowerPoint Slides

- Web Crossword Puzzle

- WebCheck Reinforcement Exercises 4.1, 4.2

- Self-Help Exercises

- Electronic Study Guide

chapter 5
Possessive Nouns

Objectives

When you have completed the materials in this chapter, you will be able to do the following:

Level I

- Distinguish between possessive nouns and noun plurals.
- Follow five steps in using the apostrophe to show ownership.

Level II

- Use apostrophe construction for animate nouns.
- Distinguish between descriptive nouns and possessive nouns.
- Pluralize compound nouns, combined ownership nouns, organization names, and abbreviations.
- Understand incomplete possessives.
- Avoid awkward possessives.

Level III

- Determine whether an extra syllable can be pronounced in forming a possessive.
- Make proper nouns possessive

Underline any incorrect possessive forms. Write correct versions in the spaces provided.

1. All customers inquiries will be answered immediately. _Customers'_
2. Kevin's sales this month are greater than Anthonys. _Anthony's_
3. Prospective tenants must pay two months rent in advance. _months'_
4. Mr. Ross real talent lies in the electronics field. _Mr. Ross'_
5. The Sanchezes real estate holdings are in San Diego. _Sanchezes'_

1. customers'   2. Anthony's   3. months'   4. Ross' or Ross's   5. Sanchezes'

Thus far you have studied four kinds of nouns (concrete, abstract, common, and proper), and you have learned how to make nouns plural. In this chapter you will learn how to use the apostrophe in making nouns possessive.

Showing Possession With Apostrophes

Notice in the following phrases how possessive nouns show ownership, origin, authorship, or measurement:

Wendy Nguyen's computer (ownership)

Alaska's citizens (origin)

Steven King's writings (authorship)

three years' time (measurement)

In expressing possession, speakers and writers have a choice. They may show possession with an apostrophe construction, or they may use a prepositional phrase with no apostrophe:

the computer of Wendy Nguyen

the citizens of Alaska

the writings of Steven King

the time of three years

The use of a prepositional phrase to show ownership is more formal and tends to emphasize the ownership word. The use of the apostrophe construction to show ownership is more efficient and more natural, especially in conversation. In writing, however, placing the apostrophe can be perplexing. Here are five simple but effective steps that will help you write possessives correctly.

Five Steps in Using the Apostrophe Correctly

1. **Look for possessive construction.** Usually two nouns appear together. The first noun shows ownership of (or a special relationship to) the second noun.

   the man['s] computer

   the children['s] games

   a year['s] time

   both doctors['] offices

   the musicians['] instruments

2. **Reverse the nouns.** Use the second noun to begin a prepositional phrase. The object of the preposition is the ownership word.

   computer of the *man*

   games of the *children*

   time of a *year*

   offices of both *doctors*

   instruments of the *musicians*

Career Tip

"Everything comes to those who hustle while they wait."
—Will Rogers

Spot the Blooper

From Lois and Selma DeBakey's collection of bad medical writing: "The receptionist called the patients names." (How does the missing apostrophe alter the meaning?)

Study Tip

Whenever you have any doubt about using an apostrophe, always put the expression into an "of" phrase. You'll immediately recognize the ownership word and see whether it ends in an *s*.

3. **Examine the ownership word.** To determine the correct placement of the apostrophe, you must know whether the ownership word ends in an *s* sound (such as *s*, *x*, or *z*).

4. **If the ownership word does not end in an *s* sound, add an apostrophe and *s*.**

   the man's computer

   the children's games

   a year's time

5. **If the ownership word does end in an s sound, usually add only an apostrophe.**

   both doctors' offices

   musicians' instruments

A word of caution: Do *not* use apostrophes for nouns that simply show more than one of something. In the sentence *These companies are opening new branches in the West*, no apostrophes are required. The words *companies* and *branches* are plural; they are not possessive. In addition, be careful to avoid changing the spelling of singular nouns when making them possessive. For example, the *secretary's* desk (meaning one secretary) is *not* spelled *secretaries'*.

Pay particular attention to the following possessive constructions. Perhaps the explanations and hints in parentheses will help you understand and remember these expressions.

   a day's work (the work of one single day)

   three days' work (the work of three days)

   a dollar's worth (the worth of one single dollar)

   your money's worth (the worth of your money)

   today's weather (there can be only one today)

   tomorrow's work (there can be only one tomorrow)

   the stockholders' meeting (we usually assume that a meeting involves more than one person)

The guides for possessive construction presented thus far cover the majority of possessives found in business writing.

Now complete the reinforcement exercises for Level I.

Level II

Problem Possessive Constructions

You can greatly improve your skill in using apostrophes by understanding the following special cases.

- **Animate versus inanimate nouns.** As a matter of style, some careful writers prefer to reserve the apostrophe construction for people and animals. For other nouns use prepositional phrases or simple adjectives.

roof of the car, or car roof (better than *car's roof*)

color of the desk, or the desk color (better than *desk's color*)

heat of the motor, or motor heat (better than *motor's heat*)

- **Descriptive versus possessive nouns.** When nouns provide description or identification only, the possessive form is *not* used. Writers have the most problems with descriptive nouns ending in *s*, such as *Claims* Department. No apostrophe is needed, just as none is necessary in *Legal* Department.

  Sales Department (not *Sales' Department*)

  the electronics industry (not *electronics' industry*)

  Los Angeles Dodgers (not *Los Angeles' Dodgers*)

- **Compound nouns.** Make compound nouns possessive by adding an apostrophe or an *'s* to the final element of the compound.

  his father-in-law's property

  onlookers' interest

  notary public's seal

- **Incomplete possessives.** When the second noun in a possessive noun construction is unstated, the first noun is nevertheless treated as possessive.

  You'll find bond paper at the stationer's [store].

  Let's meet at Patrick's [home] after the game.

  This year's sales are higher than last year's [sales].

- **Separate or combined ownership.** When two names express separate ownership, make both names possessive. When two names express combined ownership, make only the *second* name possessive.

Separate Ownership	Combined Ownership
landlords' and tenants' rights	the husband and wife's business
Mike's and Sam's stereos	my aunt and uncle's house

- **Names of organizations.** Organizations with possessives in their names may or may not use apostrophes. Follow the style used by the individual organization. (Consult the organization's stationery or a directory listing.)

Malibu West Homeowners Assn.	Ben & Jerry's Homemade
State Teachers' Retirement System	Sears

- **Abbreviations.** Make abbreviations possessive by following the same guidelines as for animate nouns.

AMA's ruling	all R.N.s' credentials
NBC's coverage	May Co.'s advertisement

- **Awkward possessives.** When the addition of an apostrophe results in an awkward construction, show ownership by using a prepositional phrase.

  Awkward: my sister's attorney's advice

  Improved: advice of my sister's attorney

Awkward:	your neighbor's doctor's telephone number
Improved:	telephone number of your neighbor's doctor
Awkward:	my instructor, Valerie Rodgers', office
Improved:	office of my instructor, Valerie Rodgers

Now complete the reinforcement exercises for Level II.

Spot the Blooper

From *The Ft. Lauderdale Sun-Sentinel*: "It was he and his wife's anniversary."

L e v e l   I I I

You have learned to follow five steps in identifying possessive constructions and in placing the apostrophe correctly. The guides presented thus far cover most possessive constructions. The possessive form of a few nouns, however, requires a refinement of the final step.

Additional Guideline

Let us briefly review the five-step plan for placing the apostrophe in noun possessives. Having done so, we will then add a refinement to the fifth step.

Spot the Blooper

Announcement pasted on top of each Domino's pizza box: "We accept all competitors coupons."

- Look for possessive construction. (Usually, but not always, two nouns appear together.)
- Reverse the nouns.
- Examine the ownership word.
- If the ownership word does *not* end in an *s* sound, add an apostrophe and *s*.
- If the ownership word does end in an *s* sound, usually add just an apostrophe. However, if an extra syllable can be easily pronounced in the possessive form, most writers will add an apostrophe and an *s* to singular nouns.

Singular Noun Ending in an *s* Sound; **Extra Syllable Can Be Easily Pronounced**	**Add Apostrophe and *s***
station of the waitress[s]	waitress's station
desk of the boss[s]	boss's desk
den of the fox[s]	the fox's den

Making Difficult Proper Nouns Possessive

Of all possessive forms, individuals' names—especially those ending in *s* sounds—are the most puzzling, and understandably so. Even experts don't always agree on the possessive form for singular proper nouns.

Traditionalists, as represented in *The Chicago Manual of Style* and *The Modern Language Association Style Manual*, prefer adding an apostrophe and *s* to troublesome *singular proper* nouns that end in *s* sounds. On the other hand, writers of more popular literature, as represented in *The Associated Press Stylebook and Libel Manual*, prefer the simpler style of adding just an apostrophe to singular proper nouns. You may apply either style, but be consistent. Please note in the following examples that the style choice applies *only* to singular names ending in *s* sounds. Plural names are always made possessive with the addition of an apostrophe only. Study the examples shown.

Study Tip

The word *the* preceding a name is a clue that the name is being used in a plural sense. For example, *the Rosses* means the entire Ross family.

Singular Name	Singular Possessive—Traditional	Singular Possessive—Popular	Plural Possessive
Mrs. Jones	Mrs. Jones's	Mrs. Jones'	the Joneses'
Mr. Morris	Mr. Morris's	Mr. Morris'	the Morrises'
Mrs. Lopez	Mrs. Lopez's	Mrs. Lopez'	the Lopezes'
Mr. Horowitz	Mr. Horowitz's	Mr. Horowitz'	the Horowitzes'

Here's a summary of the possessive rule that should be easy to remember: If an ownership word does not end in an *s*, add an apostrophe and *s*. If the ownership word does end in an *s*, add just an apostrophe—unless you can easily pronounce an extra syllable. If you can pronounce that extra syllable, add an apostrophe and *s*.

HOTLINE QUERIES

Q: Where should the apostrophe go in *employee's handbook*?

A: This is tricky because the writer of that phrase must decide whether he or she considers the handbook from one employee's point of view or from all employees' points of view. Depending on the point of view, the apostrophe could be justified for either position. The trend today seems to favor the singular construction (*employee's handbook, driver's license, user's manual*).

Q: I work for the Supreme Court in Arizona, and I have a problem with the following sentence: *The plaintiff was in fact fired ostensibly for violating Denny's alcoholic beverage service policy.* How do I make possessive a proper name that is already possessive?

A: As you suspected, you can't add another apostrophe. In the interests of clarity, I would consider the name descriptive, thus avoiding an additional *'s*. You would write *Denny's alcoholic beverage service policy*. By the same reasoning, you would not add another apostrophe to anything possessed by *McDonald's*.

Q: Why does *Martha's Vineyard* have an apostrophe while *Harpers Ferry* doesn't?

A: The federal government maintains a Board on Geographic Names in the U.S. This board has a policy that "geographic names in the U.S. should not show ownership of a feature." British maps, says board secretary Roger Payne, are "littered with apostrophes." To avoid such clutter, the board allows no possessive on any federal maps or documents, unless previously dispensated. Only four geographic names have dispensations: Martha's Vineyard, (Massachusetts), Carlos Elmer's Joshua View (Arizona), Ike's Point (New Jersey), and John E.'s Pond (Rhode Island).

Q: I'm addressing a letter to the American Nurses Association. What salutation shall I use? One person in our office suggested *Gentlewomen*. Is this being used?

A: I recommend that you use *Ladies and Gentlemen* since both male and female nurses are members of the association. In fact, this salutation is appropriate for any organization in which men and women may be represented in management. I would not use *Gentlewomen* because it sounds artificial. Businesses and individuals can avoid sexism in language without using stilted constructions. Salutations such as *Dear Sir* and *Gentlemen* are no longer used. Today we are more sensitive to women as employees, managers, and executives. The use of awkward terms like *Gentlewomen* or *Gentlepersons*, however, is an overreaction and should be avoided. Probably the best approach is to write specific people. Find the name of the individual you should be addressing.

Q: Should *undercapitalized* be hyphenated? I can't find it in my dictionary.

A: The prefixes *under* and *over* are not followed by hyphens.

Q: Is there an apostrophe in *Veterans Day*, and if so, where does it go?

A: *Veterans Day* has no apostrophe, but *New Year's Day* does have one.

Q: My boss has dictated, *I respectfully call <u>you</u> and your client's attention to. . .* What's wrong with this? How can I make *you* possessive?

A: The best way to handle this awkward wording is to avoid using the possessive form. Instead, use a prepositional phrase (*I respectfully call to the attention of you and your client . . .*).

Q: Here at the Cancer Society we have a bureau of speakers. Where should the apostrophe go when we use the possessive form of the word *speakers*?

A: *Speakers' bureau.*

Name _____

Level I

A. (Self-check) Rewrite the following phrases avoiding the use of the apostrophe. Use a prepositional phrase. Does the ownership word end in an *s* sound?

	Revision	End in *s* Sound?
Example: the trainee's hours	hours of the trainee	No
1. the defendant's pleas	pleas of the defendant	N
2. our children's futures	the future of our children	N
3. three men's suggestions	suggestions of the 3 men	N
4. our company's policy	policy of our company	N
5. your money's worth	worth of your money	N
6. a beginner's luck	luck of a beginner	N
7. two years' time	time of two years	Y
8. all drivers' engines	engines of all drivers	Y
9. this customer's e-mail message	e-mail messages of this customer	N
10. her parents' wishes	wishes of her parents	Y

Check your answers below.

B. Using apostrophes, change the following prepositional phrases into possessive constructions. Ownership words are italicized.

Example: compensation of *women*	women's compensation
1. qualifications of the *engineer*	engineer's qualifications
2. rights of *patients*	patients' rights
3. permit for a *seller*	seller's permit
4. interest for six *months*	six months' interest
5. addresses of *customers*	customers' addresses
6. stock of this *company*	company's stock
7. prices of *competitors*	competitors' prices
8. duties of the *secretary*	secretary's duties
9. delay of a *month*	a month's delay
10. meeting of *stockholders*	stockholders' meeting

C. Underline the errors in possessive construction in the following sentences. Write the correct form in the space provided. If the sentence is correct as it stands, write *C*.

Example: Some <u>students</u> cars were ticketed.   _students'_

1. Search engines can find only a fraction of the <u>Webs</u> vast contents.   _Web's_

2. Customers expect a <u>dollars</u> worth of value for a dollar spent.   _dollar's_

3. In just one <u>days</u> e-mail, the manager receives as many as 250 messages.   _day's_

4. All administrative <u>assistants'</u> salaries will be reviewed next quarter.   _____

5. Worldwide competition continues to compress profits for all companies. ~~C~~ *Correct*   _____

6. Most <u>students'</u> difficulties lie in recognizing possessives.   _____

7. Many management firms will tailor their services and charges to a <u>clients</u> needs.   _____

8. Several bakeries in our neighborhood provide excellent loaves of bread. C   _____

9. Three <u>months'</u> interest will be due in four days.   _____

10. Success depends on a <u>companies</u> capacity to deliver.   _____

11. The four <u>astronomers'</u> theories created international news.   _____

12. A <u>customers</u> credit card may be used as safely on the Internet as in a restaurant.   _____

13. Some companies are cutting expenses by requiring employees, customers, and vendors to communicate by e-mail. C   _____

14. An <u>inventors</u> patent protects an invention for seventeen years.   _____

15. At each <u>buyers</u> expense, quality upgrades may be substituted.   _____

16. You have exactly four days in which to find new fire and liability insurance policies for the <u>buildings.</u> C   _____

17. All <u>taxpayers</u> returns are checked by our computer.   _____

18. Many of <u>Disneys</u> animated films are now made in Vancouver, which is North America's second largest film production center.   _____

19. Jeong <u>Lees</u> salary is higher than that of other clerks because he has greater responsibilities.   _____

20. When the bill receives the <u>governors</u> signature, it will become law.   _____

A. (Self-check) For each of the following sentences, underline any possessive construction that could be improved. Write an improved form in the space provided. If the sentence is acceptable as it stands, write *C*.

Examples: Our office's roof is leaking.   **The roof of our office**
             The meeting Friday is at Ellens.   **Ellen's**

1. This car's brakes are worn.   _____

2. The St. Louis' Cardinals are having a good season.   _____

3. Jennifer's and Jason's new car was very expensive.   _____

4. This company's product line is superior to that companys. _____

5. The first runner-ups prize of $200 went to Chandra Lewis. _____

6. Small aircraft sales were stimulated by the FAAs new ruling. _____

7. All teachers contribute to the State Teacher's Retirement System. _____

8. A notary publics seal is required on these documents. _____

9. All ladies and mens raincoats are reduced in price. _____

10. Is your sister-in-laws job downtown?   _____

Check your answers below.

B. For each of the following sentences, underline any possessive construction that could be improved. Write an improved form in the space provided. If the sentence is acceptable as it stands, write *C*.

1. What is that sticky substance on the computer's keys?   _____

2. Web graphics must be designed with the audience's browsers in mind.   _____

3. On the second floor is the chief of staffs office.   _____

4. This year's computer sales outdistanced last years.   _____

5. All beneficiaries names must be submitted when policies are issued.   _____

6. NASAs goal is to scale down its projects to save time and money.   _____

7. Our Human Resource's manager commanded the group's attention.   _____

8. One of the CEOs children works in the mail room.   _____

9. Numerous employees personnel folders will be reviewed.   _____

10. You can download many news releases promoting software programs.   _____

11. Both the husband's and wife's signatures must be secured before the sale is valid.   _____

12. Most of this companys customers are concentrated nearby.   _____

13. At least a dozen buyers and sellers finances were scrutinized.   _____

7. Teachers'   8. notary public's   9. ladies', men's   10. sister-in-law's
1. brakes of the car or car brakes   2. St. Louis   3. Jennifer   4. company's   5. runner-up's   6. FAA's

14. Some air-freight lines and all bus lines are subject to the ICCs latest regulation. _____

15. Your totals for the last three columns are certainly different from Kims. _____

16. Because of the gravity of the offense, the district attorneys staff is investigating. _____

17. Lyon & Co.s annual sale is scheduled to begin in three days. _____

18. Two of the table's legs were damaged in transit. _____

19. They took their complaint to small claim's court. _____

20. Were you at Anns last Saturday night? _____

C. Rewrite these sentences to remedy awkward or incorrect possessives.

Example: My sister's friend's car is available.

The car of my sister's friend is available.

(*Hint:* **Start your sentence with the word that is owned.**)

1. His company's accountant's suggestions are wise. _____
   _____
   _____

2. Michael Jordan's father's support was instrumental to the athlete's success. _____
   _____
   _____

3. Were both your brothers-in-law's cars ticketed on the same day? _____
   _____
   _____

4. The engineer's secretary's computer held all the necessary equations. _____
   _____
   _____

5. My boss's friend's motor home is always parked in the company lot. _____
   _____
   _____

L e v e l   I I I

A. **(Self-check)** Select an acceptable possessive form.

1. Have you seen Annie (a) Leibovitz' or Leibovitz's, (b) Leibovitzes' photographs? _____

2. We can't locate (a) Russes', (b) Russ' or Russ's employee record. _____

3. Is that a realtor's sign on the (a) Morris' or Morris's, (b) Morrises' home? _____

4. Only one (a) waitress's, (b) waitresses' service was criticized. _____

5. Anh Le took Dr. (a) Fox' or Fox's, (b) Foxes' prescription to a pharmacy. _____

6. All (a) creditor's, (b) creditors' claims will be honored. _____

7. Several of the (a) seamstresses', (b) seamstress's machines were broken. _____

8. Please verify Mrs. (a) Lopezes', (b) Lopez's or Lopez' hours. _____

9. Have you noticed that the (a) Horowitzes, (b) Horowitzes' have a new car? (Tricky!) _____

10. Are you using a computer to schedule your (a) bosses', (b) boss's appointments? (One boss.) _____

Check your answers below.

B. Fill in the singular possessive forms for the two styles shown.

	Traditional Style	**Popular Style**
Example: [Mr. Jones] suit	**Mr. Jones's suit**	**Mr. Jones' suit**
1. [Ms. Pitts] motorcycle		
2. [Chris] car		
3. [Mr. Harris] desk		
4. [Dr. Cortez] office		
5. [Miss Metz] letter		

C. Correct any errors in possessives in the following sentences.

1. Elvis home, Graceland, is located in Memphis, Tennessee. _____

2. His landlord said that four months rent was due. _____

3. Mrs. Lopez paycheck did not reflect the deduction. _____

4. We were all invited to the party at the Thomas. _____

5. Despite a weeks delay the package finally arrived. _____

6. Chuck Norris films are enjoyed by fans of the martial arts. _____

7. Our records show that Mr. Murray account has an error. _____

8. After seven years time the property reverts to state ownership. _____

9. I can find other peoples errors but not my own. _____

10. Three companys tax returns were audited by the IRS. _____

D. Writing Exercise. Compose original sentences illustrating the possessive forms of the words shown in parentheses. Underline the possessive in each of your sentences.

Example: (two years) **You must have two years' experience to apply for the job.** _____

1. (Tiffany) _____

2. (driver) _____

3. (Jason and Serena) _____

4. (waitress) _____

5. (customers) _____

6. (mother-in-law) _____

1.a 2.b 3.b 4.a 5.a 6.b 7.a 8.b 9.a 10.b

Editor's Challenge

The following personal business letter contains intentional errors in sentence structure, spelling, plural nouns, possessive nouns, and proofreading. You should mark 30 changes.

2320 Navajo Road
Phoenix, AZ 84690
February 9, 200x

Mr. Jonathon Benson
Benson Brothers Management Services
3328 Big Mesa Road
Scottsdale, AZ 85042

Dear Mr. Bensen:

SUBJECT: MANAGING APARTMENT COMPLEX IN SCOTTSDALE

Please send me more information about your companys managment service for apartment owner's I especially would like answers to the following questions.

What are your fees to manage an apartment complex with six unit? Do you take care of renting the units when they become vacant. What percentage of all renters payments do you keep?

Will you enforce a list of do's and don't's that the owner provides? Do you require the last months rent in advance do you maintain attornies to handle legal problems?

Its now my responsibility to care for my father-in-laws six-unit apartment complex in Scottsdale, this complex is 23 years old and currently all units are occupied. Although we expect to have two vacancys in April. your firms management services' may be exactly what I need. Since I am not living near the apartment complex. Please respond to my questions before March 1. So that I may evaluate the pro's and con's of your services.

Sincerely,

Yolanda Morales

Yolanda Morales

Your boss is irritated by unwanted e-mail messages, such as "Earn Big Money Working at Home!" She asks you to use the Web to find a way to stop this misuse of her computer. You decide to use a well-known search engine, AltaVista.

Goal: To learn to refine search terms.

1. With your Web browser on the screen, key the following URL in the location box: **<http://www.altavista.com>**. Press **Enter.**

2. Look at the AltaVista opening page. Try to ignore the clutter and banner advertisements (the price we pay for free search engines). Locate the **Find** box.

3. Key the following search term: **e-mail.** Press **Enter** or click **Search**. Wait for AltaVista to complete its search.

4. Scroll down to the **Web Pages** box and note how many were found. You will see that over 40 million pages include the word *e-mail*. Look over the site titles presented. See any relevant sites?

5. To reduce the number of "hits," you must refine your search term. Scroll back to the top of the screen and locate the **Find** box again. Key a new search term: **unwanted e-mail.**

6. Scroll down to see the number of hits. This refined search term still brings over 2 million hits.

7. Scroll back to the **Find** box and insert a new search term. Include quotation marks: **"unwanted e-mail/spam."** This time AltaVista will find only those sites that include "unwanted e-mail/spam" as a unit.

8. Scroll down to the numbered Web pages found. Click on one of the pages that looks most promising. Find an answer to this question: What can an e-mail user do about unwanted messages (spam)?

9. If you have no success with AltaVista, try another search engine such as **<http://www.google.com>**.

10. Find and print one or two pages with advice on how to deal with unwanted e-mail.

11. End your session by clicking the **X** in the upper right corner of your browser. Turn in all printed copies.

POSTTEST

Underline any incorrect possessive forms. Write correct versions.

1. New dividends were announced at the stockholders meeting. _____

2. This month's sales figures were better than last months. _____

3. In just two years time, your profits will likely double. _____

4. Mrs. Alvarez secretary located all the accounts receivable. _____

5. The three witnesses testimonies required seven court days. _____

1. stockholders' 2. last month's 3. years' 4. Alvarez' or Alvarez's 5. witnesses'

chapter 6
Personal Pronouns

Objectives

When you have completed the materials in this chapter, you will be able to do the following:

Level I

- Use personal pronouns correctly as subjects and objects.
- Distinguish between personal possessive pronouns (such as *its*) and contractions (such as *it's*).

Level II

- Choose the correct pronoun in compound constructions, comparatives, and appositives.
- Use reflexive pronouns correctly.

Level III

- Use nominative case pronouns with subject complements.
- Select the correct pronouns for use with the infinitive *to be*.

Underline the correct pronouns.

1. The contract was signed by Ms. Murphy and (I, me, myself) last week.

2. (Us, We) employees receive additional health benefits in September.

3. Only one of the job applicants can keyboard as fast as (her, she).

4. Are you sure it was (he, him) who called me yesterday morning?

5. Good workers like you and (he, him) are difficult to recruit.

As you will remember from Chapter 2, pronouns are words that substitute for nouns and other pronouns. They enable us to speak and write without awkward repetition. Grammatically, pronouns may be divided into seven types (personal, relative, interrogative, demonstrative, indefinite, reflexive, and reciprocal). Rather than consider all seven pronoun types, this textbook will be concerned only with those pronouns that cause difficulty in use.

L e v e l   I

Guidelines for Using Personal Pronouns

Personal pronouns indicate the person speaking, the person spoken to, or the person or object spoken of. Notice in the following table that personal pronouns change their form (or *case*) depending on who is speaking (called the *person*), how many are speaking (the *number*), and the sex (or *gender*) of the speaker. For example, the third person feminine objective singular case is *her*. Most personal pronoun errors by speakers and writers involve faulty usage of case forms. Study this table to avoid errors in personal pronoun use.

	Nominative Case*		Objective Case		Possessive Case	
	Sing.	**Plural**	**Sing.**	**Plural**	**Sing.**	**Plural**
First Person (person speaking)	I	we	me	us	my, mine	our, ours
Second Person (person spoken to)	you	you	you	you	your, yours	your, yours
Third Person (person or things spoken of)	he, she, it	they	him, her, it	them	his, her, hers, its	their, theirs

*Some authorities prefer the term *subjective case*.

Basic Use of the Nominative Case

Nominative case pronouns are used primarily as the subjects of verbs. Every verb or verb phrase, regardless of its position in a sentence, has a subject. If that subject is a pronoun, it must be in the nominative case.

I thought *he* had left the office.

They asked if *we* had valid passports.

Basic Use of the Objective Case

Objective case pronouns most commonly are used in two ways.

- **Object of a verb.** When pronouns act as direct or indirect objects of verbs, they must be in the objective case.

Give *them* a building map.

Bill asked *her* for help.

Study Tip

This list is so important that you must memorize it. You must also know how these pronouns function in sentences.

Spot the Blooper

Vanity Fair interview with famous Hollywood action hero: "If I got married, it would be a unique situation where me and the woman would have a certain kind of format . . ."

Spot the Blooper

On KNCB-TV, Los Angeles, a reporter twice said, "The gunman shot at she and her fellow officers."

- **Object of a preposition.** The objective case is used for pronouns that are objects of prepositions.

    Supplies were sent to *them*.

    An excellent report was given by *him*.

    Just between *you* and *me*, profits are slipping.

When the words *between, but, like,* and *except* are used as prepositions, errors in pronoun case are likely to occur. To avoid such errors, isolate the prepositional phrase, and then use an objective case pronoun as the object of the preposition. (*Every employee [but Craig and him] completed the form.*)

Basic Use of the Possessive Case

Possessive pronouns show ownership. Unlike possessive nouns, possessive pronouns require no apostrophes. Study these five possessive pronouns: *hers, yours, ours, theirs, its.* Notice the absence of apostrophes. Do not confuse possessive pronouns with contractions. Contractions are shortened (contracted) forms of subjects and verbs, such as *it's* (for *it is*), *there's* (for *there is*), *they're* (for *they are*), and *you're* (for *you are*). In these examples the apostrophes indicate omitted letters.

Possessive Pronouns	Contractions
Theirs is the first car in line.	*There's* no stationery left.
The cat is cleaning *its* fur.	*It's* a dangerous situation.
Your presentation was excellent.	*You're* the next speaker.

Now complete the reinforcement exercises for Level I.

L e v e l   I I

Problems in Using Personal Pronouns

Choosing the correct personal pronouns in compound constructions, comparatives, and appositives requires a good understanding of the following guidelines.

Compound Subjects and Objects

When a pronoun appears in combination with a noun or another pronoun, special attention must be given to case selection. Use this technique to help you choose the correct pronoun case: Ignore the extra noun or pronoun and its related conjunction, and consider separately the pronoun in question to determine what the case should be.

    Tou-Mai asked [you and] *me* for advice. (Ignore *you and*.)

    [Larry and] *he* enrolled in the class. (Ignore *Larry and*.)

    Will you permit [Tony and] *them* to join you? (Ignore *Tony and*.)

Notice in the first sentence, for example, that when *you and* is removed, the pronoun *me* must be selected because it functions as the object of the verb.

Study Tip

Never use *it's* unless you can substitute *it is*. Because they'd rather be safe than sorry, many writers mentally say *it is* every time they use *it's*.

Comparatives

In statements of comparison, words are often implied but not actually stated. To determine pronoun case in only partially complete comparative statements introduced by *than* or *as*, always mentally finish the comparative by adding the implied missing words.

> Each month Jon saves as much as they. (Jon saves as much as *they* [not *them*] save.)
>
> Lisa spells better than he. (. . . better than *he* [not *him*] spells.)
>
> Tardiness annoys Mr. Britton as much as *me*. (. . . as much as it annoys *me* [not *I*].)

Appositives

Appositives explain or rename previously mentioned nouns or pronouns. A pronoun in apposition takes the same case as that of the noun or pronoun with which it is in apposition. In order to determine more easily what pronoun case to use for a pronoun in combination with an appositive, temporarily ignore the appositive.

> *We* [consumers] are protected by laws. (Ignore *consumers*.)
>
> Precautions were taken by *us* [neighbors]. (Ignore *neighbors*.)

Reflexive (or Compound Personal) Pronouns

Reflexive pronouns that end in *-self* emphasize or reflect on their antecedents (the nouns or pronouns previously mentioned).

> The president *himself* presented the award. (Emphasizes *president*.)
>
> The matter should resolve *itself*. (Reflects on *matter*.)

Errors result when reflexive pronouns are used instead of personal pronouns. If no previously mentioned noun or pronoun is stated in the sentence, use a personal pronoun instead of a reflexive pronoun.

> Bring the proposed agenda to either Brad or *me*. (Not *myself*.)
>
> Dalia Amaya and *I* analyzed the possibilities. (Not *myself*.)

Please note that *hisself* and *themself* are substandard and should always be avoided. Now complete the reinforcement exercises for Level II.

L e v e l   I I I

Advanced Uses of Nominative Case Pronouns

Although the following applications appear infrequently, careful speakers and writers try to understand why certain pronouns are used.

Subject Complement

As we saw earlier in this chapter, nominative case pronouns usually function as subjects of verbs. Less frequently, nominative case pronouns also perform as subject complements. A pronoun that follows a linking verb and renames the subject

Spot the Blooper

From *Family Circle* magazine: "After all, [Susan] Sarandon is not much older than me, and she, too, is the mother of two young children."

Spot the Blooper

Television commercial for Continental Insurance Co.: "Nobody does it better than us."

Spot the Blooper

From the KOB-TV [Albuquerque, NM] weather reporter: "Good news for we skiers!"

Spot the Blooper

From *The Chicago Tribune*: "The turn of the year is always a feast for we lovers of lists . . . ."

must be in the nominative case. Be especially alert to the linking verbs *am, is, are, was, were, be, being,* and *been.*

> It *was I* who placed the order.
>
> I'm sure it *is she* who usually answers the telephone.
>
> If you *were I*, what would you do?

When a verb of several words appears in a phrase, look at the final word of the verb. If it is a linking verb, use a nominative pronoun.

> It *might have been they* who made the bid.
>
> The driver *could have been he*.
>
> If the teacher *had been she*, my grade might have been higher.

In conversation it is common to say, *It is me,* or more likely, *It's me.* Careful speakers and writers, though, normally use nominative case pronouns after linking verbs. If the resulting constructions sound too "formal," revise your sentences appropriately. For example, instead of *It is I who placed the order*, use *I placed the order.*

Infinitive *To Be* Without a Subject

Infinitives are the present forms of verbs preceded by *to*—for example, *to sit, to run,* and *to walk.* Nominative pronouns are used following the infinitive *to be* when the infinitive has no subject. In this instance the infinitive joins a complement (not an object) to the subject.

> Mikhail was mistakenly thought to be *I*. (The infinitive *to be* has no subject; *I* is the complement of the subject *Mikhail*.)
>
> Why would Jennifer want to be *she*? (The infinitive *to be* has no subject; *she* is the complement of the subject *Jennifer*.)

Infinitive *To Be* With a Subject

When the infinitive *to be* has a subject, any pronoun following it will function as an object. Therefore, the pronoun following the infinitive will function as its object and take the objective case.

> The teacher believed Jennifer to be *her*. (The subject of the infinitive *to be* is *Jennifer*; therefore, the pronoun functions as an object. Try it another way: *The teacher believed her to be Jennifer.* You would not say, *The teacher believed she to be Jennifer.*)
>
> John expected the callers to be *us*. (The subject of the infinitive *to be* is *callers*; therefore, the pronoun functions as an object.)
>
> Regis judged the winner to be *him*. (The subject of the infinitive *to be* is *winner*; therefore, use the objective case pronoun *him*.)

Whenever you have selected a pronoun for the infinitive *to be* and you want to test its correctness, try reversing the pronoun and its antecedent. For example, *We thought the winner to be her* (*We thought her [not she] to be the winner*).

Study Tip

Whenever a pronoun follows a linking verb, that pronoun will be in the nominative case.

Study Tip

This memory device may help you remember the correct pronoun to use with the infinitive *to be*: No subject, then nominative. That is, if the infinitive *to be* has no subject, supply a nominative pronoun. For example, *I was thought to be she.*

Summary of Pronoun Cases

Spot the Blooper

Sign at Bob's Big Boy restaurant in Monrovia, CA: One side says, "There back!" The other side says, "Their back!" [Which side is correct?]

The following table summarizes the uses of nominative and objective case pronouns.

Nominative Case	
Subject of the verb	*They* are sky divers.
Subject complement	That is *he.*
Infinitive *to be* without a subject	Josh pretended to be *he.*

Objective Case	
Direct or indirect object of the verb	Give *him* another chance.
Object of a preposition	Send the order to *him.*
Object of an infinitive	Ann hoped to call *us.*
Infinitive *to be* with subject	We thought the guests to be *them.*

Now complete the reinforcement exercises for Level III.

Types of Pronouns

For those of you interested in a total view, here is a summary of the seven types of pronouns, with sentences illustrating each type. This list is presented for your interest alone, not for potential testing.

Spot the Blooper

Advice from a Canadian telephone company booklet: "Hang up if the caller doesn't say anything, at the first obscene word, or if the caller doesn't identify themself to your satisfaction."

- **Personal pronouns** replace nouns or other pronouns. Examples:

  Nominative Case: I, we, you, he, she, it, they

  Objective Case: me, us, you, him, her, it, them

  Possessive Case: my, mine, our, ours, your, yours, his, hers, its, their, theirs.

  Mr. Benton said *he* put *his* signature on *it* yesterday.

- **Relative pronouns** join subordinate clauses to antecedents. Examples: *who, whose, whom, which, that, whoever, whomever, whichever, whatever.*

  He is the candidate *whom* we all admire.

- **Interrogative pronouns** replace nouns in a question. Examples: *who, whose, whom, which, what.*

  Whose seat is this?

- **Demonstrative pronouns** designate specific persons or things. Examples: *this, these, that, those.*

  This must be the work request we need.

- **Indefinite pronouns** replace nouns. Examples: *everyone, anyone, someone, each, everybody, anybody, one, none, some, all,* and so on.

  Everybody needs adequate nourishment.

- **Reflexive pronouns (compound personal)** emphasize or reflect on antecedents. Examples: *myself, yourself, himself, herself, itself, oneself,* and so on.

  The president *himself* answered that letter.

- **Reciprocal pronouns** indicate mutual relationship. Examples: *each other, one another*.

  All three chief executive officers consulted *one another* before making the announcement.

Q: On the radio I recently heard a talk-show host say, *My producer and myself. . . .* A little later that same host said, *Send any inquiries to the station or myself at this address.* This sounded half right and half wrong, but I would have trouble explaining the problem. Can you help?

A: The problem is a common one: use of a reflexive pronoun (*myself*) when it has no preceding noun on which to reflect. Correction: *My producer and I* and *Send inquiries to the station or me.* Reflexive pronouns like *myself* should be used only with obvious antecedents, such as *I, myself, will take the calls.* Individuals in the media often misuse reflexive pronouns, perhaps to avoid sounding egocentric with overuse of *I* and *me.*

Q: I have a question about the use of *etc.* in this sentence: *We are installing better lighting, acoustical tile, sound barriers, and etc.* Should I use two periods at the end of the sentence, and does a comma precede *etc.*?

A: Although the use of *etc.* (meaning "and so forth") is generally avoided, do not, if it is to be used, include the redundant word *and*. When *etc.* is found at the end of a sentence, one comma should precede it. When *etc.* appears in the middle of a sentence, two commas should set it off. For example, *Better lighting, acoustical tile, and sound barriers, etc., are being installed.* *Never* use two periods at the end of a sentence, even if the sentence ends with an abbreviation such as *etc.*

Q: We're having a disagreement in our office about the word *healthy.* Is it correct to write *Exercise is healthy*?

A: Strictly speaking, *healthy* means "to have or possess good health." For example, *The rosy-cheeked schoolchildren look healthy.* The word *healthful* means "to promote or be conducive to good health." Your sentence should read: *Exercise is healthful.*

Q: Should a hyphen be used in the word *dissimilar*?

A: No. Prefixes such as *dis, pre, non,* and *un* do not require hyphens. Even when the final letter of the prefix is repeated in the initial letter of the root word, no hyphens are used: *disspirited, preenroll, nonnutritive.*

Q: I thought I knew the difference between *to* and *too,* but could you provide me with a quick review?

A: *To* may serve as a preposition (*I'm going to the store*), and it may also serve as part of an infinitive construction (*to sign his name*). The adverb *too* may be used to mean "also" (*Andrea will attend too*). In addition, the word *too* may be used to indicate "to an excessive extent" (*the letter is too long*).

Q: I have a lot of trouble with the word *extension,* as in the expressions *extension* cord and telephone *extension.* Is the word ever spelled *extention*?

A: You are not alone in having trouble with *extension.* No, it is never spelled with the familiar suffix *tion.* Perhaps you could remember it better if you associate the word *tension* with *extension.*

Name _____

Level I

A. (Self-check) Select the correct form.

1. We are sure that (he, him) graduated from Tidewater Community College. — *he*

2. All employees except (she, her) use e-mail regularly. — *her*

3. Send the fax to (they, them) at their Florida address. — *them*

4. (They, Them), as well as some other employees, volunteered for the project. — *They*

5. It seems strange that someone like (he, him) could be given the assignment. *him* — *~~he~~*

6. Please discuss it with Dewayna Scott and (she, her) before proceeding. — *her*

7. All the purchases made by (she, her) were billed incorrectly. — *her*

8. Are you sure (there's, theirs) time to complete the form? — *there's*

9. Courtney said that (its, it's) your turn next. — *it's*

10. Sean is certain that nobody but (he, him) can open the lock. — *him he*

Check your answers below.

B. In the spaces provided, list five personal pronouns that can be used as subjects of verbs and five that can be used as objects of verbs or objects of prepositions.

As subjects: 1. *he* 2. *she* 3. *we* 4. *it* 5. *they*

As objects: 1. *me* 2. *you* 3. *him* 4. *her* 5. *it*

C. In this set of sentences, all the omitted pronouns serve as subjects of verbs. Write the correct pronoun for each sentence.

1. The project director and (she, her) worked on the program budget. — *she ~~her~~*

2. I know that Mary Nerburn and (he, him) will be purchasing the franchise as a joint venture. — *he ~~him~~*

3. Until the auditions were completed, Rick and (she, her) had no idea who had been chosen. — *she*

4. When the product was introduced, other salespeople and (they, them) attended four training sessions. — *~~they~~ them*

5. We are pleased to learn that (he, him) will be transferred to our division. — *he*

In the next set of sentences, all the omitted pronouns serve as objects of verbs or prepositions. Selected prepositions have been italicized to help you recognize them. Write the correct pronoun for each sentence.

6. Tambi Arnold asked if the terms of the proposal were satisfactory *to* (we, us). — *us*

7. A substantial investment in the McDonald's franchise was made *by* (he, him). — *him*

8. Send Minh Ngo and (I, me) your latest prices for Model T-S40. — *me*

9. Everyone *but* (they, them) invested in growth stocks.   ~~them~~ *us*

10. When you finish with it, please give the video *to* (we, us).   *us*

D. In the spaces provided, write the correct letter to indicate how the italicized pronouns function in these sentences.

a = subject of a verb   b = object of a verb   c = object of a preposition

Example: Please ask *her* for their fax number.   **b**

1. Professor Amoroso asked *me* for my homework.   *a* b

2. Cheryl and *she* were late for their counseling appointments.   *a*

3. When Mike completed the difficult task, the supervisor praised *him*.   *b*

4. The secret agreement between Hana Pak and *him* was not revealed.   *a* c

5. *They* made an offer to purchase the four-acre plot.   *a*

E. Select the correct pronoun.

1. Please have (he, <u>him</u>) notarize this document.   _____

2. The city was proud of (it's, <u>its</u>) recycling record.   _____

3. Nobody but (he, <u>him</u>) has been authorized to use the equipment.   _____

4. Are you sure that this apartment is (there's, <u>theirs</u>, their's)?   _____

5. Just between you and (I, <u>me</u>), who will be our next company president?   _____

6. Jean Powers sent the documents to (they, <u>them</u>) for their signatures.   _____

7. (It's, <u>Its</u>) roof may collapse under the weight of the wet snow.   _____

8. After Betty Dooley and (<u>he</u>, ~~him~~) became partners, they launched a fashion magazine that became very profitable.   _____

L e v e l   I I

A. **(Self-check)** Select the correct pronoun and write it in the space provided.

1. A profit-sharing plan was offered to (we, <u>us</u>) employees in place of cost-of-living raises.   *us*

2. No one worked harder on the project than (<u>he</u>, him).   _____

3. His bank and (<u>he</u>, him) worked out a schedule of payments.   _____

4. Both girls, Alicia and (<u>she</u>, her), will be able to work this weekend.   _____

5. (Us, <u>We</u>) delegates stayed in the Omni Hotel during the convention.   _____

6. Catherine Bean and (myself, <u>I</u>, me) were singled out for commendation.   _____

7. Proposals submitted by (<u>her and me</u>, she and I) were considered first.   _____

8. No one but my friend and (<u>I</u>, me) spoke up during the discussion.   _____

9. Separate planes were taken by the business manager and (~~he~~, <u>him</u>).   _____

10. The tragedy shocked Professor Munoz as much as (she, <u>her</u>).   _____

Check your answers below.

1. us   2. he   3. he   4. she   5. We   6. I   7. her and me   8. me   9. him   10. her

B. Select the correct pronoun and write it in the space provided.

1. Her friend and (she, her) ordered double-dip Dutch chocolate ice cream cones.   *She*

2. Cory is more responsive than (she, her).   _____

3. An attorney is in charge of (we, us) trainees.   _____

4. Our CEO, Shirley Leung, said that no other employees were quite like Steve and (he, him).   _____

5. The violent movie disturbed him as much as (I, me).   _____

6. He has no one but (hisself, himself) to blame.   _____

7. It's interesting that (us, we) accountants were audited this year.   _____

8. The production manager told a reporter and (he, him) that computerization had virtually eliminated the need for paperwork.   _____

9. The co-pilots, Kyle and (he, him), requested permission to land.   _____

10. An argument between Nikki and (he, himself, him) caused problems in the office.   _____

11. Dr. Eleanor Davidson and (I, me, myself) will make the announcement very soon.   _____

12. Believe me, no one knows that problem better than (I, me).   _____

13. News of the merger pleased President Mary Goodman as much as (I, me).   _____

14. All employees but Mr. Herzog and (I, me) agreed to the economy measures.   _____

15. Several of (we, us) salespeople surpassed our monthly selling goals.   _____

16. Do you think Theresa can complete the work more quickly than (he, him)?   _____

17. Campaign literature was sent to (we, us) homeowners prior to the elections.   _____

18. The signatures on the letter appear to have been written by you and (she, her).   _____

19. Contracts were sent to the authors, Pat Tallent and (she, her).   _____

20. Everyone except two drivers and (he, him) has checked in with the dispatcher.   _____

C. Writing Exercise. Provide sentences that use the words shown.

Example: Anita Abernathy and (pronoun)

    Anita Abernathy and he agreed to market their invention. _____

1. My friend and (pronoun)

    _____

2. The two students, Marc and (pronoun),

    _____

3. Just between you and (pronoun),

    _____

4. Except for Yumiko and (pronoun),

    _____

5. The manager expected Jeff and (pronoun)

    _____

6. its

_____

7. ours

_____

Level III

A. (Self-check) Select the correct pronoun and write it in the space provided.

1. Was it (they, them) who left the concert early? _____

2. If you were (he, him), would you have sent the e-mail message? _____

3. President Darlene McClure asked the team and (I, me) to write a proposal. _____

4. If I were (she, her), I would withdraw my endorsement. _____

5. Hyong Than said that it was (he, him) who used the printer last. _____

6. We all assumed the new president would be (she, her). _____

7. It might have been (they, them) who called in the alarm. _____

8. The audience didn't discover that Marcelle was (she, her) until the final act. _____

9. They thought Marcelle to be (she, her). _____

10. I was asked to contact you and (they, them) immediately. _____

Check your answers below.

B. Select the correct pronoun.

1. When Kristie answered the telephone, she said, "This is (she, her)." _____

2. If you were (I, me), would you take an internship? _____

3. The librarian showed Emily and (I, me) how to use the on-line catalog. _____

4. Most committee members assumed that the chairperson would be (her, she). _____

5. Surely it was (they, them) who left the gift last night. _____

6. An attempt was made to reach (he and she, him and her) in Geneva. _____

7. Voter polls indicate that the new supervisor will be (he, him). _____

8. I'm sure that it was (she, her) who called this morning. _____

9. The lifeguard credited with the rescue was thought to be (he, him). _____

10. If the instructor had been (he, him), I might not have passed. _____

11. Dr. Kim Walsh judged the winner to be (her, she). _____

12. The committee invited Professor Susan Foreman and (he, him) to speak at the conference. _____

13. Megawati and Jennifer were certain it was not (they, them) who created the shortage. _____

14. The intruder was taken to be (he, him). _____

1. they 2. he 3. me 4. she 5. he 6. she 7. they 8. she 9. her 10. them

15. When Christopher opened the door, he expected to see you and (he, <u>him</u>). _____

16. <u>It</u> must have been (<u>they</u>, them) who reported the missing funds. _____

17. We hope to obtain Jan Halverson and (she, <u>her</u>) as keynote speakers. _____

18. If the caller is (<u>he</u>, him), please get his telephone number. _____

19. The office staff expected the new manager to be (she, <u>her</u>). _____

20. Are you certain it was (<u>she</u>, her) who called this morning? _____

C. **Review.** Underline any errors in possessive nouns or personal pronouns in the following sentences. For each sentence write a corrected form in the space provided. Be alert! Some sentences have more than one correction. If a sentence is correct, write *C* in the space.

1. Many small business owners', like Deborah and I, must equip offices in our homes. _____

2. On the way to the airport, Rachel and me passed a white stretch limousine that was stalled at the side of the road with it's hood up. _____

3. The governor invited Hillary and I to dinner, but Hillaries invitation was never delivered. _____

4. Although I'm sure it was him who sent the e-mail announcement, the CEO doesn't seem to remember it at all. _____

5. Our companys Web site describing our new graphic's design capabilities stimulated many inquiries. _____

6. Just between you and me, I think all passengers luggage except our's will be opened and inspected. _____

7. If chocolate could teach, Marta and me would now be extremely well-educated. _____

8. Since the envelope was addressed to Mark and I, he and I should receive the free gift. _____

9. Theirs just one problem: neither Craig nor I have credit cards. _____

10. All our customers names and addresses are stored in Mr. Betz database. _____

11. Both the manager and me were principally concerned about the fax machine and it's tendency to produce paper jams. _____

12. Although Tonya and me agreed to pay two months rent in advance, the landlord would not rent to her and me. _____

13. No one makes more use of the Internet than me. _____

14. All of we sales associates began to receive faxes announcing First Federal's grand opening. _____

15. After reviewing our insurance policy and the companys explanation, my wife and I are certain their is a mistake in the reimbursement amount. _____

16. Some people think vacations are a necessary evil, but we in management believe that recharging one's batteries away from the office really works wonders. _____

17. No matter how rich a gardens soil may be, seeds must be sown and nutrients added to produce a harvest. _____

18. If you were me, would you step into the managers shoes at this time? _____

19. Please send all RSVP's to Tracy or I before December 1. _____

20. Although Neda Mehrabani protested, I'm convinced it was her who sent the gift to Robert and I. _____

Editor's Challenge

The following memo has 35 intentional errors illustrating principles you have studied thus far. Use proofreading marks to make corrections. Your instructor may ask you to print the revised memo on your computer printer or to handwrite it on a separate sheet. Leave side margins of about 1 1/4 inches and a top margin of at least 1 inch. Double-space if your instructor directs.

DATE: July 25, 200x

TO: Anita Musto, Vice President

FROM: Rick Juarez, Research Analyst

SUBJECT: ANALYSIS OF PEPSI XL

Here is a summary of the research project assigned to David Quimby and I regarding Pepsi XL this is the reduced-sugar cola drink being introduced by our companies No. 1 competitor.

In just under a years time, Pepsi-Cola developed this new drink. Containing a mix of 50 percent sugar (high-fructose corn syrup) and 50 percent artificial sweetener (aspartame). Apparently, Pepsi-Colas plan is to spend over $8 million to introduce the drink and to assess consumers reactions to it. It will be tested on the shelfs of grocerys, mass merchants, and convenience stores in five citys in Florida.

The companys spokesperson said, "The 'X' stands for excelent taste, and the 'L' for less sugar." Aimed at young adult's who don't like the taste of aspartame but who want to control calories, the new cola is a hybrid sugar and diet drink. Our studys show that similar drinks tried in this country in the 1980's were unsuccessful. On the other hand, a 50-calorie low-sugar cola introduced in Canada two year ago was well received a 40-calorie soda is now marketed sucessfully by Coca-Cola in Japan.

However, neither Mr. Quimby nor myself believe that theres any reason for this countrys consumers to be interested in a midcalorie cola. In fact, all of we analysts in the lab were surprised at Wall Streets favorable response to Pepsis announcement of it's new drink Pepsi-Colas stock value rose slightly.

If the decision were up to Mr. Quimby or I, him and I would take a wait-and-see attitude. Toward the interduction of our own low-sugar drink.

When you are working on your own computer, you will want to *bookmark* or save the URLs of your favorite Web pages.

> **Goal:** To learn to bookmark favorite pages.

1. With your Web browser on the screen, key the following URL in the location box and press **Enter**: **<http://www.westwords.com/guffey/students.html>**

2. Because you will be returning to this page, bookmark it by clicking **Bookmark** in the upper section of your browser. Click **ADD Bookmark** (or whatever your browser says). Check the list to see whether the page was added. Close this box.

3. Return to the location box and key this URL: **<http://www.refdesk.com>**

4. This page claims to be the "single best source for facts on the Net." What kind of information is available? Bookmark this page.

5. Click on several of the links under "Facts of the Day" or "Reference Resources." Print one page that interests you or take notes if you cannot print.

6. Return to the Guffey Student Web Site by clicking **Bookmark** and the appropriate link. Print one page.

7. End your session and turn in all printed copies or notes.

POSTTEST

Underline the correct pronouns.

1. My friend and (I, me, myself) will be traveling together.

2. The questionnaires were addressed to (we, us) homeowners.

3. I'm convinced that no one will try harder than (she, her).

4. James said it was (they, them) who picked up the order today.

5. Just between you and (I, me), which is the better investment?

1. I 2. us 3. she 4. they 5. me

CHECKLIST OF BONUS LEARNING RESOURCES

The following additional learning resources are available to you. Your instructor will tell you which to complete.

- Web Editor's Challenge Exercise

- Web Interactive Chapter Review

- Web PowerPoint Slides

- Web Crossword Puzzle

- WebCheck Reinforcement Exercises 6.1, 6.2, 6.3

- Self-Help Exercises

- Electronic Study Guide

chapter 7 Pronouns and Antecedents

Objectives

When you have studied the materials in this chapter, you will be able to do the following:

Level I

- Make personal pronouns agree with their antecedents in number and gender.
- Understand the traditional use of common gender and be able to use its alternatives with sensitivity.

Level II

- Make personal pronouns agree with subjects joined by *or* or *nor*.
- Make personal pronouns agree with indefinite pronouns, collective nouns, and organization names.

Level III

- Understand the functions of *who* and *whom*.
- Follow a three-step plan in selecting *who* or *whom*.

Underline the correct word.

1. Every one of the girls was surprised by (her, their) picture.

2. Before voting, the committee took a poll of (its, their) members.

3. Either of the departments may send (its, their) manager to the meeting.

4. (Who, Whom) would you recommend for the supervisory position?

5. Send the brochures to (whoever, whomever) requested them first.

1. her 2. its 3. its 4. Whom 5. whoever

Pronouns enable us to communicate efficiently. They provide short forms that save us from the boredom of repetitious nouns. But they can also get us in trouble if the nouns to which they refer—their *antecedents*—are unclear. This chapter shows you how to avoid pronoun–antecedent problems. It also presents solutions to a major problem for sensitive communicators today—how to handle the *his/her* dilemma.

Level I

Fundamentals of Pronoun–Antecedent Agreement

When pronouns substitute for nouns, the pronouns must agree with their antecedents in number (either singular or plural) and gender (either masculine, feminine, or neuter). Here are suggestions for using pronouns effectively.

Making Pronoun References Clear

Do not use a pronoun if your listener or reader might not be able to identify the noun it represents.

Unclear:	Soo Lee told Lisa that *she* should verify the balance.
Clear:	Soo Lee told Lisa to verify the balance.
Unclear:	In that restaurant *they* do not allow *you* to smoke.
Clear:	The restaurant management does not allow its patrons to smoke. *Or:* Smoking is not allowed in that restaurant.
Unclear:	Kevin's boss said that *he* deserved a raise.
Clear:	Kevin's boss said that Kevin deserved a raise.

Making Pronouns Agree with Their Antecedents in Number

Pronouns must agree in number with the nouns they represent. For example, if a pronoun replaces a singular noun, that pronoun must be singular.

Michelangelo felt that *he* was a failure. (Singular antecedent and pronoun.)

Great *artists* often doubt *their* success. (Plural antecedent and pronoun.)

If a pronoun refers to two nouns joined by *and*, the pronoun must be plural.

The *president* and the *stockholders* discussed *their* differences. (Plural antecedent and pronoun.)

Kyle and *James* asked that suggestions be sent to *them*. (Plural antecedent and pronoun.)

Pronoun–antecedent agreement can be complicated when words or phrases come between the pronoun and the word to which it refers. Disregard phrases such as those introduced by *as well as*, *in addition to*, and *together with*. Find the true antecedent and make the pronoun agree with it.

The *general*, together with the chiefs of staff, is considering *his* strategy carefully. (Singular antecedent and pronoun.)

The *chiefs* of staff, along with the general, have submitted *their* plans. (Plural antecedent and pronoun.)

A female *member* of the group of protesting students demanded that *she* be treated equally. (Singular antecedent and pronoun.)

Making Pronouns Agree with Their Antecedents in Gender

Pronouns exhibit one of three *genders*: masculine (male), feminine (female), or neuter (neither masculine nor feminine). Pronouns must agree with their antecedents in gender.

John read *his* assignment. (Masculine gender.)

Nancy studied *her* notes. (Feminine gender.)

The idea had *its* limits. (Neuter gender.)

Choosing Alternatives to Common-Gender Antecedents

Occasionally, writers and speakers face a problem in choosing pronouns of appropriate gender. English has no all-purpose singular pronoun to represent indefinite nouns (such as *a student* or *an employee*). For this reason writers and speakers have, over the years, used masculine, or common-gender, pronouns to refer to nouns that might be either masculine or feminine. For example, in the sentence *A student has his rights*, the pronoun *his* referred to its antecedent *student*, which might name either a feminine or masculine person.

Communicators today, however, avoid masculine pronouns (*he, his*) when referring to indefinite nouns that could be masculine or feminine. Critics call these pronouns "sexist" because they exclude women. To solve the problem, sensitive communicators rewrite those sentences requiring such pronouns. Although many alternatives exist, here are three common options:

Common Gender: An employee has *his* job to do.

Alternative No. 1:   Employees have *their* jobs to do.

Alternative No. 2:   An employee has *a* job to do.

Alternative No. 3:   An employee has *his or her* job to do.

Wrong: An employee has *their* job to do.

In Alternative No. 1 the subject has been made plural to avoid the need for a singular common-gender pronoun. In Alternative No. 2 the pronoun is omitted, and an article is substituted, although at the cost of making the original meaning less emphatic. In Alternative No. 3 both masculine and feminine references (*his or her*) are used. Because the latter construction is wordy and clumsy, frequent use of it should be avoided. Substituting the plural pronoun *their* is incorrect since it does not agree with its singular antecedent, *employee*.

Now complete the reinforcement exercises for Level I.

Did You Know?

Despite efforts for the past 140 years, no one has yet come up with an acceptable multi-purpose, unisex pronoun. Suggested replacements: *ne* (1850), *le* (1884), *se*, (1938), *ve* (1970), *e* (1977), and *ala* (1988). What would you suggest to fill the void in our language?

Spot the Blooper

Television commercial for *Encyclopedia Britannica*: "Every parent has a wish list for their child."

Problems with Pronoun–Antecedent Agreement

The following guidelines will help you avoid errors in pronoun-antecedent agreement in special circumstances, such as when the antecedents are joined by *or* or *nor*, when they are indefinite pronouns, or when they are collective nouns or company names.

Antecedents Joined by *or* or *nor*

When antecedents are joined by *or* or *nor*, the pronoun should agree with the antecedent closer to it.

> Either Alice or *Vicki* left *her* coat in the office.

> Neither the manager nor the *employees* objected to *their* salary cuts.

You may be wondering why antecedents joined by *and* are treated differently from antecedents joined by *or/nor*. The conjunction *and* joins one plus one to make two antecedents; hence, a plural pronoun is used. The conjunctions *or/nor* require a choice between two antecedents. Always match the pronoun to the closer antecedent.

Indefinite Pronouns as Antecedents

Pronouns such as *anyone, something*, and *anybody* are called *indefinite* because they refer to no specific person or object. Some indefinite pronouns are always singular; others are always plural.

	Always Singular		Always Plural
anybody	everything		both
anyone	neither		few
anything	nobody		many
each	no one		several
either	nothing		
everybody	somebody		
everyone	someone		

When indefinite pronouns function as antecedents of pronouns, make certain that the pronoun agrees with its antecedent. Do not let prepositional phrases obscure the true antecedent.

> *Somebody* in the men's league left *his* lights on.

> *Each* of the corporations had *its* own home office.

> *Few* of the vendors missed the show to demonstrate *their* equipment.

> *Several* of our branches communicate *their* documents electronically.

Career Tip

Businesspeople today strive to avoid "sexist" and biased language. For example, use parallel terms (instead of *men and ladies*, say *men and women*). Use neutral titles (*salesperson* instead of *salesman*, *server* instead of *waitress*). Avoid implied gender (instead of *managers and their wives* say *managers and their spouses*).

The words *either* and *neither* can be confusing. When these words stand alone and function as pronoun subjects, they are always considered singular. When they are joined with *or* or *nor* to form conjunctions, however, they may connect plural subjects. These plural subjects, then, may act as antecedents to plural pronouns.

Either of the women is able to drive her car. (*Either* is a singular pronoun and functions as the subject of the sentence.)

Neither man is willing to admit his error. (*Neither* is a singular pronoun and functions as subject of the sentence.)

Either the woman *or* her friends left *their* packages. (*Either/or* is used as a conjunction to join the two subjects, *woman* and *friends*. The pronoun *their* agrees with its plural antecedent, *friends*.)

Collective Nouns as Antecedents

Words such as *jury*, *faculty*, *committee*, *union*, *team*, and *group* are called *collective* nouns because they refer to a collection of people, animals, or objects. Such words may be either singular or plural depending on the mode of operation of the collection to which they refer. When a collective noun operates as a unit, it is singular. When the elements of a collective noun operate separately, the collective noun is plural.

Our *staff* reaffirmed *its* position on bargaining. (*Staff* operating as one unit.)

The management *team* of Rosen and Garcia, Inc., is planning *its* strategy. (*Team* operating as one unit.)

The *jury* were divided in *their* opinions. (*Jury* operating as individuals.)

However, if a collective noun is to be used in a plural sense, the sentence can often be made to sound less awkward by the addition of a plural noun (*The jury members were divided in their opinions*).

Company and Organization Names as Antecedents

Company and organization names are generally considered singular. Unless the actions of the organization are attributed to individual representatives of that organization, pronouns referring to organizations should be singular.

Sears is having *its* biggest annual sale ever.

The United Nations, in addition to other organizations, is expanding *its* campaign to fight hunger.

Smith, Felker & Torres, Inc., plans to move *its* corporate headquarters.

The Antecedents *each*, *every*, and *many a*

If the limiting adjectives *each*, *every*, and *many a* describe either noun or both nouns in a compound antecedent, that antecedent is considered singular.

Every player and coach on the men's team has *his* assigned duties.

Many a daughter and mother will receive *her* award at the banquet.

Now complete the reinforcement exercises for Level II.

Study Tip

When *either* or *neither* is followed by an "of" phrase, it's functioning as a singular pronoun. For example, *Either of the books is available.*

Spot the Blooper

From *The Daily Herald* (Arlington Heights, IL): "Neither men see the goal of bringing permanent peace to the area within a year as attainable."

Spot the Blooper

From *The New York Times*: "Neither Gore nor Bush could bring themselves to utter a word in defense of scientific truth."

Hot Link

To reinforce and test your pronoun skills, visit the Utah Valley State College On-line Writing Lab **<http://www.uvsc.edu/owl/handouts/proant.html>**.

Spot the Blooper

Famous singer on NBC's "Today" show: "I began to recognize whom I am, and I wasn't afraid of whom I was."

Spot the Blooper

Heading in the [Cleveland] *Browns News/Illustrated*: "Whom Will It Be?"

Spot the Blooper

From a cartoon in *The New Yorker* in which a bird says to a cat who's stalking a mouse hole, "Whom shall I say is calling?"

Advanced Pronoun Use

The use of *who* and *whom* presents a continuing dilemma for speakers and writers. In conversation the correct choice of *who* or *whom* is especially difficult because of the mental gymnastics necessary to locate subjects and objects. The following guidelines explain when to use *who* and *whom*.

The Problem of *who* and *whom*

In conversation, speakers may have difficulty analyzing a sentence quickly enough to use the correct *who/whom* form. In writing, however, an author has ample time to scrutinize a sentence and make a correct choice—if the author understands the traditional functions of *who* and *whom*. *Who* is the nominative case form. Like other nominative case pronouns, *who* may function as the subject of a verb or as the subject complement of a noun following the linking verb. *Whom* is the objective case form. It may function as the object of a verb or as the object of a preposition.*

> *Who* do you think will be chosen to direct the play? (*Who* is the subject of *will be chosen*.)
>
> Paula asked *who* your friend is. (*Who* is the complement of *friend*.)
>
> *Whom* should we hire? (*Whom* is the object of *should hire*.)
>
> She is the clerk to *whom* I spoke. (*Whom* is the object of *to*.)

How to Choose Between *who* and *whom*

The choice between *who* and *whom* becomes easier if the sentence in question is approached according to the following procedure:

1. Isolate the *who/whom* clause.
2. Invert the clause, if necessary, to restore normal subject–verb–object order.
3. Substitute the nominative pronoun *he* (*she* or *they*) for *who*. Substitute the objective pronoun *him* (*her* or *them*) for *whom*. If the sentence sounds correct with *him*, replace *him* with *whom*. If the sentence sounds correct with *he*, replace *he* with *who*.

Study the following sentences and notice how the choice of *who* or *whom* is made:

Here are the records of those (who/whom) we have selected.

Isolate:	_____ we have selected
Invert:	we have selected _____
Substitute:	we have selected __him__
Equate:	we have selected __whom__
Complete:	Here are the records of those *whom* we have selected.

Whom may also function as the subject or object of an infinitive. Since little confusion results from these constructions, they will not be discussed.

Do you know (who/whom) his doctor is?

Isolate: _____ his doctor is

Invert: his doctor is _____ (*or* _____ is his doctor)

Substitute: his doctor is __he__ (*or* __he__ is his doctor)

Equate: his doctor is __who__ (*or* __who__ is his doctor)

Complete: Do you know *who* his doctor is?

In choosing *who* or *whom*, ignore parenthetical expressions such as *I hope*, *we think*, *I believe*, and *you know*.

Edward is the candidate (who/whom) we believe is best.

Isolate: _____ we believe is best

Ignore: _____ [we believe] is best

Substitute: __he__ is best

Equate: __who__ is best

Complete: Edward is the candidate *who* we believe is best.

Examples:

Whom do you think we should call? (Invert: You do think we should call him/*whom*.)

The person to *whom* the article referred was Mr. Phan. (Invert: The article referred to him/*whom*.)

Do you know *who* the manager is? (Invert: The manager is he/*who*.)

Whom would you like to see appointed to that position? (Invert: You would like to see him/*whom* appointed to that position.)

The Use of *whoever* and *whomever*

Whoever, of course, is nominative and *whomever* is objective. The selection of the correct form is sometimes complicated when *whoever* or *whomever* appears in clauses. These clauses may act as objects of prepositions, objects of verbs, or subjects of verbs. Within the clauses, however, you must determine how *whoever* or *whomever* is functioning in order to choose the correct form. Study the following examples and explanations.

Give the surplus to *whoever needs it*. (The clause *whoever needs it* is the object of the preposition *to*. Within the clause itself, *whoever* acts as the subject of *needs* and is therefore in the nominative case.)

Special provision will be made for *whoever* meets the conditions. (The clause *whoever meets the conditions* is the object of the preposition *for*. Within the clause, *whoever* acts as the subject of *meets* and is therefore in the nominative case.)

We will accept the name of *whomever they nominate*. (The clause *whomever they nominate* is the object of the preposition *of*. Within the clause, *whomever* is the object of *they nominate* and is therefore in the objective case.)

Now complete the reinforcement exercises for Level III.

Spot the Blooper

From *The Minneapolis Star-Tribune*: ". . . he'll do a chapter on Steve Forbes, whom he swears is an alien being because he never blinks his eyes."

Spot the Blooper

From *Newsweek*: "Why did Clinton nominate someone whom advisers knew would be a lightening rod?"

Q: In an article in *U.S. News & World Report* about the U.S. Embassy's proposal to purchase new dishware, I saw this sentence: *The location of the crest on the teacups and demitasse cups shall be centered so that when held with the right hand, the crest can be seen by* whomever *is sitting directly in front of the person holding the cup.* Is this correct?

A: Hey, you've found a bona fide blooper! Many writers think that an objective case pronoun MUST follow the preposition *by*. In this case, however, an entire clause follows the preposition. Within that clause *whoever* functions as the subject. Good detective work! *Whomever* should be *whoever*.

Q: My friend insists that the combination *all right* is shown in her dictionary as one word. I say that it's two words. Who's right?

A: *All right* is the only acceptable spelling. The listing *alright* is shown in many dictionaries to guide readers to the acceptable spelling, *all right*. Do not use *alright*. By the way, some individuals can better remember that *all right* is two words by associating it with *all wrong*.

Q: I don't seem to be able to hear the difference between *than* and *then*. Can you explain it to me?

A: The conjunction *than* is used to make comparisons (*your watch is more accurate than mine*). The adverb *then* means "at that time" (*we must complete this task; then we will take our break*) or "as a consequence" (*if all the angles of the triangle are equal, then it must be equilateral as well*).

Q: What is the order of college degrees and which ones are capitalized?

A: Two kinds of undergraduate degrees are commonly awarded: the associate's degree, a two-year degree; and the bachelor's degree, a four-year degree. A variety of graduate degrees exist. The most frequently awarded are the master's degree and the doctorate. Merriam-Webster dictionaries do not capitalize the names of degrees: *associate of arts degree, bachelor of science, master of arts, doctor of philosophy*. However, when used with an individual's name, the abbreviations for degrees are capitalized: *Bruce Gourlay, M.A.; Cynthia L. Phillips, Ph.D.*

Q: Why does the sign above my grocery market's quick-check stand say *Ten or less items*? Shouldn't it read *Ten or fewer items*?

A: Right you are! *Fewer* refers to numbers, as in *fewer items*. *Less* refers to amounts or quantities, as in *less food*. Perhaps markets prefer *less* because it has fewer letters.

Q: If I have no interest in something, am I *disinterested*?

A: No. If you lack interest, you are *uninterested*. The word *disinterested* means "unbiased" or "impartial" (*The judge was disinterested in the cases before him*).

Q: Everyone says "consensus of opinion." Yet, I understand that there is some objection to this expression.

A: Yes, the expression is widely used. However, since *consensus* means "collective opinion," the addition of the word *opinion* results in a redundancy.

Q: I'm disgusted and infuriated at a New York University advertisement I just saw in our newspaper. It says, *It's not just* who *you know*. . . Why would a leading institution of learning use such poor grammar?

A: Because it sounds familiar. But familiarity doesn't make it correct. You're right in recognizing that the proper form is *whom* (isolate the clause *you know him* or *whom*). The complete adage—or more appropriately, cliché—correctly stated is: *It's not what you know but* whom *you know.*

Name _____

Level I

A. (Self-check) Select the correct word(s) to complete the following sentences.

1. When a customer complains, (his, her, <u>his or her</u>, their) problem is dealt with immediately.   _____

2. In addition to other family members, the winner was sent tickets for (his, her, <u>his or her</u>, their) personal use.   _____

3. The visiting scientist and our resident engineer had (his, her, his or her, <u>their</u>) problems finding the control center.   _____

4. No veterinarian's assistant will be assigned to that task until (he is, she is, <u>he or she is</u>, they are) trained.   _____

5. One of the members of the boys' choir lost (<u>his</u>, their) robe.   _____

6. After a contractor signs, (he is, she is, <u>he or she is</u>, they are) responsible for fulfilling the terms of the contract.   _____

7. One of the women asked how many sick days (<u>she</u>, they) had accumulated.   _____

8. All flight attendants must have (her, his, his or her, <u>their</u>) uniforms cleaned regularly.   _____

9. Norberto, after consulting the production staff and others, made (<u>his</u>, their) pricing decision.   _____

10. No employee must automatically retire when (he reaches, she reaches, <u>he or she reaches</u>, they reach) the age of 65.   _____

Check your answers below.

B. Select the correct word(s) to complete the following sentences.

1. Workers in the four plants asked that (his, <u>their</u>) working conditions be improved.   _____

2. An office manager, as well as the other members of management, must do (his, her, <u>his or her</u>, their) best to promote good employee relations.   _____

3. A judge often feels that (he, she, <u>he or she</u>, they) should review the charges for the jury.   _____

4. Both Dr. Clark and Dr. Jellesed have given (her, <u>their</u>) approval.   _____

5. Lisa Lee, one of the clerks in the front office, asked that (<u>her</u>, their) vacation be changed.   _____

6. In that mall (you, <u>shoppers</u>) aren't allowed to smoke.   _____

7. Unless careful, an employee might not get all the health care benefits to which (he is, she is, <u>he or she is</u>, they are) entitled.   _____

1. his or her 2. his or her 3. their 4. he or she is 5. his 6. he or she is 7. she 8. their 9. his 10. he or she reaches

8. Mr. Tomkins and Mr. Ramos were not eager to have (his, <u>their</u>) complaints discussed in public.

_____

9. If the insured party causes an accident, (he, she, <u>he or she</u>, they) will be charged an additional fee in future premiums.

_____

10. The human resources manager advised each candidate of (his, her, his or her, <u>their</u>) opportunities for advancement within the organization.

_____

C. **Writing Exercise.** Rewrite the following sentences to avoid the use of common-gender pronouns. Show three versions of each sentence.

1. Every driver must have *his* car registered before January 1.

Every driver must have their car re _____

_____

_____

2. Be sure that each new employee has received *his* orientation packet.

their _____

_____

_____

3. A patient who doesn't accurately report *his* history to the doctor runs the risk of misdiagnosis.

his or her _____

_____

_____

D. **Writing Exercise.** Rewrite these sentences to make the pronoun references clear.

1. The article reported that Comcard had acquired Datacard and that it had sold its foreign subsidiaries.

The article reported that Datacard, acquired by Comcard, had its foreign subsidiaries sold.

2. They make you wear shoes and shirts in that restaurant.

_____

3. Because Mr. Redman was replaced by Mr. Carlos, his parking space was changed.

_____

4. Speer was Hitler's companion until the final days of the war when he turned against him.

_____

5. Mrs. Hartman talked with Courtney about her telecommuting request, but she needed more information.

_____

L e v e l   I I

A. **(Self-check)** Select the correct word(s) to complete the following sentences.

1. Someone left (his, her, <u>his or her</u>, their) keys on the counter.

_____

2. Apparently, neither the memorandum nor the letters had (<s>its</s>, <u>their</u>) contents proofread very carefully.

3. Dun and Bradstreet bases (its, their) financial ratings on accounting reports. _____

4. Someone on the girls' team lost one of (her, their) shoes. _____

5. Each man, woman, and child in the club made (his, her, his or her, their) own contribution to the canned-food drive. _____

6. Either Paula Roddy or Mary Xavier will present (her, their) research findings at the meeting. _____

7. Nobody in the boisterous crowd could hear (his, her, his or her, their) name when called. _____

8. The president asked for budget cuts, and Congress indicated (its, their) willingness to legislate some of them. _____

9. Neither of the men would admit (his, their) part in causing the accident. _____

10. The Small Business Administration sent (its, their) experts to aid flood victims. _____

Check your answers below.

B. Select the appropriate pronoun(s) to complete the following sentences.

1. Every worker and supervisor was notified when (his, her, his or her, their) yearly physical examination was due. _____

2. Neither the dog nor the cat has had (their, its) annual shots. _____

3. As directed, the committee submitted (its, their) annual report. _____

4. Not one of the creditors would allow (his, her, his or her, their) claims to be decreased. _____

5. Did someone say that (his, her, his or her, their) test copy was illegible? _____

6. The Supreme Court will announce (its, their) decision in June. _____

7. Every one of the drawers had (its, their) contents dumped. _____

8. The inspection team will have (its, their) decision on your desk Monday. _____

9. Neither the glamour nor the excitement of the job had lost (its, their) appeal. _____

10. Any new subscriber may cancel (his, her, his or her, their) subscription within the first ten days. _____

11. Union members elected (its, their) officers by mailed ballot. _____

12. Has everybody on the girls' team had (her, their) picture taken? _____

13. Either of the companies may move (its, their) headquarters to Irvine. _____

14. Every renter and homeowner should exercise (his, her, his or her, their) right to vote. _____

15. If anyone needs assistance, Ms. Sakima will help (him, her, him or her, them). _____

1. his or her 2. their 3. its 4. her 5. his or her 6. her 7. his or her 8. its 9. his 10. its

Chapter 7 Pronouns and Antecedents 111

16. Our staff agreed that (its, their) stand must be unified. _____

17. *Contemporary Homes and Gardens* announced a plan to change (their, its) method of marketing. _____

18. Each of the supermarkets featured (its, their) advertisements on Thursday. _____

19. Every one of the girls was pleased with (her, their) internship program. _____

20. Neither the father nor his sons wanted (his, their) stocks to be sold. _____

L e v e l I I I

A. **(Self-check)** Select the correct word and write it in the space provided.

1. I know perfectly well (who, whom) you are. _____

2. Are you the individual (who, whom) submitted an application? _____

3. The contract will be awarded to (whoever, whomever) submits the lowest bid. _____

4. (Who, Whom) do you think we should interview for the newsletter? _____

5. Angelina Cicero is the investment counselor of (who, whom) I spoke. _____

6. When I return the call, for (who, whom) should I ask? _____

7. (Who, Whom) did you say would drop by? _____

8. Will you recommend an attorney (who, whom) can handle this case? _____

9. To (who, whom) did you address the invitation? _____

10. Cash prizes were awarded to (whoever, whomever) the judges selected. _____

Check your answers below.

B. Select the correct word and write it in the space provided.

1. Do you know (who, whom) the telephone caller is? _____

2. He is a graphics designer (who, whom) we believe developed their prize-winning Web site. _____

3. The position will be filled by (whoever, whomever) the manager hires. _____

4. Nadine King, (who, whom) recently passed the bar exam, immediately hung out her shingle. _____

5. (Who, Whom) have you asked to study our need to promote our products on the Internet? _____

6. For (who, whom) does the bell toll? _____

7. I have a pizza for (whoever, whomever) placed the telephone order. _____

1. who (subject complement)   2. who   3. whoever   4. Whom   5. whom   6. whom   7. Who   8. who 9. whom   10. whomever

8. The economics expert to (who, whom) the professor referred was Milton Friedman.

9. Leila Nasar is the one (who, whom) we think should be made supervisor.

10. You'll never guess (who, whom) we saw in town.

11. Rob Evans is the player against (who, whom) offensive interference was called.

12. Do you know (who, whom) will be taking your place?

13. Dr. Song will see (whoever, whomever) is next in line.

14. I wonder (who, whom) the speaker is talking about.

15. In making introductions, who should be introduced to (who, whom)?

16. Betty Stiles asked us (who, whom) we think should train Kelly.

17. Please direct my inquiry to (whoever, whomever) is in charge of quality control.

18. (Who, Whom) shall I say is calling?

19. The instructor (who, whom) won the teaching award is Paige Baker.

20. (Who, Whom) would you like to work with?

Editor's Challenge

The following business letter contains 36 intentional errors in sentence structure, spelling, proofreading, plural nouns, possessive nouns, and pronouns. Use proofreading marks to show your corrections.

❖ BENSON BROTHERS' MANAGEMENT SERVICES ❖

3328 Big Mesa Road
Scottsdale, AZ 85042

(602) 358-2249   E-mail: bensonbros@world.com   Web: www.bensonbros.com

February 17, 200x

Ms. Yolanda Morales

2320 Navajo Road

Phoenix, AZ 84690

Dear Ms. Morales:

My partner and myself are certin that our rental management service can help you care for you're fathers-in-law apartment complex in Scottsdale. Here are answers to you're questions.

To manage a clients rental units, we charge 10 percent of all fees collected we will advertise whenever a unit becomes vacant. We charge an additional 10 percent on the first years rent whenever we fill a vacant unit. Whether we charge the last months rent in advance is between you and I. Our firms two attornies are available to assist you and I If necesary.

During the 1990's we expanded, and our's is now the only firm to offer maintenance and cleaning services to their customers.

Ms. Morales, we currently manage over 75 rental propertys in the greater Phoenix area. We are available to whomever needs rental assistance. Either for private residences or for multiple units. One client wrote to us saying, "You've managed my units much better than me, and you're firm has made life much easier for my husband and I." Not one of our clients has ever canceled their contract with us. To allow us to ease the burden of your responsibilitys, please call my partner or I at 358-2249.

Sincerely yours,

Johathon Benson

Jonathon Benson

As you become more familiar with the Web, you may begin to think that the Web is the perfect place for all research. Wrong! The Web does not include all useful data, and what it does contain is not always accurate. The following exercise helps you learn to think more critically about what you find on the Web.

Goal: To learn to evaluate Web site credibility.

1. With your Web browser on the screen, go to the Guffey site (which you may have bookmarked): **<http://www.westwords.com/guffey/students.html>**.

2. Click on **Internet.** Scroll down to **Assessing the Quality of Web Documents** and click. Glance over the list of sites provided.

3. Then click **The ICYouSee Guide to Critical Thinking About What You See on the Web.**

4. Read the six suggestions provided.

5. Take the pop quiz by clicking **Exhibit One** and **Exhibit Two.** Use the **Back** key to return to the ICYou site. Which of the two exhibit sites looks more reliable?

6. Look at the ICYou page that summarizes the author's six suggestions. Make a list of five or more questions that you might ask in deciding whether a Web site is reliable. (Look for the questions inside of the blue boxes.)

7. End your session by clicking the **X** in the upper right corner. Turn in your list of five questions.

POSTTEST

Underline the correct word.

1. Did anyone on the boys' team leave (his, their) shoes in the gym?

2. The entire faculty sent (its, their) support to the president.

3. Neither of the companies could identify (its, their) equipment.

4. (Who, Whom) would you like to see as the next department manager?

5. Give the prize to (whoever, whomever) earned the most points.

1. his 2. its 3. its 4. Whom 5. whoever

CHECKLIST OF BONUS LEARNING RESOURCES

The following additional learning resources are available to you. Your instructor will tell you which to complete.

- Web Editor's Challenge Exercise

- Web Interactive Chapter Review

- Web PowerPoint Slides

- Web Crossword Puzzle

- WebCheck Reinforcement Exercises 7.1, 7.2

- Self-Help Exercises

- Electronic Study Guide

Name _____

Techniques for Effective Sentences

The basic unit in writing is the sentence. Sentences come in a variety of sizes, shapes, and structures. As business communicators, we are most interested in functional sentences that say what we want to say correctly and concisely. In this workshop you'll concentrate on two important elements: writing complete sentences and writing concise sentences.

Writing Complete Sentences

To be complete, a sentence must have a subject and a predicate and it must make sense. As you learned in Chapter 3, incomplete sentences are fragments. Let's consider four common fragment errors you'll want to avoid.

1. The fragment contains a subject and a predicate, but it begins with a subordinate word (such as *because, as, although, since,* or *if*) and fails to introduce a complete clause. You can correct this problem by joining the fragment to a relevant main clause.

   Fragment: Because world markets and economies are becoming increasingly intermixed.

   Revision: Because world markets and economies are becoming increasingly intermixed, Americans will be doing more business with people from other cultures.

   Fragment: Although Americans tend to come to the point directly.

   Revision: Although Americans tend to come to the point directly, people from some other cultures prefer indirectness.

2. The fragment does not contain a subject and a predicate, but a nearby sentence completes its meaning.

   Fragment: In the spring of every year in Las Vegas. That's when computer vendors stage a huge show.

   Revision: In the spring of every year in Las Vegas, computer vendors stage a huge show.

3. The fragment starts with a relative pronoun such as *which, that,* or *who.* Join the fragment to a main clause to form a complete sentence.

   Fragment: Which is a precious item to North Americans and other Westerners.

   Revision: Concise business letters save time, which is a precious item to North Americans and other Westerners.

4. The fragment starts with a noun followed by a *who, that,* or *which* clause. Add a predicate to form a complete sentence.

   Fragment: The visiting Asian executive who was struggling to express his idea in English.

   Revision: The visiting Asian executive who was struggling to express his idea in English appreciated the patience of his listener.

Skill Check 2.1 Eliminating Sentence Fragments

Each of the following consists of a fragment and a sentence, not necessarily in that order. Use proofreading marks to eliminate the fragment.

Example: Speak in short sentences and use common words. If you want to be understood abroad.

1. Although you should not raise your voice. You should speak slowly and enunciate clearly.

2. A glazed expression or wandering eyes. These alert a speaker that the listener is lost.

3. In speaking with foreign businesspeople, be careful to avoid jargon. Which is special terminology that may confuse listeners.

4. Kevin Chambers, who is an international specialist and consultant. He said that much of the world wants to like us.

5. Graciously accept the blame for not making your meaning clear. If a misunderstanding results.

Skill Check 2.2 Completing Sentences

Expand the following fragments into complete sentences. Add your own ideas. Be ready to explain why each fragment is incomplete and what you did to remedy the problem.

Example: If we keep in mind that Americans abroad are often accused of talking too much.

Revision: If we keep in mind that Americans abroad are often accused of talking too much, we'll become better listeners.

1. The businessperson who engages a translator for important contracts _____
_____

2. Assuming that a nod, a yes, or a smile indicates agreement _____
_____

3. If you learn greetings and a few phrases in the language of the country where you are visiting
_____
_____

4. Although global business transactions are often conducted in English _____
_____

5. Which is why Americans sometimes put words in the mouths of foreign friends struggling to express an idea _____
_____

Writing Concise Sentences

Businesspeople value concise, economical writing. Wordy communication wastes the reader's time and sometimes causes confusion. You can make your sentences more concise by avoiding opening fillers, revising wordy phrases, and eliminating redundant words.

Avoiding Opening Fillers

Openers such as *there is, it is,* and *this is to inform you that* fill in sentences but generally add no meaning. These fillers reveal writers spinning their wheels until deciding where the sentence is going. Train yourself to question these constructions. About 75 percent can be eliminated, almost always resulting in more concise sentences.

Wordy: *There are* three students who volunteered to help.

Revised: Three students volunteered to help.

Wordy: *This is to inform you that* our offices will be closed on Monday.

Revised: Our offices will be closed on Monday.

Revising Wordy Phrases

Some of our most common and comfortable phrases are actually full of "word fat." When examined carefully, these phrases can be pared down considerably.

Wordy Phrases	Concise Substitutes
at the present time	now
at this point in time	now
due to the fact that	because
for the purpose of	to
in all probability	probably
in connection with	for
in spite of the fact that	even though
in the amount of	for
in the event that	if
in the near future	soon
in the neighborhood of	about
in view of the fact that	since
with regard to	about

Notice how you can revise wordy sentences to make them more concise:

Wordy: *Due to the fact that* fire damaged our distribution center, we must delay some shipments.

Revised: *Because* fire damaged our distribution center, we must delay some shipments.

Wordy: We expected *in the neighborhood of* 15 applicants.

Revised: We expected *about* 15 applicants.

Eliminating Redundant Words

Words that are needlessly repetitive are said to be "redundant." Business writers must be alert to eliminating redundant words and phrases, such as the following:

advance warning	exactly identical	perfectly clear
alter or change	few in number	personal opinion
assemble together	free and clear	positively certain
basic fundamentals	grateful thanks	potential opportunity
collect together	great majority	proposed plan
consensus of opinion	integral part	refer back
contributing factor	last and final	serious interest
dollar amount	midway between	true facts
each and every	new changes	very unique
end result	past history	visible to the eye

Wordy:	We studied the past history of each and every potential donor.
Revised:	We studied the history of every potential donor.
Wordy:	Please collect together all the true facts before proceeding.
Revised:	Please collect all the facts before proceeding.

Skill Check 2.3 Writing Concise Sentences

In the space provided, rewrite the following sentences to make them more concise.

1. There is a free booklet that shows all the new changes in employee benefits.

_____

_____

2. In view of the fact that health care benefits are being drastically altered, this is to inform you that an orientation meeting will be scheduled in the near future.

_____

_____

3. A great majority of students will in all probability support the proposed satellite parking plan.

_____

_____

4. In the event that McDonald's offers new menu items for the purpose of increasing sales, experts think that there is every reason to believe that the effort will be successful.

_____

_____

5. There will be a special showing of the orientation training film scheduled at 10 a.m. due to the fact that there were so few in number who were able to attend the first showing.

_____

_____

6. This is to give you advance warning that we plan to alter or change the procedures for submitting travel expenses in the very near future.

_____

_____

Skill Check 2.4 Proofreading a Memo

In the following memo we have deliberately introduced sentence fragments and wordy writing. Use proofreading marks to make all sentences complete and concise. You should make 30 corrections. (When you replace a wordy phrase with one word, it counts as one correction.)

Writing Application 2.1. After you edit the following memo, your instructor may ask you to respond to it. In a memo on a separate sheet, assume that you have received this memo. Show your appreciation to Jason Corzo for his advice. Explain that you are both excited and worried about your new assignment. Use your imagination to tell why. Describe how you expect to prepare for the new assignment. You might say that you plan to start learning the language, to read about the culture, and to talk with colleagues who have worked in Japan. Put this in your own words and elaborate.

Becktelman Worldwide Contractors

Interoffice Memo

TO: Marcia Murphy
FROM: Jason Corzo
DATE: August 20, 200x
SUBJECT: CONGRATULATIONS ON YOUR ASSIGNMENT TO JAPAN

Your assignment to Kansai, Japan, as office manager of our International Business Relations Department. That's cause for celebration! This is to inform you that although I'm a little late in responding to your request, I do have some experiences and advice that may interest you.

When I was on assignment in connection with our firm in Japan. My job was to help us break into the construction business. I found it very difficult to locate a Japanese construction firm. That would act as a subcontractor for us. In time, I did find a company and eventually we began to win contracts. In spite of the fact that the process was slow and frustrating.

Despite the slow pace of qualifying for and winning contracts. I am optimistic with regard to expanding our business in Asian countries. In my personal opinion, an important contributing factor in our successful entrance into Pacific Rim markets is how willing we are to play the game according to Asian rules. In the event that we are willing to work from the inside and show our long-term commitment. I am positively certain that we can succeed in gaining a great majority of Asia's construction business in the near future.

On a personal level, Marcia, there are a few things that really helped me in communicating with the Japanese. I learned to smile a lot due to the fact that a smile is perfectly clear to everyone. I also learned to listen without interrupting, and I learned to accept blame each and every time a communication misunderstanding occurred.

Due to the fact that you are in all probability midway between assignments. This message may take a while to catch up with you. Regardless, I congratulate you on this promotion, Marcia. It is the consensus of opinion in our office that you will be very successful in managing our Kansai office in Japan.

unit 3 Showing the Action

chapter 8 Verbs: Kinds, Voices, Moods

Objectives

When you have completed the materials in this chapter, you will be able to do the following:

Level I

- Distinguish between transitive and intransitive verbs.
- Identify at least ten linking verbs.

Level II

- Recognize active and passive voice verbs.
- Convert sentences written in the passive voice to sentences in the active voice.

Level III

- Recognize sentence constructions requiring the subjunctive verb mood.
- Create sentences using the subjunctive mood correctly.

Underline the appropriate answers.

1. In the sentence *Kari listened to her attorney*, the verb *listened* is (a) transitive, (b) intransitive, (c) linking.

2. In the sentence *Her check was returned*, the verb phrase *was returned* is in the (a) active voice, (b) passive voice, (c) subjunctive mood, (d) intransitive mood.

3. In the sentence *Jane Rada taught the class*, the verb *taught* is in the (a) active voice, (b) passive voice, (c) subjunctive mood, (d) intransitive mood.

4. Jackie acts as if she (a) was, (b) were the professor.

5. Judith Easley moved that a vote (a) is taken, (b) be taken.

1.b 2.b 3.a 4.b 5.b

Verbs express an action, an occurrence, or a state of being.

> Tyler <u>purchased</u> a new computer. (Action)
>
> The winter holidays <u>end</u> the fall term. (Occurrence)
>
> Marcia <u>is</u> the new product manager. (State of being)

In relation to subjects, verbs generally tell what the subject is doing or what is being done to the subject. Verbs may also link to the subject words that describe the subject or identify it.

The verb is the most complex part of speech. A complete treatment of its forms and uses would require at least a volume. Our discussion of verbs will be limited to practical applications for businesspeople.

In our discussion of sentences in Chapter 3, you became familiar with three basic sentence patterns: (1) subject–verb, (2) subject–active verb–object, and (3) subject–linking verb–complement. Sentence patterns are determined by their verbs. You have already learned to identify active and linking verbs. Let's now consider how these verbs actually function.

Spot the Blooper

In *The Denver Post*, a city councilperson was quoted as saying, "I will not be guilted into this idea." (Is this an actual verb?)

L e v e l   I

Kinds of Verbs

Active verbs may be divided into two categories: transitive and intransitive. When an active verb directs its action toward an object, it is *transitive*. When the action is complete in itself and requires no object, the verb is *intransitive*. When verbs are transitive, they may create subject–active verb–object sentence patterns. When active verbs are intransitive, they may create subject–verb sentence patterns.

Transitive Verbs

A verb expressing an action directed toward a person or thing is said to be *transitive*. An action verb used transitively needs, in addition to its subject, a noun or pronoun to complete its meaning. This noun or pronoun functions as the direct object of the transitive verb. Notice in the following sentences that the verbs direct action toward objects.

> Stockholders <u>demanded</u> improved <u>dividends</u>. (Subject, verb, object.)
>
> Yesterday the <u>president</u> <u>called</u> <u>him</u>. (Subject, verb, object.)
>
> <u>McDonald's</u> <u>sells</u> <u>hamburgers</u> by the millions. (Subject, verb, object.)

Objects usually answer the questions *what*? or *whom*? In the first example, the stockholders demanded *what*? The object is *dividends*. In the second example, the president called *whom*? The object is *him*.

Intransitive Verbs

An action verb that does not require an object to complete its action is said to be *intransitive*.

Hot Link

For a quick online overview of verbs, visit the University of Ottawa site **<http://www.uottawa.ca/academic/arts/writcent/hypergrammar/useverb.html>**.

Tran Phuong <u>worked</u> in our Human Resources Department last summer.

E-commerce <u>grows</u> rapidly because of the Internet.

Tanya <u>listened</u> carefully to the directions.

Notice that the verbs in these sentences do not express actions directed toward persons or things. Prepositional phrases (*in the human resources office, of the Internet, to the directions*) and adverbs (*rapidly, carefully*) do not receive the action expressed by the verbs. Therefore, prepositional phrases and adverbs do not function as objects of verbs.

Linking Verbs

You will recall that linking verbs *link* to the subject words that rename or describe the subject. A noun, pronoun, or adjective that renames or describes the subject is called a *complement* because it *completes* the meaning of the subject.

Angie <u>is</u> the <u>manager</u>. (*Manager* is a noun complement that completes the meaning of the sentence by renaming *Angie*.)

Her salary <u>is</u> <u>excellent</u>. (*Excellent* is an adjective complement that completes the meaning of *salary*.)

The caller <u>was</u> <u>he</u>. (*He* is a pronoun complement that completes the meaning of *caller*.)

Notice in the preceding sentences that the noun, pronoun, or adjective complements following these linking verbs do not receive action from the verb; instead, the complements *complete* the meaning of the subject.

You are already familiar with those linking verbs that are derived from the *to be* verb form: *am, is, are, was, were, be, being, been.* Other words that often serve as linking verbs are *feels, appears, tastes, seems, sounds, looks,* and *smells.* Notice that many of these words describe sense experiences. Verbs expressing sense experiences may be followed by complements just as the *to be* linking verbs often are.

They <u>feel</u> <u>bad</u> about the sale of the company. (*Bad* is an adjective complement following the linking verb *feel*. An adjective—not the adverb *badly*—is needed here to describe the senses.)

Settlement of the strike <u>appears</u> <u>imminent</u>. (*Imminent* is an adjective complement following the linking verb *appears*.)

The use of adjectives following such verbs will be discussed more completely in Chapter 12.

The function of a verb in a sentence determines its classification. The verb *write*, for example, is intransitive when it has no object (*Kevin writes*). The same verb is transitive when an object follows (*Kevin writes e-mail*). The verb *felt* is linking when it is used to connect a complement describing the subject (*Maria felt marvelous*). The same verb is transitive when it directs action to an object (*Maria felt the wet desk*). To distinguish between classifications, study carefully the constructions in which the verbs appear.

To review briefly:

- Action verbs—two kinds:

  a. Transitive: need objects to complete their meaning

  b. Intransitive: do not need objects to complete their meaning

- Linking verbs: form a link to words that rename or describe the subject

Now complete the reinforcement exercises for Level I.

Verb Voices

You will recall that a verb expressing an action directed toward a person or thing is said to be transitive. Transitive verbs fall into two categories depending on the receiver of the action of the verbs.

Active Voice

When the verb expresses an action directed by the subject toward the object of the verb, the verb is said to be in the *active voice*.

> Allison answered the telephone. (Action directed to the object, *telephone*.)

Verbs in the active voice are direct and forceful; they clearly identify the doer of the action. For these reasons, writing that frequently uses the active voice is vigorous and effective. Writers of business communications strive to use the active voice; in fact, it is called the *voice of business*.

Passive Voice

When the action in a verb is directed toward the subject, the verb is said to be in the *passive voice*. Study the following pairs:

Passive:	Computers are used daily.
Active:	We use computers daily.
Passive:	The lottery was won by Mr. Chavez.
Active:	Mr. Chavez won the lottery.
Passive:	Three errors were made in the report.
Active:	The accountant made three errors in the report.

Because the passive voice can be used to avoid mentioning the performer of the action, the passive voice is sometimes called the *voice of tact*. Notice how much more tactful the passive version of the last example shown above is. Although directness in business writing is generally preferable, in certain instances the passive voice is used when indirectness is desired.

Now complete the reinforcement exercises for Level II.

Study Tip

In the passive voice, verbs always require a *helper*, such as *is, are, was, were, being,* or *been*.

Verb Moods

Three verb moods are available to enable a speaker or writer to express an attitude toward a subject: (a) the *indicative mood* is used to express a fact (*We need the contract*); (b) the *imperative mood* is used to express a command (*Send the contract immediately*); (c) the *subjunctive mood* is used to express a doubt, a conjecture, or a suggestion (*If the contract was sent, we haven't received it*). The subjunctive mood may cause speakers and writers difficulty and therefore demands special attention.

Subjunctive Mood

Although the subjunctive mood is seldom used today, it is still employed by careful individuals in the following constructions.

- **If *and* wish *clauses.*** When a statement that is doubtful or contrary to fact is introduced by *if, as if,* or *wish,* the subjunctive form *were* is substituted for the indicative form *was.*

  If Lori *were* here, we could proceed. (Lori is *not* here.)

  She acts as if she *were* the boss. (She is *not* the boss.)

  José wishes he *were* able to type. (José is *not* able to type.)

  But if the statement could possibly be true, use the indicative form.

  If Chris *was* in the audience, I missed him. (Chris might have been in the audience.)

- **That *clauses.*** When a *that* clause follows a verb expressing a command, recommendation, request, suggestion, or requirement, the subjunctive verb form *be* is used for *to be* verbs. For third-person singular verbs, the *s* or *es* is dropped.

  The doctor recommended that everyone *be* [not is] inoculated.

  Our manager ordered that all reports *be* [not are] proofread twice.

  The Secret Service requires that everyone near the president *receive* [not *receives*] top security clearance.

- **Motions.** When a motion is stated, a subjunctive verb form should be used in the following *that* clause.

  Gary moved that a vote *be* [not *is*] taken.

  It has been seconded that the meeting *be* [not *is*] adjourned.

Caution: In a sentence without *that* clauses, do not mix subjunctive and indicative verbs.

Right: If she *were skilled*, she *would receive* job offers. (Both verbs are subjunctive.)

Right: If she *is skilled*, she *will receive* job offers. (Both verbs are indicative.)

Wrong: If she *were skilled*, she *will receive* job offers. (One subjunctive verb and one indicative verb.)

Now complete the reinforcement exercises for Level III.

Q: Which is better: *The jet plane carried canisters of highly flammable or inflammable liquid?*

A: Actually, both *flammable* and *inflammable* mean "easily set on fire." Either would be correct in your sentence. However, *flammable* is preferred because its meaning is less likely to be confused. Since the prefix *in* often means "not," the word *inflammable* could be misunderstood. Therefore, use *flammable* in technical matters, particularly if you wish to suggest a warning. You may use *inflammable* or its derivatives for nontechnical descriptions, such as *Her words were inflammatory*.

Q: I have a sentence that begins *Beside(s) providing financial aid...* Is there any real difference between *beside* and *besides*?

A: Yes, indeed! *Beside* is a preposition meaning "by the side of" (*come sit beside me*). *Besides* is an adverb meaning "in addition to" (*besides paper we must order ribbons*). In your sentence use *besides*.

Q: I received a magazine advertisement recently that promised me a *free gift* and a *15 percent off discount* if I subscribed. What's wrong with this wording?

A: You've got a double winner here in the category of redundancies. The word *gift* suggests *free*; therefore, to say *free gift* is like *saying I'm studying English English*. It would be better to say *special gift*. In the same way, *15 percent off discount* repeats itself. Omit *off*.

Q: When do you use *may* and when do you use *can*?

A: Traditionally, the verb *may* is used in asking or granting permission (*yes, you may use that desk*). *Can* is used to suggest ability (*you can succeed in business*). In informal writing, however, authorities today generally agree that *can* may be substituted for *may*.

Q: I just checked the dictionary and found that *cooperate* is now written as one word. It seems to me that years ago it was *co-operate* or *coöperate*. Has the spelling changed?

A: Yes, it has. And so has the spelling of many other words. As new words become more familiar, their spelling tends to become more simplified. For example, *per cent* and *good will* are now shown by most dictionaries as *percent* and *goodwill*. By the same token, many words formerly hyphenated are now written without hyphens: *strike-over* is now *strikeover*, *to-day* is *today*, *editor-in-chief* is *editor in chief*, *vice-president* is *vice president*, and *passer-by* is now *passerby*. Current dictionaries reflect these changes.

Q: On my computer I'm using a program that checks the writer's style. My problem is that it flags every passive voice verb and tells me to consider using active voice verbs. Are passive voice verbs totally forbidden in business writing?

A: Of course not! Computer style checkers capitalize on language areas that can be detected mechanically, and a passive voice verb is easily identified by a computer. Although active voice verbs are considered more forceful, passive voice verbs have a genuine function in business writing. Because they hide the subject and diffuse attention, passive verbs are useful in sensitive messages where indirect language can develop an impersonal, inconspicuous tone. For example, when a lower-level employee must write a persuasive and somewhat negative message to a manager, passive voice verbs are quite useful.

Q: What's the correct verb in this sentence? *Tim recognized that, if his company (was or were) to prosper, it would require considerable capital.*

A: The verb should be *were* because the clause in which it functions is not true. Statements contrary to fact that are introduced by words like *if* and *wish* require subjunctive mood verbs.

Name _____

Level I

A. (Self-check) In the spaces provided indicate whether the italicized verbs are transitive (*T*), intransitive (*I*), or linking (*L*).

Example: Kelly *is* the supervisor in that department.　　　L _____

1. Despite medication, Ann *feels* worse.　　L _____
2. Roberto *flipped* hamburgers until he finished his schooling.　　T _____
3. Before the conference, delegates *met* in the foyer.　　I _____
4. Jeanette Walgren *is* the professor who won the award.　　L _____
5. Mary *expects* Mr. Chudabala to return to the office soon.　　T _____
6. It *was* he who devised the current work schedule.　　L _____
7. The production manager *called* over four hours ago.　　I _____
8. Emily Adams *feels* certain that her work calendar is clear.　　L _____
9. Well-written business letters *get* results.　　T _____
10. We *sent* a replacement order to you as soon as we received your letter.　　T _____

Check your answers below.

B. Each of the following sentences contains a verb that is either transitive or intransitive. If the verb is intransitive, underline it and write *I* in the space provided. If the verb is transitive, underline it, write *T* in the space provided, and also write its direct object.

Example: After his presentation the manager <u>left</u>.　　I _____

Employees <u>brought</u> their lunches.　　T (lunches)

1. Good managers <u>solve</u> problems.　　T _____
2. Traffic <u>stopped</u>.　　I _____
3. FedEx <u>maintains</u> a busy Web site for its customers.　　T _____
4. Our suppliers <u>raised</u> their prices.　　T _____
5. Storm clouds <u>gathered</u>.　　I _____
6. Over the years our assets <u>increased</u>.　　I _____
7. Bill Gates <u>sends</u> many e-mail messages.　　T _____
8. The telephone <u>rang</u>.　　I _____
9. Gregory <u>answered</u> it.　　T _____
10. Many employees <u>drive</u> their cars to work.　　T _____

C. Linking verbs are followed by complements that identify, rename, or describe the subjects. The most common linking verbs are the forms of *be* (*am, is, are, was,* and so on) and the verbs of the senses (*feels, appears, tastes, smells,* and so on). The following sentences all contain linking verbs. For each sentence underline the linking verb or verb phrase and write its complement in the space provided.

Example: Joanna <u>feels</u> good about her project.   **good**

       Our current director <u>is</u> Ms. Abzug.   **Ms. Abzug**

1. Employees <u>are</u> happy about pay increases.   *happy*
2. Our trip <u>was</u> long and tiring.   *long*
3. The roses on her desk <u>smell</u> fragrant.   *fragrant*
4. Over the telephone his voice <u>sounds</u> resonant.   *resonant*
5. It <u>was</u> she who called you earlier.   *she*
6. Maureen Jackson <u>was</u> the campaign chairperson last year.   *c.p.*
7. This sweater <u>feels</u> warm and comfortable today.   *warm & c.*
8. The manager of that department might <u>be</u> Ignacio.   *Ignacio*
9. That table will <u>be</u> fine.   *fine*
10. It <u>seems</u> unusually cold in here today.   *cold*

D. In the following sentences selected verbs have been italicized. For each sentence indicate whether the italicized verb is transitive (*T*), intransitive (*I*), or linking (*L*). In addition, if the verb is transitive, write its object. If the verb is linking, write its complement.

Example: The new employee *is* Janet Oso.   **L (Janet Oso)**

       Our computer *prints* the mailing list.   **T (list)**

1. The senior scientist on the project *is* Marie Mueller.   *L Marie*
2. Traffic *moves* from the suburbs along three major arteries.   *I*
3. General Motors *offered* a warranty on certain engine parts.   *T warranty*
4. It *is* he who processes all software requests.   *L He*
5. Please *lay* the keys on the desk when you finish with them.   *T keys*
6. Her report *appears* accurate, but some data must be verified.   *L Accurate*
7. Mitchell *feels* marvelous about his recent promotion.   *L marvelous*
8. Producers *move* goods to market to meet seasonal demands.   *T goods*
9. It *must have been* they who made the anonymous gift.   *L They*
10. The economy *appears* bright despite a recent rise in interest rates.   *L bright*
11. Beverly Westbrook *is* the person whom you should call.   *L*
12. Despite vigorous consumer protests, the airline *ended* its service.
13. Please *raise* the window before you leave.
14. Your report *is lying* on the boss's desk.
15. All of us *feel* bad about her transfer.

A. (Self-check) Transitive verbs in the following sentences have been italicized. For each sentence write *active* or *passive* to indicate the voice of the italicized verb.

Example: Two important omissions in the report *were found* by the committee.   <u>**passive**</u>

1. Our company *monitors* the Internet activity of all employees.   *active/active*

2. The Internet activity of all employees *is monitored* by our company.   *passive*

3. Communication and computer skills *are required* by many hiring companies.   *passive*

4. Many hiring companies *require* communication and computer skills.   *active*

5. Fannie Johnson *manages* a number of apartments and other properties.   *active*

6. The new plan *was devised* to make premium payment completely automatic.   *passive*

7. Jennifer immediately *sent* e-mail messages to all committee members.   *active*

8. E-mail messages *were sent* immediately to all committee members.   *passive*

9. Funds for the youth campaign *were collected* from private donors.   *passive*

10. Private donors *made* contributions to the campaign because they believed in the merit of the project.   *active*

Check your answers below.

B. In the spaces provided, write *active* or *passive* to indicate the voice of the italicized verbs in the following sentences.

1. Judy Welch *prepared* the certified check.   *passive/active*

2. The certified check *was prepared* by Judy Welch.   *passive*

3. Intranets and wireless devices *are being used* in many companies.   *passive*

4. You *withdrew* the funds in question on May 29.   *act*

5. From his gross income, Amir Liba *deducts* medical expenses and contributions.   *acti*

6. Jim Perez *was told* to visit the Human Resources Department.   *pss.*

7. Contract arbitration *will be conducted* by the union and the manufacturer.   *passive*

C. *Writing Exercise.* Careful writers strive to use the active voice in business communications. This is an important skill for you to develop. To give you practice, rewrite the following sentences changing their passive voice verbs to active voice. Normally you can change a verb from passive to active voice by making the doer of the action—usually contained in a *by* phrase—the subject of the sentence.

1. active   2. passive   3. passive   4. active   5. active   6. passive   7. active   8. passive   9. passive   10. active

Example: (Passive) Production costs must be reduced by manufacturers.

           (Active) Manufacturers must reduce production costs.

1. Pollution was greatly reduced by General Motors when the company built its new plant. (*Hint: Who* greatly reduced pollution? Start your new sentence with that name.)

2. Funds for the multipurpose shopping complex were contributed by federal, state, and private groups.

    Federal, state and prices groups contributed funds for the ......

3. Massive short-term financing is used by Nike to pay off its production costs during its slow season.

D. **Writing Exercise**. Some sentences with passive voice verbs do not identify the doer of the action. Before these sentences can be converted, a subject must be provided.

Example: (Passive) New subscribers will be offered a bonus. (By whom?—by Time, Inc.)

           (Active) Time, Inc., will offer new subscribers a bonus.

In each of the following sentences, first answer the question *by whom?* Then rewrite the sentence in the active voice, beginning with your answer as the subject.

1. Our office was recently reorganized to increase efficiency and production. (By whom?)

2. Net income before taxes must be calculated carefully when you fill out your tax return. (By whom?)

3. Only a few of the many errors and changes were detected during the first proofreading. (By whom?)

Level III

A. **(Self-check)** Select the correct word and write it in the space provided.

1. If Susan Randles (was, <u>were</u>) our manager, she would not have approved these work rules. _____

2. Do we have a motion that the meeting (is, <u>be</u>) adjourned? _____

3. If I (was, <u>were</u>) you, I'd get a new alarm clock. _____

4. Did your manager suggest that you (be, are) given time off to attend classes? _____

5. If Lauren LoPresti (<u>was</u>, were) at the opening session, she did not announce herself. _____

6. Dale Rosenberg recommended that everyone (<u>meet</u>, meets) in the parking lot. _____

7. If you were in my place, I'm sure you (will, <u>would</u>) agree. _____

8. Sandi Escalante suggested that additional chairs (are, <u>be</u>) set up for the afternoon session. _____

9. He acts as if he (<u>was</u>, ⃝were) the only employee who had to work overtime. _____

10. It is extremely important that all applications (are, <u>be</u>) completed by the 15th of the month. _____

Check your answers at the bottom of the page.

B. Underscore any verbs that are used incorrectly in the following sentences. Write the correct forms in the spaces provided. Write *C* if correct.

1. Angela wished that she <u>was</u> able to vacation in Hawaii. *were*

2. I move that Craig <u>is</u> appointed acting president for the remainder of this year. *be*

3. The CEO recommended that each employee <u>is</u> given full benefits. *be*

4. If a better employee benefit program <u>was</u> available, recruiting would be easier. *were*

5. A stockholder moved that dividends <u>are</u> declared immediately. *be*

6. If he were in my place, he <u>will</u> be more understanding. *would*

7. I wish that our server was working so that I could read my mail. *C*

8. Billie Miller Cooper, the management consultant, strongly advised that antiglare shields are installed. *be*

9. Michael said he wished that you were able to accompany him. *C*

10. If Frances Martinez were in the office that day, I did not see her. *was*

C. Writing Exercise. Complete the following sentences.

1. I wish that I (was, were) _____

2. If my boss (was, were) _____

3. If you (was, were) in my position, _____

Editor's Challenge

The following e-mail message contains 25 intentional errors in spelling, proofreading, and grammar principles you have studied thus far. Use proofreading marks to correct them.

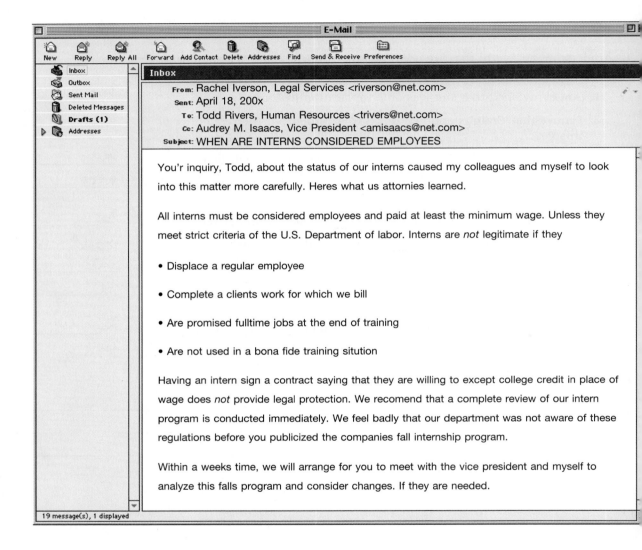

Many colleges and universities provide grammar hotline services. Generally, you can submit a question by e-mail or by telephone and receive a response from a trained language specialist. Let's assume you want to ask a question and need to know the closest hotline service.

Goal: To learn about online grammar hotlines.

1. With your Web browser on the screen, enter the URL of your favorite search engine. (Do you have it bookmarked? We always try Alta Vista first.)

2. With your search engine on the screen, enter "Grammar Hotline" as your search term.

3. Click the listing for the "Grammar Hotline Directory" at Tidelands Community College.

4. What kind of questions can you expect a grammar hotline to answer?

5. Print the first page of the Tidelands directory.

6. To find the closest hotline, scroll down and click the letter of the alphabet corresponding to the first letter of your state name.

7. For the hotline closest to you, note the name, telephone number, and/or e-mail address.

8. End your session and submit your printed page and listing.

POSTTEST

Underline the appropriate answers.

1. In the sentence *Karen Fischer wrote the memo*, the verb *wrote* is (a) transitive, (b) intransitive, (c) subjunctive, (d) passive.

2. In the sentence *Shelby Walsh hired four employees*, the verb *hired* is in the (a) active voice, (b) passive voice, (c) subjunctive mood, (d) intransitive mood.

3. In the sentence *Patricia Lenndy was given the award*, the verb phrase *was given* is in the (a) active voice, (b) passive voice, (c) subjunctive mood, (d) intransitive mood.

4. If Clara Smith (a) was, (b) were the instructor, the class would be full.

5. Professor St. Clair recommended that students (a) be, (b) are admitted free.

1.a 2.a 3.b 4.b 5.a

chapter 9 Verb Tenses and Parts

Objectives

When you have completed the materials in this chapter, you will be able to do the following:

Level I

- Write verbs in the present, past, and future tenses correctly.

Level II

- Recognize and use present and past participles.
- Write the correct forms of 60 irregular verbs.

Level III

- Supply correct verb forms in the progressive and perfect tenses.

Underline the correct verb.

1. Anthony and she (came, come) over last night to use my computer.
2. After they had (gone, went), I was able to do my own homework.
3. When last seen, the papers were (laying, lying) near the desk.
4. The value of our stock has been steadily (raising, rising) all day.
5. The condominium project has (set, sat) there untouched for a year.

Hot Link

For ESL (English as a Second Language) students, try searching the Web for "ESL Verbs." You will find many links to sites offering learning tips and helpful exercises.

English verbs change form (inflection) to indicate number (singular or plural), person (first, second, or third), voice (active or passive), and tense (time). In contrast to French and German, English verbs are today no longer heavily inflected; that is, our verbs do not change form extensively to indicate number or person. To indicate precise time, however, English employs three rather complex sets of tenses: primary tenses, perfect tenses, and progressive tenses. Level I will focus on the primary tenses and helping verbs. Level II will consider participles and irregular verbs. Level III will treat the perfect and progressive tenses.

Level I

Primary Tenses

Let's begin our discussion of verbs with the primary tenses. These tenses are used to indicate the present, the past, and the future.

Present Tense

Verbs in the present tense express current or habitual action. Present tense verbs may also be used in constructions showing future action.

We *order* office supplies every month. (Current or habitual action.)

He *flies* to Washington tomorrow. (Future action.)

Past Tense

Verbs in the past tense show action that has been completed. Regular verbs form the past tense with the addition of *d* or *ed.*

Mr. Pasternak *needed* the forms yesterday.

Our vendor *provided* toner cartridges.

She *used* to have a cell phone.

Future Tense

Verbs in the future tense show actions that are expected to occur at a later time. Traditionally, the helper verbs *shall* and *will* have been joined with principal verbs to express future tense. In business writing today, however, the verb *will* is generally used as the helper to express future tense. Careful writers continue to use *shall* in appropriate first-person constructions. (*I/we shall attend the meeting.*)

Andy *will look* for a new apartment next month.

You *will receive* your order on Thursday.

Summary of Primary Tenses

The following table summarizes the various forms employed to express the primary tenses:

	Present Tense		Past Tense		Future Tense	
	Sing.	**Plural**	**Sing.**	**Plural**	**Sing.**	**Plural**
First person:	I need	we need	I needed	we needed	I will need	we will need
Second person:	you need	you need	you needed	you needed	you will need	you will need
Third person:	he, she, it, needs	they need	he, she, it needed	they needed	he, she, it will need	they will need

Problems With Primary Tense

Most adult speakers of our language have few problems using present, past, and future tense verbs. A few considerations, however, merit mention.

- **Using the -s form verbs.** Note that third-person singular verbs require an -s ending (*he needs*). Although you might drop the -s or -es in speaking, be sure to include it in business writing.

  She *comes* to work on the bus. (Not *come.*)

  This equipment *breaks* down too often. (Not *break.*)

  Matt *drives* a pickup truck. (Not *drive.*)

- **Expressing "timeless" facts.** Present tense verbs are used to express "timeless" facts, even if these verbs occur in sentences with other past tense verbs.

  What did you say his duties *are?* (Not *were*, if he continues to perform these duties.)

  We were told often that a penny saved *is* a penny earned. (Not *was.*)

  What did you say the caller's name *is?* (Not *was.*)

- **Spelling verbs that change form.** Use a dictionary to verify spelling of verbs that change form. One must be particularly careful in spelling verbs ending in *y* (*hurry, hurries, hurried*) and verbs for which the final consonant is doubled (*occurred, expelled*).

Helping (Auxiliary) Verbs

A verb that combines with a main verb to convey information about tense, mood, or voice functions as a helping or auxiliary verb. The most common helping verbs are forms of *be (am, is, are, was, were, being, been)*, forms of *do (does, did)*, and forms of *have (has, had)*. As you will recall, the verb *be* and all its forms also function as linking verbs.

Spot the Blooper

From the Princeton Review Book for the Scholastic Aptitude Test II: "You don't have to be a genus."

Our manager *is* a funny guy. (The linking verb *is* joins the complement *guy* to the subject.)

Our manager *is using* his computer. (The helping verb *is* combines with the main verb *using* to form a verb phrase whose object is *computer.*)

Whether functioning as a linking verb or as a helping verb, the verb *be* should be used in standard forms.

Erin *is looking* for a new job. (Not *be looking.*)

She *is* lucky to have a computer. (Not *be.*)

Now complete the reinforcement exercises for Level I.

Present and Past Participles

To be able to use all the tenses of verbs correctly, you must understand the four principal parts of verbs: present, past, present participle, and past participle. You have already studied the present and past forms. Now, let's consider the participles.

Present Participle

The present participle of a regular verb is formed by adding *ing* to the present tense of the verb. When used in a sentence as part of a verb phrase, the present participle is generally preceded by a helping verb, such as *am, is, are, was, were, be,* and *been.*

> Ryan *is working* at home.
>
> You *are doing* a fine job.

Past Participle

The past participle of a regular verb is usually formed by adding a *d* or *t* sound to the present tense of the verb. Like present participles, past participles must combine with one or more helping verbs (such as *has* or *have*):

> Mark *has checked* his calculations.
>
> His calculations *have been checked* by Mark.
>
> The developer *should have built* better garages for the homes.
>
> New roads to the vacation development *should have been built.*

Irregular Verbs

Up to this point, we have considered only regular verbs. Regular verbs form the past tense by the addition of *d* or *ed* to the present tense form. Many verbs, however, form the past tense and the past participle irregularly. (More specifically, irregular verbs form the past tense by a variation in the root vowel and, commonly, the past participle by the addition of *en.*) A list of the more frequently used irregular verbs follows. Learn the forms of these verbs by practicing in patterns such as:

Present tense: Today I __drive__.

Past tense: Yesterday I __drove__.

Past participle: In the past I have __driven__.

Frequently Used Irregular Verbs

Present	Past	Past Participle
arise	arose	arisen
be (am, is, are)	was, were	been
bear (to carry)	bore	borne

Present	Past	Past Participle
become	became	become
begin	began	begun
bite	bit	bitten
blow	blew	blown
break	broke	broken
bring	brought	brought
build	built	built
choose	chose	chosen
come	came	come
do	did	done
draw	drew	drawn
drink	drank	drunk
drive	drove	driven
eat	ate	eaten
fall	fell	fallen
fly	flew	flown
forbid	forbade	forbidden
forget	forgot	forgotten *or* forgot
forgive	forgave	forgiven
freeze	froze	frozen
get	got	gotten *or* got
give	gave	given
go	went	gone
grow	grew	grown
hang (to suspend)	hung	hung
hang (to execute)	hanged	hanged
hide	hid	hidden *or* hid
know	knew	known
lay (to place)	laid	laid
leave	left	left
lie (to rest)	lay	lain
lie (to tell a falsehood)	lied	lied
pay	paid	paid
prove	proved	proved *or* proven
raise (to lift)	raised	raised
ride	rode	ridden

Spot the Blooper

From *The New York Times*: "But Van Hellemond said he had blew his whistle . . . ."

Spot the Blooper

From a Dunkin' Donuts advertisement: "The trouble with supermarket doughnuts is there's no telling how long they've been laying around."

Spot the Blooper

From *The Arizona Republic*'s report on the plane crash site of actor Patrick Swayze: ". . . and the rest of the beer was drank by construction workers the day after the crash landing."

Spot the Blooper

From the *Arizona Republic*: "The great tree uprooted the back fence, causing it to raise 5 feet in the air."

Present	Past	Past Participle
ring	rang	rung
rise (to move up)	rose	risen
run	ran	run
see	saw	seen
set (to place)	set	set
shake	shook	shaken
shrink	shrank	shrunk
sing	sang	sung
sink	sank	sunk
sit (to rest)	sat	sat
speak	spoke	spoken
spring	sprang	sprung
steal	stole	stolen
strike	struck	struck *or* stricken
swear	swore	sworn
swim	swam	swum
take	took	taken
tear	tore	torn
throw	threw	thrown
wear	wore	worn
write	wrote	written

Spot the Blooper

From Walt Disney Company: "Honey, I Shrunk the Kids."

Spot the Blooper

From *The Times-Union* [Albany, NY]: "Jane Fonda's Beverly Hills hairdresser sweared the thick blond braid she's been sporting . . . is her real hair."

Three Pairs of Frequently Misused Irregular Verbs

The key to the correct use of the following pairs of verbs lies in developing the ability to recognize the tense forms of each and to distinguish transitive verbs and constructions from intransitive ones.

Lie–Lay

Study Tip

Whenever you use *lay* in the sense of "placing" something, you must provide a receiver of the action: *Please lay the book down.* If nothing receives action, you probably want the verb *lie*, which means "resting."

These two verbs are confusing because the past tense of *lie* is spelled in exactly the same way that the present tense of *lay* is spelled. To be safe, you'll want to memorize these verb forms:

	Present	Present Participle	Past	Past Participle
Intransitive:	lie (to rest)	lying	lay	lain
Transitive:	lay (to place)	laying	laid (*not layed*)	laid

The verb *lie* is intransitive; therefore, it requires no direct object to complete its meaning.

> Today I *lie* down. (Note that *down* is not a direct object.)
>
> "*Lie* down," Mark told his dog. (Commands are given in the present tense.)
>
> Yesterday I *lay* down for a nap. (Past tense.)
>
> The papers are *lying* on the desk. (Present participle.)
>
> They have *lain* there for some time. (Past participle.)

The verb *lay* is transitive and must have a direct object to complete its meaning.

> *Lay* the bricks over there. (Command in the present tense.)
>
> The mason is *laying* bricks. (Present participle.)
>
> He *laid* the bricks in a row. (Past tense.)
>
> He has *laid* bricks all his life. (Past participle.)

Sit–Set

Less troublesome than *lie–lay,* the combination of *sit–set* is nevertheless perplexing because the sound of the verbs is similar. The intransitive verb *sit* (past tense, *sat;* past participle, *sat*) means "to rest" and requires no direct object.

> Do you *sit* here often? (Used intransitively; *here* is not an object.)
>
> Are you *sitting* here tomorrow? (Present participle.)

The transitive verb *set* (past tense, *set;* past participle, *set*) means "to place" and must have a direct object.

> Letty usually *sets* her books there. (*Books* is the direct object.)
>
> She is *setting* her books here today. (Present participle.)

Rise–Raise

The intransitive verb *rise* (past tense, *rose;* past participle, *risen*) means "to go up" or "to ascend" and requires no direct object.

> The sun *rises* every morning in the east. (*Every morning* is an adverbial phrase, not an object.)
>
> Our elevator is *rising* to the seventh floor. (Present participle.)
>
> The bread dough *rose* nicely. (Past tense.)
>
> Prices have *risen* substantially. (Past participle.)

The transitive verb *raise* (past tense, *raised;* past participle, *raised*) means "to lift up" or "to elevate" and must have a direct object.

> Please *raise* the window. (*Window* is a direct object.)
>
> Datamax is *raising* prices next month. (*Prices* is a direct object.)

Now complete the reinforcement exercises for Level II.

Spot the Blooper

From the Santa Barbara [CA] *News Press*: "Young people risk getting skin cancer because they insist on laying in the sun."

Spot the Blooper

From *The Detroit News*: "Emerick allegedly fired one shot in his wife's back as she lied on the floor."

Study Tip

To help you remember that these verbs are intransitive, look at the second letter of each:
l*i*e
s*i*t
r*i*se
Associate *i* with *in*-transitive.

Progressive and Perfect Tenses

Thus far in this chapter, you have studied the primary tenses and irregular verbs. The remainder of this chapter focuses on two additional sets of verb tenses: the perfect and the progressive. Most native speakers and writers of English have little difficulty controlling these verb forms because they have frequently heard them used correctly. This largely descriptive section is thus presented for individuals who are not native speakers and for those who are eager to study the entire range of verb tenses.

Progressive Tenses

Present Progressive Tense

	First Person	Second Person	Third Person
Active:	I am hearing we are hearing	you are hearing	he, she, it is hearing they are hearing
Passive:	I am being heard we are being heard	you are being heard	he, she, it is being heard they are being heard

Past Progressive Tense

	First Person	Second Person	Third Person
Active:	I was hearing we were hearing	you were hearing	he, she, it was hearing they were hearing
Passive:	I was being heard we were being heard	you were being heard	he, she, it was being heard they were being heard

Future Progressive Tense

	First Person	Second Person	Third Person
Active:	I will be hearing we will be hearing	you will be hearing	he, she, it will be hearing they will be hearing
Passive:	I will be being heard we will be being heard	you will be being heard	he, she, it will be being heard they will be being heard

Spot the Blooper

In *Skyway News/ Freeway News*, describing a restaurant in Mantonville [MN]: "Proprietor Paul J. Pappas extends his hostility to tour groups. Call for reservations."

We *are exporting* grain to numerous countries. (Present progressive tense expresses action in progress.)

Many textile companies *were sending* delegates to the government conference. (Past progressive tense indicates action that was begun in the past.)

They *will be receiving* the announcement shortly. (Future progressive tense indicates action in the future.)

Perfect Tenses

Present Perfect Tense

	First Person	Second Person	Third Person
Active:	I have heard we have heard	you have heard	he, she, it has heard they have heard
Passive:	I have been heard we have been heard	you have been heard	he, she, it has been heard they have been heard

Past Perfect Tense

	First Person	Second Person	Third Person
Active:	I had heard we had heard	you had heard	he, she, it had heard they had heard
Passive:	I had been heard we had been heard	you had been heard	he, she, it had been heard they had been heard

Future Perfect Tense

	First Person	Second Person	Third Person
Active:	I will have heard we will have heard	you will have heard	he, she, it will have heard they will have heard
Passive:	I will have been heard we will have been heard	you will have been heard	he, she, it will have been heard they will have been heard

He has just *heard* the news. (Present perfect tense expresses action just completed or *perfected*.)

The check *had cleared* the bank before I canceled payment. (Past perfect tense shows an action finished before another action in the past.)

The polls *will have been closed* two hours when the results are telecast. (Future perfect tense indicates action that will be completed before another future action.)

Summary of Tenses

The following table summarizes the four sets of tenses.

Primary Tenses	Progressive Tenses	Perfect Tenses
Present	Present progressive	Present perfect
Past	Past progressive	Past perfect
Future	Future progressive	Future perfect

Now complete the reinforcement exercises for Level III.

Hot Link

For a different perspective on verbs and more examples, take a look at "An On-Line English Grammar" <http://www.edunet.com/english/grammar/verb1.html>. If the URL changes, find the site using a search engine.

Q: We have a new electronic mail system, and one of its functions is "messaging" people. When folks say, *I'll message you*, it really grates on my nerves. Is this correct?

A: "Messaging" is certainly a hot term with the explosion of e-mail. As to its correctness, I think we've caught language in the act of evolving. What's happened here is the reinstitution of a noun (*message*) as a verb. Converting nouns into verbs is common in English (he *cornered* the market, we *tabled* the motion, I *penciled* it in on my calendar, the farmer *trucked* the vegetables to market). Actually, *message* was sometimes used as a verb nearly a century ago (in 1896 *the bill was messaged over from the house*). However, its recent use has been almost exclusively as a noun. Today, it is increasingly being used again as a verb. New uses of words usually become legitimate when the words fill a need and are immediately accepted. Some word uses, though, appear to be mere fads, like *The homeless child could not language her fears*. Forcing the noun *language* to function as a verb is unnecessary since a good word already exists for the purpose: *express*. But other "nouns-made-verbs" have been in use long enough to sound reasonable: I *faxed* the document, he *videotaped* the program, she *keyed* the report.

Q: I'm embarrassed to ask this because I should know the answer—but I don't. Is there an apostrophe in this: *its relevance to our program?*

A: No. Use an apostrophe only for the contraction *it's*, meaning "it is" (*it's a good plan*). The possessive pronoun *its*, as used in your example, has no apostrophe (*the car had its oil changed*).

Q: I thought I knew the difference between *principal* and *principle*, but now I'm not so sure. In a report from management I saw this: *The principal findings of the market research are negative*. I thought *principal* always meant your "pal," the school principal.

A: You're partly right and partly wrong. *Principal* may be used as a noun meaning "chief" or "head person." In addition, it may be used as an adjective to mean "chief" or "main." This is the meaning most people forget, and this is the meaning of the word in your sentence. The word *principle* means a "law" or "rule." Perhaps it is easiest to remember *principle* = *rule*. All other uses require *principal*: the *principal* of the school, the *principal* of the loan, the *principal* reason.

Q: Even when I use a dictionary, I can't tell the difference between *affect* and *effect*. What should the word be in this sentence? *Changes in personnel (affected/effected) our production this month*.

A: No words generate more confusion than do *affect/effect*. In your sentence use *affected*. Let's see if we can resolve the *affect/effect* dilemma. *Affect* is a verb meaning "to influence" (*smoking affects health; government policies affect citizens*). *Affect* may also mean "to pretend or imitate" (*he affected a British accent*). *Effect* can be a noun or a verb. As a noun, it means "result" (*the effect of the law is slight*). As a verb (and here's the troublesome part) *effect* means "to produce a result" (*small cars effect gasoline savings; GM effected a new pricing policy*).

Q: I'm editing a screenplay for a studio, and I know something is grammatically wrong with this sentence: *The old man left the room hurriedly after discovering a body laying near the window.*

A: As you probably suspected, the verb *laying* should be *lying*. *Lay* means "to place" and requires an object (*he is laying the report on your desk now*). *Lie* means "to rest" and requires no object (*the document is lying on your desk*).

Q: As the holiday season approaches, I'm wondering whether it's *Season's Greetings* or *Seasons' Greetings*.

A: If you are referring to one season, it's *Season's Greetings*.

Q: I learned that the verb *set* is transitive and requires an object. If that's true, how can we say that the sun *sets* in the west?

A: Good question! The verb *set* is generally transitive, but it does have some standardized intransitive uses, such as the one you mention. Here's another: *Glue sets up quickly.* I doubt that anyone would be likely to substitute *sit* in either of these unusual situations. While we're on the subject, the verb *sit* also has some exceptions. Although generally intransitive, *sit* has a few transitive uses: *Sit yourself down* and *The waiter sat us at Table 1.*

Q: My son is studying a foreign language; and he asked me, a teacher of business English, why we capitalize the personal pronoun *I* in English when we don't capitalize other pronouns.

A: That's a fascinating topic, and a little research on the Web revealed that linguists ponder the same question. In a linguistic journal, they discussed some relevant theories. One linguist thought that perhaps the lowercase *i* was too easily confused with the number *1* or with similar looking *i*'s, *u*'s, and *v*'s in medieval handwriting. Another attributed the word's capital letter to our egocentric nature. Another suggested that since the pronoun *I* usually appeared as the first word in a sentence, it was capitalized for that reason. In earlier centuries before the language was standardized, most nouns and pronouns were capitalized haphazardly. One linguist thought that a better question to ask would be why all of the other pronouns lose their capital letters and *I* retains its.

Name _____

Level I

A. (Self-check) Select the correct verb. Use your dictionary to verify spelling if necessary.

1. New York's mayor (denyed, <u>denied</u>) any wrongdoing in the campaign.   _____

2. What did you say your boss's name <u>(is</u>, was)?   _____

3. The machine (jamed, <u>jammed</u>) when conflicting instructions were entered.   _____

4. Bill knew that the distance between Madison and Milwaukee <u>(is</u>, was) 90 miles.   _____

5. We (hurryed, <u>hurried</u>) through the rehearsals.   _____

6. Shirley's maiden name <u>(is</u>, was) Eiseman.   _____

7. His case was (refered, <u>referred</u>) to the Motor Vehicle Department.   _____

8. This old equipment (need, <u>needs</u>) to be replaced.   _____

9. The salespeople who called this morning said that they (be, <u>are</u>, were) with Halston, Inc.   _____

10. He (write, <u>writes</u>) a dozen or more e-mail messages daily.   _____

Check your answers below.

B. In the following sentences, provide three tenses for each verb.

Example: He (*arrive*) at the office at 7:45 a.m.

Past _arrived_ Present _arrives_ Future _will arrive_

1. The nation's tax system (need) to stimulate investment.

Past _ed_ Present _s_ Future _will_

2. Our administrative assistant (copy) contracts for clients.

Past _ied_ Present _ies_ Future _will_

3. Lori (hurry) to catch the bus.

Past _ied_ Present _ies_ Future _will_

4. Jason (try) to improve his writing skills.

Past _ied_ Present _ies_ Future _will_

5. Dr. Darlene Neuman (cover) the same material.

Past _ed_ Present _s_ Future _will_

6. Monsanto (label) its plastic soft-drink bottle.

Past _ed_ Present _s_ Future _will_

7. Courtney (plan) to major in business management.

Past _ed_____ Present ___S____ Future _will_____

8. Colleges (invest) in child-care facilities for student parents.

Past _ed_____ Present ___S____ Future _will_____

9. First Federal (open) its new branch office downtown today.

Past _ed_____ Present ___S____ Future _will_____

10. Questionnaires (sample) customers' reactions to our new product.

Past _ed_____ Present _____ Future _will_____

C. **Writing Exercise.** Compose sentences using the verbs shown.

1. (Past tense of *bury*) _____

_____

2. (Present tense of *apply*) _____

_____

3. (Future tense of *study*) _____

_____

4. (Past tense of *cancel*) _____

_____

5. (Present tense of *learn*) _____

_____

L e v e l   I I

A. **(Self-check)** Write the correct verb. Do not add a helper verb.

Example: He wished he had (eat) before he left.   **eaten**_____

1. His ancestors (come) from Ireland on a freighter.   came_____

2. Have you (see) the Miami contract anywhere?   seen_____

3. That helicopter has (fly) over the intersection twice.   flown_____

4. Yesterday Lon (swim) the length of the pool.   swam_____

5. Our e-mail manual was (write) by Nancy Metzinger.   written_____

6. This morning's mild earthquake (shake) the dishes in the cabinet.   shook_____

7. Over the past year Dr. Karen Howie (give) freely of her services.   gave_____

8. Have you (speak) with the supervisor yet?   spoken_____

9. I wish Scott had (know) about the scholarship earlier.   known_____

10. All employees should have (go) to the software demonstration.   gone_____

Check your answers below.

B. Underline any verb errors you find in the following sentences. Write the correct forms in the spaces provided. Do not add helper verbs. Write *C* if the sentence is correct as it stands.

Example: Janet said she <u>seen</u> the accident.   *saw*

1. Because of advances in technology, the world has <u>shrank</u>.   *shrunk*
2. Real estate sales <u>sunk</u> to an all-time low.   *sank*
3. The office staff must <u>chose</u> a new letterhead stationery.   *choose*
4. Coach Meyers has <u>wore</u> his lucky shirt for the entire tournament.   *worn*
5. Leslie and Mark have <u>went</u> to the lecture in Royce Hall.   *gone*
6. Her friend asked if she had <u>ate</u> dinner yet.   *eaten*
7. His car was <u>stole</u> over the weekend.   *stolen*
8. We should have thrown out that old printer long ago.   *C*
9. The water bill was not <u>payed</u> last month.   *paid*
10. Is that the dog that has <u>bit</u> two passersby?   *bitten*
11. An agreement binding both parties was recently <u>wrote</u>.   *written*
12. The telephone has <u>rang</u> only twice in the past hour.   *rung*
13. Mark <u>brang</u> his bike to the mall.   *brought*
14. Howling winds have blown all day, making outside work difficult.   *C*
15. The first pitch of the season was <u>threw</u> out by the president.   *thrown*

C. *Lie–Lay.* Write the correct forms of the verb.

Present	Present Participle	Past	Past Participle
lie (to rest):			
lay (to place):			

Select the correct verb.

1. Judy Easley told her dog to (lay, <u>lie</u>) down.   ~~lay~~ *lie*
2. Stacy (layed, laid) the mail on Mrs. Tong's desk.   *laid*
3. The contracts had been (lying, laying) there for some time.   ~~laying~~ ~~lay~~ *lying*
4. In fact, they had (laid, lain) there over a week.   *lain*
5. Every day at 2 p.m. Jean (lies, lays) down to rest.   *lies*

D. *Sit–Set; Rise–Raise.* Write the correct forms of the verbs.

Present	Present Participle	Past	Past Participle
sit (to rest):	sitting	sat	sat
set (to place):	setting	set	set
rise (to go up):	rising	rose	risen
raise (to lift):	raising	raised	raised

Select the correct verb.

1. Please (raise, rise) the windows to let in fresh air. _____
2. We'll never finish if Marcy (sits, sets) there all day. _____
3. Working computers (raise, rise) the temperature in a room. _____
4. My temperature (raises, rises) when I exercise vigorously. _____
5. Managers are (sitting, setting) goals for the production and sales staffs. _____
6. The value of gold (rises, raises) or falls in relation to the dollar. _____
7. Brenda Woodward (raised, rose) the question of retroactive benefits. _____
8. Julie and Luis Suarez always (sit, set) near the door. _____
9. The employee parking lot (sits, sets) some distance away. _____
10. Consumer prices have (risen, raised) faster than consumer income. _____

E. **Writing Exercise.** Compose original sentences using the verbs shown.

1. choose _____
2. blown _____
3. shrank _____
4. laid _____
5. rose _____

L e v e l   I I I

A. **(Self-check)** Verbs in the following sentences have been italicized. In the space provided, indicate the tense of each of these verbs. Refer to the text to guide you.

Example: Your credit cards *had been recovered* by the time you reported the loss.
past perfect, passive

1. You *will have heard* the news before we have heard it. _____
2. Those orders *are being sent* to your Dallas office. _____
3. Mr. Adams' case *will have been heard* in six weeks. _____
4. I cannot believe what I *am hearing*. _____
5. Carolyn Seefer *had been told* to pick up the prize money at once. _____
6. We *have* just *seen* your product advertised on television. _____
7. The manager's suggestions for reduced paper use *have been followed* by all employees. _____
8. You *will be seeing* many changes in our Web site shortly. _____
9. The Birches *have lived* in that neighborhood for years. _____
10. We *are* now *experiencing* the effects of the last cutback. _____

Check your answers below.

1. future perfect 2. present progressive, passive 3. future perfect, passive 4. present progressive 5. past perfect, passive 6. present perfect 7. present perfect, passive 8. future progressive 9. present perfect 10. present progressive

B. Write the proper verb form.

Example: They (drive) all night before they found a motel. (Past perfect)   **had driven** _____

1. Before the office announcement was made, we (hear) rumors about layoffs. (Past perfect) _____

2. When the fire alarm sounded, Miss Waters (help) Shwan Chin Wu. (Past progressive) _____

3. By next April, RamCo (open) four branch outlets. (Future perfect) _____

4. I'm sure they (tell) about their trip when they return. (Future progressive) _____

5. Plans (develop) to reduce administrative costs. (Present progressive, passive) _____

6. Our campus (think) about developing a student child-care center. (Present progressive) _____

7. We are certain they (receive) our proposal by now. (Present perfect) _____

8. By 5 p.m. the contract (finish) and faxed to our client. (Past perfect, passive) _____

C. *Review.* These sentences review Chapters 1 through 9. Underline any errors. Then write corrected forms in the spaces provided. Some sentences require more than one correction. If a sentence is correct, write *C* in the space.

1. Fees for visits to a doctors office have rose steadily over the decade. _____

2. Although some policys allow you to chose any doctor, the plan selected for us office workers offers less freedom. _____

3. Jeff and me could have forgave her if she had softened her tone. _____

4. Brets dirt bike looks as if it has been drove through a mud puddle. _____

5. Donna Kimmerling advised every graduate to submit their résumé in scannable form. _____

6. During it's first month of operation, the recycling program has broke records for reducing waste. _____

7. Everyone except Dalton Robinson and I was impressed by the months recycling profits. _____

8. Many larger facilitys can recycle at no net cost because there haulers are taking away less trash. _____

9. Has everyone on the womens team submitted their doctor's release form? _____

10. Lorraine Ganz contract, which is laying on the desk, must be delivered immediately. _____

11. The vice president has swore that no one would work harder than him to meet the deadline. _____

12. Not one of the job candidates who we interviewed has wrote a thank-you letter. _____

13. Although I told James dog to lay down, it jumped up and knocked me over. _____

14. Because it has took two hours to complete the test, I will be late. _____

15. Next Monday is Memorial Day, hence we won't need the ride you offered to Beth and I. _____

16. The product had sank so low in the eyes of consumers' that it was removed from store shelfs. _____

17. Our research shows that the average retail part-time employee has stole over $300 worth of merchandise in a years time. _____

18. You may set the printer on this desk until a better location is found. _____

19. Cheryl said she seen you and him at Marcos party. _____

20. Because to many computers were running, the rooms temperature had raised to 95 degrees. _____

Editor's Challenge

The following memo contains 30 intentional errors in spelling, proofreading, and grammar principles you have studied thus far. Use proofreading marks to indicate your changes. If three words replace one word, it counts as one change.

DATE: January 21, 200x

TO: All Employees

FROM: Vice President, Human Resources

SUBJECT: CHANGE IN FLOATING HOLIDAY POLICY

The senior executive staff has approved a change in the companys floating holiday plan. Employees in the past vote on a single date to be took by all workers as there floating holiday.

Now, however, each employee will be allowed to chose the date that they wish to use as a floating holiday.

To reserve your floating holiday, Please notify your supervisor or I. Approval will be based on your units staffing needs. If a supervisor or myself receive several requests for the same date, employment seniority will govern.

A question has arose about how to record these holidays. I have spoke to Payroll, and they say you should use the Attendance Bonus code on your time card. This method will be used until Payroll has went over all employees records and modified it.

We wish it was possible for everyone to have their holiday exactly when desired, but we must urge you to be flexible. Because your supervisor has all ready began a schedule of employees floating holidays. It's not too early for you to submit your request.

Assume you're on the job and a new employee needs a little instruction in the use of e-mail. You decide to use the Web to provide a quick tutorial.

Goal: To learn to use an e-mail tutorial.

1. With your Web browser on the screen, key the following URL: **<http://www.fvrl.bc.ca/learn/tutorial/e-mail.html>.**

2. Read the five sections on this page.

3. How does e-mail save natural resources?

4. How are multiple addresses entered in the "**Cc**" field?

5. This site provides a quick online tutorial for introducing e-mail. But it suffers from some writing lapses. Can you find two comma splices?

6. Print two pages from this site, underline the answers to our questions, submit your printouts, and end your session.

POSTTEST

Underline the correct verb.

1. After we (saw, seen) the advertisement, we bought the machine.

2. Your telephone has (rung, rang) only twice while you were gone.

3. The contracts have (laid, lain) on your desk for over a week.

4. Soil temperatures will slowly (raise, rise) during the spring.

5. Mr. Jones has (worn, wore) the same suit every day this week.

1. saw 2. rung 3. lain 4. rise 5. worn

CHECKLIST OF BONUS LEARNING RESOURCES

The following additional learning resources are available to you. Your instructor will tell you which to complete.

- Web Editor's Challenge Exercise

- Web Interactive Chapter Review

- Web PowerPoint Slides

- Web Crossword Puzzle

- WebCheck Reinforcement Exercises 9.1, 9.2

- Self-Help Exercises

- Electronic Study Guide

chapter 10 Verb and Subject Agreement

Objectives

When you have completed the materials in this chapter, you will be able to do the following:

Level I

- Locate the subjects of verbs despite intervening elements and inverted sentence structure.
- Make verbs agree with true subjects.
- Make verbs agree with subjects joined by *and*.

Level II

- Make verbs agree with subjects joined by *or* or *nor*.
- Select the correct verbs to agree with collective nouns and indefinite pronouns.

Level III

- Make verbs agree with quantities, fractions, portions, clauses, and *a number/the number*.
- Achieve subject–verb agreement within *who* clauses.

Underline the correct verb.

1. One of our plans for reducing costs (require, requires) considerable capital.

2. The manager, along with his administrative assistant and accountant, (was, were) invited to the conference.

3. Neither the supervisor nor his team (is, are) satisfied with the level of service.

4. Behind this building (lies, lie) the parking lot and swimming pool.

5. The number of e-mail users (is, are) increasing daily.

1. requires 2. was 3. is 4. lie 5. is

Subjects must agree with verbs in number and person. Beginning a sentence with *He don't* damages a speaker's credibility and limits a communicator's effectiveness.

If an error is made in subject–verb agreement, it can generally be attributed to one of three lapses: (a) failure to locate the subject, (b) failure to recognize the number (singular or plural) of the subject after locating it, or (c) failure to recognize the number of the verb. Suggestions for locating the true subject and determining the number of the subject and its verb follow.

Spot the Blooper

On the label of Heinz 57 sauce: "Its' unique tangy blend of herbs and spices bring out the natural taste of steak." (Did you spot two bloopers?)

Hot Link

For help in locating sentence subjects, visit the Howard Payne University English Department site **<http://www.hputx. edu/Faculty/English/ subsandverbs.htm>**.

Spot the Blooper

From third grade teacher's letter to the editor in *The San Francisco Chronicle*: "Every one of our classrooms are linked to the Internet."

L e v e l   I

Locating Subjects

All verbs have subjects. Locating these subjects can be difficult, particularly when (a) a prepositional phrase comes between the verb and its subject, (b) an intervening element separates the subject and verb, (c) sentences begin with *there* or *here*, and (d) sentences are inverted.

Prepositional Phrases

Subjects of verbs are not found in prepositional phrases. Therefore, you must learn to ignore such phrases in identifying subjects of verbs. Some of the most common prepositions are *of, to, in, from, for, with, at,* and *by.* Notice in these sentences that the italicized prepositional phrases do not contain the subjects of the verbs.

> Only <u>one</u> *of the company executives* is fully insured. (The verb *is* agrees with its subject *one.*)
>
> We wondered if the <u>invoice</u> *for the two shipments* was lost. (The verb *was* agrees with its subject *invoice.*)
>
> The <u>range</u> *of skill requirements* allows for upward growth potential. (The verb *allows* agrees with the subject *range.*)

Some of the less easily recognized prepositions are *except, but, like,* and *between.* In the following sentences, distinguish the subjects from the italicized prepositional phrases.

> All <u>employees</u> *but Tom* are to report early. (The verb *are* agrees with its subject *employees.*)
>
> <u>Everyone</u> *except the Harrises* is able to attend. (The verb *is* agrees with its subject *everyone.*)

Intervening Elements

Groups of words introduced by *as well as, in addition to, such as, including, together with,* and *other than* do *not* contain sentence subjects.

> The priceless <u>book</u>, *as well as other valuable documents*, was lost in the fire.

In this sentence the writer has elected to emphasize the subject *book* and to de-emphasize *other valuable documents.* The writer could have given equal weight to these elements by writing *The priceless book <u>and</u> other valuable documents were lost in the fire.* Notice that the number (singular or plural) of the verb changes when both *book* and *documents* are given equal emphasis. Here are additional examples involving intervening elements:

Our president, *together with her entire staff of employees*, sends her greetings. (The singular subject *president* agrees with the singular verb *sends*.)

Other students *such as Kyle* have completed the assignment. (The plural subject *students* agrees with the plural verb *have*.)

The Adverbs *there* and *here*

In sentences beginning with *there* or *here*, look for the true subject *after* the verb. As adverbs, *here* and *there* cannot function as subjects.

There are four candidates who applied for the position. (The subject *candidates* follows the verb *are*.)

Here is the fuel oil consumption report. (The subject *report* follows the verb *is*.)

Inverted Sentence Order

Look for the subject after the verb in inverted sentences and in questions.

Attending the conference are salespeople from four states. (Verb precedes subject.)

Have the product specifications been submitted? (Subject separates verb phrase.)

How important are salary, benefits, and job security? (Verb precedes subjects.)

How do law and ethics relate to everyday business? (Verb precedes subjects.)

Basic Rules for Verb–Subject Agreement

Once you have located the sentence subject, decide whether the subject is singular or plural and select a verb that agrees in number.

Subjects Joined by *and*

When one subject is joined to another by the word *and*, the subject is plural and requires a plural verb.

Carolyn and her brother work at Baker's.

The proposed law and its amendment are before the legislature.

Company Names and Titles

Even though they may appear to be plural, company names and titles of publications are singular; therefore, they require singular verbs.

Country Homes and Gardens makes an excellent magazine gift.

American Airlines is advertising the lowest fare to Hawaii.

Richards, Bateman, and Richards, Inc., is offering the bond issue.

Now complete the reinforcement exercises for Level I.

Career Tip

Skillful writers avoid starting sentences or clauses with *there*, a word-wasting filler. Usually sentences can be rewritten without it.

Spot the Blooper

Sign above a group of photographs in a Service Merchandise store, Ft. Myers [FL]: "HERE'S OUR STORE MANAGERS."

Spot the Blooper

From *The Saint John's* [Newfoundland] *Evening Telegram*: "It's important that we have in that position someone who's judgment, integrity, and incompetence is beyond question." (Did you spot three bloopers?)

Spot the Blooper

From the "WSU Update" at Winona State University [MN]: "All students, faculty, and staff is invited to donate blood."

Special Rules for Verb–Subject Agreement

Making sure your subjects agree with your verbs sometimes requires the application of special rules. This is especially true when dealing with subjects joined by *or* or *nor*, indefinite pronouns as subjects, and collective nouns as subjects.

Subjects Joined by *or* or *nor*

When two or more subjects are joined by *or* or *nor*, the verb should agree with the closer subject.

Study Tip

Unlike subjects joined by *and*, subjects joined by *or/nor* require a choice between Subject No. 1 and Subject No. 2.

Neither the webmaster nor the <u>clerks</u> <u>know</u> her password.

Either Leslie or <u>you</u> <u>are</u> in charge of ordering supplies.

The manufacturer or the <u>distributors</u> <u>carry</u> spare parts.

Indefinite Pronouns as Subjects

As you may recall from Chapter 7, some indefinite pronouns are always singular, while other indefinite pronouns are always plural. In addition, some may be singular or plural depending on the words to which they refer.

Spot the Blooper

Headline in *The San Francisco Chronicle*: "One in 11 Have Trouble Speaking California's Official Language."

	Always Singular		**Always Plural**	**Singular or Plural**
anyone	every	nobody	both	all
anybody	everyone	nothing	few	more
anything	everybody	someone	many	most
each	everything	somebody	several	some
either	many a	something		any
	neither			none

Either of the two applicants *is* qualified.

Everybody in the lottery *has* an equal chance.

A *few* of the workers *are* applying for stock shares.

Neither of the Web sites *is* particularly helpful.

Indefinite pronouns such as *all*, *more*, and *most* provide one of the few instances in which prepositional phrases become important in determining agreement. Although the prepositional phrase does not contain the subject of the sentence, it does contain the noun to which the indefinite pronoun refers.

Most of the applicants *are* women. (*Most* is plural because it refers to *women*.)

Most of the work *is* completed. (*Most* is singular because it refers to *work*.)

If the indefinite pronouns *each*, *every*, or *many a* are used to describe two or more subjects joined by *and*, the subjects are considered separate. Therefore, the verb is singular.

Study Tip

To help you select correct verbs, temporarily substitute *it* for singular subjects or *they* for plural subjects. Then you can more easily make verbs agree with their subjects.

Many a semicolon and colon *is* misused.

Every man, woman, and child *is* affected by the tax cut.

The indefinite pronouns *anyone*, *everyone*, and *someone* are generally spelled as two words when followed by *of* phrases.

Any one of the police officers is available for special duty.

Every one of the candidates was questioned about illegal contributions.

Collective Nouns as Subjects

Words such as *faculty*, *committee*, and *council* may be singular or plural depending on their mode of operation. When a collective noun operates as a single unit, its verb should be singular. When the elements of a collective noun operate separately, the verb should be plural.

Our <u>faculty</u> *has approved* the proposal. (*Faculty* is operating as a single unit.)

The <u>council</u> *were* sharply *divided* over the budget. (*Council* members were acting separately. While technically correct, the sentence would be less awkward if it read *The council* <u>*members*</u> were sharply. . .)

Now complete the reinforcement exercises for Level II.

Level III

Additional Rules for Verb–Subject Agreement

In some instances it's difficult to know whether a subject is singular or plural. Here are a few additional rules to guide you in selecting appropriate verbs for such subjects.

The Distinction Between *the number* and *a number*

When the word *number* is the subject of a sentence, its article (*the* or *a*) becomes significant. *The* is specific and therefore implies *singularity*; *a* is general and therefore implies *plurality*.

The number of managers *is* declining. (Singular)

A number of e-mail messages *were* lost. (Plural)

Quantities, Measures

When they refer to *total* amounts, quantities and measures are singular. If they refer to individual units that can be counted, quantities and measures are plural.

Three years *is* the period of the loan. (Quantity as a total amount.)

Three years *are* needed to renovate the property totally. (Quantity as individual units.)

Fractions, Portions

Fractions and portions may be singular or plural depending on the nouns to which they refer.

Spot the Blooper

From *The Atlantic City Press*: "[O]ne in five adults don't know how to use a road map."

Spot the Blooper

From the *Evansville* [IN] *Press:* "Although a large crowd were gathered . . ."

Spot the Blooper

From *The Times-Union* [Albany, NY]: "The interim superintendent of schools said that 'a large number of students arrives without the basic skills we expect them to have.'"

Two-thirds of the cassettes *are* satisfactory.

Over half of the contract *was* ratified.

A majority of employees *agree* with the proposal.

A minimum of work *is* required to receive approval.

Part of the delegates *are* in favor of the plan.

Part of the proposal *is* ambiguous.

Who Clauses

Verbs in *who* clauses must agree in number and person with the nouns to which they refer. In *who* clauses introduced by *one of*, the verb is usually plural because it refers to a plural antecedent. In *who* clauses introduced by *the only one of*, the verb is singular.

Janice Salles is *one of* those managers who always support the employees.

Tyler is *one of* those people who are late sleepers.

Maria is *the only one of* the girls who is prepared.

Verbs must agree in person with the nouns or pronouns to which they refer.

It is you who are responsible for security.

Could it be I who am to blame?

Phrases and Clauses as Subjects

Use a singular verb when the subject of a sentence is a phrase or clause.

Knowing automotive design and construction is unnecessary for the typical driver.

That verbs must agree with subjects is accepted.

Subject Complements

In Chapter 8 you learned that linking verbs are followed by complements. Although a complement may differ from the subject in number, the linking verb should always agree with the subject.

The best part of the show is the singing and dancing. (The singular subject *part* agrees with the singular verb *is* despite the plural complement *singing and dancing*.)

The reason for his bankruptcy is poor investments in stocks.

To avoid awkwardness, it is better to reconstruct such sentences. One alternative is to place the plural element first: *The singing and dancing are the best part of the show.* An even better alternative is to make both the subject and its complement agree in number: *The reason for his bankruptcy is a poor stock investment strategy* or *The reasons for his bankruptcy are poor stock investments.*

Now complete the reinforcement exercises for Level III.

Study Tip

For sentences with *one of those who* clauses, begin reading with the word *of*: *Of those people who are late sleepers, John is one.* The verb will always be plural. However, if the sentence is limited by *only one*, the verb is always singular.

Spot the Blooper

From *The Atlanta Journal and Constitution*: "Initiation fee and dues information also is top secret."

Q: My uncle insists that *none* is singular. My English book says that it can be plural. Who's right?

A: Times are changing. Thirty years ago *none* was almost always used in a singular sense. Today, through usage, *none* may be singular or plural depending on what you wish to emphasize. For example, *None are more willing than we*. But, *None of the students is* (or *are* if you wish to suggest many students) *failing*.

Q: When do you use *all together*, and when do you use *altogether*?

A: *All together* means "collectively" or "all the members of a group" (*we must work all together to reach our goal*). *Altogether* means "entirely" (*he was altogether satisfied*).

Q: Please help me with this sentence that I'm transcribing for a medical laboratory: *A copy of our analysis, along with our interpretation of its results, (has or have) been sent to you.*

A: The subject of your sentence is *copy*; thus the verb must be *has*. Don't let interrupting elements obscure the real sentence subject.

Q: After looking in the dictionary, I'm beginning to wonder about this: *We have alot of work yet to do*. I can't find the word *alot* in the dictionary, but it must be there. Everyone uses it.

A: The two-word phrase *a lot* is frequently used in conversation or in very informal writing (*the copier makes a lot of copies*). *Alot* as one word does not exist. Don't confuse it with *allot* meaning "to distribute" (*the company will allot to each department its share of supplies*).

Q: Should *reevaluate* be hyphenated?

A: No. It is not necessary to use a hyphen after the prefix *re* unless the resulting word may be confused with another word (*to re-mark the sales ticket, to re-cover the chair*).

Q: I'm totally confused by job titles for women today. What do I call a woman who is a *fireman*, a *policeman*, a *chairman*, or a *spokesman*? And what about the word *mankind*?

A: As more and more women enter nontraditional careers, some previous designations are being replaced by neutral, inclusive titles. Here are some substitutes:

actor	for *actress*
firefighter	for *fireman*
mail carrier	for *mailman*
police officer	for *policeman*
flight attendant	for *steward* or *stewardess*
reporter or journalist	for *newsman*

Words like *chairman*, *spokesman*, and *mankind* traditionally have been used to refer to both men and women. Today, though, sensitive writers strive to use more inclusive language. Possible substitutes are *chair*, *spokesperson*, and *humanity*.

Q: I'm never sure how to handle words that are used to represent quantities and proportions in sentences. For example, what verb is correct in this sentence: *A large proportion of voters (was or were) against the measure.*

A: Words that represent fractional amounts (such as *proportion, fraction, minimum,* and *majority*) may be singular or plural depending on the words they represent. In your sentence *proportion* represents *voters*, which is plural. Therefore, use the plural verb *were*.

Name _____

Level I

A. (Self-check) Select the correct word to complete each sentence below. Write it in the space provided.

1. Everyone except Marco and two other employees (<u>is</u>, are) using e-mail daily. _____

2. The copy machine in our department, along with those on the second and third floors, (need, <u>needs</u>) servicing. _____

3. Here (<u>is</u>, are) one of the reasons we are establishing a Web site. _____

4. (Has, ⟨Have⟩) any of our work orders been completed yet? _____

5. No one but the Human Resources director and a few managers ever (talk, <u>talks</u>) about balancing work and family issues. _____

6. The computer and the monitor, along with the printer, (<u>cost</u>, costs) less than we expected. _____

7. Addressing the conference (is, <u>are</u>) members of our management team. _____

8. We understand that United Airlines (<u>is</u>, are) interviewing flight attendants. _____

9. A set of guidelines to standardize input and output (<u>was</u>, were) developed. _____

10. *Workplace Communication Strategies* by Eleanor M. Yueda (appear, <u>appears</u>) to be our departmental selection. _____

Check your answers below.

B. For each of the following sentences, circle the sentence subject. Then, cross out any phrases that separate the verb from its subject. Choose the correct verb and write it in the space provided.

Examples: The ⟨supervisor,⟩ ~~together with two of his assistants,~~ (is, are) here. **is** ____

Our ⟨catalog⟩ ~~of gift ideas~~ (is, are) being sent to you. **is** ____

1. Our company's ~~full range of products and services~~ (is, <u>are</u>) available through our local dealers. _____

2. A ⟨description⟩ ~~of the property, along with several other legal documents,~~ (<u>was</u>, were) filed with my attorney. _____

3. ⟨Everyone⟩ ~~except the mailing room and shipping department workers~~ (is, <u>are</u>) being trained on the new computer. _____

4. The ⟨list⟩ ~~of vendors providing leased machines~~ (<u>was</u>, were) recently revised. _____

5. All ⟨cooperatives⟩ ~~except the Lemon Growing Exchange~~ (has, <u>have</u>) been able to provide supplies at reduced prices. _____

6. ~~Although the economy is booming~~, only one of the major automobile manufacturers _____ (is, are) showing profits.

7. Outstanding salespeople ~~like Mrs. Love~~ (has, have) helped make our company a _____ leader in the field.

8. One of your duties ~~in addition to the tasks already described~~, (is, are) the budget- _____ ing of funds for both departments.

C. Assume that the following phrases serve as sentence subjects. For each item, circle the simple subject(s). Then indicate if it is singular or plural.

	Plural	Singular
Example: the controller and the treasurer of the county	✓	_____
1. a list of management objectives	✓	_____
2. the instructor together with his students	_____	✓
3. other services such as HTML coding and graphics	✓	_____
4. the production cost and the markup of each item	_____	✓
5. one of the most interesting Web sites on the Internet	_____	✓
6. current emphasis on product safety and consumer protection	_____	_____
7. Madison, Lee & Cassidy, Inc., an executive placement service	_____	_____
8. the tone and the wording of the letter	_____	_____

D. Select the correct verb and write it in the space provided.

1. Here (is, are) the full list of names and addresses. _____

2. Seated next to the Alvarados (is, are) Joe Miranda. _____

3. There (is, are) two things you must do immediately. _____

4. He (doesn't, don't) mind working extra hours this weekend. _____

5. Our president, along with the general manager and three salespeo- _____ ple, (plan, plans) to attend the conference.

6. Not one of our four service representatives (is, are) available. _____

7. Southwestern Airlines (is, are) featuring a low fare to San Diego. _____

8. Lying on my desk (is, are) my itinerary and plane tickets. _____

9. Kerr, McClellan, and Huynh, Inc., a legal firm in Oklahoma City, _____ (specializes, specialize) in patent law.

10. Considerable time and money (was, were) spent on the plans. _____

11. How important (is, are) location, benefits, and salary? _____

12. A continuing decline in test scores (is, are) a disgrace to the district. _____

L e v e l   I I

A. **(Self-check)** Write the correct form.

1. A task force of four men and five women (is, are) to be appointed. _____

2. Either Rhonda Behrens or Valerie Evans (has, have) approved the _____ report.

3. The inventory and the report (is, are) now being prepared. _____

4. Each of the classifications (contains, contain) four parts. _____

5. All union members (has, have) to vote on the proposed contract. _____

6. Every one of the new dot-com companies (is, are) seeking venture capital. _____

7. Many a clerk and receptionist (has, have) complained about the switchboard. _____

8. (Everyone, Every one) of the wills can be produced on word processing equipment. _____

9. All that work (is, are) yet to be logged in. _____

10. Each clerk, administrative assistant, and word processing specialist (was, were) asked to complete a questionnaire. _____

Check your answers below.

B. Write the correct form.

1. The Council on Consumer Prices (has, have) taken a firm position. _____

2. Neither Judith McDermid nor Bonnie Ideal (is, are) afraid of hard work. _____

3. (Everyone, Every one) of the surgical reports required careful editing. _____

4. Several of the proposals (contain, contains) complex formulas. _____

5. Either the judge or the attorneys (has, have) asked for a recess. _____

6. The group of players, coaches, and fans (plan, plans) to charter a plane. _____

7. Either of the two companies (is, are) satisfactory. _____

8. Something about these insurance claims (appear, appears) questionable. _____

9. Every one of the employees who attended the meeting (was, were) opposed to the wage proposal. _____

10. An online version of *U.S. News & World Report*'s college rankings (is, are) now available. _____

11. (Was, Were) any of the members of the organization present that afternoon? _____

12. (Is, Are) either of the letters ready for signature? _____

13. The jury (has, have) announced its verdict. _____

14. Preservation of the ocean and its creatures (is, are) a major concern. _____

15. Either of the photocopies (is, are) acceptable for our purposes. _____

16. A map showing the homes of celebrities (is, are) sold in Hollywood. _____

17. Either a book or an article (has, have) to be read to fulfill the assignment. _____

18. Our program, along with the efforts of other civic-minded businesses, (is, are) aimed at urban renewal. _____

19. Any one of the stockholders (has, have) the right to delegate his or her proxy. _____

20. Some of the handwriting in the sales reports (is, are) illegible. _____

1. is 2. has 3. are 4. contains 5. have 6. is 7. has 8. Every one 9. is 10. was

C. Writing Exercise. Use your imagination in expanding the following sentences.

1. The staff (is, are) _____

_____

2. Our city council (has, have) _____

_____

3. Not one of the plans (was, were) _____

_____

4. Some of the jury members (believe, believes) _____

_____

5. Somebody in the bus filled with students (was, were) _____

_____

L e v e l   I I I

A. (Self-check) For each sentence write the correct verb in the space provided.

1. The number of online job applicants (is, are) greater than expected. _____

2. Part of the loss of customers (is, are) the result of poor service. _____

3. Our company president is one of those executives who (is, are) able to delegate responsibility. _____

4. Fifteen feet of pipe (is, are) exactly what was specified. _____

5. Didn't you know it is you who (is, are) to be honored at the ceremony? _____

6. A number of problems (is, are) yet to be resolved. _____

7. She is the only one of the service reps who (speak, speaks) three languages. _____

8. Whoever is named for the job (has, have) my approval. _____

9. About one third of the records (is, are) stored on microfiche. _____

10. The hardest part of the job (is, are) the bending and lifting. _____

Check your answers below.

B. Select the correct verb.

1. Thirty-five dollars (is, are) required as a deposit before one can rent a tandem bicycle. _____

2. Our latest advertisements featuring our spring clothing line (is, are) an example of the campaign. _____

3. Is it he who (is, are) the new account representative? _____

4. Carole is the only one of the lab assistants who (was, were) able to repair the malfunctioning machine. _____

5. Vacations for employees who are entitled to three or more weeks (is, are) the next item on the agenda. _____

6. Sixty days (is, are) the period of the loan. _____

7. At the rear of the building complex (is, are) the quality control lab and the science department. _____

8. Only a fraction of the conference delegates (was, were) unable to find accommodations at the Mandalay Bay resort. _____

9. Serving in the student senate (is, are) a representative from each of the twenty departments on campus. _____

10. Over 80 percent of the individuals attending the lecture series (is, are) residents of nearby communities. _____

11. Steve is one of those people who always (get, gets) along well with fellow workers. _____

12. The reason for his wealth (is, are) wise investments in oil. _____

13. Neither the staff nor the students (think, thinks) that higher fees will solve the budget crisis. _____

14. Running for mayor (is, are) the sheriff and two councilpersons. _____

15. Heinlein, Fagan & Ross, Inc., with headquarters in Chicago, (has, have) been chosen for the job. _____

16. One of the problems, in addition to those already mentioned, (seem, seems) to be resistance to change. _____

17. A chart showing all staff positions and responsibilities (was, were) prepared by the vice president. _____

18. Neither the defendant nor the plaintiffs (was, were) satisfied with the judgment. _____

19. Linda Crowl is one of those versatile professors who (teach, teaches) many subjects. _____

20. On our campus the number of successful job candidates (is, are) steadily increasing. _____

C. **Writing Exercise.** Some subject–verb constructions are grammatically correct but sound incorrect. Revise the following correct sentences so that they are not only correct but sound so. Hint: Make the subject and its complement agree in number

Example: The best part of my job is meeting people and learning new things. <u>The best parts of my job are meeting people and learning new things.</u>

1. Vacations for employees who are entitled to three or more weeks are the next item on the agenda. _____

_____

2. Abstracts and affidavits are the principal work in this office. _____

_____

3. The primary reason for his wealth is wise stock and other investment choices. _____

_____

For further practice in subject–verb agreement, write sentences using the following words as subjects of present-tense verbs. Your sentences should have 12 or more words.

Example: The number of <u>voters is increasing rapidly as we approach the election date.</u>

4. A number of _____

5. Every one of the new voters _____

6. None of the new voters _____

Editor's Challenge

The following letter proposal contains 44 intentional errors in spelling, proofreading, and grammar principles you have studied thus far. Use proofreading marks to show your corrections.

Wright Research Consultants

6592 Galveston Plaza
Houston, TX 77038

Web: http://www.wrightresearch.com   Phone: (713) 220-9184   E-mail: rwright@wrightresearch.com

April 15, 200X

Dr. Morris Edelson
Consumer Credit Service
6025 Rustic Avenue
Houston, TX 77087

Dear Dr. Edelson:

At your request, my staff and myself is submitting the following proposal regarding a survey of college students credit habits in the Austin, Texas, area.

Problem

As you point out, credit purchase's among college students is burdening them with to much debt, more than half of the full-time undergraduate students at four-year universitys now has at least one major credit card. Although students account for less than 3 percent of the domestic credit card business, a significant number of these students is having more trouble than other borrowers in repaying. Credit card use among students has rose dramatically in the past decade.

Background

We understand that your non-profit organizations principle goal is to open a credit counseling service aimed at college students in the Austin area. Specifically, you want to investigate (1) credit card habit's among college students in general, (2) credit card habits among students in the Austin area, and (3) the affectiveness of student counseling services in other college towns.

Proposed Plan

On the basis of our experience in conducting many local and national surveys, Wright Research propose to develop a short but thorough questionnaire probing the data you desire. We will submit the questionnaire for you approval, and we will consult with you regarding the exact sample and it's demographics. Data from the surveywill be analyze by our experienced team of experts. Using the latest computer systems and advanced statistical measures.

Staffing and Budget

Wright Research Consultants are a nationally recognized, experienced research consulting firm specializing in survey investigation. My staff and myself has assigned your survey to Dr. Janet Sebesy, whom is our director of research. Dr. Sebesy was trained at the University of wisconsin and has successfully supervise our research program for the past nine years. Further information about her qualifications and our staffs training is described in the attached brochure. Everyone of the members of our staff are experienced in survey research. Budget figures for this proposed survey is showed in the attach brochure.

Authorization

My staff and myself sincerely believe that our profesionally designed and administered survey are exactly what you need to enable you to make a decision about the establishment of a student credit counseling service in the Austin area. Wright Research can have the results for you by July 1. If you sign the enclosed duplicate copy of this letter and return them immediately to Dr. Sebesy or I with a retainer of $3,000. The prices in this offer is in affect only until September 1.

Sincerely,

Lawrence R. Wright

Lawrence R. Wright
President

Enclosures

learning.web.ways

Goal: To learn about netiquette.

"Netiquette" is network etiquette covering the do's and don'ts of online communication. To become familiar with some of the informal "rules of the road" in cyberspace, you will visit the "Business Netiquette International" site.

1. With your Web browser on the screen, enter the following URL: **<http://www.bspage.com/1netiq/Netiq.html>** (that's a number "1" preceding "netiq").

2. If this URL doesn't work, find the site by using a search engine **<www.google.com>** with the term **Business Etiquette International**.

3. Scroll through the Business Etiquette International site. Don't click any links.

4. What is the basic rule of etiquette in any circumstance?

5. When is it permissible to send attachments to e-mail messages?

6. Should you use first names in e-mail messages?

7. Print the first page of this site.

8. End your session and submit your printed page and written answers.

POSTTEST

Underline the correct verb.

1. At least one of our accountants (suggest, suggests) using a tax-deferred plan.

2. The cost of supplies, along with service and equipment costs, (is, are) a major problem.

3. Either the administrative assistant or the engineers (has, have) to find the original copy.

4. Appearing next on the program (was, were) Dr. Gwen Hester and Professor Janis Rollins.

5. A number of surprising events (is, are) occurring in the stock market.

1. suggests 2. is 3. have 4. were 5. are

CHECKLIST OF BONUS LEARNING RESOURCES

The following additional learning resources are available to you. Your instructor will tell you which to complete.

- Web Editor's Challenge Exercise

- Web Interactive Chapter Review

- Web PowerPoint Slides

- Web Crossword Puzzle

- WebCheck Reinforcement Exercises 10.1, 10.2

- Self-Help Exercises

- Electronic Study Guide

chapter 11 Verbals

Objectives

When you have completed the materials in this chapter, you will be able to do the following:

Level I

- Recognize gerunds and supply appropriate modifiers of gerunds.
- Identify and remedy split infinitives that result in awkward sentences.

Level II

- Correctly punctuate introductory and other verbal phrases.
- Avoid writing awkward participial phrases.

Level III

- Spot dangling verbal phrases and other misplaced modifiers.
- Rewrite sentences to avoid misplaced verbal phrases and modifiers.

Write the correct letter to describe the following sentences.

a = contains no error
b = contains error in use of verbal form
c = contains error in punctuation of verbal form

1. Opening his book to the assigned chapter, the headings were read by Paul. _B_

2. After considering the project carefully the vice president gave his approval. _C_

3. To register by mail, return the enclosed application form. _A_

4. Expertly trained in accounting techniques, the interviewer hired Kelly for the position. _B_

5. To be finished on time the report required many hours of extra effort by the staff. _c_

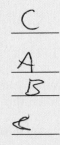

1.b 2.c 3.a 4.b 5.c

As you learned earlier, English is a highly flexible language in which a given word may have more than one grammatical function. In this chapter you will study verbals. Derived from verbs, *verbals* are words that function as nouns, adjectives, or adverbs. Three kinds of verbals are gerunds (verbal nouns), infinitives, and participles (verbal adjectives).

Level I

Gerunds

A verb form ending in *ing* and used as a noun is called a *gerund*.

Advertising is necessary. (Gerund used as the subject.)

Amarjit enjoys *skiing*. (Gerund used as the direct object.)

Using Gerunds Correctly

Study Tip

To distinguish between *ing* forms used as nouns and those used as adjectives, try the *what?* question approach. In the sentence *I admired Sara's programming,* say to yourself, "I admired what?" Answer: "I admired Sara's *programming,* not Sara." Therefore, *programming* is the object and functions as an *ing* noun.

In using gerunds, follow this rule: Make any noun or pronoun modifying a gerund possessive, as in *Karen's driving* or *Dale's computing*. Because we sometimes fail to recognize gerunds as nouns, we fail to make their modifiers possessive:

Wrong: The staff objects to *Kevin smoking*.

Right: The staff objects to *Kevin's smoking*.

The staff does not object to Kevin, as the first version states; it objects to his smoking. If we substitute a more easily recognized noun for *smoking*, the possessive form seems more natural: *The staff objects to Kevin's behavior. Behavior* is a noun, just as *smoking* is a gerund; the noun or pronoun modifiers of both must be possessive.

Mr. Drake resented *his* calling during lunch. (The gerund *calling* requires the possessive pronoun *his*, not the objective case pronoun *him*.)

We appreciate *your bringing* this matter to our attention. (Not *you bringing*.)

Spot the Blooper

From a notice to holders of Exxon credit cards: "We appreciate you choosing Exxon . . ."

Not all verbs ending in *ing* are, of course, gerunds. Some are elements in verb phrases and some act as adjectives.* Compare these three sentences:

I saw Sara programming. (The word *programming* functions as an adjective describing Sara.)

I admired Sara's programming. (As the object of the verb, *programming* acts as a gerund.)

Sara is programming. (Here *is programming* is a verb phrase.)

Infinitives

When the present form of a verb is preceded by *to*, the most basic verb form results: the *infinitive*. The sign of the infinitive is the word *to*.

Try *to sign* the papers immediately.

To write gracefully requires great skill.

*Participles will be discussed in Level II of this chapter.

Using Infinitives Correctly

In certain expressions infinitives may be misused. Observe the use of the word *to* in the following infinitive phrases. Do not substitute the conjunction *and* for the *to* of the infinitive.

Try *to call* when you arrive. (Not *try and call*.)

Be sure *to put* your initials on the letter. (Not *be sure and put*.)

Check *to see* when your appointment is. (Not *check and see*.)

When any word appears between *to* and the verb (*to carefully prepare*), an infinitive is said to be split. At one time split infinitives were considered great grammatical sins. Today most authorities agree that infinitives may be split if necessary for clarity and effect. Avoid, however, split infinitives that result in awkward sentences.

Awkward: Mr. Stokes wanted *to*, if he could find time, *recheck* his figures.

Better: If he could find time, Mr. Stokes wanted *to recheck* his figures.

Awkward: Our company has *to*, when the real estate market returns to normal, *consider* purchasing an office building.

Better: Our company has *to consider*, when the real estate market returns to normal, purchasing an office building.

Acceptable: *To* willfully *lie* under oath is perjury. (No awkwardness results from split infinitive.)

Acceptable: Mrs. Gomez expects you *to* really *work* hard. (No awkwardness results from split infinitive.)

Now complete the reinforcement exercises for Level I.

Spot the Blooper

Headline from *The Urbana* [OH] *Daily Citizen*: "Volunteers Use Sandbags to Try and Save Water Plant." (What's wrong with using *and*?)

Hot Link

Should split infinitives be condemned? Check the Bartleby.com site for the opinion of the American Heritage® Book of English Usage <http://www.bartleby.com/64/C001/059.html>.

Level II

Participles

You have already studied the present and past forms of participles functioning as parts of verb phrases. You will recall that in such constructions present and past participles always require helping verbs: *is driving, was seen, had broken*.

In this chapter we will be concerned with a second possible function of participles. Participles can function as adjectives. As adjectives, participles modify nouns or pronouns, and they do not require helping verbs. Here are sentences that illustrate the five forms of the participle.

Present participle, active: *Helping Troy with the proposal*, we are staying late. (The participial phrase *Helping Troy with the proposal* modifies *we*.)

Present participle, passive: Troy McCain, *being helped* by his colleagues, is completing the proposal. (*Being helped* is here a participle that describes Troy McCain.)

Past participle, passive: Although *helped* by three others, Troy found it difficult to admit their assistance. (The participle *helped* functions as an adjective to describe *Troy*.)

Perfect participle, active: *Having helped* Troy on many previous occasions, his colleagues were accustomed to his inability to thank them. (The participial phrase *Having helped Troy* describes *his colleagues*.)

Perfect participle, passive: Troy, *having been helped on many big projects*, was deeply indebted to his colleagues. (The participle *having been helped* functions as an adjective to describe *Troy*.)

Using Participles Correctly

Avoid using participial phrases that sound awkward, such as these:

Awkward:	Pam's having been promoted to office manager was cause for celebration.
Better:	Pam's promotion to office manager was cause for celebration.
Awkward:	Being as you have arrived early, may I leave now?
Better:	Since you have arrived early, may I leave now?

Punctuating Verbal Forms

Determining whether verbal forms require commas often causes students difficulty. Let's try to clear up this difficulty with explanations and examples.

Punctuating Introductory Verbal Forms

When verbal forms are used in introductory words or expressions, there's no question about punctuating them. A comma should be placed between an introductory verbal form and the main clause of a sentence.

Astonished, the attorney turned to the jury. (Introductory verbal form.)

To improve product distribution, Rachel hired a traffic manager. (Introductory verbal phrase.)

Receiving too many e-mail messages, Andy established filters. (Introductory verbal phrase.)

Completing forty-three years, Betty Bond retired. (Introductory verbal phrase.)

Not all verbal phrases that begin sentences, however, are considered introductory. If the verbal phrase represents the subject or part of the predicate of the sentence, *no* comma should separate it from the rest of the sentence.

Preparing a budget is Andy's responsibility. (Verbal phrase used as subject; no comma.)

To change our budget at this time is almost impossible. (Verbal phrase used as subject; no comma.)

Located in the other building is our Shipping Department. (Verbal phrase used as part of predicate; no comma.)

Career Tip

You'll win the respect of your business colleagues if you avoid using *being, being as,* or *being that* when you mean *since* or *because* (*Being it was hot . . .*). These substandard usages indicate poor education and can limit a career.

Spot the Blooper

From *Country Collectibles*: "Sitting by a blazing fire, reading a good mystery novel, a dog can jump into your lap and beg for a few playful pats on the head."

Career Tip

"A successful career requires falling in love many times with your work."
—Frank Watson

Punctuating Nonessential Verbal Phrases*

Essential (restrictive) information is needed for the reader to understand the sentence. Verbal phrases often help identify the subject. These phrases require no commas. Nonessential information could be omitted without altering the basic meaning of the sentence; thus, nonessential phrases are set off by commas.

Mrs. Ramirez, *working late at the office*, was able to meet the deadline. (The verbal phrase *working late at the office* adds additional information, but it is not essential. The subject is fully identified by name. Use commas to set off the nonessential phrase.)

The woman *working late at the office* was able to meet the deadline. (In this sentence the verbal phrase *working late at the office* is essential; it is needed to identify the subject. *Which* woman was able to meet the deadline? The woman *working late at the office*. No commas separate this essential verbal phrase.)

First Federal Bank, *opening a new branch in Lake Worth*, offered gifts to attract customers. (The verbal phrase is not essential because there is only one First Federal Bank, and it has been identified. Commas enclose this nonessential verbal phrase.)

A bank *opening a new branch in Lake Worth* offered gifts to attract customers. (This verbal phrase is essential to identify *which* bank offered gifts. No commas are needed. *Note:* Even though you pause when you reach the end of the verbal phrase, don't be tempted to add a comma.)

Notice in the preceding sentences that whenever a nonessential verbal phrase interrupts the middle of a sentence, two commas set it off.

Now complete the reinforcement exercises for Level II.

Level III

Avoiding Misplaced Verbal Modifiers

Used correctly, verbal modifiers and phrases add clarity and description to your writing. Let's consider the best way to position them within sentences.

Introductory Verbal Phrases

Introductory verbal phrases must be followed by the words they can logically modify. Such phrases can create confusion or unintended humor when placed incorrectly in a sentence. Consider this sentence: *Sitting in the car, the mountains were breathtaking.* The introductory participial phrase in this sentence is said to *dangle* because it is not followed immediately by a word it can logically modify. The sentence could be improved by revising it to read: *Sitting in the car, we saw the breathtaking mountains.* Observe how the following illogical sentences have been improved:

Study Tip

To help you understand the use of commas in dealing with nonessential (nonrestrictive) information, think of a window shade. Use commas to lower the window shade and cover the words enclosed. If words in a verbal phrase are not essential to the meaning of a sentence, use a "comma window shade" to obscure them.

Spot the Blooper

From the *Sun Cities* [AZ] *Independent*: "While pumping gas, an unoccupied car rolled into the victim's car."

Spot the Blooper

From *The Wall Street Journal*: "Looking back through American history, no Presidency raises deeper philosophical issues than Bill Clinton's."

*Many students find it easier to work with the words *essential* and *nonessential* than with the more traditional grammatical terms *restrictive* and *nonrestrictive*; therefore, the easier terminology is used here.

Illogical:	Slipping on the ice, his back was injured.
Logical:	Slipping on the ice, *he* injured his back.
Illogical:	Turning on the fan, papers flew about the office.
Logical:	Turning on the fan, *I* caused papers to fly about the office.
Illogical:	After answering the telephone, the doorbell began to ring insistently.
Logical:	After answering the telephone, Jeremy heard the doorbell ring insistently.
Illogical:	Skilled with computers, the personnel director hired Chae Lee.
Logical:	Skilled with computers, Chae Lee was hired by the personnel director.
But:	To ensure academic success, study diligently.
	To ensure academic success, (you) study diligently. (In commands, the understood subject is *you*. Therefore, this sentence is correctly followed by the word to which it refers.)

Verbal Phrases in Other Positions

In other positions within sentences, verbal phrases must also be placed in logical relation to the words they modify.

Illogical:	The missing purchase orders were found by Mrs. Seldon's secretary lying in her top desk drawer.
Logical:	Mrs. Seldon's secretary found the missing purchase orders lying in her top desk drawer.
Illogical:	Mr. Yoneji returned the envelope and its contents, recognizing his error.
Logical:	Mr. Yoneji, recognizing his error, returned the envelope and its contents.

Now complete the reinforcement exercises for Level III.

Q: Are there two meanings for the word *discreet*?

A: You are probably confusing the two words *discreet* and *discrete*. *Discreet* means "showing good judgment" and "prudent" (*the witness gave a discreet answer, avoiding gossip and hearsay*). The word *discrete* means "separate" or "noncontinuous" (*Alpha, Inc., has installed discrete computers rather than a network computer system*). You might find it helpful to remember that the *e's* are separate in *discrete*.

Q: Should I use *complimentary* or *complementary* to describe free tickets?

A: Use *complimentary*, which can mean "containing a compliment, favorable, or free" (*the dinner came with complimentary wine; he made a complimentary remark*). *Complementary* means "completing or making perfect" (T*he online edition of* The Wall Street Journal *is the perfect complement to your print subscription; the complementary colors enhanced the room*). An easy way to remember *compliment* is by thinking "*I* like to receive a *compliment*."

Q: I confuse *i.e.* and *e.g.* What's the difference?

A: The abbreviation *i.e.* stands for the Latin *id est*, meaning "that is" (*the package exceeds the weight limit, i.e., 5 pounds*). Notice the use of a comma after *i.e.* The abbreviation *e.g.* stands for the Latin *exempli gratia*, meaning "for the sake of example" or "for example" (*the manufacturer may offer a purchase incentive, e.g., a rebate or discount plan*).

Q: We're having an argument in our office about abbreviations. Can *department* be abbreviated *dep't*? How about *manufacturing* as *mf'g*? Where could we find a correct list of such abbreviations?

A: In informal writing or when space is limited, words may be contracted or abbreviated. If a conventional abbreviation for a word exists, use it instead of a contracted form. Abbreviations are simpler to write and easier to read. For example, use *dept.* instead of *dep't*; use *natl.* instead of *nat'l*; use *cont.* instead of *cont'd*. Other accepted abbreviations are *ins.* for *insurance*; *mfg.* for *manufacturing*; *mgr.* for *manager*; and *mdse.* for *merchandise*. Notice that all abbreviations end with periods. Some dictionaries show abbreviations of words along with their definitions. Other dictionaries alphabetize abbreviations within the main entries, so that a reader must know how to spell an abbreviation in order to be able to locate it. Reference manuals often have lists of abbreviations that are very helpful.

Q: I'm not sure which word to use in this sentence: *They have used all (they're, their, there) resources in combating the disease.*

A: Use *their*, which is the possessive form of *they*. The adverb *there* means "at that place or at that point" (*we have been there before*). *There* is also used as an expletive or filler preceding a linking verb (*there are numerous explanations*). *They're* is a contraction of *they* and *are* (*they're coming this afternoon*).

Q: In a letter written by my boss, how should we spell *there*: *We do not want an open invoice without there being justifiable reasons.*

A: *There* is spelled correctly, but its use creates an awkward verbal form. If your boss agrees, revise the sentence to read: *We do not want an open invoice without justification.*

Name _____

Level I

A. **(Self-check)** In the following sentences gerunds are italicized. Other *ing* words that are not italicized are not functioning as gerunds. Select appropriate modifiers.

1. She is unhappy with (you, _your_) *handling* of the order. _____

2. We saw (Rachel, Rachel's) leaving the office early. _____

3. (His, Him) *traveling* first class was questioned by the auditor. _____

4. Did Gene tell you about (Gail, Gail's) *moving* to Alaska? _____

5. Can you believe (Bill, Bill's) *missing* the plane? _____

6. The (clerk, clerk's) making the sale receives the commission. _____

7. John suggested (you, your) *making* reservations early. _____

8. I noticed Mrs. (Lee, Lee's) *handwriting* on the invoice. _____

9. I appreciate (them, their) *answering* the telephone. _____

10. The (salesperson, salesperson's) making the appointment is here. _____

Check your answers below.

B. Gerunds are again italicized. Choose the correct modifier.

1. Our success depends on (you, your) *making* the best investments. _____

2. The (person, person's) picking up the check gets to choose the restaurant. _____

3. The accuracy of this report depends on (him, _his_) *proofreading*. _____

4. They said (you, your) *printing* of the brochures was excellent. _____

5. The (firm, firm's) printing the forms went out of business. _____

6. Did the boss recommend (us, our) *attending* the demonstration? _____

7. The (customer, customer's) paying his bill complimented the service. _____

8. We are incredulous at (them, their) *winning* the series. _____

9. The (player, player's) winning the final game takes the prize. _____

10. (Him, His) *being* on time for the appointment is very important. _____

C. From each of the pairs of sentences shown, select the more acceptable version and write its letter in the space provided.

1. (a) Christine Bolt was asked to, as soon as possible, develop a Web site. _____
   (b) Christine Bolt was asked to develop a Web site as soon possible.

2. (a) Hurriedly, Vicente Aguilar began to scan his e-mail messages. _____
   (b) Vicente Aguilar began to hurriedly scan his e-mail messages.

3. (a) Be sure and stop by our booth at the trade show. _____
   (b) Be sure to stop by our booth at the trade show.

1. your 2. Rachel 3. His 4. Gail's 5. Bill's 6. clerk 7. your 8. Lee's 9. their 10. salesperson

4. (a) We wondered about his ordering so few office supplies. _____
   (b) We wondered about him ordering so few office supplies.

5. (a) The secretary started to, as the deadline approached, check the names and _____
      addresses.
   (b) As the deadline approached, the secretary started to check the names and
      addresses.

6. (a) Try to find when the meeting is scheduled. _____
   (b) Try and find when the meeting is scheduled.

7. (a) I think their being present at the hearing is crucial. _____
   (b) I think them being present at the hearing is crucial.

8. (a) Please check to see if the contract is ready. _____
   (b) Please check and see if the contract is ready.

9. (a) You may wish to, if you have time, contact your broker. _____
   (b) You may wish to contact your broker if you have time.

10. (a) The travel counselor recommended our traveling by train. _____
   (b) The travel counselor recommended us traveling by train.

D. Writing Exercise. Rewrite the following sentences to remedy any gerund or infinitive faults.

1. We plan to, if all the papers have been signed, initiate proceedings tomorrow.

   _____

2. Be sure and call to, if you haven't changed your mind, make your plane reservations.

   _____

3. I hope that you will inform your two agents that I appreciate them listening to my complaints.

   _____

4. When you are interviewed for a job, try and ask good questions about the position.

   _____

Level II

A. (Self-check) Verbal phrases in the following sentences are shown in italics. All the sentences have been punctuated correctly. Study each sentence and select the letter that explains the reason for including or omitting commas.

   a = introductory verbal phrase, comma necessary
   b = essential verbal phrase, no commas necessary
   c = nonessential verbal phrase, commas necessary
   d = verbal phrase used as a subject; no commas necessary

Examples: *To settle the matter* is extremely difficult.   d

   Elizabeth Wright, *to settle the matter*, flipped a coin.   c

1. *In preparing copies of her résumé*, Karley Cooper used a laser printer.   A

2. The student *looking for a parking place* was late to class.   B

3. Karley Cooper, *preparing copies of her résumé*, used a laser printer.   C

4. *Finding an earlier class* is very unlikely.   D

5. *Preparing copies of a résumé* is easy when one uses a laser printer.   D

6. *Consulting her astrologer,* Stella Starlet refused to set foot outside.   A

7. The person *consulting her astrologer* refused to set foot outside.   B

8. *Looking at the class schedule,* I see that I can take English.   A

9. Anyone *looking at a class schedule* can see what classes are available.   B

10. Professor Kathleen Young, *looking at a class schedule,* announced a time change.   C

Check your answers below.

B. Selected verbal words and phrases have been italicized in the following sentences. Insert commas if needed. In the space provided at the right, write the number of commas that you insert for each sentence. If no commas are added, write *0*.

Example: To complete the job before the deadline, we worked late.   1

1. *To further the cause of medicine,* he donated his body to science.   ___

2. *Setting personal goals and objectives* is one important step in career planning.   ___

3. *After studying the company's files,* Cynthia Sajid recommended a more efficient records management system.   ___

4. *Horrified,* Bridget dropped her books when she saw the collision.   ___

5. *Working in another office* are the legal secretaries who specialize in contracts.   ___

6. *Writing reports and sending frequent e-mail messages,* the manager could not get along without her computer.   ___

7. *To improve the writing of government employees,* consultants were hired.   ___

8. *Fearing detection* the embezzler could never take a day off.   ___

9. *Beginning as a sole proprietor,* H. J. Heinz eventually built a large corporation.   ___

10. *Breaking down a job cycle into separate units of work* is the first task in a time-and-motion study.   ___

C. Selected verbal phrases have been italicized in the following sentences. Insert commas if the phrases are nonessential. In the space provided, write the number of commas that you insert for each sentence. If no commas are added, write *0*.

1. Ellen Elkins, *keyboarding at her computer for as many as 14 hours a day,* developed repetitive stress injury.   ___

2. The clerk *keyboarding at her computer for as many as 14 hours a day* developed repetitive stress injury.   ___

3. CEO Marilyn Helser, *accessing her e-mail network daily,* was able to stay in contact with her business while traveling.   ___

4. You may be interested to know that any student *enrolled in the college* has full library privileges.   ___

5. The latest company contract enables employees *participating in our profit-sharing plan* to benefit from the stock split.   ___

6. Rosalba Errico *striving to qualify for a promotion* enrolled in a Saturday course.   ___

7. Anyone *striving to qualify for a promotion* should consider enrolling in college courses.   ___

8. Those employees *expecting a raise* will have to work extra hours.   ___

D. If needed, insert commas to punctuate verbal forms in the following sentences. In the space provided, indicate the number of commas added.

1. To be hired, candidates must have excellent computer and communication skills. _____

2. General Motors, facing unexpected competition from foreign suppliers, decided to close the small fabrication plant. _____

3. After considering the matter carefully, we chose to implement your suggestion. _____

4. Reducing safety and health hazards is the primary function of OSHA (Occupational Safety and Health Administration). _____

5. Anyone possessing the necessary background may apply for the position. _____

6. Our CEO, facing another year of intense pressure, resigned his post. _____

7. Reducing safety and health hazards, our division recently set a record for consecutive accident-free workdays. _____

8. Personnel Director Nan Goodman, hoping to help employees improve their job skills, organized an in-service training class. _____

9. All employees interested in improving their job skills are invited to attend the in-service programs. _____

10. To enroll in any of the programs, employees must sign up immediately. _____

Level III

A. (Self-check) From each of the sets of sentences that follow, select the sentence that is stated in the most logical manner. Write its letter in the space provided.

1. (a) Plunging 1,000 feet into the gorge, we were amazed by Yosemite Falls.
   (b) Plunging 1,000 feet into the gorge, Yosemite Falls amazed us. _____

2. (a) Sealed in an airtight crock, the Joneses savored the fine cheese.
   (b) Sealed in an airtight crock, the fine cheese was savored by the Joneses. _____

3. (a) To complete the accounting equation, one must add liabilities to equity.
   (b) To complete the accounting equation, it is necessary to add liabilities to equity. _____

4. (a) Before starting the project, permission must be obtained.
   (b) Before starting the project, one must obtain permission. _____

5. (a) In sorting the names and addresses, James discovered an error.
   (b) In sorting the names and addresses, an error was discovered by James. _____

6. (a) To graduate early, carry more units.
   (b) To graduate early, more units must be carried. _____

7. (a) After collecting author references on note cards, write the bibliography.
   (b) After collecting author references on note cards, the bibliography should be written. _____

8. (a) Having completed twenty years of service, Zivi Nunary was presented a gold watch.
   (b) Having completed twenty years of service, a gold watch was presented to Zivi Nunary. _____

9. (a) After seeing the job advertisement, a letter was sent by Miss Bruner. _____
   (b) After seeing the job advertisement, Miss Bruner sent a letter.

10. (a) To qualify for the certificate, perfect attendance must be maintained. _____
    (b) To qualify for the certificate, one must maintain perfect attendance.

Check your answers below.

B. Writing Exercise. Each of the following sentences has an illogical introductory verbal phrase. Rewrite each sentence using that introductory phrase so that it is followed by a word it can logically modify. It may be necessary to add a subject. Keep the introductory verbal phrase at the beginning of the sentence.

Example: Driving through Malibu Canyon, the ocean came into view.
   Driving through Malibu Canyon, we saw the ocean come into view.

1. Running in the Boston marathon, her dream came true. _____
   _____ her dream came true for _____

2. Comparing figures from four sources, the error in the balance sheet was finally discovered.
   _____ they finally discovered the error in the
   balance sheet

3. To be binding, a consideration must support every contract. _____
   _____

4. As a baboon growing up in the jungle, I realized Kiki had special nutritional needs.
   _____
   _____

5. Selected as Employee of the Year, the CEO presented an award to Cecile Chang.
   _____
   _____

6. After breaking into the building, the police heard the alarm set off by the burglars.
   _____
   _____

7. To be promoted, your performance appraisal must be excellent. _____
   _____

The preceding sentences had misplaced introductory verbal phrases. The next sentences have misplaced verbal phrases in other positions. Rewrite these sentences so that the verbal phrases are close to the words they can logically modify.

8. An autopsy revealed the cause of death to be strangulation by the coroner. _____
   _____

9. Noxious fumes made many office workers sick coming from the nearby auto paint shop.
   _____
   _____

10. A trellis was designed to divert attention from the large driveway, which is seen walking up to the house. _____

_____

11. He was killed while riding his bicycle by a drunken driver. _____

_____

Editor's Challenge

The following letter contains intentional errors in spelling, proofreading, and language principles covered thus far. You should make 30 changes. If one word replaces three, it's considered one change.

1320 Trexler Avenue
Allentown, PA 18105
May 12, 200x

Mr. Michael K. Topton
Attorney at Law
455 Zionsville Road
Emmaus, PA 18367

Dear Mr. Toptan:

At the suggestion of your former partner, Ms. Molly Harned. I am submiting this application for the position of legal secretery in your office. I understand that you are seeking an individual whom has communication, transcription, and microcomputer skills. Both my education and my experience, I believe, qualifies myself for this position.

Having finish two years' of schooling at Valley Community College. My skills include word processing, machine transcription, and business letter writing. To learn about working for a attorney, a course in legal procedures was completed. Being that we studied personal injury, dissolution, and unlawful detainer procedures, I now have skill in these areas. Moreover, I have took a course in legal terminology.

In addition to my education, I have complete a six-month intern ship with two attornies, Mr. Ronald W. Schultz and Ms. Linda Hagen, in Norristown. Keyboarding legal documents and updating a client data base in Mr. Schultz office has helped me learn current computer software program.

Please study the enclosed résumé to review my complete educational and employment background. Ms. Harned said that you needed some one immediately, if I was hired for this position, I would be able to start June 1. I must give at least two weeks notice to my present employer. If I meet your requirements, I would appreciate you calling me at 389-5910 to arrange a interview at a time convenent to you.

Sincerely,

Michelle a Robinson

Michelle A. Robinson

Enclosure

You've been asked to make a presentation on personal finance and credit debt. You decide that you need a good motivational (and perhaps humorous) quotation on money. Many Web sites provide free quotations. One of the best is Quoteland.com.

Goal: To find a motivational quotation.

1. With your Web browser on the screen, enter **<http://www.quoteland.com>**.

2. In the search box, enter the term "**Money**."

3. Read all of the selections provided. Print the pages and circle the quotation you like best.

4. Use a search engine and find another Web site with motivational quotations.

5. Print a selection and circle the one you like best.

6. End your session and submit your printed pages.

POSTTEST

Write the correct letter to describe the following sentences.

a = contains no errors
b = contains error in use of verbal form
c = contains error in punctuation of verbal form

1. Deciding that his first letter was unclear, a second letter was written by Mr. Holmes.

2. To supervise effectively a manager must have excellent communication skills.

3. To collect health benefits, fill out the long application.

4. Improving health and dental benefits for all employees is our primary goal.

5. Having submitted an application, benefits should be forthcoming immediately.

1. b 2. c 3. a 4. a 5. b

CHECKLIST OF BONUS LEARNING RESOURCES

The following additional learning resources are available to you. Your instructor will tell you which to complete.

- Web Editor's Challenge Exercise

- Web Interactive Chapter Review

- Web PowerPoint Slides

- Web Crossword Puzzle

- WebCheck Reinforcement Exercises 11.1, 11.2

- Self-Help Exercises

- Electronic Study Guide

Unit Review Chapters 8–11

Name _____

Begin your review by rereading Chapters 8–11. Then test your comprehension of those chapters by completing the exercises that follow. Compare your responses with the key at the end of the book.

Level I

In the blank provided, write the letter of the word or phrase that correctly completes each of the following sentences.

1. In the sentence *He seems responsible*, the verb *seems* is (a) transitive, (b) intransitive, (c) linking. _____

2. In the sentence *Dr. Amoroso is the speaker*, the word *speaker* is a(n) (a) object, (b) linking verb, (c) complement. _____

3. A keyboard with 106 characters (a) has, (b) have been developed for your computer. _____

4. The president, together with his entire staff of employees, (a) send, (b) sends greetings to you. _____

5. The president and his entire staff (a) send, (b) sends greetings to you. _____

6. Be sure (a) to write, (b) and write the name and address legibly. _____

7. We certainly appreciate (a) him, (b) his handling of the program. _____

8. Olsen, Leung, and Miller, Inc., (a) is, (b) are expecting an increase in profits this quarter. _____

9. The shipping statement for the equipment and supplies (a) was, (b) were delayed. _____

10. Is there any possibility of (a) your, (b) you coming early? _____

11. The tone and wording of a business message (a) are, (b) is very important in achieving your goal. _____

12. How effective (a) is, (b) are the company guidelines on Internet use? _____

Level II

Write the letter of the word or phrase that correctly completes each of the following sentences.

13. When converting a verb from the passive to the active voice, the writer must make the doer of the action the (a) subject, (b) object of the active voice verb. _____

14. In the sentence *Three form letters were keyed by Tomoko*, the verb is in the (a) active, (b) passive voice. _____

15. Many letters and packages have (a) laid, (b) lain, (c) lay on that desk for the past week. _____

16. If you had (a) rung, (b) rang the bell, I would have heard it. _____

17. That contract (a) laying, (b) lying on your desk must be signed. _____

18. Neither the computer nor the printers (a) is, (b) are working. _____

19. We think that (a) anyone, (b) any one of our representatives will serve you well. _____

20. Either the Web site address or his e-mail address (a) is, (b) are wrong. _____

21. The jury, consisting of six men and seven women, (a) has, (b) have come back into court. _____

Insert commas where necessary in the next group of sentences. Indicate the number of commas that you added. Write *0* for none.

22. We were very pleased to see that Rebecca working until 10 p.m. was able to complete the job. _____

23. Storing thousands of customer files became physically possible when we installed an electronic database. _____

24. Working until 10 p.m. Rebecca was able to complete the job. _____

L e v e l   I I I

In the blank provided, write the letter of the word or phrase that correctly completes each sentence.

25. The problem would have been handled differently if I (a) was, (b) were in charge. _____

26. A motion was made that members (a) be, (b) are admitted free. _____

27. The number of employees participating in elective classes (a) is, (b) are steadily increasing. _____

28. It is you who (a) is, (b) are to do the judging tomorrow. _____

29. It looks as if three fourths of the brochures (a) has, (b) have yet to be assembled. _____

30. She is one of those executives who always (a) tell, (b) tells the truth. _____

For each of the following sentences, indicate whether (a) the sentence is written correctly or (b) the sentence has a verbal phrase placed illogically. Rewrite illogical sentences.

31. To qualify for a full scholarship, applications must be made by January 1. _____

    _____

32. Skilled at programming computers, the personnel manager hired Eun Park instantly. _____

    _____

33. Driving to the office, two accidents were seen by Debbie. _____

    _____

34. To enroll early, send in your application by March. _____

    _____

35. Although her mother was in it, thieves stole a suitcase containing jewelry and clothing from the car of Mrs. Voorhees. _____

    _____

Hotline Review

36. _____ e-mail, for what purposes do you use the Internet?   _____
    a. Beside   **b.** Besides

37. State budget cuts will _____ education adversely.   _____
    a. affect   **b.** effect

38. Researcher Terry Strauss announced her _____ findings in a journal article.   _____
    a. principle   **b.** principal

39. Both plaintiffs and defendants were _____ pleased with the out-of-court   _____
    settlement.
    a. all together   **b.** altogether

40. Robert Cannon was quite _____ in discussing the students in his class.   _____
    a. complementary   **b.** complimentary

Name _____

Techniques for Effective Paragraphs

As you learned in Workshop 2, the basic unit in writing is the sentence. The next unit is the paragraph. Although no rule regulates the length of paragraphs, business writers recognize the value of short paragraphs. Paragraphs with fewer than eight printed lines look inviting and readable, whereas long, solid chunks of print appear formidable. In this workshop you will learn writing techniques for organizing sentences into readable, coherent, and clear paragraphs. The first very important technique involves topic sentences.

Organizing Paragraphs Around Topic Sentences

A well-organized paragraph has two important characteristics. First, it covers just one subject. For example, if you are writing about your booth at the Las Vegas computer expo, you wouldn't throw in a sentence about trouble with the IRS. Keep all the sentences in a paragraph related to one topic. Second, a well-organized paragraph begins with a topic sentence that summarizes what the paragraph is about. A topic sentence helps readers by preparing them for what follows.

Consider the following scenario. Let's say your company promotes an extensive schedule of team sports for employees after hours. One group enjoys weekend bicycling. You've been assigned the task of writing a memo to the members of this group stating that they must wear helmets when cycling. One paragraph of your memo covers statistics about cycling accidents and the incidence of brain injury for unhelmeted riders. Another paragraph discusses the protection offered by helmets:

Helmets protect the brain from injury. They spread the force of a crash from the point of impact to a wider area. When an accident occurs, an unhelmeted head undergoes two collisions. The first occurs when the skull slams into the ground. The second occurs when the brain hits the inside of the skull. A helmet softens the second blow and acts as a shock absorber. Instead of crushing the brain, the impact crushes the foam core of the helmet, often preventing serious brain injury.

Notice how the preceding paragraph focuses on just one topic: how helmets protect the brain from injury. Every sentence relates to that topic. Notice, too, that the first sentence functions as a topic sentence, informing the reader of the subject of the paragraph.

The best way to write a good paragraph is to list all the ideas you may include. Here's a rough draft of the list of items for the preceding paragraph. Notice that the fourth item doesn't relate to the topic sentence. By listing the ideas to be included in a paragraph, you can immediately see what belongs—and what doesn't. Once the list is made, you can easily write the topic sentence.

1. Helmets spread force of impact.

2. Crashes cause two collisions, the first when the skull hits the ground and the second when the brain hits the skull.

3. The foam core of the helmet absorbs the impact.

4. The federal government has issued biking regulations requiring helmets.

Topic Sentence: Helmets protect the brain from injury.

Skill Check 1 Organizing a Paragraph

In a memo to the college president, the athletic director is arguing for a new stadium scoreboard. One paragraph will describe the old scoreboard and why it needs to be replaced. Study the following list of ideas for that paragraph.

1. The old scoreboard is a tired warhorse that was originally constructed in the 1960s.

2. It's now hard to find replacement parts for it when something breaks.

3. The old scoreboard is not energy efficient.

4. Coca-Cola has offered to buy a new sports scoreboard in return for exclusive rights to sell soda pop on campus.

5. The old scoreboard should be replaced for many reasons.

6. It shows only scores for football games.

7. When we have soccer games or track meets, we're without any functioning scoreboard.

    a. Which sentence should be the topic sentence? _____

    b. Which sentence(s) should be developed in a different paragraph? _____

    c. Which sentences should follow the topic sentence? _____

Writing Coherent Paragraphs

Effective paragraphs are coherent; that is, they hold together. Coherence is a quality of good writing that doesn't happen accidentally. It is consciously achieved through effective organization and through skillful use of three devices. These writing devices are (a) repetition of key ideas or key words, (b) use of pronouns that refer clearly to their antecedents, and (c) use of transitional expressions.

Repetition of Key Ideas or Key Words. Repeating a key word or key thought from a preceding sentence helps guide a reader from one thought to the next. This redundancy is necessary to build cohesiveness into writing. Notice how the word *deal* is repeated in the second sentence.

> For the past six months, college administrators and Coca-Cola have been working on a *deal* in which the college would receive a new sports scoreboard. The *deal* would involve exclusive rights to sell soda pop on the 12,000-student campus.

Use of Pronouns That Refer Clearly to Their Antecedents. Pronouns such as *this, that, they, these, those,* and *it* help connect thoughts in sentences. But these pronouns are useful only when their antecedents are clear. Often it's better to make the pronoun into an adjective joined with its antecedent to ensure that the reference is absolutely clear. Notice how the pronoun *this* is clearer when it is joined to its antecedent *contract.*

Confusing: The Coca-Cola offer requires an exclusive contract committing the college for ten years without any provision preventing a price increase. *This* could be very costly to students, staff, and faculty.

Improved: The Coca-Cola offer requires an exclusive contract committing the college for ten years without any provision preventing a price increase. *This contract* could be very costly to students, staff, and faculty.

Avoid vague pronouns, such as *it* in the following example.

Confusing: If your kitten will not drink cold milk, put *it* in the microwave oven for a few seconds.

Improved: If your kitten will not drink cold milk, put the cold milk in the microwave oven for a few seconds.

Use of Transitional Expressions.
One of the most effective ways to achieve paragraph coherence is through the use of transitional expressions. These expressions act as road signs. They indicate where the message is headed, and they help the reader anticipate what is coming. Some common transitional expressions follow:

although	furthermore	moreover
as a result	hence	nevertheless
consequently	however	of course
for example	in addition	on the other hand
for this reason	in this way	therefore

Other words that act as connectives are *first, second, finally, after, meanwhile, next, after all, instead, specifically, thus, also, likewise, as,* and *as if.*

The following paragraph achieves coherence through use of all three techniques. (1) The key idea of *surprising battle* in the first sentence is echoed in the second sentence with repetition of the word *battle* coupled with *unexpected,* a synonym for *surprising.* (2) The use of a pronoun, *This,* in the second sentence connects the second sentence to the first. (3) The transitional words *however* and *as a result* in following sentences continue to build coherence.

A *surprising battle* between two global cola giants was recently fought in Venezuela. *This battle* was *unexpected* because Venezuelans had always been loyal Pepsi drinkers. *However,* when the nation's leading bottler sold half of its interest to Coca-Cola, everything changed. *As a result*, Coca-Cola turned the Pepsi-drinking nation of Venezuela into Coke drinkers almost overnight.

Skill Check 2 Improving Paragraph Coherence

In the space below or on a separate sheet of paper, use the information from Skill Check 1 to write a coherent paragraph about replacing the sports scoreboard. Remember that this paragraph is part of a memo from the athletic director to the college president. Include a topic sentence. Strive to illustrate all three techniques to achieve coherence.

_____

_____

_____

_____

_____

_____

Developing Parallel Construction

Paragraph clarity can be improved by expressing similar ideas with similar grammatical structures. For example, if you are listing three ideas, do not use *ing* words for two of the ideas and a *to* verb with the third idea: *reading, eating, and studying* (not *to study*). Use adjectives with adjectives, verbs with verbs, phrases with phrases, and clauses with clauses. In the following list, use all verbs: *the machine sorted, stamped, and counted* (not *and had a counter*). For phrases, the wording for all parts of the list should be matched; *safety must be improved in the home, in the classroom, and on the job* (not *for office workers*).

Poor: Miss Tanaga is energetic, resourceful and she can be relied on.

Improved: Miss Tanaga is energetic, resourceful, and reliable. (Matches adjectives.)

Poor: The new shredder helped us save money, reduce pollution, and paper could be recycled.

Improved: The new shredder helped us save money, reduce pollution, and recycle paper. (Matches verb–noun construction.)

Skill Check 3 Improving Parallel Construction

Revise each of the following sentences to improve parallel construction.

1. Your job is to research, design, and the implementation of a diversity program.

_____

_____

2. Few managers are able to write letters accurately, concisely, and with efficiency.

_____

_____

3. The new software totals all balances, gives weekly reports, and statements are printed.

_____

_____

4. Our objectives are to make our stock profitable, to operate efficiently, and developing good employee relations.

_____

_____

Writing Application 3.1. On a separate sheet revise the following paragraph. Add a topic sentence and improve the organization. Correct pronouns with unclear antecedents, wordiness, and misplaced verbal modifiers (which you learned about in Chapter 11). Add transitional expressions if appropriate.

You may be interested in applying for a new position within the company. The Human Resources Department has a number of jobs available immediately. The positions are at a high level. Current employees may apply immediately for open positions in production, for some in marketing, and jobs in administrative support are also available. To make application, these positions require immediate action. Come to the Human Resources Department. We have a list showing the open positions, what the qualifications are, and job descriptions are shown. Many of the jobs are now open. That's why we are sending this now. To be hired, an interview must be scheduled within the next two weeks.

Writing Application 3.2. On a separate sheet revise the following poorly written paragraph. Add a topic sentence and improve the organization. Correct misplaced modifiers, pronouns with unclear antecedents, wordiness, and any other writing faults. Add transitional expressions if appropriate.

As you probably already know, this company (Lasertronics) will be installing new computer software shortly. There will be a demonstration April 18, which is a Tuesday. We felt this was necessary because this new software is so different from our previous software. It will be from 9 to 12 a.m. in the morning. This will show employees how the software programs work. They will learn about the operating system, and this should be helpful to nearly everyone. There will be information about the new word processing program, which should be helpful to administrative assistants and product managers. For all you people who work with payroll, there will be information about the new database program. We can't show everything the software will do at this one demo, but for these three areas there will be some help at the Tuesday demo. Oh yes, Paula Roddy will be presenting the demonstration. She is the representative from Quantum Software.

Writing Application 3.3. Assume you work in the Human Resources Department of Bank of America. You must write an announcement describing a special program of classes for your employees. Use the following information to write a well-organized paragraph announcement. Explain that Bank of America will reimburse any employee the full cost of tuition and books if that employee attends classes. Describe the plan. Skyline Community College, in cooperation with Bank of America, will offer a group of courses for college credit at very convenient locations for our employees. Actually, the classes will be offered at your downtown and East Bay branches. Tell employees that they should call Jean Fujimoto at Ext. 660 if they are interested. You'd better mention the tuition: $80 for a semester course. Explain that we (Bank of America) are willing to pay these fees because we value education highly. However, make it clear that employees must receive a grade of *C* or higher before they are eligible for reimbursement of course and book fees. It might be a good idea to attach a list of the courses and the times that they will be offered. Include a deadline date for calling Jean.

unit 4 Modifying and Connecting Words

chapter 12 Modifiers: Adjectives and Adverbs

Objectives

When you have completed the materials in this chapter, you will be able to do the following:

Level I

- Form the comparative and superlative degrees of regular and irregular adjectives and adverbs.
- Use articles correctly and avoid double negatives.

Level II

- Use adjectives after linking verbs and use adverbs to modify verbs, adjectives, and other adverbs.
- Punctuate compound and successive independent adjectives correctly.

Level III

- Compare degrees of absolute adjectives and make comparisons within a group.
- Place adverbs and adjectives close to the words they modify.

Spot the Blooper

Headline in Florida newspaper: "MAN EATING PIRANHA SOLD AS PET FISH"

Underline the correct word.

1. This is the (worse, worst) business report I've ever read.
2. It is (a, an) honor to be selected by the interviewing committee.
3. If you did (good, well) enough in the interview, you will be hired.
4. Our (six-year-old, six year old) lease must be renegotiated.
5. The (newly repaired, newly-repaired) copier seems to be working well.

1. worst 2. an 3. well 4. six-year-old 5. newly repaired

210

Both adjectives and adverbs act as modifiers; that is, they describe or limit other words. Since many of the forms and functions of adjectives and adverbs are similar and since faulty usage often results from the confusion of these two parts of speech, adjectives and adverbs will be treated together in this chapter.

Level I

Basic Functions of Adjectives and Adverbs

Adjectives describe or limit nouns and pronouns. As you have already learned, they often answer the questions *what kind? how many?* or *which one?* Adjectives in the following sentences are italicized.

> *Short* visits are *the best* visits.
>
> *Large government* grants were awarded to *the eight top* institutions.

Adverbs describe or limit verbs, adjectives, or other adverbs. They often answer the questions *when? how? where?* or *to what extent?*

> *Yesterday* our work went *slowly*.
>
> He answered *quite decisively*.

Comparative and Superlative Forms

Most adjectives and adverbs have three forms, or degrees: positive, comparative, and superlative. The following examples illustrate how the comparative and superlative degrees of regular adjectives and adverbs are formed.

	Positive	**Comparative**	**Superlative**
Adjective:	warm	warmer	warmest
Adverb:	warmly	more warmly	most warmly
Adjective:	careful	more careful	most careful
Adverb:	carefully	more carefully	most carefully

The positive degree of an adjective or an adverb is used in merely describing or in limiting another word. The comparative degree is used to compare two persons or things. The superlative degree is used in the comparison of three or more persons or things.

The comparative degree of short adjectives (nearly all one-syllable and most two-syllable adjectives ending in *y*) is formed by adding *r* or *er* (*warmer*). The superlative degree of short adjectives is formed by the addition of *st* or *est* (*warmest*). Long adjectives, and those difficult to pronounce, form the comparative and superlative degrees, as do adverbs, with the addition of *more* and *most* (*more careful, most beautiful*). The following sentences illustrate degrees of comparison for adjectives and adverbs.

Adjectives:	Sales are unusually *high*.	(Positive degree.)
	Sales are *higher* than ever before.	(Comparative degree.)
	Sales are the *highest* in years.	(Superlative degree.)

Adverbs:	He drives *carefully*.	(Positive degree.)
	He drives *more carefully* now.	(Comparative degree.)
	He drives *most carefully* at night.	(Superlative degree.)

Do not create a double comparative form by using *more* and the suffix *er* together (such as *more neater*) or by using *most* and the suffix *est* together (such as *most fastest*).

A few adjectives and adverbs form the comparative and superlative degrees irregularly. Some common irregular adjectives are *good* (*better, best*); *bad* (*worse, worst*); and *little* (*less, least*). Some common irregular adverbs are *well* (*better, best*); *many* (*more, most*); and *much* (*more, most*).

Modifiers that Deserve Special Attention

Adjectives as Articles

The articles *a, an,* and *the* merit special attention. When describing a specific person or thing, use the article *the,* as in *the film.* When describing persons or things in general, use *a* or *an,* as in *a film* (meaning *any* film). The choice of *a* or *an* is determined by the initial sound of the word modified. *A* is used before consonant sounds; *an* is used before vowel sounds.

Before Vowel Sounds		Before Consonant Sounds	
an operator		a shop	
an executive		a plan	
an hour ⎫	*h* is not voiced;	a hook ⎫	
an honor ⎭	vowel is heard	a hole ⎭	*h* is voiced
an office ⎫	*o* sounds	a one-man show ⎫	*o* sounds like
an onion ⎭	like a vowel	a one-week trip ⎭	the consonant *w*
an understudy ⎫	*u* sounds	a union ⎫	*u* sounds like
an umbrella ⎭	like a vowel	a unit ⎭	the consonant *y*
an X-ray ⎫	*x* and *m* sound		
an M.D. ⎭	like vowels		

Adverbs and Double Negatives

When a negative adverb (*no, not, nothing, scarcely, hardly, barely*) is used in the same sentence with a negative verb (*didn't, don't, won't*), a substandard construction called a *double negative* results. Such constructions are considered to be illogical and illiterate. In the following examples, notice how eliminating one negative corrects the double negative.

Incorrect:	Calling her *won't* do *no* good.
Correct:	Calling her will do no good.
Correct:	Calling her won't do any good.

Incorrect:	We *couldn't hardly* believe the news report.
Correct:	We could hardly believe the news report.
Correct:	We couldn't believe the news report.

Study Tip

The sound, not the spelling, of a word governs the choice between *a* and *an*. When the letter *u* sounds like a *y*, it is treated as a consonant: a *u*tility, a *u*sed car.

Did You Know?

At one time in the history of the English language multiple negatives were used to emphasize an idea. (*Don't never say nothing wicked!*) But in the 18th century, grammarians adopted Latin logic and decreed that two negatives created a positive.

Incorrect:	Drivers *can't barely* see in the heavy fog.
Correct:	Drivers can barely see in the heavy fog.
Correct:	Drivers can't see in the heavy fog.

Incorrect:	He didn't have nothing to do with it.
Correct:	He had nothing to do with it.
Correct:	He didn't have anything to do with it.

The Adjectives *this/that* and *these/those*

The adjective *this*, and its plural form *these*, indicates something nearby. The adjective *that*, and its plural form *those*, indicates something at a distance. Be careful to use the singular forms of these words with singular nouns and the plural forms with plural nouns: *this shoe, that road, these accounts, those records.* Pay special attention to the nouns *kind*, *type*, and *sort*. Match singular adjectives to the singular forms of these nouns and plural adjectives to the plural forms.

Incorrect:	Job candidates should be prepared for these type questions.
Correct:	Job candidates should be prepared for this type of question.
Correct:	Job candidates should be prepared for these types of questions.

Now complete the reinforcement exercises for Level I.

Level II

Problems with Adjectives and Adverbs

In the following discussion you will learn to avoid confusing adjectives with adverbs. You will also learn to express compound adjectives and independent adjectives.

Confusion of Adjectives and Adverbs

Because they are closely related, adjectives are sometimes confused with adverbs. Here are guidelines that will help you choose the appropriate adjective or adverb.

- Use adjectives to modify nouns and pronouns. Note particularly that adjectives (not adverbs) should follow linking verbs.

  This orange tastes *sweet*. (Not *sweetly*.)

  I feel *bad* about the loss. (Not *badly*.)

  He looks *good* in his uniform. (Not *well*.)

- Use adverbs to describe verbs, adjectives, or other adverbs.

  The engine runs *smoothly*. (Not *smooth*.)

  It runs *more smoothly* than before. (Not *smoother*.)

  Listen *carefully* to the directions. (Not *careful*.)

  The assignment went *easily*. (Not *easy*.)

Hot Link

To learn more about the antiquity of the double negative, visit **<http://www.bartleby.com/185/45.html>**. Is a double negative bad grammar and vulgar?

Spot the Blooper

From a Citibank brochure: "Your Citibank card will only access your checking account for these type purchases."

Career Tip

The misuse of *badly* for *bad* is one of the most frequent errors made by educated persons. Following the linking verb *feel*, use the adjective *bad*, not the adverb *badly*.

Spot the Blooper

Host to guest on radio program, station WOR, New Haven [CT]: "You look wonderfully!"

It should be noted that a few adverbs have two acceptable forms: *slow, slowly; deep, deeply; direct, directly;* and *close, closely.*

> Drive *slowly*. (Or, less formally, *slow*.)
>
> Pack the fruits *closely*. (Or, less formally, *close*.)

Compound Adjectives

Writers may form their own adjectives by joining two or more words. When these words act as a single modifier preceding a noun, they are temporarily hyphenated. If these same words appear after a noun, they are generally not hyphenated.

Words Temporarily Hyphenated Before a Noun	Same Words Not Hyphenated After a Noun
never-say-die attitude	attitude of never say die
eight-story building	building of eight stories
state-sponsored program	program that is state sponsored
a case-by-case analysis	analysis that is case by case
high-performance computer	computer that has high performance
income-related expenses	expenses that are income related
four-year-old child	child who is four years old
out-of-warranty repair	repair that is out of warranty

Compound adjectives shown in your dictionary with hyphens are considered permanently hyphenated. Regardless of whether the compound appears before or after a noun, it retains the hyphens. Use a current dictionary to determine what expressions are always hyphenated. Be sure that you find the dictionary entry that is marked *adjective*. Here are samples:

Permanent Hyphens Before Nouns	Permanent Hyphens After Nouns
first-class service	the service was first-class
up-to-date news	the news is up-to-date
old-fashioned attitude	attitude that is old-fashioned
short-term loan	loan that is short-term
well-known author	author who is well-known
well-rounded program	program that is well-rounded

Don't confuse adverbs ending in *ly* with compound adjectives: *newly decorated office* and *highly regarded architect* would not be hyphenated.

As compound adjectives become more familiar, they are often simplified and the hyphen is dropped. Some familiar compounds that are not hyphenated are *high school student, charge account customer, income tax return, home office staff,* and *data processing center.*

Spot the Blooper

From the Harvard Medical School's *Heart Letter*: "Do not feel too badly about missing dosages of your pills."

Spot the Blooper

Newspaper headline: "Squad Helps Dog Bite Victim"

Spot the Blooper

Under a photograph in *Science* magazine: "Museum staffer Ed Rodley checks out 65 million year-old eggs." (How does the missing hyphen alter the meaning?)

Independent Adjectives

Two or more successive adjectives that independently modify a noun are separated by commas. No comma is needed, however, when the first adjective modifies the combined idea of the second adjective and the noun.

Two Adjectives Independently Modifying a Noun	First Adjective Modifying a Second Adjective Plus a Noun
confident, self-reliant woman	efficient administrative assistant
economical, efficient car	blue sports car
stimulating, provocative book	luxurious mobile home

Study Tip

To determine whether successive adjectives are independent, mentally insert the word *and* between them. If the insertion makes sense, the adjectives are probably independent and require a comma.

Special Cases

The following adjectives and adverbs cause difficulty for some writers and speakers. With a little study, you can master their correct usage.

almost (adv.—nearly): *Almost* (not *Most*) everybody wants to work.

most (adj.—greatest in amount): *Most* people want to work.

farther (adv.—actual distance): How much *farther* is the market?

further (adv.—additionally): To argue the matter *further* is fruitless.

sure (adj.—certain): He is *sure* of victory.

surely (adv.—undoubtedly): He will *surely* be victorious.

later (adv.—after expected time): The contract arrived *later* in the day.

latter (adj.—the second of two things): Of the two options, I prefer the *latter*.

fewer (adj.—refers to numbers): *Fewer* requests for tours were granted this year.

less (adj.—refers to amounts or quantities): *Less* time remains than we anticipated.

real (adj.—actual, genuine): The *real* power in the company lies with the chairman of the board.

really (adv.—actually, truly): Jan wondered if she could *really* learn to operate the equipment in five hours.

good (adj.—desirable): A number of *good* plans were submitted.

well { (adv.—satisfactorily): Amy did *well* on the test.
{ (adj.—healthy): Jamal feels quite *well* since the operation.

Now complete the reinforcement exercises for Level II.

Level III

Other Uses of Adjectives and Adverbs

In this section you will learn how to use absolute modifiers, how to make comparisons within a group, and how to place adjectives and adverbs appropriately in sentences.

Absolute Modifiers

Adjectives and adverbs that name perfect or complete (absolute) qualities cannot logically be compared. For example, to say that one ball is more *round* than another ball is illogical. Here are some absolute words that should not be used in comparisons.

round	dead	complete
perfect	true	right
unique	correct	straight
perpendicular	endless	unanimous

Authorities suggest, however, that some absolute adjectives may be compared by the use of the words *more nearly* or *most nearly*.

> Ron's account of the disagreement was *more nearly accurate* than Sue's version. (Not *more accurate*.)

> Which of the children's drawings shows the *most nearly round* ball? (Not *roundest*.)

Comparisons Within a Group

Spot the Blooper

From a radio commercial for The Club, a device to prevent auto theft: "The Club works where other cheap imitations fail." (Does this statement say that The Club is a cheap imitation?)

When the word *than* is used to compare a person, place, or thing with other members of a group to which it belongs, be certain to include the words *other* or *else* in the comparison. This inclusion ensures that the person or thing being compared is separated from the group with which it is compared.

Illogical: Miami is larger than any city in Florida. (This sentence suggests that Miami is larger than itself.)

Logical: Miami is larger than any *other* city in Florida.

Illogical: Our team had more points than any league team.

Logical: Our team had more points than any *other* league team.

Illogical: Alex works harder than anyone in the office.

Logical: Alex works harder than anyone *else* in the office.

Placing Adverbs and Adjectives

Spot the Blooper

Headline from *The Concord Monitor* [Concord, NH]: "How Can You Expect a Child Who Can't Tell Time to Only Get Sick During Office Hours?"

The position of an adverb or adjective can seriously affect the meaning of a sentence. Study these examples.

> *Only* I can fix this copy machine. (No one else can fix it.)

> I can *only* fix this copy machine. (I can't fix anything else.)

> I can fix *only* this copy machine. (I can't fix any other copy machine.)

To avoid confusion, adverbs and adjectives should be placed close to the words they modify. In this regard, special attention should be given to the words *only*, *merely*, *first*, and *last*.

Confusing: He *merely* said that all soldiers couldn't be generals.

Clear: He said *merely* that all soldiers couldn't be generals.

Confusing: Seats in the five *first* rows have been reserved.

Clear: Seats in the *first* five rows have been reserved.

Now complete the reinforcement exercises for Level III.

Q: One of my favorite words is *hopefully*, but I understand that it's often used improperly. How should it be used?

A: Language purists insist that the word *hopefully* be used to modify a verb (*We looked at the door hopefully, expecting Mr. Guerrero to return momentarily*). The word *hopefully* should not be used as a substitute for *I hope that* or *We hope that*. Instead of saying *Hopefully, interest rates will decline*, one should say *I hope that interest rates will decline*.

Q: Is it necessary to hyphenate a *25 percent* discount?

A: No. Percents are not treated in the same way that numbers appearing in compound adjectives are treated. Thus, you would not hyphenate a *15 percent* loan, but you would hyphenate a *15-year* loan.

Q: Should hyphens be used in a *point-by-point analysis*?

A: Yes. When words are combined in order to create a single adjective preceding a noun, these words are temporarily hyphenated (*last-minute decision, two-semester course, step-by-step procedures*).

Q: In my writing I want to use *firstly* and *secondly*. Are they acceptable?

A: Both words are acceptable, but most good writers prefer *first* and *second*, because they are more efficient and equally accurate.

Q: How many hyphens should I use in this sentence? *The three, four, and five year plans continue to be funded.*

A: Three hyphens are needed: *three-, four-, and five-year plans*. Hyphenate compound adjectives even when the parts of the compound are separated or suspended.

Q: Why can't I remember how to spell *already*? I want to use it in this sentence: *Your account has already been credited with your payment.*

A: You—and many others—have difficulty with *already* because two different words (and meanings) are expressed by essentially the same sounds. The adverb *already* means "previously" or "before this time," as in your sentence. The two-word combination *all ready* means "all prepared," as in *The club members are all ready to board the bus*. If you can logically insert the word *completely* between *all* and *ready*, you know the two-word combination is needed.

Q: I never know how to write *part time*. Is it always hyphenated?

A: The dictionary shows all of its uses to be hyphenated. *She was a part-time employee* (used as adjective). *He worked part-time* (used as adverb).

Q: Here are some expressions that caused us trouble in our business letters. We want to hyphenate all of the following. Right? *Well-produced play, awareness-generation film, decision-making tables, one-paragraph note, swearing-in ceremony, commonly-used book.*

A: All your hyphenated forms are correct except the last one. Don't use a hyphen with an *ly*-ending adverb.

Q: Why are these two expressions treated differently: *two-week* vacation and *two weeks'* vacation?

A: Although they express the same idea, they represent two different styles. If you omit the *s*, *two-week* is hyphenated because it is a compound adjective. If you add the *s*, as in *two weeks' vacation*, the expression becomes possessive and requires an apostrophe. Don't use both styles together (not *two-weeks' vacation*).

Name _____

Level I

A. (Self-check) Write the correct forms in the spaces provided.

1. These are the (worse, <u>worst</u>) grades I have ever received. _____

2. My grades are much (<u>worse</u>, worst) this semester than last semester. _____

3. (<u>This type</u>, These types) of problem can be avoided with careful planning. _____

4. I can't think of a (<u>better</u>, more better) plan. _____

5. We (<u>can</u>, can't) hardly work in this room without air conditioning. _____

6. Andrew claimed that he didn't have (nothing, <u>anything</u>) to do with it. _____

7. Examine closely the blades on (<u>this</u>, these) pair of scissors. _____

8. Driving to the bank and back requires at least (a, <u>an</u>) hour's time. _____

9. Rainfall for this year (<u>has</u>, hasn't) been barely ten inches. _____

10. The outcome of the race between Connors and Morelli will determine the (<u>faster</u>, fastest) driver. _____

Check your answers below.

B. Write the correct forms in the spaces provided.

1. (That kind, <u>Those kinds</u>) of rumors can cause stock prices to plunge. _____

2. Bill Gates is the (more, <u>most</u>) powerful of the software manufacturers. _____

3. It takes (a, <u>an</u>) hour to complete this questionnaire. _____

4. The mortgage company (don't have no, <u>doesn't have any</u>) reason to deny the loan. _____

5. Ask the tailor whether (<u>this</u>, these) pair of pants is ready. _____

6. After paying his taxes, Mark complained that he (<u>has</u>, hasn't) barely a dollar left. _____

7. Health care and communications are two service industries growing at (a, <u>an</u>) unusually fast pace. _____

8. Susan said she couldn't see (no, <u>any</u>) other way to install the program. _____

9. Of the four brothers and sisters, he is the (younger, <u>youngest</u>). _____

10. Which of these two colors is (<u>better</u>, best) for the hall? _____

11. Dennis complained that the owner didn't have (no, <u>any</u>) right to keep the deposit. _____

12. The company knew that it couldn't give (nothing, <u>anything</u>) to its favorite charity this year. _____

1. worst 2. worse 3. This type 4. better 5. can 6. anything 7. this 8. an 9. has 10. faster

219

C. Supply the proper article (*a* or *an*) for the following words.

Example: _an_ adjustment

1. _a_ number	7. _a_ warehouse	13. _an_ insult
2. _an_ honor	8. _an_ agency	14. _an_ X-ray
3. _an_ inventory	9. _a_ combination	15. _an_ illegible letter
4. _a_ pattern	10. _an_ idea	16. _a_ one-year lease
5. _a_ Hawaiian	11. _a_ utility	17. _an_ eight-year lease
6. _an_ orange	12. _an_ airplane	18. _an_ oil glut

D. In the space provided write the correct comparative or superlative form of the adjective shown in parentheses.

Example: Of the three filing systems, which is (good)?   **best**

1. Kareem is the (tall) player on the team.   tallest
2. This is the (good) illustration submitted thus far.   best
3. Please send me the (current) figures you can find.   most current
4. The 20-pound stationery is (heavy) than the 16-pound paper.   heavier
5. Purchasing a home is (costly) than renting an apartment.   more costly
6. Of all the employees, Richard is the (little) talkative.   least
7. Ms. Hansen is (businesslike) than the office manager she replaced.   more businesslike
8. Have you ever met a (kind) individual than Lien Phuong Pham?   kinder
9. This is the (bad) winter we've had in years.   worst
10. Which is the (interesting) of the two novels?   more interesting

Level II

A. (Self-check) Write the correct forms in the spaces provided.

1. The defendant looked (calm, calmly) as the verdict was read.   calm
2. The lighthouse is (farther, further) away than it first appeared.   farther
3. Better service is ensured if a purchaser has (face-to-face, face to face) dealings with the manufacturer.   face to face
4. (Fewer, Less) homes have been constructed than ever before.   fewer
5. Unless sales data can be processed (quicker, more quickly), we lose business to our competitors.   more quickly
6. Mr. Burton (sure, surely) made his personal feelings apparent when he announced the policy change.   surely
7. Because he forgot your birthday, Matthew felt (bad, badly).   bad
8. Of probationary and permanent employees, only the (later, latter) are eligible for tuition reimbursement.   latter
9. Some small businesses barely exist from (year-to-year, year to year).   year to year

10. Asked about her health, Aunt Edna said she felt (good, well).   *well*

Check your answers below.

B. Write the correct words in the spaces provided.

1. For about a week our new copier worked just (beautiful, <u>beautifully</u>).   _____

2. Because of the construction decline, (fewer, ~~less~~) housing is available.   _____

3. Lee thought that she did (good, <u>well</u>) in her interview.   _____

4. Honeydew melons taste <u>(good</u>, well) with lemon juice.   _____

5. Global investment will (sure, <u>surely</u>) increase in coming years.   _____

6. Since its tune-up, the engine runs (smoother, <u>more smoothly</u>).   _____

7. Lavonda wasn't (real, (really)) sure she could attend the meeting.   _____

8. I hope you won't take this comment (personal, <u>personally</u>).   _____

9. Does this coffee taste (<u>bitter</u>, bitterly) to you?   _____

10. Your new suit certainly fits you (good, <u>well</u>).   _____

11. The new suit looks very (<u>good</u>, well) on you.   _____

12. She wanted to debate the question (<u>further</u>, farther).   _____

13. He completed the aptitude test (satisfactory, <u>satisfactorily</u>).   _____

14. If you write (<u>fewer</u>, less) checks, your service charges will decline.   _____

15. Rick feels (sure, <u>surely</u>) that part-time salaries will improve.   _____

16. (Most, <u>Almost</u>) everyone agreed that work is the price you pay for money.   _____

17. Four specialists keyed the lengthy report (perfect, <u>perfectly</u>).   _____

18. To reduce costs, they pressed for a settlement (quick, <u>quickly</u>).   _____

19. Mr. Turner was (sure, <u>surely</u>) proud of his pilot's license.   _____

20. Recovering from his illness, Luis said he felt (good, <u>well</u>).   _____

C. Select the correct group of words below. Write its letter in the space provided.

1. (a) coast to coast broadcast   _____   6. (a) book that is up to date   _____
   (b) coast-to-coast broadcast   (b) book that is up-to-date

2. (a) well-documented report   _____   7. (a) data-processing service   _____
   (b) well documented report   (b) data processing service

3. (a) child who is ten-years-old   _____   8. (a) arm-twisting tactics   _____
   (b) child who is ten years old   (b) arm twisting tactics

4. (a) ten-year-old child   _____   9. (a) last-minute preparations   _____
   (b) ten year old child   (b) last minute preparations

5. (a) fully certified nurse   _____   10. (a) widely-acclaimed cure   _____
   (b) fully-certified nurse   (b) widely acclaimed cure

D. Place commas where needed in the following groups of words.

1. red sports car

2. narrow, winding path

3. concise, courteous letter

4. snug, cheerful apartment

5. imaginative, daring designer

6. efficient clerical employee

E. Writing Exercise. Compose sentences using the compound adjectives shown. Be sure that the compound adjectives precede nouns.

Example: (up to the minute)

Your up-to-the-minute report arrived today. _____

1. (three year old) _____

_____

2. (once in a lifetime) _____

_____

3. (month by month) _____

_____

4. (work related) _____

_____

5. (state of the art) _____

_____

F. Writing Exercise. Compose sentences using the following words.

1. (farther) _____

_____

2. (latter) _____

_____

3. (fewer) _____

_____

L e v e l   I I I

A. (Self-check) Underline any errors in the following sentences and write their corrected forms in the spaces provided. If a sentence is correct as it is written, write *C*.

Example: Taylor is the <u>most unique</u> individual I know.

most nearly unique

1. Because he used a ruler, his line is <u>more straight</u> than mine.

more nearly straight

2. Professor Anita Musto is the most conscientious teacher I have.

C

3. She is more conscientious than any teacher I've ever had.

any other

4. We were told to answer the ten last questions.

last ten questions

5. Larry has the most perfect sales routine in the business.

most nearly perfect

6. We are concerned only with your welfare and happiness.

with only

7. He merely thought you wanted one page copied.

you wanted merely

8. Western mountains are more perpendicular than Eastern mountains.

more nearly

9. San Francisco is the most cosmopolitan city in California.

C

10. It is more cosmopolitan than any city in the state.

any other

Check your answers below.

B. Underline errors and write corrected forms in the spaces provided. If correct, write C.

1. Her three last books have been best-sellers.

last three

2. The *Times* story about the embezzlement is more accurate than the *Globe* article.

① more nearly

3. Colonel Bauer asserted that the Army was safer for women than any organization in America.

any other

4. Is this the most correct answer among all the applicants' tests?

most nearly

5. I only have one dollar in my wallet.

have only

6. Las Vegas is the largest city in Nevada.

C

7. Las Vegas is larger than any city in Nevada.

any other city

8. That brand of cosmetic is only sold by door-to-door sales-people.

sold only

9. Kinko's offers the most complete office service in town.

most nearly complete

10. The two first applicants presented excellent résumés.

first two

C. *Review of Levels I, II, and III.* For each sentence below, underline any error. Then write a corrected form in the space provided.

1. His only record of the salary offer was a e-mail message from the CEO.

an

2. Is Model Z3 or Model X10 best for our office needs?

better

3. Sandy said that she couldn't barely hear you when you called.

could barely

4. Because of excessive costs, designer Donna Karan made less trips to the Far East and Africa in search of "creative inspiration."

fewer

5. Mr. Wu interviewed a Canadian official and an European diplomat concerning the proposed two-year trade program.

a

6. If deliveries can't be made more quicker, we will change carriers.

quickly

7. In using our newly-installed voice mail system, be sure to leave clear, complete messages.

voice-mail

8. One applicant felt that he had done good on the skills test.

well

9. I like this job better than any job I've ever had.

any other job

10. Management thought that most everyone would want expanded health care benefits.

almost

1. more nearly straight 2. C 3. any other teacher 4. last ten questions 5. most nearly perfect 6. with only 7. you merely wanted or you wanted merely 8. more nearly perpendicular 9. C 10. any other city

Chapter 12 Modifiers: Adjectives and Adverbs   **223**

11. Today's smart nimble companies are turning out world-class products in head-to-head international competition.

smart, nimble

12. We only try to file necessary paperwork.

try only

13. Did you say that the two first rows had empty seats?

first two

14. He passed my desk so quick I hardly saw him.

quickly

15. Bonnie Jeffers made a point by point comparison of the machines.

point-by-point

Editor's Challenge

The following memo proposal contains intentional errors representing language principles covered thus far, spelling, and proofreading. You should mark 35 changes. If one word replaces three, it's considered one change.

Rawlinson Enterprises
Interoffice Memo

DATE: June 5, 200x

TO: Larry LaGrange, Vice President, Operations

FROM: Elyse Ellerman, Manager, Accounting

SUBJECT: INSTALLATION OF UNDERCARPET WIRING

Proposal

Because the Accounting Department needs a flexible economical wiring system that can accommodate our ever changing electrical needs. That's why I propose that we install a flat undercarpet wiring system.

Present System

At this time the Accounting Department has an out of date system of floor wiring and power poles that limit us to surface wiring. This network of surface wiring appear to be totally overwhelmed by the demands we are now placing on them. The operation of 27 pieces of equipment in addition to 34 telephone lines require extensive electrical circuits and cabling. Moreover, our overhead lighting, which consist of fluorescent fixtures in a suspended egg-crate structure, contains excessive wiring above the ceiling. Technicians whom have came to our office have said that its the worse system theyve ever saw.

Advantages of Proposed System

Cabling for telephone, power, and data are now available in a flat form only .043 inches thick. This flat flexible cable can be install underneath existing carpeting. Thus preventing costly and disruptive renovation. Undercarpet wiring would mean less office power poles. Moreover, flat cables can be moved easy, giving we accountants greater flexibility when we need to add equipment. Installation of a undercarpet wiring system in the Accounting Department would also enable the company to evaluate the systems affectiveness before considering it for other departments.

Cost and Savings

Suppliers and consultants estimates that an undercarpet wiring system for the Accounting department would cost about $50,000. If we was to use conventional methods to install round wiring, we would have to renovate our entire department, costing over $200,000. Equally important, however, is the savings in terms of productivity and employee satisfaction. Which would deteriorate if renovation was required.

Goal: To use an online newspaper

Your boss heard a news story on the way to work, and she asks you to verify it. Many newspapers have online editions that provide the latest news at no cost.

1. With your Web browser on the screen, go to **<www.usatoday.com>**.

2. Make a list of the headlines for three top news stories. Click on one of the stories. Write one or two sentences summarizing the story.

3. To look at another newspaper, key this URL: **<www.meguffey.com>**. Click **Research tools;** then click **U.S. and World Newspapers**. Click on a newspaper that interests you.

4. Make a list of the headlines for three top news stories. Click on one of the stories. Write one or two sentences summarizing the story.

5. End your session and submit your lists and summaries.

POSTTEST

Underline the correct word.

1. We seem to have (fewer, less) applications than ever before.

2. Please use (a, an) orange marking pen to highlight the report.

3. Jason was certain that he had done (good, well) in his job interview.

4. Erin completed a (page by page, page-by-page) check of the book.

5. Employees liked their (completely-redecorated, completely redecorated) office.

1. fewer 2. an 3. well 4. page-by-page 5. completely redecorated

CHECKLIST OF BONUS LEARNING RESOURCES

The following additional learning resources are available to you. Your instructor will tell you which to complete.

- Web Editor's Challenge Exercise

- Web Interactive Chapter Review

- Web PowerPoint Slides

- Web Crossword Puzzle

- WebCheck Reinforcement Exercises 12.1, 12.2

- Self-Help Exercises

- Electronic Study Guide

chapter 13 Prepositions

Objectives

When you have completed the materials in this chapter, you will be able to do the following:

Level I

- Use objective case pronouns as objects of prepositions.
- Avoid using prepositions in place of verbs and adverbs.

Level II

- Use eight troublesome prepositions correctly.
- Omit unnecessary prepositions and retain necessary ones.
- Construct formal sentences that avoid terminal prepositions.

Level III

- Recognize those words and constructions requiring specific prepositions (idioms).

Underline the correct word.

1. Speed is important, but proofreading is necessary (to, too).

2. (As, Like) I said, all our documents must be accurate.

3. Do you plan (on taking, to take) a two-week vacation?

4. Management and workers alike agreed (to, with) the contract.

5. The printer should be placed (beside, besides) the computer.

1. too   2. As   3. to take   4. to   5. beside

Prepositions are connecting words. They show the relationship of a noun or pronoun to another word in a sentence. This chapter reviews the use of objective case pronouns following prepositions. It also focuses on common problems that communicators have with troublesome prepositions. Finally, it presents many words in our language that require specific prepositions (idiomatic expressions) to sound "right."

L e v e l   I

Common Uses of Prepositions

In the following list, notice that prepositions may consist of one word or several.

about	below	from	on
according to	beside	in	on account of
after	between	in addition to	over
along with	but	in spite of	to
among	by	into	under
around	during	like	until
at	except	of	upon
before	for	off	with

Objective Case Following Prepositions

As you will recall from Chapter 6, pronouns that are objects of prepositions must be in the objective case.

We received pledges *from him* and *her* for the charity bike ride.

The disagreement is with the distributor, not *with* you and *me.*

Give the account balances *to* Ms. Love and *him.*

To review further, recall that some prepositions—such as *like, between, but,* and *except*—are particularly likely to lead to confusion in determining pronoun case. Consider the following examples.

Just *between you and me,* will the two companies merge? (Not *between you and I.*)

Volunteers *like Mr. Sheldon and him* are rare. (Not *like Mr. Sheldon and he.*)

Applications from everyone *but them* have arrived. (Not *but they.*)

Fundamental Problems With Prepositions

In even the most casual speech or writing, the following misuses of prepositions should be avoided.

- ***Of* for *have.*** The verb phrases *should have* and *could have* should never be written as *should of* or *could of.* The word *of* is a preposition and cannot be used in verb phrases.

  Juan *should have* called first. (Not *should of.*)

  He *could have* given some advance notice. (Not *could of.*)

- *Off* **for** *from.* The preposition *from* should never be replaced by *off* or *off of*.

    My colleague borrowed money *from* me. (Not *off of*.)

    Shannon said she got the CD *from* you. (Not *off* or *off of*.)

- *To* **for** *too.* The preposition *to* means "in a direction toward." Do not use the word *to* in place of the adverb *too*, which means "additionally," "also," or "excessively."

    Dividends are not distributed *to* stockholders unless declared by the directors.

    No dividends were declared because profits were *too* small.

    Contributions of services will be accepted *too*.

You will recall that the word *to* may also be part of an infinitive construction.

    She is learning *to* program the computer.

Now complete the reinforcement exercises for Level I.

Spot the Blooper

Colorado Springs traffic sign: "Following to close." (City officials blamed the sign company, which had shortened "Following too closely" because it didn't fit.)

Level II

Troublesome Prepositions

Be particularly careful to use the following prepositions properly.

- *Among, between.* *Among* means "in or through the midst of" or "surrounded by." It is usually used to speak of three or more persons or things; *between* means "shared by" and is usually used for two persons or things.

    The disagreement was *between* him and his partner.

    Supplies were distributed *among* the four divisions.

- *Beside, besides.* *Beside* means "next to"; *besides* means "in addition to."

    Please sit *beside* me at the assembly.

    Besides calling, you should write a letter of apology.

- *Except.* The preposition *except*, meaning "excluding" or "but," is sometimes confused with the verb *accept*, which means "to receive."

    Everyone *except* Melanie and her was able to come.

    Please *accept* this gift as a token of our appreciation.

- *In, into.* *In* indicates a position or location. *Into* indicates direction or movement to an interior location.

    We store copy paper *in* the supply cabinet. (Preposition *in* indicates location.)

    Bring the boxes *into* the storeroom. (Preposition *into* indicates movement to an interior location.)

Some constructions may employ *in* as an adverb preceding an infinitive:

    They went *in* to see the manager. (Adverb *in* precedes infinitive *to see*.)

Hot Link

An excellent place to learn more about prepositions is Capital Community College's site **<http://cctc2 .commnet.edu/ grammar/ prepositions.htm>**.

Study Tip

Look at the word(s) following *like*. If many words follow, chances are they function as a clause; use *as, as if,* or *as though* instead of *like*.

Spot the Blooper

From *The Tampa Tribune*: "Like he's done so many times before, Daryl Strawberry tried to put the past behind him."

Spot the Blooper

From an Ann Landers column: ". . . [They] might get their eyes opened up." [Is <u>up</u> a needed preposition?]

• **Like.** The preposition *like* should be used to introduce a noun or pronoun. Do not use *like* to introduce a clause (a group of words with a subject and a predicate). To introduce clauses, use *as, as if,* or *as though*.

> She looks *like* her sister. (*Like* used as a preposition to introduce the object, *her sister*.)
>
> She looks *as if she is tired*. (*As if* used to introduce the clause *she is tired*.)
>
> *As I said earlier*, the order was sent. (Do not use *like* to introduce the clause *I said earlier*.)

Necessary Prepositions

Don't omit those prepositions necessary to clarify a relationship. Be particularly careful when two prepositions modify a single object.

> We have every desire *for* and hope *of* an early settlement. (Do not omit *for*.)
>
> What type *of* coupler do you need? (Do not omit *of*.)
>
> Mr. Munoz is unsure *of* where to place the machine. (Do not omit *of*.)
>
> Salaries for temporary positions seem to be higher than *for* permanent positions. (Do not omit *for*.)
>
> When did you graduate *from* high school? (Do not omit *from*.)*

Unnecessary Prepositions

Omit unnecessary prepositions, particularly the word *of*.

> Leave the package *inside* the door. (Not *inside of*.)
>
> Both Web sites are useful. (Not *of the Web sites*.)
>
> All the letters require stationery. (Not *of the*.)
>
> Where is the meeting? (Not *meeting at*.)
>
> She could not help laughing. (Rather than *help from*.)
>
> Keep the paper near the printer. (Not *near to*.)

Ending a Sentence With a Preposition

In the past, language authorities warned against ending a sentence (or a clause) with a preposition. In formal writing today most careful authors continue to avoid terminal prepositions. In conversation, however, terminal prepositions are acceptable.

> **Informal:** What organization is he a member *of*?
>
> **Formal:** *Of* what organization is he a member?
>
> **Informal:** What is the medicine prescribed *for*?
>
> **Formal:** *For* what is the medicine prescribed?

*See Hotline Query on p. 235 regarding the expression "graduating from college."

Informal:	How many forms did you write *on*?
Formal:	*On* how many forms did you write?
Informal:	We don't know whom you spoke *to* when you called.
Formal:	We don't know *to* whom you spoke when you called.

Now complete the reinforcement exercises for Level II.

Spot the Blooper

From *The Sun* [San Bernardino, CA]: "Authorities had asked for the public's help in finding a silver Mercedes-Benz Jenkins had been seen driving away from Saturday's fire in."

Level III

Idiomatic Use of Prepositions

Every language has idioms (word combinations that are peculiar to that language). These combinations have developed through usage and often cannot be explained rationally. A native speaker usually is unaware of idiom usage until a violation jars his or her ear, such as "He is capable *from* (rather than *of*) violence."

The following list shows words that require specific prepositions to denote precise meanings. This group is just a sampling of the large number of English idioms. Consult a dictionary when you are unsure of the correct preposition to use with a particular word.

acquainted with	You must become *acquainted with* the new equipment.
addicted to	Miss Saguchi was *addicted to* jelly beans.
adept in	Are you *adept in* programming?
adhere to	All employees must *adhere to* certain office rules.
agree to (a proposal)	Did they *agree to* the plan for splitting shifts?
agree with (a person)	In this matter I certainly *agree with* you.
angry at (a thing)	Customers are understandably *angry at* the delay.
angry with (a person)	How can you be *angry with* the child?
buy from	You may *buy from* any one of several vendors.
capable of	She is *capable of* remarkable accomplishments.
comply with	We must *comply with* governmental regulations.
concur in (an action)	Four countries *concur in* a plan to promote peace.
concur with (a person)	Do you *concur with* Andrew about profits?
conform to	These machine parts do not *conform to* specifications.
contrast with	The white boat *contrasts* sharply *with* the blue ocean.
correspond to (match)	A bird's wing *corresponds to* a person's arm.
correspond with (write)	Madge *corresponds with* several distant friends.
desire for	A *desire for* wealth may create greed.
desirous of	Mr. Lee is *desirous of* acquiring blue-chip stocks.
differ from (things)	Checking accounts *differ from* savings accounts.
differ with (person)	I *differ with* you in small points only.

different from (not *than*)	This product is *different from* the one I ordered.
disagree with	Do you *disagree with* him?
expert in	Dr. Rand is an *expert in* electronics.
guard against	*Guard against* infection by covering wounds.
identical with or to	This house key is *identical with* (or *to*) yours.
independent of	Living alone, the young man was *independent of* his parents.
infer from	I *infer from* your remark that you are dissatisfied.
interest in	Jerry has a great *interest in* personal computers.
negligent of	*Negligent of* his diet, the old man became ill.
oblivious of or to	Mr. McClain was *oblivious of* (or *to*) his surroundings.
plan to (not *on*)	We *plan to* expand the marketing of our products.
prefer to	Do you *prefer to* work a four-day week?
reason with	We tried to *reason with* the unhappy customer.
reconcile with (match)	Checkbook figures must be *reconciled with* bank figures.
reconcile to (accept)	He has never become *reconciled to* retirement.
responsible for	William is *responsible for* locking the building.
retroactive to	The salary increase is *retroactive to* last July 1.
sensitive to	Mrs. Choy is unusually *sensitive to* cold.
similar to	Your term paper topic is *similar to* mine.
standing in (not *on*) line	How long have you been *standing in* line?
talk to (tell something)	The speaker *talked to* the large group.
talk with (exchange remarks)	After his lecture, the speaker *talked with* club members informally.

Now complete the reinforcement exercises for Level III.

Spot the Blooper

From the *Patriot-Ledger* [Quincy, MA]: "Clemens is able to come off the disabled list Sunday, but tests by Dr. Arthur Pappas led to the conclusion that Clemens' groin is still too weak to pitch in a game."

HOTLINE QUERIES

Q: Another employee and I are collaborating on a report. I wanted to write this: *Money was lost due to poor attendance.* She says the sentence should read: *Money was lost because of poor attendance.* My version is more concise. Which of us is right?

A: Most language authorities agree with your coauthor. *Due to* is acceptable when it introduces an adjective phrase, as in *Success was due to proper timing.* In this sense, *due to* is synonymous with *attributable to*. However, *because of* should introduce adverbial phrases and should modify verbs: *Money was lost because of poor attendance. Because of* modifies the verb phrase *was lost*.

Q: What's wrong with saying *Lisa graduated college last year*?

A: The preposition *from* must be inserted for syntactical fluency. Two constructions are permissible: *Lisa graduated from college* or *Lisa was graduated from college*. The first version is more popular; the second is preferred by traditional grammarians.

Q: Should *sometime* be one or two words in the following sentence? *Can you come over (some time) soon?*

A: In this sentence you should use the one-word form. *Sometime* means "an indefinite time" (*the convention is sometime in December*). The two-word combination means "a period of time" (*we have some time to spare*).

Q: I saw this printed recently: *Some of the personal functions being reviewed are job descriptions, job specifications, and job evaluation.* Is *personal* used correctly here?

A: Indeed not! The word *personal* means "private" or "individual" (*your personal letters are being forwarded to you*). The word *personnel* refers to employees (*all company personnel are cordially invited*). The sentence you quote requires *personnel*.

Q: Is there any difference between *proved* and *proven*?

A: As a past participle, the verb form *proved* is preferred (*he has proved his point*). However, the word *proven* is preferred as an adjective form (*that company has a proven record*). *Proven* is also commonly used in the expression *not proven*.

Q: We're writing a letter to our subscribers, and this sentence doesn't sound right to me: *Every one of our subscribers benefit . . .*

A: As you probably suspected, the verb *benefit* does not agree with the subject *one*. The sentence should read as follows: *Every one of our subscribers benefits . . .* Don't let intervening phrases obscure the true subject of a sentence.

Q: In my dictionary I found three ways to spell the same word: *life-style, lifestyle,* and *life style.* Which should I use?

A: The first spelling shown is usually the preferred one. In your dictionary a second acceptable form may be introduced by the word *also.* If two spellings appear side by side (*ax, axe*), they are equally acceptable.

Q: How should I write *industry wide*? It's not in my dictionary.

A: A word with the suffix *wide* is usually written solid: *industrywide, nationwide, countrywide, statewide, worldwide.*

Name _____

Level I

A. (Self-check) Select the correct word and write it in the space provided.

1. Between (we, us) two, we should be able to finish by noon.   _____

2. Thomas thought that he (should of, should have) been allowed extra time.   _____

3. Dr. Bernstein has (to, too) little patience for that job.   _____

4. Everyone received the e-mail announcement but (I, me).   _____

5. You might be able to get the lecture notes (off of, from) Holly.   _____

6. Should photocopies be made for Mrs. Korkosz and (her, she)?   _____

7. Government, too, has (to, too) consider the effects of inflation.   _____

8. Can you borrow a stapler (off of, from) Enrique?   _____

9. With additional study Gregory (could of, could have) earned an *A*.   _____

10. No one in the group except her and (I, me) will miss the field trip.   _____

Check your answers below.

B. Underline any errors you find in the following sentences. Write the correct forms in the spaces provided. Write *C* if the sentence is correct as written.

Example: Performers like Hayley and she are crowd pleasers.   **her**

1. Everyone in the office except she uses the Internet regularly.   *her*

2. If asked, Armando could of worked some overtime hours.   *have*

3. We got your address off of Richard before he left.   *from*

4. Many customers are eager to make appointments with Mr. Jerome or him.   *C*

5. Our union said that management's offer was "too little and to late."   *too*

6. Diana Abernathy told Andrew and me that we should have read the directions more carefully.   *C*

7. It's to soon to tell whether the young tree will bear edible fruit.   *too*

8. Along with Tim and me, Mr. De la Torre will check sales prices.   *C*

9. Just between you and I, the difference between a job and a career is the difference between 40 and 60 hours a week.   *me*

10. You could of attended the premier showing last evening.   *have*

11. Our manager, together with Tanya and he, helped to close the sale.   *him*

12. If you could of delivered the disks earlier, we might have finished on time.   *could have*

13. One can always rely on friends like Renee and <u>she</u> for assistance in time of need. — *her*

14. Everyone except him and <u>I</u> received the announcement too late to respond. — *me*

15. To address the letter properly, you must use information <u>off of</u> their stationery. — *from*

16. Last year we tried to order supplies <u>off of</u> them too. — *from*

17. All the checkers except <u>she and he</u> have the holiday off. — *her & him*

18. Some of the paper is <u>to</u> long for our everyday use. — *too*

19. If you <u>could of</u> seen the shipment when it arrived, you would have refused it too. — *could have*

20. CEO Christine Gerbig spoke with the marketing manager and <u>I</u> about sales. — *me*

L e v e l   I I

A. (Self-check) Select the correct word(s).

1. The inheritance will be divided (between, <u>among</u>) all the heirs. _____

2. Ruth Martin moved (in, <u>into</u>) the office next door. _____

3. Identifying serial numbers are engraved (<u>inside</u>, inside of) the machines. _____

4. Located (besides, <u>beside</u>) the computer store is the food court. _____

5. It looks (like, <u>as if</u>) we'll be working late tonight. _____

6. You will be billed later if you (except, <u>accept</u>) the shipment. _____

7. Despite his salary and new title, Tony feels (<u>like</u>, as) a technician. _____

8. Differences (<u>between</u>, among) the two brothers affected their management styles. _____

9. When the door was opened, the contracts blew ((off), off of) the desk. _____

10. In her job search, Marcia used many resources (beside, <u>besides</u>) the Web. _____

Check your answers below.

B. In the following sentences, cross out unnecessary prepositions and insert necessary ones.

Examples: What type ^of^ wheel bearings are needed?
Where are you going ~~to~~?

1. The time for submitting entries is over ~~with~~.

2. A new shopping center is being built opposite ~~to~~ the college.

3. Special printing jobs must be done outside ~~of~~ the office.

4. Charles had great respect and interest ~~in~~ ^for^ astronomy.

1. among 2. into 3. inside 4. beside 5. as if 6. accept 7. like 8. between 9. off 10. besides

238   **Chapter 13**   Prepositions

5. Who can tell me where the meeting is scheduled at?

6. What style *of* clothes is recommended for the formal dinner?

7. As the huge stack of boxes tumbled, Randy couldn't help from laughing.

8. Where shall we move the extra desks and chairs to?

9. After graduating college in June, Tuan Nguyen sent out résumés.

10. Exactly what type *of* printer do you need?

11. Please write up her performance appraisal quickly.

12. She complained because her desk was too near to the air conditioner.

C. Select the correct word(s).

1. Relief funds were divided (among, between) all earthquake victims. _____

2. (As, Like) the president said, we must increase productivity. _____

3. Sitting (beside, besides) the speaker is the program chair. _____

4. All three candidates have gone (in, into) the conference room. _____

5. Your laptop computer looks just (like, as) mine. _____

6. The advertising campaign looks (like, as if) it will be quite successful. _____

7. Has anyone been (in to, into) see me this morning? _____

8. We cannot (accept, except) the shipment without an invoice. _____

9. After the interview, Courtney felt (like, as if) she would be offered the position. _____

10. If he (accepts, excepts) the job, he would live in Columbus. _____

11. (Beside, Besides) Randy Marks and Leticia Lopez, whom have you invited? _____

12. It looks (like, as if) Dr. Helen Grattan will be the next CEO. _____

D. Writing Exercise. The following sentences have prepositions that end clauses. Rewrite the sentences so that the prepositions precede their objects.

Example: Here is the information you asked about.

   Here is the information about which you asked.

1. Whom did you address the letter to? _____

_____

2. Please locate the disk directory you put the letter in. _____

_____

3. What did I come into this room for? _____

_____

4. We have a number of loyal members we can rely upon. _____

_____

5. What salesperson did these brochures come from? _____

_____

A. (Self-check) Underline any errors in the use of prepositions in the following sentences, and write the correct form in the space provided. Write *C* if the sentence is correct as written.

1. Al Fernandez is exceptionally adept <u>with</u> woodworking. ___in___

2. We find it impossible to comply <u>to</u> the latest safety regulations. ___with___

3. In a televised address, the president will talk <u>with</u> the nation at 6 p.m. ___to___

4. Brenda said that she plans <s>on sleeping</s> late during her vacation. ___to sleep___

5. Taking calculated risks is quite different <u>than</u> being rash. ___from___

6. Virginia Tong is very angry <u>at</u> her boss for being transferred. ___with___

7. How can one reconcile this new business venture with their recent bankruptcy? ___C___

8. Isolated from neighbors, the hermit was independent <u>with</u> local laws. ___of___

9. A car very similar <u>with</u> yours is for sale. ___to___

10. Her desire <u>of</u> wealth and power made her unhappy throughout her life. ___for___

Check your answers below.

B. Underline any errors in the use of prepositions in the following sentences, and write a correction in the space provided. Write *C* if the sentence is correct as written.

1. How does stock differ <u>with</u> bonds? ___from___

2. All hourly raises are retroactive <u>for</u> January 1. ___to___

3. Nike officials plan <s>on expanding</s> their marketing in Latin America. ___to expand___

4. Does Judith McNeely concur with other board members in raising tuition? ___C___

5. Have you become acquainted <u>to</u> your new database software yet? ___with___

6. That film is much different <u>than</u> what I expected. ___from___

7. All procedures must adhere <u>with</u> the company manual. ___to___

8. The white letters on the sign do not sufficiently contrast <u>from</u> the yellow background. ___with___

9. Do you hire an interpreter when your company corresponds <u>to</u> Japanese customers? ___with___

10. We had to increase parking lot security to guard <u>from</u> auto thefts. ___against___

C. Writing Exercise. Write complete sentences using the expressions show in parentheses.

1. (oblivious of) ___He was oblivious to his surroundings___

_____

1. adept in 2. comply with 3. talk to 4. plans to sleep 5. different from 6. angry with 7. C 8. independent of 9. similar to 10. desire for

240   **Chapter 13   Prepositions**

2. (adhere to) He will not adhere to the rules

3. (retroactive to) His pay was retroactive to Feb 24

4. (independent of) His decision was independent of outside influence.

5. (differs from) His decision differs from mine

Editor's Challenge

The following short report contains intentional errors representing spelling, proofreading, and language principles covered thus far. You should mark 30 changes. If one word replaces three, it's considered one change.

RESULTS OF SMOKING POLICY SURVEY

by Craig Abrams, Human Resources

Background

A number of requests has been received from employees asking that smoking be banned in open offices. Second hand smoke represent a health risk with significant compensation implications for our company and it's stockholders. To gather information about managers and employees feelings, Human Resources distributed a questionnaire to 158 employees, a total of 138 responses were received.

Findings

A tally of the returned surveys show that a clear majority of our employees favors a nonsmoking policy. A total of 110 employees, or nearly 80 percent of the respondents', indicated there approval of an non smoking policy. To implement this policy, excellent suggestions were made by respondents. Which are discussed from the attached printouts.

Conclusion

The results of this survey suggests that our managers and many other employes would support a nonsmoking policy. They feel that a carefully planned sensitively implemented non-smoking policy could be successful about our organization.

Recommendations

A well managed cessation program should offer support and practical advice to those who want to use the opportunity to quit. Employees should be allowed sometime to take part in group counseling activitys. High visibility displays should promote participation. Whether to provide smoking areas for those employees who do not stop are a matter a committee must work on.

Goal: To use an online encyclopedia.

Your company is thinking of expanding its business into Malaysia, and Sri Lanka is a prime target. You want to learn more about trade in Sri Lanka.

1. With your Web browser on the screen, go to the Encyclopedia Britannica site **<http://www.britannica.com>.**

2. In the search box near the top of the screen, key your search term, **Sri Lanka**. Be sure to use quotation marks.

3. Click **See complete article**. Read about Sri Lanka and print one page of the article.

4. When did the country officially become Sri Lanka? What was it formerly called? What is its chief problem in regard to trade?

5. To select another online encyclopedia, go to the Guffey site **<www.meguffey. com>**. Click **Research Tools** and then **Reference Tools**.

6. From the list of encyclopedias, click one and compare the findings for Sri Lanka. Print one page.

7. End your session by clicking the **X** in the upper right corner of your browser. Turn in all printed pages and your answers to the questions.

POSTTEST

Underline the correct word.

1. The memo was (to, too) long to fit on one page.

2. It looks (like, as if) the company must relocate.

3. Is it necessary for all documents to comply (to, with) the new guidelines?

4. Dividends will be distributed (between, among) stockholders.

5. (Beside, Besides) Ann, who is able to work Saturday?

1. too   2. as if   3. with   4. among   5. Besides

CHECKLIST OF BONUS LEARNING RESOURCES

The following additional learning resources are available to you. Your instructor will tell you which to complete.

- Web Editor's Challenge Exercise
- Web Interactive Chapter Review
- Web PowerPoint Slides
- Web Crossword Puzzle
- WebCheck Reinforcement Exercises 13.1, 13.2, 13.3
- Self-Help Exercises
- Electronic Study Guide

chapter 14 Conjunctions to Join Equals

Objectives

When you have completed the materials in this chapter, you will be able to do the following:

Level I

- Distinguish between simple and compound sentences.
- Punctuate compound sentences joined by *and, or, nor*, and *but*.

Level II

- Punctuate compound sentences using conjunctive adverbs such as *therefore, however,* and *consequently*.

Level III

- Recognize correlative conjunctions such as *either . . . or, not only . . . but also,* and *neither . . . nor*.
- Use a parallel construction in composing sentences with correlative conjunctions.

Insert commas and semicolons to punctuate the following sentences correctly.

1. Sales on the West Coast have increased; therefore we are assigning more sales representatives to that area.

2. It is important, however, that we also continue to cover all other sales territories.

3. Eleanor Uyeda prefers to remain in Fullerton, but Bonnie Albert is considering the San Diego area.

4. As many as 20 agents will move; nevertheless the transition must be made smoothly.

Underline the letter of the sentence that is more effective.

5. (a) Not only is this copier faster but it also is cheaper than the other.
   (b) This copier is not only faster but also cheaper than the other.

1. increased; therefore, 2. important, however, 3. Fullerton, 4. move; nevertheless, 5. b

Conjunctions are connecting words. They may be separated into two major groups: those that join grammatically equal words or word groups and those that join grammatically unequal words or word groups. This chapter focuses on those conjunctions that join equals. Recognizing conjunctions and understanding their patterns of usage will, among other things, enable you to use commas and semicolons more appropriately.

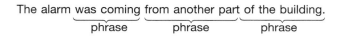

L e v e l   I

Coordinating Conjunctions

Coordinating conjunctions connect words, phrases, and clauses of equal grammatical value or rank. The most common coordinating conjunctions are *and, or, but,* and *nor*. Notice in these sentences that coordinating conjunctions join grammatically equal elements.

> We think your action is *illogical, unfair,* and *arbitrary*. (Here the word *and* joins equal words.)
>
> Give serious thought *to your letters* and *to reader reaction*. (Here *and* joins equal phrases.)
>
> *Mr. Freeman opens the mail*, but *Miss Santana fills the orders*. (Here *but* joins equal clauses.)

Phrases and Clauses

A group of related words without a subject and a verb is called a *phrase*. You are already familiar with verb phrases and prepositional phrases. It is not important that you be able to identify the other kinds of phrases (infinitive, gerund, participial), but it is very important that you be able to distinguish phrases from clauses.

> The alarm was coming from another part of the building.
>   phrase   phrase   phrase

A group of related words including a subject and a verb is a clause.

> We interviewed three applicants, and we decided to hire Mr. Lee.
>   clause   clause
>
> Karen is interested in a job in marketing, but she wants to travel also.
>   clause   clause
>
>   phrase   phrase
> Salaries begin at $35,000 annually, and they can reach over $75,000.
>   clause   clause

Simple and Compound Sentences

A *simple sentence* has one independent clause; that is, a clause that can stand alone. A *compound sentence* has two or more independent clauses.

> We agreed to lease the equipment. (Simple sentence.)
>
> Our Travel Department planned the sales trip, but some salespeople also made private excursions. (Compound sentence.)

Hot Link

For a colorful look at "A Brief Explanation of Conjunctions," go to <http://www.gsu.edu/~wwwesl/egw/bryson.htm>. If this site is not available, search for "coordinating conjunctions" with your favorite search engine.

Study Tip

Clauses have subjects and verbs. Phrases do not. Clauses may have phrases within them.

Spot the Blooper

Advertisement published in the *Los Angeles Times*: "Brother Word Processor with Grammer Check and Word Spell"

Punctuating Compound Sentences

When coordinating conjunctions join clauses in compound sentences, a comma precedes the conjunction unless the clauses are very short (four or fewer words in each clause).

> We can ship the merchandise by air, *or* we can ship it by rail.
>
> Ship by air *or* ship by rail. (Clauses are too short to require a comma.)

Do not use commas when coordinating conjunctions join compound verbs, objects, or phrases.

> The <u>bank</u> <u>will notify</u> you of each transfer, or <u>it</u> <u>will send</u> you a monthly statement. (Comma used because *or* joins two independent clauses.)
>
> The <u>bank</u> <u>will notify</u> you of each transfer or <u>will send</u> you a monthly statement. (No comma needed because *or* joins the compound verbs of a single independent clause.)
>
> <u>Thomas Edison</u> <u>said</u> that colleges should not have to choose between lighting their buildings *and* enlightening their students. (No comma needed because *and* joins the compound objects of a prepositional phrase.)
>
> <u>Stockholders</u> <u>are expected</u> to attend the meeting *or* to send their proxies. (No comma needed because *or* joins two infinitive phrases.)
>
> <u>Analyze</u> all your possible property risks, *and* <u>protect</u> yourself with insurance. (Comma needed to join two independent clauses; the subject of each clause is understood to be *you*.)

Now complete the reinforcement exercises for Level I.

Level II

Conjunctive Adverbs

Conjunctive adverbs may also be used to connect equal sentence elements. Because conjunctive adverbs are used to effect a transition from one thought to another, and because they may consist of more than one word, they have also been called *transitional expressions*. The most common conjunctive adverbs follow.

accordingly	in fact	on the other hand
consequently	in the meantime	that is
furthermore	moreover	then
hence	nevertheless	therefore
however	on the contrary	thus

In the following compound sentences, observe that conjunctive adverbs join clauses of equal grammatical value. Note that semicolons (*not* commas) are used before conjunctive adverbs that join independent clauses. Commas should immediately follow conjunctive adverbs of two or more syllables. Note also that the word following a semicolon is not capitalized—unless, of course, it is a proper noun.

Electricians rewired the equipment room; *nevertheless*, fuses continued to blow.

Some equipment requires separate outlets; *consequently*, we installed new outlets.

Equipment expenditures are great this quarter; *on the other hand*, new equipment will reduce labor costs.

The growing use of hand-held phones in cars endangers safety; thus several communities are giving away free bumper stickers that say, "Drive Now, Talk Later."

Competition among computer manufacturers is intensive; *hence* prices have decreased sharply.

Generally, no comma is used after one-syllable conjunctive adverbs such as *hence*, *thus*, and *then* (unless a strong pause is desired).

Study Tip

Use a semicolon only when you are joining two complete sentences.

Distinguishing Conjunctive Adverbs From Parenthetical Adverbs

Many words that function as conjunctive adverbs may also serve as *parenthetical* (interrupting) *adverbs* that are employed to effect transition from one thought to another. Use semicolons *only* with conjunctive adverbs that join independent clauses. Use commas to set off parenthetical adverbs that interrupt the flow of a sentence.

Mr. Jackson is, *however*, a fine administrator. (Adverb used parenthetically.)

Mr. Jackson is a fine administrator; *however*, he is a poor fund-raiser. (Conjunctive adverb used to join two clauses.)

The Federal Reserve System, *moreover*, is a vital force in maintaining a sound banking system and a stable economy. (Adverb used parenthetically.)

The Federal Reserve System is a vital force in maintaining a sound banking system; *moreover*, it is instrumental in creating a stable economy. (Conjunctive adverb joins two clauses.)

We believe, *on the other hand*, that cellular phone sales will continue to grow. (Adverb phrase used parenthetically.)

We agree that cell phones are convenient; *on the other hand*, they must be used responsibly. (Conjunctive adverb phrase used to join two clauses.)

Now complete the reinforcement exercises for Level II.

L e v e l   I I I

Other Conjunctions

We have studied thus far two kinds of conjunctions used to join grammatically equal sentence elements: coordinating conjunctions (used to join equal words, phrases, and clauses) and conjunctive adverbs (used to join grammatically equal clauses in compound sentences). *Correlative conjunctions* form the third and final group of conjunctions that join grammatically equal sentence elements.

Correlative Conjunctions

Correlative conjunctions are always paired: *both . . . and, not only . . . but (also), either . . . or,* and *neither . . . nor.* When greater emphasis is desired, these paired conjunctions are used instead of coordinating conjunctions.

Your cell phone is lying on the counter *or* on the table.

Your cell phone is lying *either* on the counter *or* on the table. (More emphatic.)

In using correlative conjunctions, place them so that the words, phrases, or clauses being joined are parallel in construction.

Parallel: He was working *either* in Scottsdale *or* in Phoenix.

Not parallel: *Either* he was working in Scottsdale *or* in Phoenix.

Parallel: She was *not only* gracious *but also* kind.

Not parallel: She was *not only* gracious, *but* she was *also* kind.

Parallel: I have *neither* the time *nor* the energy for this.

Not parallel: I *neither* have the time *nor* the energy for this.

Additional Coordinating Conjunctions

At Level I you studied the four most commonly used coordinating conjunctions: *and, or, nor,* and *but.* Three other coordinating conjunctions should also be mentioned: *yet, for,* and *so.*

The words *yet* and *for* may function as coordinating conjunctions, although they are infrequently used as such.

We have only two hours left, *yet* we hope to finish.

The weary traveler was gaunt and ill, *for* his journey had been long and arduous.

The word *so* is sometimes informally used as a coordinating conjunction. In more formal contexts the conjunctive adverbs *therefore* and *consequently* should be substituted for the conjunction *so.*

Informal: The plane leaves at 2:15, *so* you still have time to pack.

Improved: The plane leaves at 2:15; *therefore,* you still have time to pack.

To avoid using *so* as a conjunction, try starting your sentence with *because* or *although.*

Informal: Cell phone calls in public can be exasperating, so they are banned in some places.

Improved: Because cell phone calls in public can be exasperating, they are banned in some places.

Now complete the reinforcement exercises for Level III.

Spot the Blooper

From a New York sport columnist: "While checking my bags at the counter, Magic Johnson arrived in a stretch limo."

Q: A friend of mine gets upset when I say something like, *I was so surprised by her remark.* She thinks I'm misusing *so.* Am I?

A: Your friend is right, if we're talking about formal expression. The intensifier *so* requires a clause to complete its meaning. For example, *I was so surprised by her remark that I immediately protested.* It's like waiting for the other shoe to drop when one hears *so* as a modifier without a qualifying clause. *He was so funny.* So funny that what? *He was so funny that he became a stand-up comedian.*

Q: Please help me decide which *maybe* to use in this sentence: *He said that he (maybe, may be) able to help us.*

A: Use the two-word *may be*, which is the verb form. *Maybe* is an adverb that means "perhaps" (*maybe she will call*).

Q: At the end of a printed line, is it acceptable to type part of an individual's name on one line and carry the rest to the next line?

A: Full names may be divided between the first and last names or after the middle initial. For example, you could type *John R.* on one line and *Williamson* on the next line. Do not, however, separate a short title and a surname (such as *Mr./Williamson*), and do not divide a name (such as *William/son*). By the way, many computer programs make unacceptable line-ending decisions. Be sure to inspect your copy, either on the screen or on the printout, so that you can correct poor hyphenation and unacceptable word separations.

Q: What should the verb in this sentence be? *There (has, have) to be good reasons . . .*

A: Use the plural verb *have*, which agrees with the subject *reasons*. In sentences that begin with the word *there*, look for the subject after the verb.

Q: Does *Ms.* have a period after it? Should I use this title for all women in business today?

A: *Ms.* is probably a blend of *Miss* and *Mrs.* It is written with a period following it. Some women in business prefer to use *Ms.,* presumably because it is a title equal to *Mr.* Neither title reveals one's marital status. Many other women, however, prefer to use *Miss* or *Mrs.* as a title. It's always wise, if possible, to determine the preference of the individual.

Q: I just typed this sentence: *He was given a new title in lieu of a salary increase.* I went to my dictionary to check the spelling of *in lieu of,* but I can't find it. How is it spelled and what does it mean?

A: The listing in the dictionary is under *lieu*, and it means "instead of." Many authorities today are recommending that such phrases be avoided. It's easier and clearer to say "instead of."

Q: Can you help me with the words *averse* and *adverse*? I've never been able to straighten them out in my mind.

A: *Averse* is an adjective meaning "disinclined" and generally is used with the preposition *to* (*the little boy was averse to bathing; she is averse to statistical typing*). *Adverse* is also an adjective, but it means "hostile" or "unfavorable" (*adverse economic conditions halted the company's growth; the picnic was postponed because of adverse weather conditions*). In distinguishing between these two very similar words, it might help you to know that the word *averse* is usually used to describe animate (living) objects.

Q: What should I write: *You are our No. 1 account*, or *You are our number one account*? Should anything be hyphenated?

A: Either is correct, but I prefer *No. 1* because it is more easily recognizable. No hyphen is required.

Name _____

Level I

A. (Self-check) Select *a*, *b*, or *c* to identify the sentences below.

   a. A comma correctly punctuates a compound sentence.

   b. The sentence is not compound; thus the comma should be omitted.

   c. Although the sentence is compound, the clauses are too short to require a comma.

   Example: It rained most of the morning, but stopped in the afternoon when the sun began to shine.   **b**

1. A New York restaurant received so many complaints about cell phone users that it set up a cell phone lounge, and banished their use elsewhere.   *b*

2. The value-added tax is quite popular in Europe, but it has received little support in this country.   *a*

3. We did not expect a profit, and did not fear a loss.   *b*

4. Listen well, and look carefully.   *c*

5. Word processing specialists must possess excellent English skills, and they must be skilled at keyboarding.   *a*

6. The concert did not begin until 8 p.m., but a large crowd began to gather at noon.   *a*

7. Danielle types and Koshi edits.   *c*

8. Albert Einstein was four years old before he could speak, and seven years old before he could read.   *b*

9. The Human Resources Director will be interviewing applicants Monday and Tuesday, and will make a decision on the appointment by Friday.   *b*

10. The city of Bombay originally rested on seven islands, but the islands were joined by landfill long ago.   *a*

Check your answers below.

B. A simple sentence has one independent clause. A compound sentence has two or more independent clauses. Indicate with a check mark whether the following sentences, all of which are punctuated correctly, are simple or compound. *Hint:* A sentence is not compound unless the words preceding and following a conjunction form independent clauses. If these groups of words could not stand alone as sentences, the sentence is not compound.

	Simple	Compound
1. Janet Polesak attended a computer trade show, and she shared what she learned with other members of the staff.		✓
2. Janet Polesak attended a computer trade show and shared what she learned with other members of the staff.	✓	

1. b 2. a 3. b 4. c 5. a 6. a 7. c 8. b 9. b 10. a

	Simple	Compound
3. We will allow you our discount of 10 percent and also a cash rebate of over $50 for each purchase.	✓	
4. The recently constructed corporate headquarters contained attractive executive offices, but the structure had few support facilities for employees.		✓
5. The recently constructed corporate headquarters contained attractive executive offices but few support facilities for employees.		
6. Management trainees are sent to all our branch offices in this country and to some of the branch offices in South America and Europe.	✓	
7. Children become adults when they stop asking their parents for allowances and begin requesting loans instead.		
8. Fill in all the answers on the application, and send the form to the human resources director.		✓
9. Send copies of the project report to me and to other management personnel in our three subsidiaries.		
10. Supplies for three offices arrived today, but most of our order will not arrive until later.	✓	

C. Insert commas where appropriate in the following sentences. Then, in the space provided, indicate the number of commas you have added for each sentence. If no comma is needed, write *0*.

Example: Kevin attended classes on Monday̭but he went to the beach on Tuesday.   1_____

1. Some employees think their e-mail should be confidential but courts generally uphold an employer's right to monitor messages. _____

2. CEO Ann Aron authorized the expenditure and directed the purchasing agent to place an order immediately.   0_____

3. Mr. Peterson was not pleased with the delay but he did not seem to be angry with the vendor. _____

4. Please keyboard this letter and fax it.   0_____

5. People will forget how fast you did a job but they will remember how well you did it. _____

6. Today's software can detect potentially troublesome words or identify high-pressure sales tactics in outgoing e-mail messages.   0_____

7. Charles Goodyear invented a process leading to the manufacture of rubber but he failed to benefit from it and died in poverty. _____

8. Raw materials and supplies are available but machinery and equipment must be replaced before production can begin.   1_____

9. Consider the alternatives and act accordingly. _____

10. You may be interested in a career in this country or you may be interested in working abroad.   1_____

A. (Self-check) In the following sentences, insert commas and semicolons. In the space provided, indicate the number of punctuation marks you added. Be prepared to explain your choices.

Example: Too many staff members missed the seminar; therefore, future attendance will be mandatory.   **2**

1. A person with a watch knows what time it is, however, a person with two watches is never sure.   2

2. Our Reprographics Department is currently understaffed thus we are behind on our production schedule.   _____

3. We are, however, able to make single copies quickly.   2

4. The bill of lading did not match the order consequently the shipment was refused.   _____

5. Property may be insured in excess of its actual value; however, damages will be paid for no more than the actual loss.   2

6. Kelly did nevertheless pick up the printed copies she needed immediately.   _____

7. Ozana Costellano appears to be best qualified; on the other hand, Shanell Alexander has excellent recommendations.   2

8. Tracee considered the possibility of changing jobs but was unwilling to accept the risks involved.   _____

9. Kevin, on the other hand, changed jobs whenever the urge impelled him.   2

10. Your account is now three months overdue hence we have only one alternative left open to us.   _____

B. In the following sentences, insert commas and semicolons. In the space provided, indicate the number of punctuation marks you added. Be prepared to explain your choices.

Example: Some loans must be secured, therefore, the borrower must supply collateral.   **2**

1. Julie had years of on-the-job experience however she returned to school to learn new technologies and to improve her communications skills.   _____

2. Microwave relay stations have reduced telephone costs moreover cable and satellite circuits reduce costs even more.   _____

3. Our company is faced nevertheless with unusually expensive communication costs.   _____

4. We are drowning in information but starving for knowledge.   _____

5. Insurance is controlled by the law of averages thus increased losses send the average cost of premiums upward.   _____

6. The car came with an automatic transmission nevertheless it provided better-than-average gas mileage.   _____

7. We are moreover pleased with its maneuverability and handling.   _____

1. (2) it is; however, 2. (1) understaffed; 3. (2) are, however, 4. (2) order; consequently, 5. (2) value; however, 6. (2) did; nevertheless, 7. (2) qualified; on the other hand, 8. (0) 9. (2) Kevin, on the other hand, 10. (1) overdue;

Chapter 14 Conjunctions to Join Equals   **255**

8. A new directory will be released later in the month in the meantime use the old book and the information service. _____

9. Automobile repair costs are skyrocketing consequently car insurance costs are rising sharply. _____

10. Please place your order immediately or you will not be eligible for the discount. _____

11. Members of our management staff moreover are interested in hiring a consultant to train customer service personnel on the new equipment. _____

12. Data concerning cellular phone use was needed therefore Nokia conducted a survey. _____

13. We are mailing over 3,000 questionnaires to business organizations thus we will need a postal permit for metered mail. _____

14. We are currently using envelopes made from kraft paper and find that some of our deliveries are arriving in damaged condition. _____

15. ColorImage has produced on the other hand a program with remarkable graphic features and excellent accessibility. _____

16. The company gave each employee a holiday bonus therefore Christmas checks were considerably larger this year. _____

17. This apprenticeship program on the contrary combines classroom instruction with on-the-job training. _____

18. Sessions for business managers start on Tuesday but seminars for sales representatives do not begin until Wednesday. _____

C. Write compound sentences using the conjunctions shown below.

1. (*consequently* as a conjunctive adverb) _____

_____

2. (*consequently* as a parenthetical adverb) _____

_____

3. (*but* as a coordinating conjunction) _____

_____

4. (*nevertheless* as a conjunctive adverb) _____

_____

5. (*nevertheless* as a parenthetical adverb) _____

_____

Level III

A. **(Self-check)** Select the more effective version of each of the following pairs of sentences. Write its letter in the space provided.

1. (a) Either turn in your time sheet to your manager or to me.
   (b) Turn in your time sheet to either your manager or me. _____

2. (a) Cindy Conley is not able to represent us and neither is Marcelo Zavala.
   (b) Neither Cindy Conley nor Marcelo Zavala is able to represent us. _____

3. (a) Our objectives are both to improve customer relations and increasing sales.
   (b) Our objectives are both to improve customer relations and to increase sales. _____

4. (a) She neither called nor explained her absence. _____
   (b) Neither did she call nor explain her absence.

5. (a) Cheryl needed more time for her studies, so she asked for a part-time assign- _____
      ment.
   (b) Because Cheryl needed more time for her studies, she asked for a part-time
      assignment.

6. (a) Our new copier is not only faster but also cheaper. _____
   (b) Not only is our new copier faster, but it also is cheaper.

7. (a) Neither did the staff finish the proposals nor the contracts. _____
   (b) The staff finished neither the proposals nor the contracts.

8. (a) He has had no formal education, yet he is very well-read. _____
   (b) He has had no formal education; yet he is very well-read.

9. (a) A three-hour time difference separates us; so you should fax immediately. _____
   (b) A three-hour time difference separates us; therefore, you should fax immedi-
      ately.

10. (a) You must either e-mail or fax the proposal quickly. _____
    (b) Either you must e-mail or fax the proposal quickly.

Check your answers below.

B. Which of these sentence pairs is more effective?

1. (a) Either send the proposal to Tina Chang or to me. _____
   (b) Send the proposal either to Tina Chang or to me.

2. (a) Our travel counselor will both plan your trip and make your reservations. _____
   (b) Our travel counselor will both plan your trip and reservations will be made.

3. (a) We planned the event carefully; yet we exceeded our budget. _____
   (b) We planned the event carefully, yet we exceeded our budget.

4. (a) Not only does a product carry an expressed warranty, but it also carries an _____
      implied warranty.
   (b) A product carries not only an expressed warranty but also an implied warranty.

5. (a) We must receive either your payment or a reason for nonpayment. _____
   (b) We must either receive your payment, or you must give us a reason for non-
      payment.

C. Rewrite the following sentences to make them more effective.

1. Either bankruptcy can be declared by the debtor or it can be requested by the
   creditors.

   _____

   _____

2. Neither the staff was happy with the proposed cutbacks in class offerings, and
   nor were the students.

   _____

   _____

1. b 2. b 3. b 4. a 5. b 6. a 7. b 8. a 9. b 10. a

3. Not only do banks use computers to sort checks, but they also use computers for disbursing cash automatically.

_____

_____

4. Users of cell phones are often guilty of boorish behavior, so many restaurants and other public places have imposed bans on the devices.

_____

_____

_____

Editor's Challenge

The following e-mail message contains intentional errors representing spelling, proofreading, punctuation, and language principles covered thus far. You should mark 30 changes.

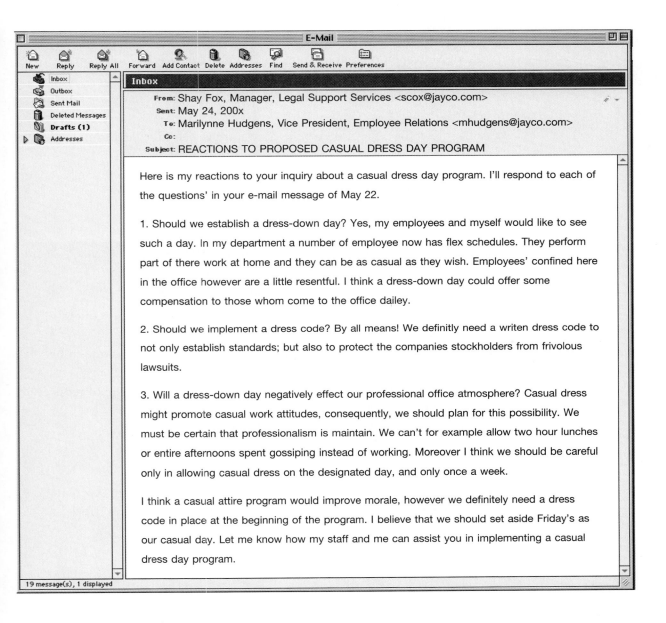

Goal: To learn about "cookies."

You've heard that "cookies" are dangerous and can be used to gather sensitive information from your computer. You decide to find out more.

1. With your Web browser on the screen, go to the Cookies and Privacy FAQ site of Netscape Communications Security **<http://www.cookiecentral.com/n_cookie_faq.htm>**.

2. Read over the FAQs (Frequently Asked Questions) and answers. Print three pages.

3. What are cookies? Can they be used to retrieve sensitive data from your computer?

4. End your session by clicking the **X** in the upper right corner of your browser. Turn in all printed pages and your answers.

POSTTEST

Add commas or semicolons to the following sentences.

1. We are having difficulty hiring qualified programmers consequently we must recruit overseas.

2. We are convinced nevertheless that our products will continue to be competitive in today's market.

3. We are searching for other suppliers and we are also trying to reduce transportation costs.

4. One supplier is located in the state of Washington however we have been unable to find anyone closer.

Underline the letter of the sentence that is more effective.

5. (a) Neither can we ship the printer nor the computer until April 1.
   (b) We can ship neither the printer nor the computer until April 1.

1. programmers; consequently, 2. convinced, nevertheless, 3. suppliers, and 4. Washington; however, 5. b

CHECKLIST OF BONUS LEARNING RESOURCES

The following additional learning resources are available to you. Your instructor will tell you which to complete.

- Web Editor's Challenge Exercise

- Web Interactive Chapter Review

- Web PowerPoint Slides

- Web Crossword Puzzle

- WebCheck Reinforcement Exercises 14.1, 14.2

- Self-Help Exercises

- Electronic Study Guide

chapter 15 Conjunctions to Join Unequals

Objectives

When you have completed the materials in this chapter, you will be able to do the following:

Level I

- Distinguish among phrases, dependent clauses, and independent clauses.
- Expand dependent clauses into complete sentences.

Level II

- Punctuate introductory and terminal dependent clauses.
- Punctuate parenthetical, essential, and nonessential dependent clauses.

Level III

- Recognize simple, compound, complex, and compound-complex sentences.
- Convert simple sentences into a variety of more complex patterns.

Insert appropriate commas in the following sentences. Mark *C* if correct.

1. When you finish this work, remember that you must back up all files.

2. If possible, we will stop work a little early on Friday.

3. The employee who submits the best suggestion will win the bonus trip.

4. We understand that Susan Jones, who works in Legal Services, will be leaving next month.

5. Although several applicants passed the test, no one has been hired yet.

In Chapter 14 you learned about conjunctions that joined equal sentence elements such as words, phrases, and clauses. These equal sentence parts were joined by co-ordinate conjunctions (such as *and, or, nor, but*), conjunctive adverbs (such as *therefore, however, consequently*), and correlative conjunctions (such as *either . . . or*). Now let's look at a special group of conjunctions that join unequal sentence parts.

L e v e l   I

Subordinating Conjunctions

To join unequal sentence elements, such as independent and dependent clauses, use *subordinating conjunctions*. A list of the most common subordinating conjunctions follows.

after	because	since	when
although	before	so that	where
as	if	that	whether
as if	in order that	unless	while
as though	provided	until	

You should become familiar with this list of conjunctions, but do not feel that you must at all times be able to recall every subordinating conjunction. Generally, you can recognize a subordinating conjunction by the way it limits, or subordinates, the clause it introduces. In the clause *because he always paid with cash*, the subordinating conjunction *because* limits the meaning of the clause it introduces. The clause is incomplete and could not stand alone as a sentence.

Independent and Dependent Clauses

Main clauses that can stand alone are said to be *independent*. They have subjects and verbs and make sense by themselves.

Business writing should be concise. (One main clause.)

Business writing should be concise, and it should be clear as well. (Two main clauses.)

Shauna Cox writes many e-mail messages, but Kathleen Young writes more letters. (Two main clauses.)

Clauses that cannot stand alone are said to be *dependent*. They have subjects and verbs, but they depend on other clauses for the completion of their meaning. Dependent clauses are often introduced by subordinating conjunctions.

When Ms. Cox wants a quick reply, she sends an e-mail message. (Dependent clause precedes the main clause.)

Since Ms. Young works with customers, she writes many letters. (Dependent clause precedes the main clause.)

Business letters are important because they represent the company. (Dependent clause, *because they represent the company*, comes after the main clause.)

Study Tip

Dependent clauses should never be written or punctuated as if they were complete sentences.

Relative Pronouns

The relative pronouns *who, whom, whose, which,* and *that* actually function as conjunctions when they introduce dependent clauses. *Who* is used to refer to persons. It may introduce essential or nonessential clauses. *That* refers to animals or things and should be used to introduce essential clauses. *Which* refers to animals or things and introduces nonessential clauses.

The tricky part is deciding whether a clause is essential or nonessential. Nonessential clauses contain information that the reader does not need to know; the main clause is understandable without this extra information. In some cases, only the writer knows whether a clause is intended to be essential or nonessential. If it is nonessential, it should be set off from the rest of the sentence by commas. You'll learn more about punctuating these sentences shortly.

Hot Link

If you have a fast Internet connection and a sound card, visit *SchoolHouse Rock* at **<http://genxtvland. simplenet.com/ SchoolHouseRock/ index-lo.shtml>**. Click on "Grammar Rock" for a cartoony look at parts of speech and catchy tunes.

Anyone *who* (not *that*) has a computer can create a Web site. (The relative pronoun *who* refers to a person, and it introduces an essential clause.)

A company *that* (not *who* or *which*) values its employees is likely to succeed. (The relative pronoun *that* introduces an essential clause.)

Software giant Microsoft, *which* is headquartered in Redmond, has many other offices in the state of Washington. (The relative pronoun *which* introduces a nonessential clause and is set off by commas.)

Microsoft is the company *that* (not *which*) is headquartered in Redmond. (The relative pronoun *that* introduces an essential clause and requires no commas.)

Lisa Meyers, *who* has excellent recommendations, is applying for a position in our department. (The relative pronoun *who* introduces a nonessential clause and is set off by commas.)

Now complete the reinforcement exercises for Level I.

L e v e l   I I

Punctuation of Sentences with Dependent Clauses

Business writers are especially concerned with clarity and accuracy. A misplaced or omitted punctuation mark can confuse a reader by altering the meaning of a sentence. The following guidelines for using commas help ensure clarity and consistency in writing. Some professional writers, however, take liberties with accepted conventions of punctuation, particularly in regard to comma usage. These experienced writers may omit a comma when they feel that such an omission will not affect the reader's understanding of a sentence. Beginning writers, though, are well advised to first develop skill in punctuating sentences by following traditional guidelines.

Introductory Dependent Clauses

Use a comma after a dependent (subordinate) clause that precedes an independent clause.

Before they left the office, they finished the proposal.

Until he returns, we cannot continue.

When you are ready to start, let me know.

Use a comma after an introductory dependent clause even though the subject and verb may not be stated.

As [it is] expected, the shipment is overdue.

If [it is] possible, send a replacement immediately.

When [they are] printed, your brochures will be distributed.

Terminal Dependent Clauses

Generally, a dependent clause introduced by a subordinating conjunction does not require a comma when the dependent clause falls at the end of a sentence.

They finished the proposal *before* they left the office.

We cannot continue *until* he returns.

Let me know *when* you are ready to start.

If, however, the dependent clause at the end of a sentence interrupts the flow of the sentence and sounds as if it were an afterthought, a comma should be used.

I know the canceled check was returned, *although* I cannot find it now.

We will ship the goods within the week, *if* that is satisfactory with you.

Parenthetical Clauses

Within sentences, dependent clauses that interrupt the flow and are unnecessary for the grammatical completeness of the sentence are set off by commas.

The motion, *unless* you want further discussion, will be tabled until our next meeting.

At our next meeting, *provided* we have a quorum, the motion will be reconsidered.

Relative Clauses

You learned earlier that the relative pronouns *who, that,* and *which* may introduce essential (restrictive) or nonessential (nonrestrictive) clauses. Remember that an essential clause is needed to identify the noun to which it refers; therefore no commas should separate this clause from its antecedent.

Any employee *who wants an August vacation* must apply soon. (The dependent clause is essential because it is needed to identify which employees must apply soon.)

Parking permits *that were issued in the fall* must be validated for the spring. (The dependent clause is essential because it is needed to identify which permits must be validated.)

A *nonessential clause* supplies additional information that is not needed to identify its antecedent; therefore, commas are used to separate the nonessential information from the rest of the sentence. Notice that *two* commas are used to set off internal nonessential dependent clauses.

Spot the Blooper

From classified ads in local newspapers: "LAWNMORE SHOP" and a house for sale with "walking closets."

Study Tip

Careful writers use the word *that* for essential clauses and the word *which* for nonessential clauses. Remember that dependent clauses introduced by *which* require commas.

Matt Ferranto, *who wants an August vacation*, must apply soon. (The antecedent of the dependent clause, Matt Ferranto, is clearly identified.)

Lot C parking permits, *which were issued in the fall*, must be validated for the spring. (The antecedent of the dependent clause is clearly identified.)

Punctuation Review

The following three common sentence patterns are very important for you to study and understand. Notice particularly how they are punctuated.

Independent clause() + { and / or / nor / but } + Independent clause. — (Comma used when a coordinating conjunction joins independent clauses.)

Independent clause() + { therefore, / consequently, / however, / nevertheless, } + Independent clause. — (Semicolon used when a conjunctive adverb joins independent clauses.)

{ Since / If / As / When } Dependent clause() + Independent clause. — (Comma used after a dependent clause introduced by a subordinate conjunction.)

Now complete the reinforcement exercises for Level II.

L e v e l   I I I

Sentence Variety

To make messages more interesting, good writers strive for variety in sentence structure. Notice the monotony and choppiness of a paragraph made up entirely of simple sentences:

Rena Pocrass founded a dessert business in 1995. She specialized in molded containers made of French chocolate. Her 350 designs were unique. She copyrighted them. Another chocolatier copied her spiral chocolate seashell. Rena sued. She won.

Compare the following version of this paragraph, which uses dependent clauses and other structures to achieve greater sentence variety:

Rena Pocrass, who founded a dessert business in 1995, specialized in molded containers made of French chocolate. Because her 350 designs were unique, she copyrighted them. When another chocolatier copied her spiral chocolate seashell, Rena sued and won.

Recognizing the kinds of sentence structures available to writers and speakers is an important step in achieving effective expression. Let's review the three kinds of sentence structures that you have been studying and include a fourth category as well.

Spot the Blooper

An advertisement from *Patient Information & News* [Edmonds, WA]: "Dentistry at it's best."

Kind of Sentence	Minimum Requirement	Example
Simple	One independent clause	Rena Pocrass founded a dessert business in 1995.
Compound	Two independent clauses	Rena founded a dessert business in 1995, and she specialized in molded containers of French chocolate.
Complex	One independent clause and one dependent clause	Rena Pocrass, who founded a dessert business in 1995, specialized in molded containers of French chocolate.
Compound-complex	Two independent clauses and one dependent clause	Rena's chocolate designs were copyrighted; therefore, when another chocolatier copied one, she sued and won.

Developing the ability to use a variety of sentence structures to facilitate effective communication takes practice and writing experience.

Now complete the reinforcement exercises for Level III.

HOTLINE QUERIES

Q: I don't think I'll ever be able to know the difference between *that* and *which*. They sound alike to me. Any advice for keeping them straight?

A: The problem usually is the substitution of *which* for *that*. Whenever you're tempted to use *which*, remember that it requires a comma. Think *which + comma*. If the sentence doesn't sound right with a comma, then you know you need *that*. One eminent language specialist, William Strunk, advised careful writers to go *which*-hunting and remove all defining *whiches*. Examples: *The lawn mower that is broken is in the garage* (defines which one). *The lawn mower, which is broken, is in the garage.* (Adds a fact about the only mower in question.)

Q: Can the word *that* be omitted from sentences? For example, *She said [that] she would come.*

A: The relative pronoun *that* is frequently omitted in conversation and casual writing. For absolute clarity, however, skilled writers include it.

Q: Is there some rule about putting periods in organization names that are abbreviated? For example, does *IBM* have periods?

A: When the names of well-known business, educational, governmental, labor, and other organizations or agencies are abbreviated, periods are normally not used to separate the letters. Thus, no periods would appear in IBM, ITT, UCLA, AFL-CIO, YWCA, or AMA. The names of radio and television stations and networks are also written without periods: Station WJR, KNX-FM, PBS, WABC-TV. Geographical abbreviations, however, generally do require periods: U.S.A., U.S.S.R., S.A. The two-letter state abbreviations recommended by the U.S. Postal Service require no periods: NY, OH, CA, MI, NJ, OR, MA, and so on.

Q: As a command, which is correct: *lay down* or *lie down*?

A: Commands are given in the present tense. You would never tell someone to *closed the door*, because commands are not given in the past tense. To say *lay down* (which is the past tense form of *lie*) is the same as saying *closed the door*. Therefore, use the present tense: *lie down*.

Q: In this sentence which word should I use? *Your order will be sent to you in the (later or latter) part of the week.*

A: Use *latter*. The word *latter* designates the second of two persons or things. In addition, *latter* can be used to mean "further advanced in time or sequence," or *latter* can be used to contrast with *former*. In your sentence, the *latter* part of the week contrasts with the *former* part of the week.

Q: We're having a sale on *nonChristmas* items. Should a hyphen follow *non*? In my dictionary the prefix *non* is not hyphenated when it is joined to other words.

A: A hyphen is not used when a prefix is joined to most words: *nonessential, prewar, unwelcome, anticlimax*. A hyphen is used, however, when a prefix is joined to a proper (capitalized) noun: *non-Christmas, pre-Columbian, un-Christian, anti-American*.

Q: I have a lot of trouble with verbs in sentences like this: *He is one of the 8 million Americans who (has or have) a drinking problem.*

A: You're not alone. Make your verb agree with its antecedent (*Americans*). One easy way to work with sentences like this is to concentrate on the clause that contains the verb: *Of the 8 million Americans who have a drinking problem, he is one.*

Name _____

Level I

A. (Self-check) Indicate whether the following word groups are phrases (*P*), independent clauses (*I*), or dependent clauses (*D*). (Remember that phrases do not have both subjects and verbs.)

Example: in the spring of the year   **P** _____

1. which is where I want to work   D _____
2. paralegals and administrative assistants worked together   ~~P~~I _____
3. at the crack of dawn to finish studying   ~~D~~P _____
4. as he stated earlier in the lecture   D _____
5. she answered immediately   I _____
6. recently they acquired an option to purchase the property   I _____
7. before anyone had an opportunity to examine it carefully   D _____
8. during the middle of the four-year fiscal period from 1998 through 2002   P _____
9. unless the human resources department rejects John's application   D _____
10. our new pricing schedule takes effect January 1   ~~P~~I _____

Check your answers below.

B. Indicate whether the following word groups are phrases (*P*), independent clauses (*I*), or dependent clauses (*D*). For the clauses, underline the subjects once and the verbs twice.

Example: until <u>we</u> <u><u>are</u></u> able to assess the damage   **D** _____

1. as you prepare for your employment interview   P _____
2. in order that employees may attend   D _____
3. many businesses sell services rather than products   I _____
4. on the first page of the Web site   ~~I~~ P _____
5. after he complimented Gregorio Morales's work   D _____
6. she swerved just in time   I _____
7. might have been considered   D _____
8. since Charles began working as a marketing representative   ~~I~~ D _____
9. Division Manager Kelsey analyzed the data   P ~~I~~ _____
10. during our lunch hour last week   ~~P~~I _____

C. After each sentence write the correct word in the space provided. Remember that the relative pronoun *which* should be used only to introduce nonessential clauses and, as such, requires commas.

1. We're shopping for software (which, that) we can use without customizing. _____

2. Is that the dog (who, that, which) frightened the mail carrier? _____

3. The IRS, (who, that, which) audits only 2 percent of all income tax returns, is choked with paperwork. _____

4. Any bank (who, that, which) adds an outside ATM can reduce the number of its inside tellers. _____

5. Our team, (who, that, which) has authority to set its own work schedules, tries to rotate the hardest jobs. _____

6. General Electronics is known as a company (who, that, which) emphasizes customer service. _____

7. I have a friend (who, that, which) cannot study alone. _____

8. Western rattlesnakes, (who, that, which) are the most common rattlers in the West, hibernate together in large numbers during the winter months. _____

9. We plan to use our new Web site as a research tool (who, that, which) will enhance our print coverage. _____

10. Employers are looking for workers (who, that, which) have good vocabularies, grammar, and manners. _____

D. Sort this group of words into three lists and write them below: and, however, if, but, moreover, although, nor, because, consequently, or, thus, since.

Coordinating Conjunctions	Conjunctive Adverbs	Subordinating Conjunctions
and	however	since
but	moreover	because
nor	consequently	although
or	thus	if

E. Writing Exercise. Use your imagination to write the following complete sentences. Remember that clauses must contain subjects and verbs.

1. A sentence using *and* to connect two independent clauses. _____

   _____

2. A sentence using *but* to connect two independent clauses. _____

   _____

3. A sentence using *because* to introduce a dependent clause. _____

   _____

4. A sentence using *although* to introduce a dependent clause. _____

   _____

5. A sentence using *after* to introduce a dependent clause. _____

   _____

A. (Self-check) Where appropriate, insert commas in the following sentences. In the space provided after each sentence, indicate the number of commas you have added to that sentence. Do not add any commas that you cannot justify.

Example: After we hiked to the summit, we pitched our tent.   **1** _____

1. Debra Bohlman, who just returned from two weeks in Hawaii, called me.   2 _____

2. As predicted, interest rates will climb during any period of inflation.   1 _____

3. Money for the child-care program, which included salaries for five teachers and three assistants, came from the federal government.   2 _____

4. A magazine that is featuring the 100 best places to work is now on the newsstands.   0 _____

5. Tiffany English, who was the top salesperson in the country, received a Porsche convertible as a bonus.   1 _____

6. Any salesperson who sells more than the weekly quota will receive a bonus.   0 _____

7. If possible, send the report that shows your current sales figures compared with last year's.   1 _____

8. The latest production model, unless it is drastically altered, looks as if it will be a winner.   2 _____

9. Please consider our budget deficit before you make a decision.   0 _____

10. A profit-sharing plan for employees is now available, although I believe the announcement will not be made until next week.   1 _____

Check your answers below.

B. Where appropriate, insert commas in the following sentences. In the space provided after each sentence, indicate the number of commas that you added. Be prepared to discuss the reasons for the commas you use.

1. Lynn Machen, who developed an innovative Web site, received the top award.   2 _____

2. A journalist who developed an innovative Web site received the top award.   0 _____

3. If you want a place in the sun, you may have to put up with a few blisters.   1 _____

4. We were notified that the computer server would be down for six hours, although we were not told why.   2 _____

5. I will edit and process the Microsoft order tomorrow morning, if that meets with your approval.   1 _____

6. When completed, the newly created Web site will enable customers to track shipments.   1 _____

7. All the information on my personal résumé, which I prepared myself, fills just one page.   2 _____

8. Although you said my order was shipped ten days ago, I have not yet received it.   1 _____

9. The warranty, that you refer to in your recent letter, covers only merchandise brought to our shop for repair.   2 _____

1. (2) Bohlman, Hawaii,   2. (1) predicted,   3. (2) program, assistants,   4. (0)   5. (2) English, country,   6. (0)
7. (1) possible,   8. (2) model, altered,   9. (0)   10. (1) available.

Chapter 15   Conjunctions to Join Unequals   **273**

10. Justin Edwards, who works in the Traffic Department, received last month's merit award. _2_

11. A secretary who joined our staff only two months ago received this month's merit award. _0_

_1_

12. Zone Improvement Program codes, which are better known as zip codes, are designed to expedite the sorting and delivery of mail. ___

13. I would like to give your suggestion more thought when I am not quite so preoccupied. _0_

14. The Senate will surely, when it convenes in its regular session, discuss campaign financing. _2_

15. Before you make a decision, consider carefully our strained financial condition. _1_

16. No additional tuition increases can be made, if I understand the legislation correctly. _1_

17. In order that we may complete the mailing quickly, the address list is being printed from our database. _1_

18. In the coming fiscal year, provided enough funds are available, we hope to expand our employee fitness program. _2_

19. The clerk who receives all orders, also sets the prices and makes the initial calculations. _1_

20. Marketers, that develop advertising, targeted at heavy users, are attempting to build brand loyalty. _2_

Level III

A. **(Self-check)** Indicate the structure of the following sentences by writing the appropriate letter in the spaces provided.

  a = simple sentence   c = complex sentence
  b = compound sentence   d = compound-complex sentence

Example: We expect to receive the price list shortly. _a_

  1. Our project manager suggested a daring marketing campaign. _A_

X 2. Since it passed the controversial ordinance, the city council has been besieged by calls. _B C_

X 3. A decision had to be made soon; therefore, a managers' meeting was scheduled for Monday. _A B_

X 4. We have no supplies, and other departments face a similar problem. _B_

  5. Allen was offered a sales position in Grand Rapids; therefore, he eagerly made plans to travel to Michigan, where he looked forward to beginning his sales career. _D_

X 6. The bank will charge a service fee unless you write fewer checks. _A C_

  7. The cost of the product increased, but sales continued to climb. _B_

  8. Although the letter was concise, its message was clear; moreover, it promoted goodwill. _D_

9. Laura Cooper, Lynn Seaman, My Bui, and Jane Bennett will be honored.

A

10. Because pictures are worth a thousand words, your report should include photos or graphics.

C

Check your answers below.

B. Rewrite the following groups of simple sentences into *one* sentence for each group. Add coordinating conjunctions, conjunctive adverbs, and subordinating conjunctions as needed to create more effective complex, compound, and compound-complex sentences.

> **Example:** Baskin-Robbins needed an executive assistant. It advertised in local newspapers. It finally hired a recent graduate. The graduate had excellent skills.
>
> **After advertising for an executive assistant in local newspapers, Baskin-Robbins finally hired a**
>
> **recent graduate who had excellent skills.**

1. Rusty was recently hired as a word processing specialist. She will work for DuPont. DuPont is located in Wilmington, Delaware.

   Rusty was recently hired to work for Dupont, located in Wilmington, Delaware, as a word processing specialist.

2. Each intern is assigned to a senior staff member. The staff member acts as a mentor. The staff member assists the intern with eventual job placement.

   Each intern is assigned to a senior staff member who acts as a mentor and assists with eventual job placement

3. Makers of the Rolls-Royce plan to open showrooms in Shanghai and Hong Kong. The world's largest market for Rolls-Royce is China.

   Maker of the Rolls-Royce, which largest market is China, plans to open showrooms in Shanghai and Hong Kong.

4. Cows will respond to beeps. Some Japanese ranchers learned of this phenomenon and equipped their cattle with pagers. Now they herd cattle with beepers. These ranchers need fewer workers as a result.

5. Skilled writers save time for themselves. They also save it for their readers. They organize their ideas into logical patterns. They do this before sitting down at their computers.

6. Nancy Burnett is a single parent. She has merchandising experience. Nancy started a mall-based chain of stores. These stores sell fashionable, durable clothing for children.

Editor's Challenge

The following memo contains intentional errors representing spelling, proofreading, punctuation, and language principles covered thus far. You should mark 35 changes.

Dee Kirkland Modeling and Dance Studios

MEMORANDUM

DATE: February 21, 200x

TO: Natali Aljaja   Stacy Janisse   Eduardo Solano
Robin Haynes   Mayer Rubin   Tom Winters

FROM: Dee Kirkland

SUBJECT: MARCH 1 FASHION SHOW AT WESTLAND PLAZA HOTEL

Thanks to all of you acceptional students for agreeing to participate in this years fashion show at the Westland Plaza Hotel.

Show time is 8:15 p.m., if possible you should be there at 6:30 to prepare. Rehearsals is scheduled for Tuesday, February 25, and Thursday, February 27, from 5 to 6:15 p.m. Its important for you to be promp!

Participants in the fashion show will not be payed, however, we have a bonus for you. Mr. Lon McHenry who is this years sponsor is one of those people who likes to encourage young models, so he will allow you to by any of the item in the show at 20 percent below his cost.

The cloths are all from CAL SPORT. Which specializes in informal fashions. Since shoes are not supplied everyone should bring there own casual shoes or tennis shoes.

Of all the students in the school, you were choosen to participate in the show because you have showed excellent potential and professionalism. I want you to treat this show like it was any professional paid job. This fashion show is bigger then any show in the area, please consider it a extension of your training. If you succeed here you can count on farther success as you grow in your career.

learning.web.ways

Goal: To learn about privacy policies.

1. With your Web browser on the screen, enter the URL for a search engine, such as **<www.google.com>**. Search for **"privacy policies."** Be sure to use the quotation marks.

2. Select a general article to read, such as "Privacy Policies Spread, but Privacy Doesn't" published by *PC World*.

3. What should a privacy policy include?

4. Inspect the privacy policies at three sites, such as retailer J. Crew **<http://www.jcrew.com>,** credit giant Equifax, **<http://www.equifax.com>,** and computer maker Sun Microsystems **<http://www.sun.com>**. You may have to look carefully to find a reference to a site's privacy policy. Which policy seemed most effective? Print two pages from the best policy.

5. End your session and submit your printout along with your answers.

POSTTEST

Insert appropriate commas in the following sentences. Mark *C* if the sentence is correct.

1. If the figures are available send them by e-mail to our Wichita branch office.

2. When necessary we make rush shipments of products that we have in our immediate inventory.

3. The demonstration by Victor Castro who represents Custom Software Systems will be Friday.

4. Any manager or employee who is unable to attend the Friday demonstration should call me.

5. Since many employees are interested in spreadsheets those programs will be discussed first.

CHECKLIST OF BONUS LEARNING RESOURCES

The following additional learning resources are available to you. Your instructor will tell you which to complete.

- Web Editor's Challenge Exercise

- Web Interactive Chapter Review

- Web PowerPoint Slides

- Web Crossword Puzzle

- WebCheck Reinforcement Exercises 15.1, 15.2

- Self-Help Exercises

- Electronic Study Guide

Unit Review Chapters 12–15

Name _____

Begin your review by rereading Chapters 12–15. Then test your comprehension of those chapters by completing the exercises that follow. Compare your responses with those provided at the end of the book.

Level I

In the blank provided, write the letter of the word or phrase that correctly completes each of the following sentences.

1. This is the (a) worse, (b) worst day I've ever had for computer crashes. _____

2. In comparing Papa John's and Pizza Palace, we decided that Pizza Palace's delivery service was (a) fastest, (b) faster. _____

3. If you need (a) a, (b) an example of her work, just look at her Web site. _____

4. The technician (a) could have, (b) could of repaired the equipment if he had had the parts. _____

5. Today's weather is (a) to, (b) too moist for the paint to dry. _____

6. We are fortunate to have exceptional employees like William and (a) him, (b) he. _____

7. We're seeking a bright young person (a) which, (b) whom we can train. _____

8. The group of words *if you will write us* is a(n) (a) phrase, (b) independent clause, (c) dependent clause. _____

Insert appropriate commas and semicolons in the following sentences. In the space provided, indicate the number of punctuation marks you added. Write *0* if you add none.

9. Nan Goodman came to Los Angeles in May but moved to Mississippi in July. _____

10. Hai Nguyen might be assigned to work in our legal office or he might be assigned to our administrative headquarters. _____

11. Stop at the crosswalk and look both ways. _____

12. Kristin wrote a chronological résumé but Cameron preferred a functional strategy for his résumé. _____

Level II

Write the letter of the word or phrase that correctly completes each sentence.

13. Before we proceed any (a) further, (b) farther, I must consult my attorney. _____

14. The search was conducted (a) house to house, (b) house-to-house. _____

15. If you have (a) less, (b) fewer than ten items, you may use the quick-check lane. _____

16. Mr. Jefferson said that we had done the work (a) satisfactorily, (b) satisfactory. _____

17. Power in our government is balanced (a) among, (b) between its three branches. _____

18. One of the computers must be moved (a) into, (b) in the outer office. _____

Insert appropriate commas and semicolons in the following sentences. In the space provided, indicate the number of marks you added.

19. Amy Major's paralegal service was an immediate success consequently she is considering opening a second office. _____

20. Before she started a serious job search Holly bought a book on résumés and designed hers to be computer scannable. _____

21. The employee who asked for a transfer will be moving to Atlanta. _____

22. Send all checks to Gina Caracas who is in charge of contributions. _____

23. As reported our division shows declining sales. _____

24. Management believes however that sales will pick up soon. _____

L e v e l   I I I

Write the letter of the word or phrase that correctly completes each sentence.

25. Los Angeles is larger than (a) any other city, (b) any city on the West Coast. _____

26. Examine carefully the (a) 50 first, (b) first 50 pages of the booklet. _____

27. Despite her meager income, Sally remained independent (a) of, (b) from her parents. _____

28. You will find that the test questions are not very different (a) than, (b) from the review questions. _____

29. The union asked that the salary increase be retroactive (a) to, (b) from the first of the year. _____

Insert appropriate commas and semicolons in the following sentences. In the space provided, indicate the number of marks you added.

30. If you want to create a good impression be sure to write a thank-you letter after a job interview. _____

31. When Pat Cramer joined our Michigan office sales immediately increased. _____

32. I was unable to locate the information you requested when you called our office last week. _____

33. Sales in your district have risen markedly moreover service requests are decreasing. _____

34. Although he had no use for bodyguards Elvis Presley is said to have had a very special use for two highly trained CPAs. _____

35. It has been said that the meek will inherit the earth however the strong will retain the mineral rights. _____

Hotline Review

36. She has _____ completed 34 units of credit in her program. _____
    a. all ready   b. already

37. After two years, every employee is entitled to a _____ vacation. _____
    a. two-week   b. two weeks

38. When you visit New York, be sure to spend _____ at the Metropolitan Museum of Art. _____
    a. sometime   b. some time

39. All _____ matters are now handled in human resources.   _____
    a. personnel   **b.** personal

40. Roger Allen _____ teaching the course in Tucson, Arizona.   _____
    a. maybe   **b.** may be

Memos and E-mail Messages

Memos and e-mail messages are increasingly important forms of internal communication for most companies today. Organizations are downsizing, flattening chains of command, forming work teams, and empowering rank-and-file employees. Given more power in making decisions, employees find that they need more information. They must collect, exchange, and evaluate information about the products and services they offer. Management also needs input from employees to respond rapidly to local and global market actions. This growing demand for information results in an increasing use of memos and especially e-mail. That's why anyone entering the business world today should know how to write good memos and e-mail messages.

Characteristics of Memos and E-mail Messages

Memos and e-mail messages have a number of characteristics in common:

- They begin with *To, From, Date*, and *Subject.*
- They generally cover just one topic.
- They are informal.
- They are concise.

Memos and e-mail messages use efficient standard formats, such as you see in Figure 15.1 on page 287. So that they can be acted on separately, memos and e-mail messages should discuss only one topic. Let's say you send your supervisor an e-mail message requesting a copier repair. You also tack on a comment about an article you want to appear in the company newsletter. The supervisor may act on one item and overlook the other. He might also want to forward your request for a copier repair directly to the operations manager, but he has to edit or rekey the message because of the second topic. Thus, memos and e-mail messages are most helpful when they cover just one subject.

Because they replace conversation, these messages tend to be informal. They may include first-person pronouns, such as *I* and *me*, as well as occasional contractions, such as *can't* or *haven't*. The tone, however, should not become familiar or unbusinesslike. Moreover, memos and e-mail messages should not be wordy. Concise messages save time and often are more easily understood than longer documents.

Writing Plan

For most informational and procedural messages, follow a direct writing plan that reveals the most important information first. Here are specific tips for writing the subject line, first sentence, body, and closing of memos and e-mail messages.

Subject Line. In the subject line, summarize the message. Although brief, a subject line must make sense and should capture the reader's interest. Instead of *Meeting,* for example, try *Meeting to Discuss Hiring Two New Employees.* A subject line is like a newspaper headline. It should snag attention, create a clear picture, and present an accurate summary. It should not be a complete sentence and should rarely occupy more than one line.

First Sentence. Although an explanation occasionally may precede the main idea, the first sentence usually tells the primary idea of the message. For example, an appropriate first sentence in a memo announcing a new vacation procedure follows:

> Here are new guidelines for employees taking two- or three-week vacations between June and September.

The opening of a memo may issue a polite command (*Please answer the following questions about . . .*), make a request (*Please begin research on a summer internship program*), or ask a question (*Can your department complete the printing of a . . .*). Try not to begin with a lengthy explanation. Get to the point as quickly as possible.

Skill Check 1 Opening Memos and E-mail Messages

Which subject line is better for a memo? Circle its letter.

1. a. SUBJECT: Inventory
   b. SUBJECT: Annual Pharmacy Inventory Scheduled for June 2

2. a. SUBJECT: This Memo Announces Revised Procedures for Applying for Dental Benefits
   b. SUBJECT: Revised Procedures for Dental Benefits Applications

Which opening sentence is better for a memo?

3. a. Employees interested in acquiring and improving computer skills are invited to an in-service training program beginning October 4.
   b. For some time now we have been thinking about the possibility of developing an in-service training program for some of our employees.

4. a. We have noticed recently a gradual but steady decline in the number of customer checking accounts.
   b. Please conduct a study and make recommendations regarding the gradual but steady decline of customer checking accounts.

5. Write a subject line for a memo that describes the possibility of a new sports scoreboard sponsored by Coca-Cola, a topic to be discussed at the next management council meeting.

_____

_____

6. Write a subject line for a memo announcing a demonstration of new software for all employees to be given Thursday, November 16.

_____

_____

Body of Message. Provide details of the message in the body. If you are asking for information, arrange your questions in a logical order. If you are providing information, group similar information together. Think about using side headings in bold print, such as you see in these paragraphs. They help readers understand, locate, and reference information quickly. You can also improve the readability of any message by listing items with numbers or bullets. Compare the two sets of instructions that follow:

Hard to Read

The instructions for operating our copy machine include inserting your meter in the slot, loading paper in the upper tray, and then copies are fed through the feed chute.

Improved

Here are instructions for using the copy machine:

- Insert your meter in the slot.
- Load paper in the upper tray.
- Feed copies through the feed chute.

Notice that all the items in the preceding bulleted list are parallel in construction. That means that each item uses the same form. All begin with verbs. This kind of balanced writing helps readers anticipate and understand information more readily.

Skill Check 2 Listing Information

In the space provided, revise the following paragraph so that it includes an introductory sentence and a list of four items.

> We are trying to improve budget planning, and we'd also like to control costs. To accomplish these goals, we must change our procedures for submitting requests in the future for outside printing jobs. The new procedures include first determining your exact printing specifications for a particular job. Then we want you to obtain two estimates for the job. These estimates should be submitted in writing to Kelly. Finally, you may place the outside print order—but only after receiving approval.

_____

_____

_____

_____

_____

_____

Closing a Memo or an E-mail Message. Memos and e-mail messages frequently end with a (a) request for action, (b) summary of the message, or (c) closing thought. If action on the part of the reader is sought, be sure to spell out that action clearly. A vague request such as *Drop by to see this customer sometime* is ineffective because the reader may not understand exactly what is to be done. A better request might be worded as follows: *Please make an appointment to see Rebecca Johnson before June 2 when she will be leaving.* Notice that an *end date* is given. This technique, particularly when coupled with a valid reason, is effective in prompting people to act.

Another way to close an internal message is by summarizing its major points. A closing summary is helpful if the message is complicated. When no action request is made and a closing summary is unnecessary, the writer may prefer to end the memo with a simple closing thought, such as *I'll appreciate your assistance, What do you think of this proposal?* or *Call me if I may answer questions.* Avoid tired, mechanical phrases such as *Don't hesitate to call on me,* or *Thank you for your cooperation.* If you wish to express these thoughts, find a fresh way to say them.

Figure 15.1 shows how the four parts of a writing plan combine to create a readable, efficient interoffice memo. For more information on memo and e-mail formats, see Appendix C.

Special Tips for Sending E-mail Messages

Instead of using paper to send memos, increasing numbers of businesspeople are turning to e-mail to send internal and external messages. To make the best use of e-mail, you may wish to implement the following suggestions:

Compose off line. Instead of dashing off hasty messages on line, take the time to compose off line. Consider using your word processing program and then uploading your message to the e-mail network. This avoids "self-destructing" on line (losing all your writing through some glitch or pressing the wrong key).

Get the address right. E-mail addresses are sometimes complex, often illogical, and always unforgiving. Omit one character or misread the letter *l* for the number *1*, and your message bounces. Solution: Use your electronic address book for people you write to frequently. And double-check every address that you key in manually. Also be sure that you don't reply to a group of receivers when you intend to answer only one.

Keep lines, paragraphs, and messages short. Try to keep your lines under 65 characters in length and your paragraphs no longer than eight lines. Above all, keep your message short. If it requires more than three screens, consider sending it in hard-copy form.

Care about correctness. Senders and receivers of e-mail tend to be casual about spelling, grammar, and usage. However, people are still judged by their writing; and you never know how far your message will travel. Read and edit any message before hitting the "Send" button!

Don't send anything you wouldn't want published. Because e-mail seems like a telephone call or a person-to-person conversation, writers sometimes send sensitive, confidential, inflammatory, or potentially embarrassing messages. Beware! E-mail creates a permanent record that often does not go away even when deleted. And every message is a corporate communication that can be used against you or your employer. Don't write anything that you wouldn't want your boss, your family, or a judge to read.

Special Tips for Replying to E-mail Messages

Scan all messages in your inbox before replying to each individually. Because subsequent messages often affect the way you respond, read them all first (especially all those from the same individual).

Don't automatically return the sender's message. When replying, cut and past the relevant parts. Avoid irritating your recipients by returning the entire "thread" (sequence of messages) on a topic.

Revise the subject line if the topic changes. When replying or continuing an e-mail exchange. revise the subject line as the topic changes.

Finally, remember that office computers are meant for work-related communication. Don't use company computers for personal matters. Unless your company specifically allows it, never use your employer's computers for personal messages, personal shopping, or entertainment. Assume that all e-mail is monitored. Employers legally have the right to eavesdrop on employee e-mail messages, and many do.

Figure 15.1 Interoffice Memo

TO: Michelle Young, Legal Services Department

FROM: Rasheed Polk, Human Resources Department

DATE: May 14, 200x

SUBJECT: Change in Job-Advertising Procedures

Effective today, all advertisements for departmental job openings should be routed through the Human Resources Department. — **Introduces main idea directly.**

A major problem resulted from the change in hiring procedures implemented last month. Each department has been placing newspaper advertisements for new-hires individually, when all such requests should be centralized in this office. To process applications more efficiently, please follow this procedure: — **Explains why change in procedure is necessary.**

1. Write an advertisement for a position in your department.

2. Let Human Resources place the ad in an appropriate newspaper. — **Presents new procedure in parallel list.**

3. Pick up applicant folders from Human Resources the day following the closing date provided in the ad.

Following these guidelines will save you work and will also enable Human Resources to help you fill your openings more quickly. Call Ann Edmonds at Ext. 351 if you have questions about this procedure. — **Summarizes benefits and names contact person.**

Writing Application 4.1

On a separate sheet of paper or, preferably, at a computer, revise the following poorly written memo. It suffers from wordiness, indirectness, and confusing instructions. Include a numbered list in your revised memo, and be sure to improve the subject line.

TO: All Staff Members

FROM: Roy Minami, Manager

DATE: July 11, 200x

SUBJECT: COPIER RULES

Some of you missed the demonstration of the operation of our new Turbo X copier last week. I thought you might appreciate receiving this list of suggestions from the salesperson when she gave the demonstration. This list might also be helpful to other employees who saw the demo but didn't take notes and perhaps can't remember all these pointers. It's sometimes hard to remember how to operate a machine when you do it infrequently. Here's what she told us to do. There are two paper loading trays. Load 8 1/2-X-11-inch or 8 1/2-X-14-inch paper in the two loading trays. The paper should curve upward in the tray. You should take your copy and feed it into the machine face up. However, if you have small sheets or book pages or cut-and-pasted copy, lift the copier door and place your copy face down on the glass.

Before you begin, select the number of copies to be made by pressing the touch selector panel. Don't push too hard. If copies become jammed, open the front door and see where the paper got stuck in the feed path. Remove jammed paper. Oh yes, your meter must be inserted before the machine will operate. We urge you, of course, to make only as many copies as you really need. Keep this list to use again.

Don't hesitate to call on me if you need a private demonstration.

Writing Application 4.2

As Jennifer Tovar, manager, Reprographic Services, write an e-mail message to Kevin Suzuki, manager, Technical Services. You are very worried that one of the computers of your operators may be infected with a virus. The computer belongs to Jackie Jimenez. Jackie says that each time she opens a previously stored document in her Word program, the contents of the document are immediately deleted. Fortunately, because Jackie has backup files, she hasn't lost anything yet. But obviously she can't go on using this computer. You plan to assign Jackie some temporary tasks for the rest of the day; however, she must have her computer up and running by tomorrow. You want a technician to inspect her machine before 5 p.m. today. You know that Kevin likes to learn as much about a computer problem as possible before he sends a technician, so include sufficient details to help him identify the problem.

Writing Application 4.3

As Garth M. Scavone, manager of the Customer Services Division, Milwaukee Breweries, write an e-mail message to Melissa Miller, supervisor, Customer Services. Ask Melissa to draft a form letter that can be sent to groups requesting plant tours. In your memo, explain that the brewery has always encouraged tour groups to see your home plant brewery. However, you cannot sponsor tours at this time because of extensive remodeling. You are also installing a new computer-controlled bottling system. Tours are expected to resume in September. You need a form letter that can be sent to all groups but that can be personalized for individual responses. You want the letter draft by Monday, April 6. The letter should build good customer relations, a primary goal of your tour policy. The letter might enclose a free product coupon and a brochure picturing your operations. Tell Melissa to add any information that she feels would improve the letter.

unit 5 Punctuating Sentences

chapter 16
Commas

Objectives

When you have completed the materials in this chapter, you will be able to do the following:

Level I

- Correctly place commas in series, direct address, and parenthetical expressions.
- Use commas correctly in punctuating dates, addresses, geographical items, and appositives.

Level II

- Place commas correctly in punctuating independent adjectives, verbal phrases, and prepositional phrases.
- Use commas correctly in punctuating independent, introductory, terminal, and nonessential clauses.

Level III

- Use commas correctly in punctuating degrees, abbreviations, and numerals.
- Use commas to indicate omitted words, contrasting statements, clarity, and short quotations.

Insert appropriate commas in the following sentences.

1. Our records, Mr. Thomas, indicate that your order was received May 3 and shipped May 6.

2. We have suppliers in Akron, Ohio, and in Denver, Colorado.

3. The attorney had reason to believe, by the way, that the judge was not impartial and might be biased against this case.

4. The information revolution may be responsible for the biggest peacetime economic boom in history, but keeping up with the digital flow means being chained to your computer.

5. Although tired, employees preferred the evening, not the morning, in-service training programs.

1. records, Mr. Thomas,   2. Akron, Ohio, Denver,   3. believe, way,   4. history,   5. tired, evening, morning,

When you talk with a friend, you are probably unaware of the "invisible" commas, periods, and other punctuation marks that you are using. In conversation your pauses and voice inflections punctuate your thoughts and clarify your meaning. In writing, however, you must use a conventional set of symbols, punctuation marks, to help your reader understand your meaning.

Over the years we have gradually developed a standardized pattern of usage for all punctuation marks. This usage has been codified (set down) in rules that are observed by writers who wish to make their writing as precise as possible. As noted earlier, some professional writers may deviate from conventional punctuation practices. In addition, some organizations, particularly newspapers and publishing houses, maintain their own style manuals to establish a consistent "in-house" style.

The punctuation guidelines presented in this book represent a consensus of punctuation styles that are acceptable in business writing. Following these guidelines will enable you to write with clarity, consistency, and accuracy.

Level I

Basic Guidelines for Using Commas

The most used and misused punctuation mark, the comma, indicates a pause in the flow of a sentence. *Not all sentence pauses, however, require commas.* It is important for you to learn the standard rules for the use of commas so that you will not be tempted to clutter your sentences with needless, distracting commas. Here are the guidelines for basic comma usage.

Series

Commas are used to separate three or more equally ranked (coordinate) elements (words, phrases, or short clauses) in a series. A comma before the conjunction ensures separation of the last two items. No commas are used when conjunctions join all the items in a series.

Only in June, July, and August is a lifeguard available. (Series of words. Notice that a comma precedes *and*, but no comma follows the last item, *August*.)

Wireless technology enables you to respond to customers' requests, change sales forecasts, and manage suppliers even when you are away from the office. (Series of phrases.)

Mr. Horton is the owner, Ms. Travis is the marketing manager, and Miss Savala is the executive assistant. (Series of clauses.)

We need wireless access to e-mail and Web sites and the home office. (No commas needed when conjunctions are repeated.)

Direct Address

Words and phrases of direct address are set off with commas.

You must agree, *Mr. James*, that Luis has done outstanding work.

I respectfully request, *sir*, that I be transferred.

Parenthetical Expressions

Parenthetical words, phrases, and clauses may be used to create transitions between thoughts. These expressions interrupt the flow of a sentence and are unessential to its grammatical completeness. These commonly used expressions, some of which are listed below, are considered unessential because they do not answer specifically questions such as *when? where? why?* or *how?* Set off these expressions with commas.

accordingly	hence	namely
all things considered	however	needless to say
as a matter of fact	in addition	nevertheless
as a result	incidentally	no doubt
as a rule	in fact	of course
at the same time	in my opinion	on the contrary
by the way	in other words	on the other hand
consequently	in the first place	otherwise
for example	in the meantime	therefore
furthermore	moreover	under the circumstances

In addition, your computer skills are excellent. (At beginning of sentence.)

This report is not, *however*, one that must be classified. (Inside sentence.)

You have checked with other suppliers, *no doubt*. (At end of sentence.)

The words in question are set off by commas only when they are used parenthetically and actually interrupt the flow of a sentence.

However the vote goes, we will abide by the result. (No comma needed after *however*.)

We have *no doubt* that our Web site must be revamped. (No commas needed to set off *no doubt*.)

Don't confuse short introductory essential prepositional phrases for parenthetical expressions. Notice that the following phrases are essential and, therefore, require no commas.

In the summer the size of our staff declines. (No comma is needed because the short prepositional phrase answers the question *when?*)

At our Madison branch we will hire additional personnel. (No comma is needed because the short prepositional phrase answers the question *where?*)

For this reason we will be lowering our wholesale prices. (No comma is needed because the short prepositional phrase answers the question *why?*)

With your help our production team can meet its goal. (No comma is needed because the short prepositional phrase answers the question *how?*)

Dates, Addresses, and Geographical Items

When dates, addresses, and geographical items contain more than one element, the second and succeeding elements are normally set off by commas. Study the following illustrations.

- **Dates**

  On January 3 we opened for business. (No comma needed for one element.)

  On January 3, 2001, we opened for business. (Two commas set off second element.)

  On Monday, January 3, 2001, we opened for business. (Commas set off second and third elements.)

  In June, 2001, the reorganization was effected. (Commas set off second element.)

  Note: In June 2001 the reorganization was effected. (This alternate style is acceptable in writing the month and year only.)

- **Addresses**

  Send the software to Mr. Chun Wong, 1639 East 69 Street, Cleveland, Ohio 44116, before Tuesday. (Commas are used between all elements except the state and zip code, which are in this special instance to be considered a single unit.)

- **Geographical items**

  He moved from Nashville, Tennessee, to Chicago, Illinois. (Two commas set off the state unless it appears at the end of the sentence.)

Appositives

You will recall that appositives rename or explain preceding nouns or pronouns. An appositive that provides information not essential to the identification of its antecedent should be set off by commas.

Debbie Robinson, *the DataMax sales representative*, is here. (The appositive adds nonessential information; commas set it off.)

The sales representative *Debbie Robinson* is here to see you. (The appositive is needed to identify which sales representative has arrived; therefore, no commas are used.)

One-word appositives do not require commas.

My husband *Kevin* sometimes uses my computer.

Now complete the reinforcement exercises for Level I.

Study Tip

In separating cities and states and dates and years, many writers remember the initial comma but forget the final one (*my friend from Albany, New York, called*).

Spot the Blooper

From *The Union-Leader* [Manchester, NH]: "Prince Louis Ferdinand of Prussia, a grandson of Germany's last emperor who worked in a Detroit auto plant in the 1930s and later opposed Nazi dictator Adolf Hitler, has died at age 86." [Could a comma help clarify who worked in the auto plant? Would the idea be better expressed in two sentences?]

Level II

Special Guidelines for Using Commas

At this level we will review comma usage guidelines that you studied in previous chapters, and we will add one new guideline.

Independent Adjectives

Separate two or more adjectives that equally modify a noun (see Chapter 12).

Online customers can conduct *secure, real-time* banking transactions.

We're looking for an *industrious, ambitious* person to hire.

Hot Link

For a chatty, online discussion of commas, go to "Commas: They're Not Just for English Majors Anymore" **<http://parallel.park.uga.edu/~sigalas/Commas/ie.html>**.

Introductory Verbal Phrases

Verbal phrases (see Chapter 11) that precede main clauses should be followed by commas.

> *To qualify for the position*, you must have two years' experience.
>
> *Climbing quickly*, the hikers reached the summit by noon.

Prepositional Phrases

One or more introductory prepositional phrases totaling five or more words should be followed by a comma.

> *In the spring of the year*, our thoughts may be diverted from academics.
>
> *For a period of six months*, a new employee is on probation.

Introductory prepositional phrases of fewer than five words require *no* commas.

> *In August* that stock reached its highest price.
>
> *In some instances* a single parent must work alternate hours.

Prepositional phrases in other positions do not require commas when they are essential and do not interrupt the flow of the sentence.

> We have installed *in our Chicago office* a centralized telecommunications system. (No commas are needed around the prepositional phrase because it answers the question *where?* and does not interrupt the flow of the sentence.)
>
> You may *at your convenience* complete the Adams project. (No commas are needed because the prepositional phrase answers the question *when?* and does not interrupt the flow of the sentence.)

Independent Clauses

When a coordinating conjunction (see Chapter 14) joins independent clauses, use a comma before the coordinating conjunction, unless the clauses are very short.

> In Japan the wireless Internet has become wildly successful, and companies are pushing for even more sophisticated services.

Introductory Clauses

Dependent clauses that precede independent clauses are followed by commas.

> *When you have finished*, please return the style manual.
>
> *If you need help*, please call me in the afternoon.
>
> *Since we need more clerks*, we will begin advertising.

Terminal Dependent Clauses

Use a comma before a dependent clause at the end of a sentence only if the dependent clause is an afterthought.

Please return the style manual *when you have finished*. (No comma needed.)

I plan to leave at 3:30, *if that meets with your approval*. (Dependent clause added as an afterthought.)

Nonessential Clauses

Use commas to set off clauses that are used parenthetically or that supply information unneeded for the grammatical completeness of a sentence.

> An increase in employee benefits, *as you can well understand*, must be postponed until profits improve.
>
> We received a letter from Anne Diga, *who is now living in Anchorage, Alaska*.

Do *not* use commas to set off clauses that contain essential information.

> A student *who is studying English* certainly needs an up-to-date dictionary. (No commas are necessary because the italicized clause is essential; it tells what student needs an up-to-date dictionary.)

Now complete the reinforcement exercises for Level II.

Level III

Additional Guidelines for Using Commas

The last guidelines for commas include suggestions for punctuating degrees, abbreviations, numerals, omitted words, contrasting statements, and short quotations.

Degrees and Abbreviations

Except for *Jr.* and *Sr.*, degrees, personal titles, and professional designations following individuals' names are set off by commas.

> John T. O'Dell Jr. is frequently confused with John T. O'Dell Sr.
>
> Dana Fladhammer, M.D., has a flourishing practice in Tempe, Arizona.
>
> Judith Lounsbury, Ph.D., discussed degree requirements with the college president.
>
> We have retained Robin Cittenden, Esq., to represent us.

The abbreviations *Inc.* and *Ltd.* are set off by commas if the company's legal name includes the commas.

> Blackstone & Smythe, Inc., exports goods worldwide. (Company's legal name includes comma.)
>
> Shoes Inc. operates at three locations in Tampa. (Legal name does not include comma before *Inc.*)

Numerals

Unrelated figures appearing side by side should be separated by commas.

> By 2004, 1.3 billion subscribers will be using wireless devices worldwide.
>
> A total of 150, 2001 graduates attended the reception.

Spot the Blooper

From *The Pacifica Tribune* [Pacifica, CA]: "The land was eventually sold to Andy Oddstad who built homes and also became the site of Linda Mar Shopping Center."

Study Tip

The *Chicago Manual of Style* (14th Edition) recommends that *Jr.*, *Sr.*, *II*, and *III* no longer be set off by commas.

Numbers of more than three digits require commas.

    1,760   47,950   6,500,000

However, calendar years and zip codes are written without commas within the numerals.

| Calendar Years: | 1776 | 2001 | 2004 |
| Zip Codes: | 02116 | 45327 | 90265 |

Telephone numbers, house numbers, decimals, page numbers, serial numbers, and contract numbers are also written without commas within the numerals.

Telephone Number:	(212) 555-4432
House Number:	20586 Victory Avenue
Decimal Number:	.98651, .0050
Page Number:	Page 1356
Serial Number:	36-5710-1693285763
Contract Number:	No. 359063420

Omitted Words

A comma is used to show the omission of words that are understood.

Last summer we hired 12 employees; this summer, only 3 employees. (Comma shows omission of *we hired* after *summer*.)

Contrasting Statements

Commas are used to set off contrasting or opposing expressions. These expressions are often introduced by such words as *not, never, but,* and *yet.*

The nominating committee selected Mr. Durell, not Mr. Monroe, as its representative. (Two commas set off contrasting statement that appears in the middle of a sentence.)

Our budget for equipment this year is reduced, yet quite adequate.

The harder our staff works, the further behind we seem to get. (One comma sets off contrasting statement that appears at the end of a sentence.)

Clarity

Commas are used to separate words repeated for emphasis and words that may be misread if not separated.

Susan Keegan said that it was a very, very complex contract.

Whoever goes, goes at his or her own expense.

No matter what, you know you have our support.

In business, time is money.

Spot the Blooper

From *The Boston Globe*: "Then her hair caught fire while sitting in a front seat during a fireworks display."

Short Quotations

A comma is used to separate a short quotation from the rest of a sentence. If the quotation is divided into two parts, two commas are used.

Study Tip

Here's a good rule to follow in relation to the comma: *When in doubt, leave it out!*

Alice Beasley said, "The deadline for the ATI contract is June 6."

"The deadline for the ATI contract," said Alice Beasley, "is June 6."

Now complete the reinforcement exercises for Level III.

HOTLINE QUERIES

Q: My boss always leaves out the comma before the word *and* when it precedes the final word in a series of words. Should the comma be used?

A: Although some writers omit that comma, present practice favors its use so that the last two items in the series cannot be misread as one item. For example, *The departments participating are Engineering, Accounting, Personnel, and Human Resources.* Without that final comma, the last two items might be confused as one item.

Q: Should I use a comma after the year in this sentence: *In 1999 we began operations?*

A: No. Commas are not required after short introductory prepositional phrases unless confusion might result without them. If two numbers, for example, appear consecutively, a comma would be necessary to prevent confusion: *In 1999, 156 companies used our services.*

Q: Are these three words interchangeable: *assure, ensure,* and *insure?*

A: Although all three words mean "to make secure or certain," they are not interchangeable. *Assure* refers to persons and may suggest setting someone's mind at *rest (let me assure you that we are making every effort to locate it). Ensure* and *insure* both mean "to make secure from loss," but only *insure* is now used in the sense of protecting or indemnifying against loss (*the building and its contents are insured*).

Q: It seems to me that the word *explanation* should be spelled as *explain* is spelled. Isn't this unusual?

A: Many words derived from root words change their grammatical form and spelling. Consider these: *maintain, maintenance; repeat, repetition; despair, desperate, desperation; pronounce, pronunciation.*

Q: Is *appraise* used correctly in this sentence? *We will appraise stockholders of the potential loss.*

A: No. Your sentence requires *apprise,* which means "to inform or notify." The word *appraise* means "to estimate" (*he will appraise your home before you set its selling price*).

Q: Is an apostrophe needed in this sentence? *The supervisor('s) leaving early on Thursday prevented us from finishing the job by Friday.*

A: The apostrophe is needed: *the supervisor's leaving . . .* The word *leaving* is a verbal noun (a gerund), and its modifier must be possessive. Other examples are: *the boy's whistling, the lion's roaring, my friend's driving.*

Q: Which word is correct in this sentence? *The officer (cited, sited, sighted) me for speeding.*

A: Your sentence requires *cited*, which means "to summon" or "to quote." *Site* means "a location," as in *a building site. Sight* means "a view" or "to take aim," as in *the building was in sight.*

Name _____

Level I

A. (Self-check) Insert necessary commas. In the space provided, indicate briefly the reason for the comma (for example, *series, parenthetical, direct address, date, address, essential appositive*, and so forth). Write *C* if the sentence is correct.

Example: We believe, on the contrary, that we are underfunded.   parenthetical

1. Monday, January 14, 2001, is the most important date in the history of our company.   *Date*

2. Hong Kong is, on the other hand, one of the most densely populated areas in the world.   _____

3. The Small Business Administration named Alaska, South Dakota, and New Hampshire, as the states most friendly to entrepreneurs.   _____

4. Denise lived in Palm Springs, California, before she began working in Seattle, Washington.   _____

5. Your student Troy Adkins called this morning.   _____

6. Emily Hale, your business English student, also called.   _____

7. In the winter, we always hire additional personnel in the warehouse and in the office.   _____

8. Your car, Mr. Takeda, is not properly registered.   _____

9. We have no doubt that such practices are widespread.   _____

10. Organize your thoughts and jot down some notes and then keyboard the letter from your notes.   _____

Check your answers below.

B. Insert necessary commas. In the space provided, indicate briefly the reason for the comma (for example, *series, parenthetical, direct address, date, address, essential appositive*, and so forth). Write *C* if the sentence is correct.

1. Under the circumstances, we cannot promise any faster connections to the Internet.   *Parenthetical*

2. Send the Web-enabled cell phone to Ms. Denise Hourihan, 1000 Henrietta Road, Rochester, NY 14623, as soon as possible.   *Address*

3. Nancy Stewart, our former office manager, is now a CEO in the Southwest.   *Appositive*

4. We recognize, of course, that the speed of wireless connections to the Internet is slower than that of computer hookups.   *Parenthetical*

5. In June we asked employees to offer compliments, criticism, and suggestions as feedback to management.   *Series*

6. We feel, however, that a job transfer would be appropriate.   *Parenthetical.*

7. I understand that your brother Gary is pleased with his new smart phone.

   Appositive (handwritten)

8. It is a pleasure to announce that our new wireless phone allows you to download, store, and play songs from the Internet.

   Series C (handwritten)

9. For you, Mr. Estrada, we have a three months' subscription to *Forbes*.

   Direct Address (handwritten)

10. Horst Werner joined the staff in April 1998.

    C (handwritten)

11. It is necessary, consequently, for you to pay the return postage.

    Parenthetical (handwritten)

12. Kari Abrams, who is a student at Mercer Community College, is studying office information systems.

    Appositive (handwritten)

13. In the meantime, we must make alternate flight reservations.

    Parenthetical (handwritten)

14. The special fares, by the way, are available only until July 1.

    Parenthetical (handwritten)

15. Tanya Collins is president, Jason Schumacher is vice president, and Sherry Gonzalez is secretary.

    Series (handwritten)

C. Insert necessary commas. In the space provided for each sentence, write the number of commas that you inserted. If the sentence is correct, write *C*. Be prepared to explain each comma.

1. I wonder, Ms. Gilford, when it is best to visit the San Antonio, Texas, resort hotels. _____

2. My cousin George will arrive Monday, July, 17 from Dayton, Ohio. _____

3. Allison calculated employee benefits, Jennifer managed the payroll, and Todd processed all accounts receivable and payable. _____

4. Damon Washington, the chief security officer, responded to a disturbance that awoke nearly everyone in the building at 1:30 a.m. _____

5. With your assistance, we should be able to finish the report by Friday, April 4. _____

6. Send the software to Ms. Pat McMahon, 15800 State Street, Holland, Illinois 60473, before January 1. _____

7. For that reason, our next sales letter, of course, must target key decision-makers. _____

8. In the meantime, our sales letter must include more than facts, testimonials, and guarantees. _____

9. Incidentally, we have shipped your wood sample to our designers in Portland, Oregon, and Tampa, Florida, for their inspection. _____

10. Employees may choose from aerobics, ballroom dancing, and yoga classes offered at the company gym. _____

11. I have no doubt in my mind about his competency and integrity. _____

12. Our analysis, Mr. and Mrs. Carter, shows that you owe additional taxes for 1998, 1999, and 2000. _____

13. I noticed on our company Web site, by the way, that your friend Charles was promoted. _____

14. Phillip Johnson, the eminent East Coast architect, studied our needs, developed a plan, and designed our office complex. _____

15. The architect Phillip Johnson was recently featured in *Architectural Digest*. _____

A. (Self-check) Insert necessary commas. In the space provided, indicate briefly the reason for the comma (for example, *independent adjectives, introductory verbal phrase, independent clauses,* and so forth). Write *C* if the sentence is correct.

Example: Jeremy made several constructive, imaginative suggestions.

independent adjectives

1. To succeed in life, you must be willing to fail.

IVP   IVP

2. At the end of each fiscal year, we prepare a progress report.

PP

3. By January, we are able to predict with considerable accuracy the year's profits.

C

4. It takes 43 muscles to frown, but it takes only 17 to smile.

IC

5. If the telephone is not answered by the third ring, we risk lost sales.

Intro Cl

6. We risk lost sales if the telephone is not answered by the third ring.

C

7. The work in this office is strictly confidential, as I am sure you are well aware.

DC, Afterthought

8. The person who answers the telephone sounds alert and responsive.

C

9. Dr. Morris Edelson plans to attend the conference in London, and later he expects to vacation in Europe.

IC

10. When you have completed this exercise, you are to check your answers.

Intro CL

Check your answers below.

B. Insert necessary commas. In the space provided, indicate briefly the reason for the comma (for example, *independent adjectives, introductory verbal phrase, introductory clause,* and so forth). Write *C* if the sentence is correct.

1. Today's consumers are searching for reliable, economical cars.

Independent Adj

2. Agreeing to serve as our leader, Frances Sheppard worked with students and faculty to devise an online learning program.

Intro Clause

3. If I were you, I would take a part-time job and continue school.

IVP Intro Clause

4. In 1998 Dr. Aragon traveled to Africa, and in 2000 she visited Asia.

Independent Clause

5. When you need a mortgage loan, please check our Web site for competitive rates.

Intro Clause

6. Patty Hall, who founded a chain of computer stores, addressed our class.

non-essential clause

7. A businessperson who founded a chain of computer stores addressed our class.

C

1. life, (intro. verbal phrase)   2. year, (long intro. prep. phrase)   3. C   4. frown, (independent clauses)   5. ring, (introductory clause)   6. C   7. confidential, (dependent clause, afterthought)   8. C   9. London, (independent clauses)   10. exercise, (introductory clause)

Chapter 16 Commas   303

8. Since your wife shares your checking account, she doesn't need to sign the credit application. *IVP IC*

9. Your wife doesn't need to sign the credit application since she shares your checking account.

10. The firm has been in business 11 years, and its principal offices are in Ashland. *C*

11. Any increase in salaries, as you might have expected, is presently impossible because of declining profits. *Nonessential Phrase*

12. For a period of at least six months, we cannot increase salaries. *IVP Prep*

13. In two months we may be able to expand health benefits.

14. Clearing the papers from his desk, he finally located the contract. *IVP*

15. School cafeterias try to serve nutritious, tasty meals.

C. Insert necessary commas. For each sentence write, in the space provided, the number of commas that you inserted. If the sentence is correct, write *C*. Be prepared to explain each comma.

1. If scientists are correct, the Earth's surface is composed of a number of shifting plates that move a few inches each year. *1*

2. Our current liability insurance, in view of the new law that went into effect April 1, needs to be increased. *2*

3. The happy, carefree students had just completed their examinations, although many had to leave immediately for their jobs. *2*

4. Starting as a file clerk, I moved to Accounts Payable as an accountant. *1*

5. We are looking for a reliable, experienced individual who is interested in growing with our organization. *1*

6. By the spring of next year, we hope to have completed our telecommunications network. *1*

7. In the winter, Susan Madarieta, who was recently hired away from CyberVision, will join the executive staff as chief information officer. *3*

8. Some companies have excellent voice mail systems, but other organizations use impersonal systems that frustrate and irritate callers. *1*

9. Having misplaced her keys, Kerry had to retrace her day's activities. *1*

10. Although it represents a small share of our total sales, the loss of the Phoenix territory would negatively affect our profits. *1*

11. We do not, at this time, see any reason for continuing this inefficient, profitless practice. *3*

12. When you send an e-mail message, remember that it may be forwarded to someone else. *1*

13. As Professor Brunton predicted, the resourceful, well-trained graduate was hired immediately. *2*

14. We hope that the new year will be prosperous for you, and that we may have many more opportunities to serve you.

15. You were probably concerned about your increased insurance rates, but you didn't know where to find adequate economical coverage. *1*

16. At a meeting of our advertising committee, we decided to renew our contract for a _____ one-page advertisement in your magazine.

17. Lynda Lee, who recently bought a sports car has received three speeding tickets _____ in the past six weeks.

18. In our company, a prospective policyholder is thoroughly investigated before a *C* policy is issued.

19. Renouncing her wealthy social background Florence Nightingale became a nurse _____ and is considered the founder of modern nursing.

20. You have worked here every summer, and you have always been an asset to the _____ firm.

L e v e l   I I I

A. **(Self-check)** Insert necessary commas. In the space provided, indicate briefly the reason for the comma (for example, *omitted words, contrasting statement, clarity, short quotation,* and so forth). Write *C* if the sentence is correct.

1. What it is, is a matter of principle.   *clarity*

2. The first loan was made on February 3; the second, June 1.   *omitted*

3. "Those who cannot remember the past," said George Santayana, "are   *SQ* condemned to repeat it."

4. In the fall we will need six operators; in the spring, eight.   *omitted*

5. Mayel Alwar, CPA, listed the firm's assets at $873,500.   *Degree & Abbr.*

6. At least 16, 2001 Chevy vans must be serviced.   *Numerals*

7. We are issuing Policy No. 2176800394 in your name.   *C*

8. We were expecting Miss Weber, not Mr. Allen, to conduct the audit.   *Contrasting*

9. "A résumé is a balance sheet without any liabilities," said personnel   *SQ* specialist Robert Half.

10. The octogenarians had known each other for a long, long time.   *clarity*

Check your answers below.

B. Insert necessary commas. In the space provided, indicate briefly the reason for the comma (for example, *omitted words, contrasting statement, clarity, short quotation,* and so forth). Write *C* if the sentence is correct.

1. "Nothing you can't spell," said humorist Will Rogers, "will ever work."   *SQ*

2. Did you know that on July 23, 12 additional workers will be hired?   *numerals*

3. On January 1 your Policy No. 8643219 will expire.   *C*

4. Lynn Craig, L.V.N., and Annette Juarez, R.N., work at St. Elizabeth's.   *Abb.*

5. On paper, diets often sound deceptively simple.   *clarity*

6. The longer we keep our funds invested, the greater will be the interest. *Contrastive/Clarity*

7. Major responsibility for the loan lies with the signer; secondary responsibility, with the cosigner. *omitted*

8. That task must be reserved for experienced, never inexperienced, employees. *Contrast*

9. Motion-picture producer Samuel Goldwyn said, "A verbal contract isn't worth the paper it's written on." *SQ*

10. In short, employees must be more considerate of others. *clarity*

11. Donna Meyer, Ph.D., and Victor Massaglia, M.D., spoke at the opening session. *Abb*

12. Toyota management was worried because 231, 1998 sedans had to be recalled. *numeral*

13. It was Dr. Harris, not Dr. Shimada, who performed the surgery. *contrast*

14. What it was, was an international power struggle. *Clarity*

15. Half of the payment for the shipment is due on delivery; the balance, in six weeks. *Omitted*

16. Although bored, students managed to stay awake during the lecture. *clarity*

17. Whatever it is, it is not very amusing. *Clarity*

18. In Room 201, 32 computers and 16 printers are operating. *numeral*

19. Cooperation, not criticism, is what is needed. *contrast*

20. "Frankly," said Brian, "I don't really understand his motivation." *SQ*

C. **Writing Exercise.** Select five comma rules that you think are most important. Name the rule; then write an original sentence illustrating that rule.

Comma Rule	Sentence Illustration
1. _____	_____
	_____
2. _____	_____
	_____
3. _____	_____
	_____
4. _____	_____
	_____
5. _____	_____
	_____

Editor's Challenge

The following letter illustrates *simplified* style. Notice that all lines begin at the left margin and that the salutation is replaced by a subject line in all capital letters. The complimentary close is replaced by the writer's name and title or company. This letter contains 30 intentional errors representing spelling, proofreading, punctuation, and language principles covered thus far.

Adventure Sports, Inc.

8550 Old Dairy Road
Juneau, AK 99801

E-mail: troy@alaska.net
FAX: 907-789-2319

March 7, 200x

Mr. Kevin M. Simpson
433 East South Temple
Salt Lake City, UT 84111

THANKS FOR YOUR INTEREST IN KAYAK TOURS

Enclosed is a list of current trips and other information, that you requested about our Kayak tours in Alaska. To ensure a quality wilderness experience the number of guests on a tour are limited to six people. No special experience is neccesary. Many of our guests have never been in a sea kayak, and are surprised to find that they are very stable. Moreover we teach you safe efficient operation of a kayak.

All equipment, meals and safety gear is included in the trip price. We provide charter transportation from Juneau to the trip location, however you are responsible for getting to Juneau, and for your meals and lodging before and after the trip. To reserve a trip you must make a 50 percent deposit. We will hold reservations for your party for two weeks. Anyone who must request a refund, will be charged a $50 handling fee. If we must cancel a trip a full refund will be made. In some instances, we must cancel because of to few participants, or dangerous weather.

Our most popular trip is whale watching and kayaking at Pt. Adolphus. This four day trip costs $750 which includes boat charter and fairy. We also recommend the glacier tour at Tracy Arm, and our island tour of Pt. Couverdon. By the way custom dates is available for familys or group's of three or more.

Call, write or fax to make your reservations. We look forward to providing you with the wilderness adventure of a lifetime!

Troy M. Donohue

TROY M. DONOHUE, ADVENTURE SPORTS, INC.

Enclosure

Goal: To gather job-search and career information.

Soon you will be looking for a job. You decide to learn as much as possible about wages and trends in your career area.

1. With your Web browser on the screen, go to **America's Career InfoNet** **<http://www.acinet.org>**.

2. Click **General Outlook of the U.S. Job Market**. Scroll down and click **Fastest Growing Occupations** and select an appropriate worker education level for yourself. Press **Search**.

3. Study the list of occupations. Select one. For this occupation what was employment in 1998, and what is it projected to be in 2008? What is the percent of change?

4. At the top of the screen, click **Career Exploration**. Then click **Wages and Trends—Occupation Level**. Scroll down to **Job Families**. Scroll to a job in which you might be interested. Scroll down farther and click a state, district, or territory. **Search.**

5. Print a page showing information about your job choice in your state.

6. End your session and submit your printout and your answers.

POSTTEST

Insert appropriate commas in the following sentences.

1. Your letter, Mrs. Rice, should describe the merchandise and announce the beginning of our fall clothing sale.

2. The manager thinks, on the other hand, that all service calls must receive prior authorization and that current service contracts must be honored.

3. Connie Jo Clark, Ph. D., and Patricia Flood, CPA, have been asked to speak at our Albany, New York, conference.

4. When trained, all employees in this company should be able to offer logical, effective advice to customers.

5. If you are unsure, you may ask Mrs. Cruz, not Mr. Ray, for additional information.

1. letter, Mrs. Rice, 2. thinks, hand, 3. Clark, Ph.D., Flood, CPA, Albany, New York, 4. trained, logical, 5. unsure, Cruz, Ray,

CHECKLIST OF BONUS LEARNING RESOURCES

The following additional learning resources are available to you. Your instructor will tell you which to complete.

- Web Editor's Challenge Exercise

- Web Interactive Chapter Review

- Web PowerPoint Slides

- Web Crossword Puzzle

- WebCheck Reinforcement Exercises 16.1, 16.2

- Self-Help Exercises

- Electronic Study Guide

chapter 17 Semicolons and Colons

Objectives

When you have completed the materials in this chapter, you will be able to do the following:

Level I
- Use semicolons correctly in punctuating compound sentences.
- Use semicolons when necessary to separate items in a series.

Level II
- Learn the proper and improper use of colons to introduce listed items.
- Correctly use colons to introduce quotations and explanatory sentences.

Level III
- Distinguish between the use of commas and semicolons preceding expressions such as *namely, that is,* and *for instance.*
- Understand why semicolons are sometimes necessary to separate independent clauses joined by *and, or, nor,* or *but.*
- Use colons appropriately and be able to capitalize words following colons when necessary.

Insert appropriate semicolons, colons, and commas in the following sentences.

1. Small businesses often lack credit opportunities;therefore the owners of these businesses must raise capital privately.

2. We have engaged as speakers the following individuals:Kathleen Stewart, Moraine Valley Community College;Roietta Fulgham,American River College;and Kathy Green,Phoenix College.

3. Speakers for the morning session are now scheduled;speakers for the afternoon session have not yet been arranged.

4. The programming committee,however,must proceed with its plans.

5. Although the committee had many cities from which to choose,it decided to focus on the following;namely,San Francisco, Denver, or New Orleans.

1. opportunities; therefore.   2. individuals: Stewart, College; Fulgham, College. Green, 3. scheduled;   4. committee, however,   5. choose, following; namely,

Skilled writers use semicolons and colons to signal readers about the ideas that will follow. Semicolons tell readers that two closely related ideas should be thought of together. The semicolon is a stronger punctuation mark than a comma, which signifies a pause; but the semicolon is not as strong as a period, which signifies a complete stop. Understanding the use of semicolons will help you avoid fundamental writing errors, such as the *comma splice* and the *run-on sentence*. This chapter presents basic uses and advanced applications of semicolons and colons.

L e v e l I

Basic Uses of the Semicolon

The most basic use of the semicolon occurs in compound sentences. Many business communicators use a comma when they should be using a semicolon. Study the following examples to make sure you don't make this error.

Independent Clauses Separated by Conjunctive Adverbs

Semicolons are used primarily when two independent clauses are separated by a conjunctive adverb or a transitional expression. You studied this basic semicolon use in Chapter 14. Here are some review examples.

> Companies make no profits until they recover costs; *therefore*, most companies use a cost approach in pricing. (Semicolon separates two independent clauses joined by the conjunctive adverb *therefore*.)

> Mike rose from bag boy to vice president; *thus* he knew every position well. (Semicolon separates two independent clauses joined by the conjunctive adverb *thus*.)

In addition to the application shown here, semicolons may be used in other constructions, as we'll discuss next.

Independent Clauses Without a Coordinating Conjunction or a Conjunctive Adverb

Two or more closely related independent clauses not separated by a conjunctive adverb or a coordinating conjunction (*and, or, nor, but*) require a semicolon.

> The licensing company is called the *franchisor*; the dealer is called the *franchisee*.

> Inside teller service at our branch ends at 3 p.m.; outside ATM service is available 24 hours a day.

As you learned in Chapter 3, a serious punctuation error results when separate independent clauses are joined by only a comma (a comma splice) or without any punctuation whatever (a run-on sentence).

Comma splice:	Inside teller service at our branch ends at 4 p.m., outside ATM service is available 24 hours a day.
Run-on sentence:	Inside teller service at our branch ends at 4 p.m. outside ATM service is available 24 hours a day.

Study Tip

Remember that a comma is used only after a two-syllable conjunctive adverb. And don't capitalize the word following a semicolon unless it's a proper noun.

Series Containing Internal Commas or Complete Thoughts

Semicolons are used to separate items in a series when one or more of the items contain internal commas.

> Only the company branches in Wilmington, Delaware; Tucson, Arizona; and Cincinnati, Ohio, are showing substantial profits. ???
>
> Attending the conference were Georgia Mackh, executive vice president, Cabrillo Industries; Toni Cannizzaro, president, Santa Rosa Software; and Sandy Cornish, program director, Club Mediterranean.

Semicolons are used to separate three or more serial independent clauses.

> The first step consists of surveying all available information related to the company objective so that an understanding of all problems can be reached; the second step involves interviewing consumers, wholesalers, and retailers; and the third step consists of developing a research design in which the actual methods and procedures to be used are indicated.

A series of short independent clauses, however, may be separated by commas.

> Ease of handling is excellent, passenger comfort is certainly above average, and fuel consumption is the lowest of all cars tested.

Now complete the reinforcement exercises for Level I.

L e v e l   I I

Basic Uses of the Colon

The colon is most often used to introduce formally listed items, quotations, and explanatory sentences.

Formally Listed Items

Use a colon after an independent clause that introduces one item, two items, or a formal list. A list may be shown vertically or horizontally and is usually introduced by such words as *the following, as follows, these,* or *thus.* A colon is also used when words like these are implied but not stated.

> Creating a company Web site offered *the following* advantage: improved customer service. (Independent clause introduces single item.)
>
> Some of the most commonly used manufacturers' discounts are *the following*: trade, cash, quantity, and seasonal. (Formal list with introductory expression stated.)
>
> Our company uses several delivery services for our important packages: UPS, FedEx, and Airborne. (Formal list with introductory expression only implied.)
>
> *These* are a few of the services that a correspondent bank performs for other banks:
>
> 1. Collecting checks, payments, and other credit instruments
>
> 2. Accepting letters of credit and travelers' checks
>
> 3. Making credit investigations (Formal list shown vertically.)

Do not use a colon unless the list is introduced by an independent clause. Lists often function as sentence complements or objects. When this is the case and the statement introducing the list is incomplete, no colon should be used. It might be easiest to remember that lists introduced by verbs or prepositions require no colons (because the introductory statement is incomplete).

> Three courses in this program are accounting, business English, and Computer Science 22. (No colon is used because the introductory statement is not complete; the list is introduced by a *to be* verb and functions as a complement to the sentence.)

> Awards of merit were presented to Professor Loncorich, Ms. Harned, and Dr. Konishi. (No colon is used because the introductory statement is not an independent clause; the list functions as an object of the preposition *to*.)

Do not use a colon when an intervening sentence falls between the introductory statement and the list.

> The following cities have been chosen as potential convention sites. A final decision will be made May 1.
>
> New Orleans   San Francisco
> Chicago   Orlando

> (No colon appears after *sites* because an intervening sentence comes between the introductory statement and the list.)

Quotations

Use a colon to introduce long one-sentence quotations and quotations of two or more sentences.

> Consumer advocate Lori Nahama said: "Historically, in our private-enterprise economy, consumers determine what and how much is to be produced through their purchases in the marketplace; hence the needs of consumers are carefully monitored by producers."

Incomplete quotations not interrupting the flow of a sentence require no colon, no comma, and no initial capital letter.

> The River Walk area of San Antonio is sometimes described as "the Venice of the Southwest."

Explanatory Sentences

Use a colon to separate two independent clauses if the second clause explains, illustrates, or supplements the first.

> The company's newly elected directors were immediately faced with a perplexing dilemma: they had to choose between declaring bankruptcy and investing additional funds in an attempt to recoup previous losses.

> The applicants for the position all exhibited one common trait: they were achievers who accepted nothing less than success.

Now complete the reinforcement exercises for Level II.

Special Considerations in Using Semicolons and Colons

You've just studied basic uses for semicolons and colons. Occasionally, though, these punctuation marks are used in circumstances demanding special attention.

Introductory Expressions Such As *namely*, *for instance*, and *that is*

When introductory expressions (such as *namely*, *for instance*, *that is*, and *for example*) immediately follow independent clauses, they may be preceded by either commas or semicolons. Generally, if the words following the introductory expression appear at the end of the sentence and form a series or an independent clause, use a semicolon before the introductory expression. If not, use a comma.

> Numerous fringe benefits are available to employees; *namely*, injury compensation, life insurance, health insurance, dental care, and vision care. (A semicolon is used because *namely* introduces a series at the end of the sentence.)

> Salaries of most government employees are determined by the General Schedule; *for example*, typists are classified GS-2 or GS-3. (A semicolon is used because *for example* introduces an independent clause.)

> Our company is considering better ways to evaluate employees, *for example*, an objective performance appraisal system. (A comma is used because *for example* introduces neither a series nor an independent clause.)

These same introductory expressions may introduce parenthetical words within sentences. Usually, commas punctuate parenthetical words within sentences. If the parenthetical words thus introduced are punctuated by internal commas, however, use dashes or parentheses. (Dashes and parentheses will be treated in detail in Chapter 18.)

> The biggest health problems facing workers, *namely*, drug abuse and alcoholism, cost American industry over $10 billion a year. (Commas are used because the parenthetical words contain only two items joined by *and*.)

> The pursuit of basic job issues—*for instance*, wages, job security, and working conditions—has been the main concern of American workers. (Dashes are used because the parenthetical words are punctuated with commas.)

Independent Clauses With Coordinating Conjunctions

Normally, a comma precedes a coordinating conjunction (*and*, *or*, *nor*, *but*) when it joins two independent clauses. If either of the independent clauses contains an additional comma, however, the reader might be confused about where the second independent clause begins. For this reason many writers prefer to use a semicolon, instead of the normally expected comma, to separate independent clauses when either independent clause contains a comma.

> We have examined your suggestions carefully, and it appears that they have considerable merit. (Comma precedes coordinating conjunction because no additional punctuation appears within either clause.)

Study Tip

Notice that a comma follows *namely*, *for instance*, *that is*, and *for example* when these words are used as introductory expressions.

Spot the Blooper

From a column in *The Chicago Tribune*: "[A] letter from her mother, written in Polish, for example, has the date (for we dummies in the audience) written in English."

On the basis of Diane Fisher's recommendation, we have examined your suggestions carefully; and it appears that they have considerable merit. (Semicolon precedes co-ordinating conjunction because a comma appears within one of the independent clauses.)

Other Uses of the Colon

- After the salutation of a business letter.

    Dear Mr. Paniccia: Ladies and Gentlemen: Dear Mike:

- In expressions of time to separate hours from minutes.

    2:45 p.m.   12:01 a.m.

- Between titles and subtitles.

    HOW: A Handbook for Office Workers

- Between place of publication and name of publisher.

    Guffey, Mary Ellen. *Essentials of Business Communication*. Cincinnati: South-Western College Publishing, 2001.

Capitalization Following Colons

Do not capitalize the initial letter of words or of phrases listed following a colon unless the words so listed are proper nouns or appear as a vertical array.

    The four Cs of effective letter writing are the following: clarity, courtesy, conciseness, and correctness.

    These cities will receive heavy promotional advertising: Omaha, Lincoln, Sioux City, and Council Bluffs.

    To be legally enforceable, a contract must include at least four elements:

    1. Mutual assent of all parties
    2. Parties who are competent
    3. A consideration
    4. A lawful purpose

Do not capitalize the first letter of an independent clause following a colon if that clause explains or supplements the first one (unless, of course, the first word is a proper noun).

    You will be interested in our new savings plan for one special reason: it allows you to invest up to $2,500 in a tax-free account.

Capitalize the first letter of an independent clause following a colon if that clause states a formal rule or principle.

    Experienced negotiators adhere to the following principle: Never cut what you can untie.

For a quotation following a colon, capitalize the initial letter of each complete sentence.

    Commenting on the importance of incorporation, historians Krooss and Seropian said: "A strong case can be made for the proposition that the increased use of the corporation was the most important institutional innovation of the century. The corporate form permeates American business."

A Final Word

Semicolons are excellent punctuation marks when used carefully and knowingly. After reading this chapter, though, some students are guilty of semicolon overkill. They begin to string together two—and sometimes even three—independent clauses with semicolons. Remember to use semicolons in compound sentences *only* when two ideas are better presented together. Forget about joining three independent clauses with semicolons—too unconventional and too difficult to read. In most instances, independent clauses should end with periods.

Now complete the reinforcement exercises for Level III.

Hot Link

To learn more about semicolons, visit **http://chuma.cas.usf. edu/~olson/pms/ semicolon.html** (or check updated URLs at Guffey Web site).

HOTLINE QUERIES

Q: Here's a sentence we need help with: *We plan to present the contract to whoever makes the lowest bid.* My supervisor recommends *whoever* and I suggest *whomever*. Which of us is right?

A: Your supervisor. The preposition *to* has as its object the entire clause (*whoever makes the lowest bid*). Within that clause *whoever* functions as the subject of the verb *makes*; therefore, the nominative case form *whoever* should be used.

Q: When I list items vertically, should I use a comma or semicolon after each item? Should a period be used after the final item? For example,

Please inspect the following rooms and equipment:

1. The control room

2. The power transformer and its standby

3. The auxiliary switchover equipment

A: Do not use commas or semicolons after items listed vertically, and do not use a period after the last item in such a list. However, if the listed items are complete sentences or if they are long phrases that complete the meaning of the introductory comment, periods may be used after each item.

Q: Is there a plural form of *plus and minus*?

A: The plural form is *pluses* (or *plusses*) *and minuses* (*consider all the pluses and minuses before you make a decision*).

Q: I'm setting up advertising copy, and this sentence doesn't look right to me: *This line of fishing reels are now priced . . .*

A: Your suspicion is correct. The subject of the verb in this sentence is *line*; it requires the singular verb *is*.

Q: I wonder if the possessive is correctly expressed in this sentence that I'm transcribing: *I appreciate the candor of both you and Neil in our conversation.* Shouldn't both *you* and *Neil* be made possessive?

A: No. It would be very awkward to say *your and Neil's candor*. It's much better to use the *of* construction, thus avoiding the awkward double possessive.

Q: Is this a double negative: *We can't schedule the meeting because we have no room available?*

A: No, this is not regarded as a double negative. In grammar a double negative is created when two negative adverbs modify a verb, such as *can't hardly*, *won't barely*, or *can't help but*. Avoid such constructions.

Name _____

Level I

A. **(Self-check)** For each of the following sentences, underline any errors in punctuation. Then in the space provided, write the correct punctuation mark plus the word preceding it. Write *C* if the sentence is correct.

Example: Breeding and raising horses can be profitable, consequently, large sums are being invested.

profitable;

1. Horse breeding has become a big business, and investors are supplying large sums for thoroughbreds.

business;

2. Most thoroughbreds are sold as yearlings; it is usually one year before they can race.

yearlings;

3. Investors' expectations are <u>high</u> therefore, competitive bidding for breeding animals is brisk.

high;

4. Some investors use thoroughbred horses as tax shelters, these investors "write off" the expenses of maintaining the horses.

shelters;

5. Mr. Marks invested, Mrs. Villaflor was interested, and Mr. Phipps declined.

C

6. Important breeding is being conducted at the Peachtree Ranch, Rome, Georgia; the Blue Meadows Ranch, Lexington, Kentucky; and the Flag Is Up Ranch, Buellton, California.

C

7. Stallions yield the highest <u>prices;</u> but mares can also be extremely expensive.

prices,

8. The average auction price has tripled in the last five years; profits from breeding have climbed even faster.

years;

9. Several investors may form a syndicate to buy a good <u>horse,</u> the syndicate then shares expenses and spreads risks.

horse;

10. Horse breeding can be an exciting and profitable <u>venture,</u> thus many investors are choosing horses over stocks and bonds.

venture;

Check your answers below.

B. Add any necessary commas or semicolons to the following sentences. (Do not add periods.) In the spaces provided, write the number of punctuation marks you inserted. Write *C* if a sentence is correct as written.

Example: New equipment was ordered eight weeks ago, delivery is expected within two weeks.

1

1. Consumers expect anytime, anywhere access to businesses; therefore, wireless cell phone use is growing.

2

2. Greenland is the largest island in the world; it is about ten times the size of Great Britain.

1

3. Buildings swayed, lights flickered, and dishes rattled.

2

1. business; 2. yearlings; 3. high; 4. shelters; 5. C 6. C 7. prices, 8. years; 9. horse; 10. venture;

4. Serving on the panel of experts are Pam Rippin, marketing director, Santa Rosa Associates; Evelyn Katusak, sales supervisor, Broome Products; and Carrie McFerron, market analyst, Tyler Enterprises.   _8_

5. Babies under six months old can breathe and swallow at the same time; adults cannot do this.   _1_

6. Your account is now several months past due; consequently, it is impossible for us to grant you further extensions.   _2_

7. The shortest recorded reign of any monarch was that of Louis XIX of France; it lasted only 15 minutes.   _1_

8. Every Christmas, we hire a number of temporary office workers; hence, I am writing to you to make this announcement of job openings to your students.   _3_

9. Jeremy worked, Jennifer supervised, and Jean entertained.   _2_

10. Web advertising attempts to reach large, international audiences; television advertising is aimed at national or local audiences.   _2_

11. Microsoft hired over 2,000 new employees last year; it plans to hire even more next year.   _1_

12. Computer hackers can easily decode short passwords; thus passwords should be at least six to eight characters long and be a mix of letters and numerals.   _1_

13. We have hired "white hat" hackers, and their job is to test how well our computer systems withstand assaults by real hackers.   _C 1_

14. Smart companies assume their computer networks will be broken into; consequently, they develop computer-use policies to limit the damage.   _2_

15. Among the oddly named towns in the United States are Accident, Maryland; Truth or Consequences, New Mexico; and Slap Out, Alabama.   _C 0_

16. Speakers for the afternoon session include Ms. Karen Whitman, executive vice president, Security Systems; Professor Linda Scher-Padilla, Department of Office Administration, Los Angeles City College; and Dr. Jane Mangrum, director of research, Miami Industries.   _8_

17. Employment opportunities are available in hospitals, banks, and insurance companies; however, training is often required.   _4_

18. Such training, nevertheless, can usually be completed in six to ten months; thus, you can begin earning wages in less than a year.   _4_

19. If you open your account immediately, your first 500 checks will be supplied free; moreover, you will receive a bonus gift if you are among our first 50 customers.   _3_

20. Guests on his show have included Winston, a singing dog; Polly, a talking bird; and Reggie, a water-skiing squirrel.   _5_

L e v e l   I I

A. **(Self-check)** For each of the following sentences, underline any errors in punctuation. Then in the space provided, write the correct punctuation plus the preceding word. If a colon should be omitted, write *Omit colon*. Write *C* if the sentence is correct.

Example: Special invitations were sent to: President Owens, Vice President Spears, and Treasurer Avery.   **Omit colon**

1. The most outstanding speakers at the national convention were: Leandro Castillo, Cathy Grant, and Carol Engel.   *Omit colon*

2. Our trip last summer included visits to the following historical sites: Mount Vernon, Virginia; Gettysburg, Pennsylvania; and Concord, Massachusetts.

C

3. Smart phones are available from the following three companies: Please check on prices.

Omit colon; add ^

    Motorola   Nokia
    Samsung

4. Dr. Marlyn Wiswall said; "Never underestimate the value of stories and humor in delivering and organizing your speech. People forget facts and graphs; they remember and retell memorable stories and anecdotes that illustrate your points."

said:

5. The head of the computer security firm admitted one big problem: finding good people without criminal records.

problem; C

6. Five of the worst computer passwords are: your first name, your last name, the Enter key, *Password*, and the name of a sports team.

Omit colon

7. We have requests for information from three local companies: Sterling Laboratories, Putnam Brothers, and Big Dog, Inc.

C

8. Because of the urgency of the problem, we have sent Express messages to: Evelyn Dobson, Mary Ringle, and Eunice Smith.

Omit colon

9. The most commonly observed holidays are the following: Thanksgiving, Labor Day, Christmas, July Fourth, and New Year's Day.

C

10. Arriving late for class, the student offered a convincing excuse: her car had run out of gas three miles away.

C

Check your answers below.

B. For the following sentences, add any necessary but missing punctuation marks. For each sentence indicate in the space provided the number of additions you have made. Mark *C* if the sentence is correct as it stands.

Example: Shipments of computer chips were sent to Dallas, Sacramento, Cleveland, and Zurich.   *4*

1. Three similar types of tropical storms with different names are cyclones, typhoons, and hurricanes.   *2*

2. Japan faces a serious economic threat; its dependence on oil imports endangers its future economic growth.   *1*

3. Polygraph examinations generally consist of four parts: a preexamination interview, a demonstration, questioning of the examinee, and a postexamination interview.   *1*

4. Speaking at the convention, humorist Lawrence Peter said: "Most hierarchies were established by men who now monopolize the upper levels. This deprives women of their rightful share of opportunities for incompetence."   *1*

5. The records of the following employees will be reviewed for salary evaluation. Please send the records by October 1.   *2*

    Vicki Torres   Julie Mauer
    Tony Watkins   Ivan Krakowski

1. omit colon 2. C 3. companies. 4. said: 5. C 6. omit colon 7. C 8. omit colon 9. C 10. C

6. The balance sheet is a statement of assets, liabilities, and owner's equity. _____2_____

7. Included in our introductory offer are the following: colored file folders, self-closing envelopes, and erasable ballpoint pens. _____3_____

8. Energy in this country is supplied from a number of sources: oil, natural gas, coal, nuclear fission, and hydropower. _____5_____

9. For graduation you must complete courses in mathematics, accounting, English, management, and computer applications. _____C_____

10. The law of supply and demand can function only under the following condition: producers must know what consumers want. _____C_____

11. Professor Marilyn Simonson asked that research reports contain the following parts: introduction, body, summary, and bibliography. _____4_____

12. Additional costs in selling the house are title examination, title insurance, transfer tax, preparation of documents, and closing fee. _____C_____

13. Warren Bennis said: "The factory of the future will have only two employees, a man and a dog. The man will be there to feed the dog. The dog will be there to keep the man from touching the equipment." _____1_____

14. Of all the discoveries and inventions in human history, the four greatest are said to be these: speech, fire, agriculture, and the wheel. _____C 1_____

15. Business letters generally include four parts: date, inside address, body, and closing. _____1_____

C. **Writing Exercise.** Write original sentences to illustrate the following. Talk about your experience in using the Internet and e-mail. For example: *I generally use the Internet for e-mail; however, I plan to get better at using it for research.*

1. (Semicolon with conjunctive adverb) _____

   _____

2. (Semicolon without conjunctive adverb) _____

   _____

3. (Colon with listed items) _____

   _____

L e v e l   I I I

A. **(Self-check)** Insert necessary punctuation. In the space provided, write the number of punctuation marks that you inserted. Write *C* if the sentence is correct.

1. Four employees have been recognized for achievement awards; namely, Michelle Taylor, Corrine Chan, Todd Wilde, and Bill Hevore. _____C_____

2. Foreign Service secretaries may be assigned to a number of countries; for example, India, Brazil, Finland, and France. _____C_____

3. Daily newspapers in the United States, of which there are approximately 1,800, have a combined circulation of 65 million; and daily papers that publish Sunday editions, of which there are about 700, have a combined circulation of over 52 million. _____C_____

4. The meeting started promptly at 1:15 p.m. and ended at 3:45 p.m. _____C_____

5. Many banks now offer automated transfers from savings to checking accounts; that is, money may be kept in an interest-bearing savings account until needed. — *2*

6. All employees are urged to observe the following rule: When in doubt, consult the company style manual. — *C*

7. The writer of a research report should include a variety of references; for example, books, periodicals, government publications, and newspapers. — *C*

8. Karen Desch considered naming her book *Successful Investing: A Complete Guide to Your Financial Future.* — *1*

9. For the opening session of the convention, the keynote speaker will be systems analyst Barb Kaldenberger; and for the afternoon general membership meeting, the speaker will be NASA representative Catherine Peck. — *C*

10. You may repay your loan according to one of the following plans: the annual plan, the semiannual plan, the quarterly plan, or the weekly plan. — *C*

Check your answers below.

B. For the following sentences, add necessary punctuation. For each sentence indicate the number of additions you made. Mark *C* if correct.

Example: If she completes the proposal, Sharon Allen will fly to Washington on Tuesday; if not, she will leave on Thursday. — *3*

1. When completing your résumé, be sure to include relevant activities; for example, intern experience, work-study experience, and volunteer work. — *4*

2. Because of her computer expertise, Kay Stephan was chosen as our network administrator, and because of her people skills, Karley Cooper, was chosen as trainer. — *2 ???*

3. One of the titles Christine Spindler is considering for her book is *Your First Résumé: A Complete Guide to Strategies and Techniques.* — *1*

4. Many of the best convention cities are the most expensive; for example, San Francisco, New York, and Honolulu. — *4*

5. Three times have been designated for the interviews: Thursday at 6:30 p.m., Friday at 3:30 p.m., and Monday at 10 a.m. — *~~6~~ 5*

6. An author, composer, or photographer may protect his or her product with a government-approved monopoly; namely, a copyright. — *2*

7. Our school operates on the quarter system; that is, the school year is divided into four equal quarters. — *2*

8. Victor Valdez enjoyed his current position as sales representative very much, but when a competing company offered him a substantial increase in salary, he found it very tempting. — *C*

9. Stories circulated about Henry Ford, founder, Ford Motor Company; Lee Iacocca, former CEO, Chrysler Motor Company; and Shoichiro Toyoda, former chief, Toyota Motor Company. — *6*

10. The following companies won top awards for their Web sites: IBM, Godiva Chocolates, and Nike. — *3*

Editor's Challenge

The following progress report contains intentional errors representing spelling, proofreading, punctuation, and language principles covered thus far. You should mark 40 changes.

★ LONESTAR PRODUCTIONS ★

Interoffice Memo

TO: Patrick M. Young
FROM: Kellie Whitford
DATE: February 2, 200x
SUBJECT: SITES FOR "BODEGA BAY" TELEFILM

This memo describes the progress of my search for a appropriate rustic home, villa or ranch. To be used for the wine country sequences in the upcoming telefilm "Bodega Bay." As you requested three sites has been selected for you to inspect on February 21.

Background. To prepare for this assignment I consulted Director Mario Polero who gave me his preferences for the sight. He wants a picturesque ranch home, that is located near grape vineyards, moreover he would like redwoods in the background. I also consulted Producer Tucker Setterberg who told me that the site must accommodate 55 to 70 production crew members for approximately three weeks of filming. Jocelyn Garcia who is our telefilm accountant requested that the cost of the site not exceed $24,000, for a three week lease.

Work Completed. For the past eight days I have searched the Russian River area in the Northern California wine country. Since this area is rich with history I was able to locate many possibilities including: turn-of-the-century estates, Victorian mansions and rustic farmhouses. One of the best sites is the Country Meadows Inn a 97 year old farmhouse, with a breathtaking view of vallies, redwoods and distant mountains. The most promising towns are the following Duncans Mills, Monte Rio, and Guerneville.

Work to be Completed. In the next few days I'll search the Sonoma County countryside, and inspect winerys at: Korbel, Field Stone and Napa. Many of these old winerys has charming structures, however they also attract tourists, and crowds of people.

By February 14, you'll have my final report, that describes the three better locations.

Goal: To learn to locate job listings.

You're now ready to hunt for a job, and you decide to start with online listings.

1. With your Web browser on the screen, key **<http://www.monster.com>**.

2. At the Monster.com site, click **First timers, start here.** Then click **Search Jobs.**

3. On the Monster Jobs page, scroll down to **Location Search**. Click a location of your choice.

4. Use the scroll bar along the side to move down to **Job Category Search**. Click a job title of your choice.

5. Study the jobs listed. Click one or more. Print a page from the best listing.

6. Repeat the process for another job category. Print a page.

7. If you want to see other job listing sites, go to the Guffey Student Site **<http://www.westwords.com/guffey/students.html>** and click **Job Search**.

8. End your session and submit two printed pages with job listings.

POSTTEST

Add appropriate semicolons, colons, and commas.

1. Most students prefer morning classes consequently we schedule many courses before noon.

2. The following instructors have been chosen to represent their schools at the professional meeting Joyce Birch Normandale Community College Sandra Farrar Louisiana Technical College and Paul Murphey Southwest Wisconsin Technical College.

3. All morning sessions begin at 9 a.m all afternoon sessions commence at 1 p.m.

4. Because we have little time before the deadline we are forced to choose from among the leaders for example, AT&T, Sprint, and CompuAmerica.

5. We feel however that more time should be allowed for major equipment decisions.

1. classes; consequently, 2. meeting: Birch, College; Farrar, College; Murphey, 3. a.m.; 4. deadline, leaders; 5. feel, however,

Chapter 17 Semicolons and Colons 325

CHECKLIST OF BONUS LEARNING RESOURCES

The following additional learning resources are available to you. Your instructor will tell you which to complete.

- Web Editor's Challenge Exercise

- Web Interactive Chapter Review

- Web PowerPoint Slides

- Web Crossword Puzzle

- WebCheck Reinforcement Exercises 17.1, 17.2

- Self-Help Exercises

- Electronic Study Guide

chapter 18 Other Punctuation

Objectives

When you have completed the materials in this chapter, you will be able to do the following:

Level I

- Use periods to correctly punctuate statements, commands, indirect questions, and polite requests.
- Use periods to correctly punctuate abbreviations, initials, and numerals.
- Use question marks and exclamation points correctly.

Level II

- Recognize acceptable applications of the dash.
- Use parentheses to de-emphasize material.
- Explain when to use commas, dashes, or parentheses to set off nonessential material.
- Correctly punctuate and capitalize material set off by parentheses and dashes.

Level III

- Correctly use double and single quotation marks.
- Correctly place other punctuation marks in relation to quotation marks.
- Use brackets, underscores, and italics appropriately.

Use proofreading marks to insert punctuation in the following sentences.

1. Will you please send certificates to Radene Schroeder and M. L. Vasquez.

2. Miss Lee, Mrs. Ortega, and Mr. Simon have been appointed to the FCC.

3. The chapter entitled "Principles of Persuasion" was the best one in the book Elements of Business Writing.

4. Have all candidates for the CEO position completed M.B.A. degrees?

5. Did Professor Scholl say, "There will be no class Friday."?

1. Vasquez. 2. Lee, Ortega, FCC. 3. "Principles of Persuasion." Elements of Business Writing. 4. M.B.A. degrees? 5. say, "There Friday"?

327

This chapter teaches you how to use periods, question marks, and exclamation points correctly. It also includes suggestions for punctuating with dashes, parentheses, single quotation marks, double quotation marks, brackets, and underscores (italics).

Uses for the Period

The period is used to punctuate sentences, abbreviations, and numerals. The following guidelines will help you use the period correctly.

To Punctuate Sentences

Use a period at the end of a statement, a command, an indirect question, or a polite request. Although it may have the same structure as a question, a polite request ends with a period.

> Ali Mazahri was promoted to a position with increased salary and responsibilities. (Statement.)
>
> Send our latest catalog and price list to them. (Command.)
>
> Tracy asked whether we had sent the price list. (Indirect question.)
>
> Would you please send me an introductory sample. (Polite request.)

To Punctuate Abbreviations

Because of their inconsistencies, abbreviations present problems to writers. The following suggestions will help you organize certain groups of abbreviations and provide many models. In studying these models, note the spacing, capitalization, and use of periods. Always consult a good dictionary or style manual when in doubt.

Use periods after many abbreviations beginning with lowercase letters.

a.m. (ante meridiem)	i.e. (that is)
e.g. (for example)	ft. (foot or feet)

Exceptions: mph (miles per hour), wpm (words per minute), mm (millimeter), and kg (kilogram).

Use periods for most abbreviations containing capital and lowercase letters.

Dr. (Doctor)	Mr. (Mister)
Esq. (Esquire)	No. (number)
Ms. (blend of Miss and Mrs.)	Sat. (Saturday)

Use periods with abbreviations that represent academic degrees, geographical expressions, and initials of a person's first and middle names.

B.A. (bachelor of arts)	S.A. (South America)
M.B.A. (master of business administration)	U.K. (United Kingdom)

M.D. (doctor of medicine)   U.S.A. (United States of America)

Ph.D. (doctor of philosophy)   Ms. T. L. Clem (initials of name)

Study Tip

Most abbreviations fall in this group. Note capitalized letters, lack of periods, and tight spacing.

Do *not* use periods for most capitalized abbreviations.

CEO (chief executive officer)   IBM (International Business Machines)

CIO (chief information officer)   ID (identification)

CPA (certified public accountant)   OCR (optical character reader)

CPU (central processing unit)   RAM (random-access memory)

EPA (Environmental Protection Agency)   SASE (self-addressed, stamped envelope)

EST (Eastern Standard time)   SEC (Securities and Exchange Commission)

FYI (for your information)   SOP (standard operating procedure)

GDP (gross domestic product)   URL (Universal Resource Locator)

Some abbreviations have two forms.

c.o.d., COD (collect on delivery)   f.o.b., FOB (free on board)

d.b.a., DBA (doing business as)   p.o.e., POE (port of entry)

To Punctuate Numerals

For a monetary sum use a period (decimal point) to separate dollars from cents.

The two items in question, $13.92 and $98, were both charged in the month of October.

Use a period (decimal point) to mark a decimal fraction.

Although a moderate voter turnout was predicted, only 18.6 percent of registered voters actually voted.

Uses for the Question Mark

To Punctuate Direct Questions

Use a question mark at the end of a direct question.

What qualities are necessary for a person to become a successful administrator?

Have you compiled the figures requested by CyberVision, Inc.?

Study Tip

Use a period after a polite request if you expect an action rather than a yes-or-no answer.

Do not punctuate polite requests as questions. These are considered to be commands or "please do" statements. A polite request asks the reader to perform a specific action and is usually answered by an action rather than a verbal response.

Will you please mail your check in the enclosed envelope.

To Punctuate Questions Appended to Statements

Place a question mark after a question that is appended to a statement. Use a comma to separate the statement from the question.

They have already established a Web site, haven't they?

This personnel announcement should be sent by e-mail, don't you think?

To Indicate Doubt

A question mark within parentheses may be used to indicate a degree of doubt about some aspect of a statement.

The accounting department needs two(?) temporary clerks.

A beginning salary of $3,500(?) per month is possible.

Uses for the Exclamation Point

The exclamation point is an emphatic mark of punctuation reserved for strong feelings. It is seldom seen in business writing.

To Express Strong Emotion

After a word, phrase, or clause expressing strong emotion, use an exclamation point. In business writing, however, exclamation points should be used sparingly.

Impossible! We understood the deadline to be tomorrow.

What a day! Will 5 p.m. never come?

It is incredible that my watch is still working after such punishment!

Do not use an exclamation point after mild interjections, such as *oh* and *well*.

Well, it seems we have little choice in the matter.

Now complete the reinforcement exercises for Level I.

L e v e l   I I

Uses for the Dash

The dash is a legitimate and effective mark of punctuation when used according to accepted conventions. As an emphatic punctuation mark, however, the dash loses effectiveness when it is overused. In typewritten or simple word processing-generated material, a dash is formed by typing two hyphens with no space before, between, or after the hyphens. In printed or desktop publishing-generated material, a dash appears as a solid line (an *em* dash). (Note: Many current word processors will automatically convert two hyphens to an *em* dash). Study the following suggestions for and illustrations of appropriate uses of the dash.

To Set Off Parenthetical Elements

Within a sentence a parenthetical element is usually set off by commas. If, however, the parenthetical element itself contains internal commas, use dashes (or parentheses) to set it off.

Spot the Blooper

Ad for an electronics store published in the *Journal-News* [Rockland, NY]: "Bring in any competitor's ad and we will beat the price plus 10% of the difference in price or it's your's free!"

Sources of raw materials—farming, mining, fishing, and forestry—are all dependent on energy.

Four administrative assistants—Priscilla Alvarez, Vicki Evans, Yoshiki Ono, and Edward Botsko—received cash bonuses for outstanding performance in their departments.

To Indicate an Interruption

An interruption or abrupt change of thought may be separated from the rest of a sentence by a dash.

The shipment will be on its way—you have my word—by Wednesday.

Send the disks by Friday—no, we must have them sooner.

Sentences with abrupt changes of thought or with appended afterthoughts can usually be improved through rewriting.

To Set Off a Summarizing Statement

Use a dash (not a colon) to separate an introductory list from a summarizing statement.

Variety of tasks, contact with people, opportunity for advancement—these are what I seek in a job.

Running, playing tennis, and reading—those are Bill's favorite pastimes.

To Attribute a Quotation

Place a dash between a quotation and its source.

"English is the language of men ever famous and foremost in the achievements of liberty."—John Milton

"A man has no worse enemy than himself."—Cicero

Uses for Parentheses

Parentheses are useful to set off nonessential sentence elements. Careful writers avoid overusing parentheses because they distract readers.

To Set Off Nonessential Sentence Elements

Generally, nonessential sentence elements may be punctuated as follows: (a) with commas, to make the lightest possible break in the normal flow of a sentence; (b) with dashes, to emphasize the enclosed material; and (c) with parentheses, to de-emphasize the enclosed material.

One of the blueprints, which appears on page 7, shows the internal structure of the engine clearly. (Normal punctuation.)

One of the blueprints—which appears on page 7—shows the internal structure of the engine clearly. (Dashes emphasize enclosed material.)

One of the blueprints (which appears on page 7) shows the internal structure of the engine clearly. (Parentheses de-emphasize enclosed material.)

Explanations, references, and directions are often enclosed in parentheses.

> The bank's current business hours (10 a.m. to 3 p.m.) will be extended in the near future (to 6 p.m.).

> We recommend that you use hearing protectors (see our comment on p. 618) when using this electric drill.

Additional Considerations

If the material enclosed by parentheses is embedded within another sentence, a question mark or exclamation point may be used where normally expected. Do not, however, use a period after a statement embedded within another sentence.

> We have tickets to *New York, New York* (have you seen it?) on the evening of March 9. (A question mark concludes a question enclosed by parentheses and embedded in another sentence.)

> The fire alarm sounded (but no one responded!) during the middle of our final exam. (An exclamation mark concludes an exclamation enclosed by parentheses and embedded in another sentence.)

> An air conditioner cools space (this will be discussed in detail in the next chapter) by removing heat from it. (A period is not used at the end of a statement that is enclosed by parentheses and embedded in another sentence.)

If the material enclosed by parentheses is not embedded in another sentence, use whatever punctuation is required.

> Report writers must document all references. (See the appendix for a guide to current documentation formats.)

> In fewer than ten years, the price of that article has tripled. (Who would have thought it possible?)

In sentences involving expressions within parentheses, a comma, semicolon, or colon that would normally occupy the position occupied by the second parenthesis is then placed after that parenthesis.

> When I return from my trip (in late June), I will begin work on the feasibility study. (Comma follows parenthesis.)

> Your application for a credit card was received before the deadline (November 1); however, you did not supply two financial references. (Semicolon follows parenthesis.)

Now complete the reinforcement exercises for Level II.

Level III

Uses for Quotation Marks

Quotation marks help readers understand what words were written or spoken by somebody else. They may also be used to enclose short expressions, definitions, and titles.

To Enclose Direct Quotations

Double quotation marks are used to enclose direct quotations. Unless the exact words of a writer or speaker are being repeated, however, quotation marks are not employed.

> "There is a world market for about five computers," said IBM founder Thomas J. Watson. (Direct quotation enclosed.)

> Dwight Moody said that character is what you are in the dark. (Indirect quotation requires no quotation marks.)

Capitalize only the first word of a direct quotation.

> "The best way to cheer yourself up," said Mark Twain, "is to cheer everybody else up." (Do not capitalize *is*.)

To Enclose Quotations Within Quotations

Single quotation marks (apostrophes on most keyboards) are used to enclose quoted passages cited within quoted passages.

> Linda DeLorme remarked, "In business writing I totally agree with Aristotle, who said, 'A good style must, first of all, be clear.'" (Single quotation marks within double quotation marks.)

To Enclose Short Expressions

Slang, words used in a special sense, and words following *stamped* or *marked* are often enclosed within quotation marks.

> Cheryl feared that her presentation would "bomb." (Slang.)

> Federal Reserve Banks are called "bankers' banks." (Words used in a special sense.)

> In Web terminology, robots are referred to as "bots." (Word used in a special sense.)

> The package was stamped "Handle with Care." (Words following *stamped*.)

To Enclose Definitions

Quotation marks are used to enclose definitions of words or expressions. The word or expression being defined should be underscored or set in italics.

> The Latin word *ergo* means "therefore" or "hence."

> Businessmen use the term *working capital* to indicate an "excess of current assets over current debts."

To Enclose Titles

Quotation marks are used to enclose the titles of subdivisions of literary and artistic works, such as magazine and newspaper articles, chapters of books, episodes of television shows, poems, lectures, songs, and links in Web sites.

However, italics (or underscores) are used to enclose the titles of complete works, such as the names of books, magazines, Web sites, pamphlets, movies, television series, albums, and newspapers.

Hot Link

For an online explanation of the use of quotation marks, visit the Purdue Online Writing Lab **<http://owl. english.purdue.edu/ handouts/grammar/ g_quote.html>**.

Spot the Blooper

From *The Journal-American* [Bellevue, WA]: "Youths caught breaking the law or their parents could face a $250 fine or community service."

Spot the Blooper

From *The Times & Record News* [Wichita Falls, TX]: "Do not sweep an area where there have been rodents with a broom."

One source of information for your term paper might be the magazine article "Demise of a Cash Cow," which appeared in *Newsweek* recently.

Students find the chapter entitled "E-Mail Netiquette" from *Writing in the World of Work* very helpful.

The episode "Turnabout Intruder," in which a vengeful woman took mental control of Kirk's body, ended the long-running *Star Trek* TV series.

For current online employment information, go to Dr. Mary Ellen Guffey's Web site for students, *Communication @ Work* <www.meguffey.com>, and click the link for "Job Search."

Additional Punctuation Considerations

Periods and commas are always placed inside closing quotation marks, whether single or double. Semicolons and colons are, on the other hand, always placed outside quotation marks.

Kay Stephan said, "I'm sure the package was marked 'Fragile.'"

The article is entitled "Corporate Espionage," but we can't seem to locate the magazine in which it appeared.

Our contract stipulated that "both parties must accept arbitration as binding"; therefore, the decision reached by the arbitrators is final.

Three dates have been scheduled for the seminar called "E-Commerce and You": April 1, May 3, and June 5.

Question marks and exclamation points may go inside or outside closing quotation marks, as determined by the form of the quotation.

Kalonji Watts said, "How may I apply for that position?" (Quotation is a question.)

"The next time your cell phone rings" fumed the CEO, "we will ask you to leave!" (Quotation is an exclamation.)

Do you know who it was who said, "Money is more trouble than it's worth"? (Incorporating sentence asks question; quotation does not.)

I can't believe that the check was stamped "Insufficient Funds"! (Incorporating sentence is an exclamation; quotation is not.)

When did the manager say, "Who wants to reserve a summer vacation?" (Both incorporating sentence and quotation are questions. Use only one question mark inside the quotation marks.)

Uses for Brackets

Within quotations, brackets are used by writers to enclose their own inserted remarks. Such remarks may be corrective, illustrative, or explanatory. Brackets are also used within quotations to enclose the word *sic*, which means "thus" or "so." This Latin form is used to emphasize the fact that an error obvious to all actually appears *thus* in the quoted material.

"A British imperial gallon," reported Miss Sohoori, "is equal to 1.2 U.S. gallons [4.54 liters]."

"The company's reorganization program," wrote President Theodore Bailey, "will have its greatest affect [*sic*] on our immediate sales."

Spot the Blooper

From an invitation to a dinner honoring newly elected Board of Education members [Scarborough, MA]: "Your Invited."

Spot the Blooper

Sign on I-75 in Florida: "Speed Limit Strickly Enforced"

Uses for the Underscore and Italics

The underscore or italics are normally used for titles of books, magazines, newspapers, and other complete works published separately. In addition, words under discussion in the sentence and used as nouns are italicized or underscored.

> *Creative Financing*, the latest book of author Thomas Manley, was favorably reviewed in *The Wall Street Journal*.

> Two of the most frequently misspelled words are *calendar* and *separate*. (Words used as nouns.)

Now complete the reinforcement exercises for Level III.

HOTLINE QUERIES

Q: My team and I are writing a proposal in which we say that *some of the current dot-coms are undervalued*. We can't agree on how to write *dot-coms*.

A: This playful reference to Internet companies is a little slangy, but we are hearing it more and more often. You could write it *dot.com*, but that's like saying *dot dot com*. I suggest using *dot-com* to avoid the obvious redundancy.

Q: We can't decide whether the period should go inside quotation marks or outside. At the end of a sentence, I have typed the title "Positive Vs. Negative Values." The author of the document that I'm typing wants the period outside because she says the title does not have a period in it.

A: In the U.S., typists and printers have adopted a uniform style: when a period or comma falls at the same place quotation marks would normally fall, the period or comma is always placed inside the quotation marks—regardless of the content of the quotation. In Britain a different style is observed.

Q: I'm not sure where to place the question mark in this sentence: *His topic will be "What Is a Good Health Plan (?)"* Does the question mark go inside the quotation marks? Too, should a comma precede the title of the talk?

A: First, a question mark goes inside the quotation mark because the quoted material is in the form of a question. Be sure that you do not use another end punctuation mark after the quotation mark. Second, do not use a comma preceding the title of the topic because the sentence follows normal subject-verb-complement order. No comma is needed to separate the verb and the complement.

Q: Is it correct to say *Brad and myself were chosen* . . . ?

A: No. Use the nominative case pronoun *I* instead of *myself*.

Q: What salutation should I use when addressing a letter to Sister Mary Elizabeth?

A: The salutation of your letter should be *Dear Sister Mary Elizabeth*. For more information on forms of address, consult a good dictionary or reference manual.

Q: Is anything wrong with saying *someone else's car*?

A: Although it sounds somewhat awkward, the possessive form is acceptable. The apostrophe is correctly placed in *else's*.

Q: I've looked in the dictionary but I'm still unsure about whether to hyphenate *copilot*.

A: The hyphen is no longer used in most words beginning with the prefix *co* (*coauthor, co-counsel, codesign, cofeature, cohead, copilot, costar, cowrite*). Only a few words retain the hyphen (*co-anchor, co-edition, co-official*). Check your dictionary for usage. In reading your dictionary, notice that centered periods are used to indicate syllables (*co•work•er*); hyphens are used to show hyphenated syllables (*co-own*).

Q: Can you tell me what sounds strange in this sentence and why? *The building looks like it was redesigned.*

A: The word *like* should not be used as a conjunction, as has been done in your sentence. Substitute *as if* (*the building looks as if it was redesigned*).

Name _____

Level I

A. (Self-check) In the spaces provided after each sentence, indicate whether a period, question mark, or exclamation point is needed. Use the symbol. If no additional punctuation is required, write *C*.

Example: May I have your answer by return mail⊙   .

1. Will you please send me your latest catalog as soon as possible.   *P*
2. What a great job you did on this proposal,   *EP*
3. You are not using the printer, are you?   *Q*
4. Has anyone checked the FedEx Web site to see if our package was delivered?   *Q*
5. Send for your complimentary brochure today.   *P*
6. Help! Smoke is coming from my keyboard.   *EP*
7. Juanita asked if she should come in at 7 a.m. to complete the work for LaserPro, Inc.   *P*
8. Oh, I don't believe we should worry about it at this time,   *P*
9. I wonder whether he received my e-mail message.   *P*
10. Dr. Janet G. Adams and Judy Wagner, Esq., will appear on TV at 2 p.m. EST.   *C*

Check your answers below.

B. Write the letter of the correctly punctuated sentence.

1. (a) I wonder if I could return Mr. Lee's call as early as 8 am.
   (b) I wonder if I could return Mr. Lee's call as early as 8 a.m.?
   (c) I wonder if I could return Mr. Lee's call as early as 8 a.m.   *C*

2. (a) Did our CEO interview Ms. E. W. Rasheen for the CPA position?
   (b) Did our C.E.O. interview Ms. E. W. Rasheen for the C.P.A. position?
   (c) Did our CEO interview Ms E. W. Rasheen for the CPA position?   *A*

3. (a) Isabelle asked whether jobs from the U.K. or S.A. were listed online.
   (b) Isabelle asked whether jobs from the UK or SA were listed online.
   (c) Isabelle asked whether jobs from the U.K. or S.A. were listed online?   *A*

4. (a) Tell Mr. Willett to submit his proposal immediately to InfoWorld, Inc..
   (b) Tell Mr. Willett to submit his proposal immediately to InfoWorld, Inc.
   (c) Tell Mr Willett to submit his proposal immediately to InfoWorld, Inc.   *B*

5. (a) The No 1 official at the EPA has a B.A. from Ohio State.
   (b) The No. 1 official at the E.P.A. has a BA from Ohio State.
   (c) The No. 1 official at the EPA has a B.A. from Ohio State.   *C*

1. possible! 2. proposal! 3. you? 4. delivered? 5. today. 6. keyboard! 7. Inc. 8. time. 9. message. 10. C

337

C. In the following sentences all punctuation has been omitted. Insert commas, periods, question marks, colons, and exclamation points. Some words have extra spaces between them so that punctuation may be inserted. Use a caret (∧) to indicate each insertion. In the space at the right, indicate the number of punctuation marks you inserted. Consult a reference manual or a dictionary for abbreviation style if necessary.

Example: I wonder if William R. Templeton Jr. was hired as C I O at Intel, Inc.   _3_

1. Will you please add Mary B. Mancuso, Esq. to the address list.   _5_

2. Abbreviations like a.m. and p.m. often appear in business correspondence.   _5_

3. Dr. James C. Downs was recently named C. E O at MileHigh Enterprises.   _5_

4. You did place an ad in the classified section, didn't you?   _2_

5. It was Thu Thi Tran, not Kim Sloan, who should have received the c. o.d. shipment.   _6_

6. What a dilemma the latest S E C regulations have created.   _1_

7. Stop! Don't touch that switch!   _2_

8. Deliver the signed contracts to Mr. C. P. Ryan before 5 p. m.   _5_

9. If I B M offers a full-service contract, we would be interested.   _2_

10. What a great day for a picnic!   _1_

11. Most automobiles are delivered f. o. b. Detroit.   _4_

12. After completing her A. A. degree at Miami-Dade Community College, Kim transferred and began working on a B. S. degree.   _5_

13. Ms. J. S. Neighbors has been appointed consultant for educational services to the A F L—C I O.   _4_

14. He often uses the abbreviations e. g. and i.e. in his e-mail messages.   _5_

15. Since the funds were earned in the U. K., I must consult my C P A about U. S taxes.   _5_

16. Some authorities wonder if the I Q of schoolchildren is affected by T V.   _1_

17. Has the erroneous charge of $45.95 been removed from my account?   _2_

18. The guest list includes the following individuals: Dr. Lyn Clark, Ms. Frances Hendricks, and Professor Jean Sturgill.   _6_

19. Lt. Gen. Maxwell asked whether the New York office was open until 6 p.m.   _4_

20. You did check the URL for that Web site, didn't you?   _2_

Level II

A. (Self-check) Write the letter of the correctly punctuated sentence in the space provided.

1. (a) Riding, roping, and bronco busting: these are Chet's favorite rodeo events.
   (b) Riding, roping, and bronco busting—these are Chet's favorite rodeo events.
   (c) Riding, roping, and bronco busting; these are Chet's favorite rodeo events.   _B_

2. (a) "Civilization and profits go hand in hand."—Calvin Coolidge
   (b) "Civilization and profits go hand in hand," Calvin Coolidge
   (c) "Civilization and profits go hand in hand": Calvin Coolidge   _A_

3. (a) He scored a perfect 900 (can you believe it) on the exam.
   (b) He scored a perfect 900 (can you believe it?) on the exam.
   (c) He scored a perfect 900 (can you believe it) on the exam?   *B*

4. (Emphasize parenthetical element.)   *C*
   (a) Currently our basic operating costs: rent, utilities, and wages, are
       10 percent higher than last year.
   (b) Currently our basic operating costs (rent, utilities, and wages) are
       10 percent higher than last year.
   (c) Currently our basic operating costs—rent, utilities, and wages—
       are 10 percent higher than last year.

5. (a) Loading and unloading film (see page 23 in the manual) must be done care-   *A*
       fully.
   (b) Loading and unloading film, see page 23 in the manual, must be
       done carefully.
   (c) Loading and unloading film: see page 23 in the manual, must be
       done carefully.

6. (a) Recently you applied for a position (executive assistant); however, you did not   *A*
       indicate for which branch your application is intended.
   (b) Recently you applied for a position; (executive assistant) how-
       ever, you did not indicate for which branch your application is
       intended.
   (c) Recently you applied for a position (executive assistant;) however,
       you did not indicate for which branch your application is in-
       tended.

7. (Emphasize.)   *B*
   (a) Sales, sales, and more sales: that's what we need to succeed.
   (b) Sales, sales, and more sales—that's what we need to succeed.
   (c) Sales, sales, and more sales; that's what we need to succeed.

8. (De-emphasize.)   *C*
   (a) Three Washington cities—Seattle, Everett, and Tacoma—are com-
       peting for the large industrial complex.
   (b) Three Washington cities, Seattle, Everett, and Tacoma, are com-
       peting for the large industrial complex.
   (c) Three Washington cities (Seattle, Everett, and Tacoma) are com-
       peting for the large industrial complex.

Check your answers below.

B. Insert dashes or parentheses in the following sentences. In the space provided after each
sentence, write the number of punctuation marks you inserted. Count each parenthesis
and each dash as a single mark.

Example: (Emphasize.) Three of the biggest problems with e-mail—privacy, overuse,   2
            and etiquette—will be discussed.

1. (De-emphasize.) The modernized production of Shakespeare's "As You Like It"   *3*
   (have you read the reviews?) will be opening here very shortly.

2. Fingerprints, mug shots, and arrest records—these are now stored on microforms   *1*
   by law enforcement officers.

3. "Do not squander time, for that is the stuff life is made of."—Benjamin Franklin.   *2*

1. b   2. a   3. b   4. c   5. a   6. a   7. b   8. c

4. (Emphasize.) Three branch assistant managers Courtney Young, Ramon Lopez, and Samantha Johnson will be promoted this month. _____ 2

5. (De-emphasize.) Three branch assistant managers (Courtney Young, Ramon Lopez, and Samantha Johnson) will be promoted this month. _____ 2

6. (De-emphasize.) As soon as you are able to make an appointment (try to do so before December 30), we will process your insurance forms. _____ 2

7. Quality copies, low cost, ease of operation, speedy output what more could a customer want in an economical office copy machine? _____ 1

8. Funds for the project will be released on the following dates (see Section 12.3 of the original grant): January 1, March 14, and June 30. _____ 2

9. (De-emphasize.) Although toy factories are heavily concentrated in three locations (New York, Chicago, and Boston), the largest single manufacturer is located in Hawthorne, California. _____ 2

10. The warranty period for this cordless drill is limited to sixty (60) days. _____ 2

C. Using three different forms of punctuation, correctly punctuate the following sentence. In the space provided explain how the three methods you have employed differ.

1. Numerous appeals all of which came from concerned parents prompted us to rethink the school closure.

2. Numerous appeals, all of which came from concerned parents, prompted us to rethink the school closure.

3. Numerous appeals (all of which came from concerned parents) prompted us to rethink the school closure.

Explanation: _____

_____

Level III

A. (Self-check) Indicate whether the following statements are true (T) or false (F).

1. Quotation marks are used to enclose the exact words of a writer or speaker. _T_

2. The names of books, magazines, pamphlets, and newspapers may be underscored or enclosed in quotation marks. _F_

3. Periods and commas are always placed inside closing quotation marks. _T_

4. Parentheses are used by writers to enclose their own remarks inserted into a quotation. _F_

5. A quotation within a quotation is shown with single quotation marks. _T_

6. Semicolons and colons are always placed inside closing quotation marks. _F_

7. The underscore is used to emphasize words that would be italicized in printed copy. _T_

8. If both a quotation and its introductory sentence are questions, use a question mark before the closing quotation marks. _T_

9. The word *sic* is used to show that a quotation is free of errors. _F_

10. A single quotation mark is typed by using the apostrophe key. _T_

Check your answers below.

B. Many, but not all, of the following sentences contain direct quotations. Insert all necessary punctuation.

Example: The term <u>preferred stock</u> means "stock having priority over common stock in the distribution of dividends."

1. "I have yet to hear a man," said Gloria Steinem, "ask for advice on how to combine marriage and a career."

2. Careful speakers use the word "mad" to mean "insane."

3. Dr. Upchurch's chapter entitled "Drawing the World Together" appeared in the book, *Global Links.*

4. Did the basketball coach really say, "If winning isn't important, why do they keep score?"

5. In his speech the software billionaire said, "Our goal is to link the world irregardless [*sic*] of national boundaries and restrictions."

6. Dr. Scott said that he hoped we would call him, if our team needed assistance.

7. When Garth began shouting during the argument, his friend Kendra told him to "chill."

8. The postal worker said, "Shall I stamp your package 'Fragile'?"

9. Did you see the article entitled "What People Earn" in last week's *Parade* magazine?

10. The expression *persona non grata* means one "who is not acceptable."

11. Would you please send a current catalog to Globex, Inc.?

12. (Direct quotation.) "The only thing you can get in a hurry," said the professor, "is trouble."

13. The three most important links at the *Globex Online Web* site are the following: "About Us," "Success Stories," and "Resources."

14. In *Business Week* I saw an article entitled "Communication for Global Markets."

15. (De-emphasize.) Only two dates (February 15 and March 1) are suitable for the meeting.

C. Writing Practice. On a separate sheet write a paragraph describing your favorite job. Try to include as many of the punctuation marks you have studied as possible. Include commas, semicolons, periods, question marks, exclamation points, dashes, parentheses, quotation marks, italics, and possibly even brackets. Include a quotation from your boss. Make up the name of a book or article that you could publish about this job.

Editor's Challenge

The following letter contains intentional errors representing spelling, proofreading, punctuation, and language principles covered thus far. You should mark 40 changes.

GLOBAL FOODS, INC.
814 Mission Street, Suite 205
San Francisco, CA 94104

May 15, 200x

Gulf Coast Importers, Inc
729 Bayou Street
New Orleans, LA. 70589

YOUR MAY 3 PURCHASE ORDER NO 14902

All the in stock items requested in your recent purchase order were ship to you Friday May 8 from our Oakland California warehouse.

Because of unseasonably wet weather in February; this springs supply of black teas from Sri Lanka are extremely limited. We have none of these fine tea on hand at present, however, we expect a small shipment to arrive by August 1.

We do have in our warehouse a stock of select black teas from the following sources, south China Japan and south India. Indian teas as you are well aware do not always meet some of our customers high standards. Which is why we hesitate to advice you to except the Indian tea as a substitute. Chinese and Japanese teas though are generally well regarded.

In fact one of our customers recently said "Our best sales are now from Chinese black tea. Another importer wrote "We are delighted with the recent shipment of Japanese black tea". Moreover an article in the January 8 issue of The new york times described the healthy affects of Japanese tea.

Please call us toll free at 1-800-321-8993, to tell us whether you wish to wait for the Sri Lankan black tea or whether you prefer the immediate supply of black tea from: China, Japan, or India.

BRIAN W. LEE, MANAGER

Goal: To learn more about electronic résumés.

You've just discovered that the company where you wish to apply uses a computer to scan all incoming résumés. You decide to learn more about electronic résumés.

1. With your Web browser on the screen, go to Pat Kendall's *Electronic Resumes* site **<http://www.reslady.com/electronic.html>.** This is one of the resources available at the Guffey Student Web site listed under "Résumé Resources."

2. Read the information on scannable resumes. What are three techniques you should use in preparing a scannable résumé? Print two pages from this Web site.

3. Read the information on keyword strategies. How can you determine the keywords for your profession?

4. Click on **Sample HTML Résumé**. What is distinctive about the model HTML résumé shown?

5. End your session. Submit your printouts and answers to the questions posed here.

POSTTEST

Use proofreading marks to insert necessary punctuation.

1. Will you please send me a copy of the book entitled Dynamite Résumés

2. When did we receive this envelope marked Confidential

3. The only guests who have not sent RSVPs are Miss Mendoza Mrs Gold and Mr Sims

4. The word principal was misused in the chapter entitled Writing Persuasive Letters

5. Did Professor Miles say "How many students expect to miss the test Friday"

1. Dynamite Résumés. 2. "Confidential"? 3. Mendoza, Mrs. Gold, and Mr. Sims. 4. principal "Writing Persuasive Letters." 5. say, "How Friday?"

CHECKLIST OF BONUS LEARNING RESOURCES

The following additional learning resources are available to you. Your instructor will tell you which to complete.

- Web Editor's Challenge Exercise

- Web Interactive Chapter Review

- Web PowerPoint Slides

- Web Crossword Puzzle

- WebCheck Reinforcement Exercises 18.1, 18.2

- Self-Help Exercises

- Electronic Study Guide

Unit Review Chapters 16–18

Name _____

First, review Chapters 16–18. Then, test your comprehension of those chapters by completing the exercises that follow and comparing your responses with those shown at the end of the book.

Level I

Insert necessary punctuation in the following sentences. Write *C* if the sentence is correct.

1. Because of your many years of service Ms. Labinski we are presenting you with this plaque. _____

2. However the matter is resolved, the goodwill of the customer is paramount. _____

3. Our Human Resources Department is concerned with recruiting hiring and training new employees. _____

4. A student who studies diligently and masters the principles will score well on the examination. _____

5. The management team feels on the other hand that it must hold the line on benefits and salaries. _____

6. Our field technician Ryan Ober knows the equipment thoroughly. _____

Select (a), (b), or (c) to indicate the correctly punctuated sentence.

7. (a) Some of the equipment is stored in the warehouse other equipment is now in transit. _____
   (b) Some of the equipment is stored in the warehouse, other equipment is now in transit.
   (c) Some of the equipment is stored in the warehouse; other equipment is now in transit.

8. (a) Reports have arrived from our offices in Bonn, Switzerland, Munich, Germany, and Vienna, Austria. _____
   (b) Reports have arrived from our offices in Bonn, Switzerland; Munich, Germany; and Vienna, Austria.
   (c) Reports have arrived from our offices in: Bonn, Switzerland; Munich, Germany; and Vienna, Austria.

9. (a) Investments should turn a profit; however, security is also important. _____
   (b) Investments should turn a profit, however, security is also important.
   (c) Investments should turn a profit; however security is also important.

10. (a) Would you please send the shipment COD. _____
    (b) Would you please send the shipment c.o.d.?
    (c) Would you please send the shipment COD?

Select (a), (b), or (c) to indicate the correctly punctuated sentence.

11. (a) She said she held AA and BS degrees didn't she?   _____
    (b) She said she held A.A. and B.S. degrees, didn't she?
    (c) She said she held AA and BS degrees, didn't she?

12. (a) Wow! A total of 89.9 percent of the voters approved!   _____
    (b) Wow, a total of 89 point 9 percent of the voters approved!
    (c) Wow. A total of 89.9 percent of the voters approved!

13. (a) We're looking for three qualities in an employee; honesty, intelligence, and experience.   _____
    (b) We're looking for three qualities in an employee, honesty, intelligence, and experience.
    (c) We're looking for three qualities in an employee: honesty, intelligence, and experience.

14. (a) Thus far, we have received brochures from Compaq, IBM, and Dell.   _____
    (b) Thus far, we have received brochures from, Compaq, IBM, and Dell.
    (c) Thus far, we have received brochures from: Compaq, IBM, and Dell.

15. (a) Ms. Sakoda said, "We used to depend on fixed-rate mortgages."   _____
    (b) Ms. Sakoda said: "We used to depend on fixed-rate mortgages."
    (c) Ms. Sakoda said; "We used to depend on fixed-rate mortgages."

16. (a) Three of the most populous states: Illinois, New York, and California, will receive extra federal funding.   _____
    (b) Three of the most populous states—Illinois, New York, and California—will receive extra federal funding.
    (c) Three of the most populous states, Illinois, New York, and California, will receive extra federal funding.

17. (a) Cameras, VCRs, and cell phones—these are only some of the products we carry.   _____
    (b) Cameras, VCRs, and cell phones: these are only some of the products we carry.
    (c) Cameras, VCRs, and cell phones, these are only some of the products we carry.

18. (Emphasize.)   _____
    (a) In only three months, October, November, and December, our store does 80 percent of its yearly business.
    (b) In only three months: October, November, and December, our store does 80 percent of its yearly business.
    (c) In only three months–October, November, and December–our store does 80 percent of its yearly business.

19. (a) The three Texas cities selected are Houston, Fort Worth, and Dallas.   _____
    (b) The three Texas cities selected are: Houston, Fort Worth, and Dallas.
    (c) The three Texas cities selected are—Houston, Fort Worth, and Dallas.

20. (De-emphasize.)   _____
    (a) A pilot project—refer to page 6 of the report—may help us justify the new system.
    (b) A pilot project, refer to page 6 of the report, may help us justify the new system.
    (c) A pilot project (refer to page 6 of the report) may help us justify the new system.

Select (a), (b), or (c) to indicate the correctly punctuated sentence.

21. (a) In summary reports of a hostile takeover are exaggerated.
    (b) In summary–reports of a hostile takeover are exaggerated.
    (c) In summary, reports of a hostile takeover are exaggerated. _____

22. (a) Our goal is to help, not hamper, good communication.
    (b) Our goal is to help–not hamper, good communication.
    (c) Our goal is to help, not hamper good communication. _____

23. (a) Only one department submitted its report on time, namely the Legal
        Department.
    (b) Only one department submitted its report on time, namely, the Legal
        Department.
    (c) Only one department submitted its report on time: namely, the Legal
        Department. _____

24. (a) The location of the convention has been narrowed to three sites, namely, New
        Orleans, Chicago, and San Francisco.
    (b) The location of the convention has been narrowed to three sites; namely, New
        Orleans, Chicago, and San Francisco.
    (c) The location of the convention has been narrowed to three sites; namely New
        Orleans, Chicago, and San Francisco. _____

25. (a) The computer was producing "garbage," that is, the screen showed gibberish.
    (b) The computer was producing "garbage"; that is, the screen showed gibberish.
    (c) The computer was producing "garbage;" that is, the screen showed gibberish. _____

26. (a) A cartel is defined as a "group of companies acting to control prices."
    (b) A "cartel" is defined as a 'group of companies acting to control prices.'
    (c) A *cartel* is defined as a "group of companies acting to control prices." _____

27. (a) HomeOffice, a monthly magazine for small business owners, featured an article
        called "Financial Formulas to Keep You in the Black."
    (b) *HomeOffice*, a monthly magazine for small business owners, featured an article
        called "Financial Formulas to Keep You in the Black."
    (c) "HomeOffice," a monthly magazine for small business owners, featured an article
        called *Financial Formulas to Keep You in the Black.* _____

28. (a) "An ombudsman, said Sally Stouder, is an individual hired by management to
        investigate and resolve employee complaints."
    (b) "An ombudsman," said Sally Stouder, "Is an individual hired by management to
        investigate and resolve employee complaints."
    (c) "An ombudsman," said Sally Stouder, "is an individual hired by management to
        investigate and resolve employee complaints." _____

29. (a) Who was it who said, "Never cut what you can untie."?
    (b) Who was it who said, "Never cut what you can untie?"
    (c) Who was it who said, "Never cut what you can untie"? _____

30. (a) Did the office manager really say, "Stamp this package 'Confidential'?"
    (b) Did the office manager really say, "Stamp this package 'Confidential'"?
    (c) Did the office manager really say, "Stamp this package "Confidential"? _____

Hot Line Review

Write the letter of the word or phrase that correctly completes each sentence.

31. Every measure has been taken to _____ your satisfaction.
    a. insure   **b.** ensure   _____

32. Because few stockholders were _____ of the CEO's total salary package,   _____
    no complaints were heard.
    a. appraised   **b.** apprised

33. My partner and _____ have signed an agreement.   _____
    a. I   **b.** me   **c.** myself

34. Have you ever been _____ for a speeding violation?   _____
    a. cited   **b.** sited   **c.** sighted

35. We give our Web address to _____ requests it.   _____
    a. whomever   **b.** whoever

Informational Business Letters

Business letters are forms of external communication. That is, they deliver information to individuals outside an organization. Business letters may request information, respond to requests, make claims, seek adjustments, order goods and services, sell goods and services, recommend individuals, develop goodwill, or achieve many other goals. All businesspeople have to write business letters of various kinds, but a majority of those letters will be informational.

Characteristics of Business Letters

Writers of good business letters–whether the messages are informational, persuasive, or bad news–are guided by the four Cs: conciseness, clarity, correctness, and courtesy. In earlier Writing Workshops, you learned techniques for making your writing concise and clear. You've also studied many guidelines for correct grammar and usage throughout this textbook. At this point we'll review some of these techniques briefly as they relate to business letters.

Conciseness. Concise letters save the reader's time by presenting information directly. You can make your letters concise by avoiding these writing faults: (a) wordy phrases (such as *in addition to the above* and *in view of the fact that*), (b) excessive use of expletives (such as *There are four reasons that explain . . .* or *It is a good plan*), (c) long lead-ins (such as *This message is to inform you that* or *I am writing this letter to*), (d) needless adverbs (such as *very, definitely, quite, extremely,* and *really*), and (e) old-fashioned expressions (such as *attached please find* and *pursuant to your request*).

Clarity. Business letters are clear when they are logically organized and when they present enough information for the reader to understand what the writer intended. Informational letters are usually organized directly with the main idea first. Clarity can be enhanced by including all the necessary information. Some authorities estimate that one third of all business letters are written to clarify previous correspondence. To ensure that your letters are clear, put yourself in the reader's position and analyze what you have written. What questions may the reader ask? Does your information proceed logically from one point to another? Are your sentences and paragraphs coherent?

Correctness. Two aspects of correctness are accuracy of facts and accuracy of form. In regard to facts, good business writers prepare to write by gathering relevant information. They collect supporting documents (previous letters, memos, and reports), they make inquiries, they jot down facts, and they outline the message. Correct letters require thorough preparation. In the same manner, correct letters require careful proofreading and attention to form. Typographical errors, spelling irregularities, and grammatical faults distract the reader and damage the credibility of the writer. Correct business letters also follow one of the conventional formats, such as block, modified block, or simplified style, shown in Appendix C.

Courtesy. You develop courtesy in business letters by putting yourself in the place of the reader. Imagine how you would like to be treated and show the same consideration and respect for the individual receiving your message. The ideas you express and the words used to convey those ideas create an impression on the reader. Be alert to words that may create a negative feeling, such as *you claim, unfortunately, you neglected, you forgot, your complaint*, and so forth. Create a positive feeling by presenting your message from the point of view of the reader. Try to use the word *you* more than the words *I* and *we*. Create a positive tone in business letters by using conversational language. How can you make your writing sound like conversation? Think of your reader as if he or she were sitting across from you having a friendly chat. Avoid formal, pretentious, and stuffy language, such as *the undersigned is pleased to grant your request*. In your business messages you can develop goodwill toward your company and toward yourself by putting yourself in the place of the reader, by developing a friendly tone, and by using conversational language.

Skill Check 1 Reviewing the Four Cs

1. Which of the following is most concise?
   (a) Due to the fact that we had a warehouse fire, your shipment is delayed.
   (b) This is to inform you that your shipment will be delayed.
   (c) Because of a warehouse fire, your shipment is delayed.
   (d) There was a warehouse fire, which explains why your shipment is delayed. _____

2. Which of the following is clear and logical?
   (a) If the strike is not settled quickly, it may last a while.
   (b) Flying over the rain forests of Indonesia, the trees form a solid and menacing green carpet.
   (c) This is not to suggest that Salt Lake, Denver, and Houston are not the most affordable areas for housing.
   (d) Prince Charles complained that the citizens of Britain speak and write their language poorly. _____

3. Which of the following is grammatically correct?
   (a) We hope that you and he will be in town for our next seminar.
   (b) A host of ethical issues involve business, including e-mail privacy, whistleblowing, and mission statements.
   (c) We must develop a policy on returning merchandise. So that they know about it before they are made.
   (d) Jeffrey has twenty years experience in the software industry. _____

4. Which of the following is most courteous?
   (a) During your interview, I informed you that if we were not successful in finding a suitable candidate, I would contact you.
   (b) We appreciate receiving your letter describing your treatment by our store security personnel.
   (c) In your letter of June 1, you claim that you were harassed by our store security personnel.
   (d) Unfortunately, we are unable to complete your entire order because you neglected _____ to provide a shirt size.

5. Which of the following sounds most conversational?
   (a) Attached herewith is the form you requested.
   (b) Pursuant to your request, we are forwarding the form you requested.
   (c) Under separate cover we are sending the form you requested.
   (d) You'll receive the form you requested in a separate mailing. _____

Writing Plan

Most business letters have three parts: opening, body, and closing. This three-part writing plan will help you organize the majority of your business messages quickly and effectively.

Opening. The opening of a business letter may include a subject line that refers to previous correspondence or summarizes the content of the message. A subject line should make sense but should not be a complete sentence; it is not followed by a period.

The first sentence of a business letter that requests or delivers information should begin directly with the main idea. If you are asking for information, use one of two approaches. Ask the most important question first, such as *Do you have a two-bedroom cottage on Devil's Lake available for the week of July 8-15?* A second approach involves beginning with a summary statement, such as *Please answer the following questions regarding. . . .* If the letter delivers information, begin with the most important information first, such as *Yes, we have a two-bedroom cottage on Devil's Lake available for . . . .* or *Here is the information you requested regarding . . . .* Most informational business letters should *not* begin with an explanation of why the letter is being written.

Body. The body of the letter provides explanations and additional information to clarify the first sentence. Use a separate paragraph for each new idea, being careful to strive for concise writing.

If the message lends itself to enumeration, express the items in a bulleted or numbered list. Be certain, of course, to construct the list so that each item is parallel.

Think about the individual reading your message. Will that person understand what you are saying? Have you included enough information? What may seem clear to you may not be so evident to your reader. In responding to requests, don't hesitate to include more information than was requested—if you feel it would be helpful.

Maintain a friendly, conversational, and positive tone.

Closing. Business letters that demand action should conclude with a specific request, including end dating if appropriate. That is, tell the reader when you would like the request complied with, and, if possible, provide a reason (for example, *Please send me this information by June 1 so that I can arrange my vacation*).

Letters that provide information may end with a summary statement or a pleasant, forward-looking thought (for example, *I hope this information helps you plan your summer vacation*). Business organizations may also use the closing to promote products or services.

Avoid ending your letters with mechanical phrases such as *If I can be of further service, don't hesitate to call on me*, or *Thanks for any information you can provide*. Find a fresh way to express your desire to be of service or to show appreciation.

Figure 18.1 illustrates the application of the writing plan to an information request. Notice that the subject line summarizes the main topic of the letter, while the first paragraph provides more information about the reason for writing. The body of the letter explains the main idea and includes a list of questions so that the reader can see quickly what information is being requested. The closing includes an end date with a reason.

Skill Check 2 Reviewing the Writing Plan

In the space provided, write a, b, or c to identify the letter part where each of the following might logically be found.

(a) Opening   (b) Body   (c) Closing

1. **Explanation and details**   _____

2. Subject line that summarizes main idea _____

3. End dating with reason _____

4. Enumerated or bulleted list _____

5. Main idea _____

6. Summary statement or forward-looking thought _____

Figure 18.1
Information Request

GraphicPros

264 South Halsted Street
Chicago Heights, IL 60412
FAX (708) 345-2210   VOICE (708) 345-8329   INTERNET: http://www.graphicpros.com

March 5, 200x

Ms. Kesha Scott
Micro Supplies and Software
P.O. Box 800
Fort Atkinson, WI 53538-2900

Dear Ms. Scott:

Summarizes main idea — SUBJECT: AVAILABILITY AND PRICE OF EQUIPMENT SECURITY DEVICES

Introduces purpose immediately — Please provide information and recommendations regarding security equipment to prevent the theft of office computers, keyboards, monitors, faxes, and printers.

Explains need for information — Our office now has 18 computer workstations and 6 printers that we must secure to desks or counters. Answers to the following questions will help us select the best devices for our purpose.

Groups open-ended questions into list for quick comprehension and best feedback

1. What device would you recommend that can secure a workstation consisting of a computer, monitor, and keyboard?

2. What expertise and equipment are required to install and remove the security device?

3. How much is each device? Do you offer quantity discounts, and, if so, how much?

Courteously provides end date and reason — Because our insurance rates will be increased if the security devices are not installed before May 12, we would appreciate your response by March 20.

Sincerely,

Brent R. Barnwell

Brent R. Barnwell
Office Manager

Writing Application 5.1

On a separate sheet of paper, or, preferably, at a computer, revise the following poorly written letter. Use block style (every line starts at the left margin) and mixed punctuation. This is a personal business letter; follow the format shown in Figure C.3 in Appendix C, inserting your own address in the return address block. Remember that the following letter is poorly written. Improve it!

Writer's street address
City, State Zip
Current date

Ms. Barbara L. Hernandez
Manager, Rainbow Resort
1102 West Brannan Island Road
Isleton, CA 95641-1102

Dear Ms. Hernandez:

I saw an advertisement recently in *Sunset* magazine where Rainbow Resort rents houseboats. My family and I (there are three kids and my wife and me) would like to take a vacation on a houseboat from July 17 through July 24 in the California Delta area. We've never done this before but it sounds interesting.

Please send me any information you may have. I'll have to make my vacation plans soon.

I have no idea how much this might cost. If we rent a houseboat, my wife wants to know do you provide bedding, dishes, pots and pans, and the like? I'm wondering about navigating a houseboat. Will I have to take a course or training on how to operate it? It may be too difficult for me to run. How far can we travel in the Delta area in one of your houseboats? What if we decide to stay on more than one week? I actually have two weeks of vacation, but we may want to travel in our RV part of the time. Does insurance come with the rental fee? My kids want to know if it has TV.

Yours,

Leslie E. Childers

Leslie E. Childers

Writing Application 5.2

Assume you are Barbara Hernandez. Write a response to Mr. Childers' letter. Use modified block style and mixed punctuation. Tell Mr. Childers that the rental fee, which is $175 per day or $1,000 per week, does include insurance. You have a houseboat available for July 17–24, but definite reservations must be made for that time and for the week following, if Mr. Childers decides to stay two weeks. Your houseboats can travel about 100 miles on the inland waterways of the Delta. Rainbow Resort provides bedding, dishes, and kitchenware. Yes, each houseboat has a TV set. You also provide an AM/FM radio and a stereo cassette player. Your houseboats accommodate four to ten people, and you require a deposit of $500 for a one-week reservation. Reservations must be received by June 1 to ensure a July vacation. Your houseboats are easy to operate. No special training is required, but you do give each operator about 30 minutes of instruction. Send Mr. Childers a brochure describing Rainbow Resort and the memorable holiday he and his family can enjoy. The scenery and attractions are good.

Writing Application 5.3

Write a personal business letter in response to the following problem. For your home office you ordered a combination telephone/answering machine called the Execudyne Remote 2010. Instead of troublesome cassette tapes, the Execudyne used solid-state microchips to record both incoming and outgoing messages. It had many attractive features, and you were eager to try it. When it arrived, however, you plugged it in and discovered that an irritating static sound interfered with every telephone call you made or received. Eventually you discovered that the static occurred only when the fluorescent light fixtures over your desk were turned on. When the lights were on, the telephone picked up static, making telephone calls impossible.

You returned the telephone January 15 by UPS two-day service to ElectroWare, Inc., the mail-order supplier from whom you purchased the unit. You still have a copy of the invoice, which states that merchandise may be returned for any reason within 30 days after purchase. You also have the UPS receipt proving that you returned it. However, your MasterCharge statement (No. 5390-3390-2219-0002) has not shown a credit for the return. Your last two statements show no credit for $188.90. You're wondering what happened. Did ElectroWare receive the returned telephone? Why hasn't your account been credited? If ElectroWare did not receive the machine, you want UPS to trace it. Write to ElectroWare, Inc., 22121 Crystal Creek Boulevard, Bothell, Washington 98201-2212. You have complied with their instructions regarding returning merchandise, and you want them to credit your account. You do not want another telephone/answering machine from ElectroWare. Be sure to open your letter with a direct request for the action you want taken.

unit 6 Writing With Style

chapter 19
Capitalization

Objectives

When you have completed the materials in this chapter, you will be able to do the following:

Level I

- Distinguish between common and proper nouns for purposes of capitalization.
- Decide when to capitalize proper adjectives and when not to.

Level II

- Understand when to capitalize personal titles, numbered items, and points of the compass.
- Correctly capitalize departments, divisions, committees, government terms, product names, and published titles.

Level III

- Capitalize beginning words, celestial bodies, and ethnic references.
- Apply special rules in capitalizing personal titles and terms.

Use proofreading marks to show any letters that should be capitalized in the following sentences.

1. Last spring mother took classes in art, computer technology, english, and psychology.

2. The american chemical society will meet in the st. louis room of the hilton hotel on march 25.

3. After receiving a bachelor's degree from humboldt state university, sharon became assistant to the personnel manager at bank of america.

4. Our company president and vice president met with several supervisors on the west coast last week.

5. The internal revenue service requires corporations to fill out form 1040 before the april 15 deadline.

1. Mother English 2. American Chemical Society St. Louis Room Hilton Hotel March 3. Humboldt State University Sharon Bank of America 4. West Coast 5. Internal Revenue Service Form 1040 April

Rules governing capitalization reflect conventional practices; that is, they have been established by custom and usage. By following these conventions, a writer tells a reader, among other things, what words are important. In earlier times writers capitalized most nouns and many adjectives at will; few conventions of capitalization or punctuation were then consistently observed. Today most capitalization follows definite rules that are fully accepted and practiced at all times. Dictionaries are helpful in determining capitalization practices, but they do not show all capitalized words. To develop skill in controlling capitals, study the rules and examples shown in this chapter.

Level I

Basic Rules of Capitalization

Proper Nouns

Capitalize proper nouns, including the *specific* names of persons, places, schools, streets, parks, buildings, religions, holidays, months, nicknames, agreements, and so forth. Do *not* capitalize common nouns that make *general* reference.

Proper Nouns	Common Nouns
Jackson Turner	a young man on the basketball team
Mexico, Canada	neighboring countries of the U.S.
Cypress College, Ohio University	a community college and a university
Stoner Avenue Park	a picnic in the park
Catholic, Presbyterian	representatives of two religions
Empire Room, Royal Inn	a room in the hotel
Veterans Day, Easter	on these holidays
Golden Gate Bridge	a bridge over the bay
World Trade Center	the building in the city
House of Representatives, Senate	components of government
January, February, March	first three months of the year
the Windy City, the Big Apple	nicknames of cities
Stipulation of Interest Agreement	an agreement between companies
The Online English Grammar Clinic	a Web site
Microsoft Word	a word processing program
World Wide Web, the Web	best-known area of Internet

Proper Adjectives

Capitalize most adjectives that are derived from proper nouns.

Victorian furniture	Socratic method
Danish pastry	British thermal unit
Keynesian economics	Roman numeral
Arabic alphabet	Greek symbols

Career Tip

Many large companies publish style manuals showing their preferred capitalization and the spelling of frequently used terms. One of the first tasks of a new employee is becoming familiar with the company style manual.

Study Tip

Most proper nouns retain their capital letters when they become adjectives—for example, French toast, Russian roulette, Persian cat, Spanish moss, Italian marble, and Swedish massage.

Do not capitalize those adjectives originally derived from proper nouns that have become common adjectives (without capitals) through usage. Consult your dictionary when in doubt.

mandarin collar	homburg hat
french fries	china dishes
manila folder	diesel engine
india ink	charley horse

Beginning of Sentence

Capitalize the first letter of a word beginning a sentence.

Inventory and sales data are transmitted electronically.

Geographic Locations

Capitalize the names of *specific* places such as states, cities, mountains, valleys, lakes, rivers, oceans, and geographic regions. Capitalize *county* and *state* when they follow the proper nouns.

Oregon, Washington, Idaho	Rogue River, Mississippi River
Oklahoma City, Salt Lake City	Atlantic Ocean, Indian Ocean
San Fernando Valley	New England, Texas Panhandle
Lake Michigan, Salton Sea	European Community (EC)
Broward County, Cook County (*but* the city of Chicago, the county of Cook, the state of Colorado)	New York State

Organization Names

Capitalize the principal words in the names of all business, civic, educational, governmental, labor, military, philanthropic, political, professional, religious, sports, and social organizations.

Environmental Protection Agency	United Farm Workers of America
International Association for	National Basketball Association
Administrative Professionals	San Diego Unified School District
National Association of Letter Carriers	Communications Satellite Corporation
Securities and Exchange Commission	National Park Service
Screen Actors Guild	The Boeing Company*

Generally, do *not* capitalize *company*, *association*, *board*, and other shortened name forms when they are used to replace full organization names. If these shortened names, however, are preceded by the word *the* and are used in formal or legal documents (contracts, bylaws, minutes, etc.), they may be capitalized.

*Capitalize *the* only when it is part of an organization's official name (as it would appear on the organization's stationery).

Did you know that the *company* will pay certain medical benefits? (Informal document.)

The Treasurer of the *Association* is herein authorized to disburse funds. (Formal document.)

Academic Courses and Degrees

Capitalize the names of numbered courses and specific course titles. Do not capitalize the names of academic subject areas unless they contain a proper noun.

Becky expects to enroll in Keyboarding I, Office Administration 32, and Accounting 28.

Lee excelled in business management, Spanish, and computer applications.

All accounting majors must take business English and business law.

Capitalize abbreviations of academic degrees whether they stand alone or follow individuals' names. Do not capitalize general references to degrees.

Wei-Li Tsai hopes to earn A.A., B.S., and M.S. degrees. (Associate of Arts, Bachelor of Science, and Master of Science degrees.)

Central State University offers bachelor's and master's degrees. (General reference to degrees.)

Elizabeth S. Wright, Ph.D., teaches psychology in the spring semester.

Glenda R. Hanson is a certified P.L.S. (Professional Legal Secretary).

Seasons

Do not capitalize seasons unless they are personified (spoken of as if alive).

Last winter we talked about summer vacations.

"Come, Winter, with thine angry howl . . ."—Burns

Now complete the reinforcement exercises for Level I.

L e v e l   I I

Special Rules of Capitalization

Titles of People

Capitalize courtesy titles (such as *Mr., Mrs., Ms., Miss,* and *Dr.)* when they precede names. Also capitalize titles representing a person's profession, company position, military rank, religious station, political office, family relationship, or nobility when the title precedes the name and replaces a courtesy title.

Students greeted *Ms.* Judith Bynum and *Mr.* Peter Jones. (Courtesy titles.)

Speakers included *Professor* Jackie Harless-Chang and *Dr.* Ann Lee. (Professional titles.)

Sales figures were submitted by *Budget Director* Magee and *Vice President* Anderson. (Company titles.)

Will *Major General* Donald M. Franklin assume command? (Military title.)

Appearing together were *Rabbi* David Cohen, *Archbishop* Sean McKee, and *Reverend* Thomas White. (Religious titles.)

We expect *President* Bush to offer support for *Senator* Tom Watson and *Mayor* Warren Rivers in the next campaign. (Political titles.)

Only *Aunt* Arlene and *Uncle* Keith had been to Alaska. (Family relationship.)

Onlookers waited for *Prince* Charles and *Queen* Elizabeth to arrive. (Nobility.)

Do not capitalize a person's title—professional, business, military, religious, political, family, or one related to nobility—when the title is followed by an appositive. You will recall that appositives rename or explain previously mentioned nouns or pronouns.

Only one *professor*, Malcolm Randall, favored a tuition hike.

Republican candidates asked their *president*, George W. Bush, to help raise funds.

Reva Hillman discovered that her *uncle*, Paul M. Hillman, had named her as his heir.

Do not capitalize titles or offices following names.

Leon Jones, *president* of Allied Chemical, met with Cecille Stone, *director* of Human Resources.

After repeated requests, Rose Valenzuela, *supervisor*, Document Services, announced extended hours.

George W. Bush, *president* of the U.S., conferred with Robert Hollingsworth, *senator* from Wyoming.

Alexander M. Berquist, *chief justice* of the Supreme Court, promised a ruling in June.

Generally, do not capitalize a title or office that replaces a person's name.

Neither the *president* of the company nor the *executive vice president* could be reached for comment.

An ambitious five-year plan was developed by the *director of marketing* and the *sales manager*.

The *president* conferred with the *joint chiefs of staff* and the *secretary of defense*.

At the reception the *mayor* of New York spoke with the *governor* of New Jersey.

Capitalize titles in addresses and closing lines.

Ms. Carol A. Straka	Very sincerely yours,
Executive Vice President, Planning	
Energy Systems Technology, Inc.	
8907 Canoga Avenue	Benelle H. Robinson
Canoga Park, CA 91371	Marketing Manager

Do not capitalize family titles used with possessive pronouns.

my mother	our aunt
his father	your cousin

Study Tip

Capitalize only the first word in a salutation (*My dear Ms. Jones*) or in a complimentary close (*Very truly yours*).

But do capitalize titles of close relatives when they are used without pronouns.

Please call Father immediately.

Numbered and Lettered Items

Capitalize nouns followed by numbers or letters except in page, paragraph, line, size, and verse references.

Gate 69, Flight 238	FHA Form 2900-4	Building I-63-B
Invoice No. 15891	Volume II, Appendix A	Medicare Form 72T
page 6, line 12	State Highway 5	Supplement No. 3

Points of the Compass

Capitalize *north, south, east, west,* and their derivatives when they represent *specific* regions. Do not capitalize the points of the compass when they are used in directions or in general references.

the Middle East, the Far East	heading east on the turnpike
the Midwest, the Pacific Northwest	to the west of town
the East Coast, the West Coast	eastern Maine, western Illinois
Easterners, Southerners	southern Georgia
Northern Hemisphere	in the northern corner

Departments, Divisions, and Committees

Capitalize the names of departments, divisions, or committees within your own organization. Outside your organization capitalize only *specific* department, division, or committee names.

Sue works in our Communication Services Department.

Dr. Nguyen is director of the Northeast Division of Barco.

Send your employment application to their human resources department.

Grievances are referred to our Personnel Practices Committee.

A steering committee has not yet been named.

Governmental Terms

Do not capitalize the words *federal, government, nation,* or *state* unless they are part of a specific title.

Neither the state government nor the federal government would fund the proposal.

The Federal Trade Commission regulates advertising in all the states.

Product Names

Capitalize product names only when they represent trademarked items. Except in advertising, common names following manufacturers' names are not capitalized.

Spot the Blooper

From a Wendy's International poster: "Be Cool in School! Good Grades Has Its Rewards!" (See any problem with subject-verb agreement? How about pronoun-antecedent agreement?)

Study Tip

A clue to the capitalization of a region is the use of *the* preceding it: *the East Coast, the West, the Pacific Northwest.*

Spot the Blooper

From an advertisement in *The New Yorker*: "Safer than any car Volvo's ever built."

Hot Link

For an online review of a few rules of capitalization, visit the Purdue University Online Writing Lab **<http://owl.english. purdue.edu/ handouts/ grammar/ g_caps.html>**.

Coca-Cola	DuPont Teflon	Kodak camera
Kleenex	Ray-Ban sunglasses	NordicTrack Walkfit
Magic Marker	Whirlpool washer	Styrofoam cup
Play-Doh	IBM computer	Chrysler Jeep
Q-Tip	Paper-Mate pen	Formica counter

Published and Artistic Titles

Capitalize the principal words in the titles of books, magazines, newspapers, articles, movies, plays, songs, poems, Web sites, and reports. Do *not* capitalize articles (*a, an, the*), conjunctions (*and, but, or, nor*), and prepositions with three or fewer letters (*in, to, by, for*, etc.) unless they begin or end the title.

By the way, remember that the titles of published works that contain subdivisions (such as books, magazines, pamphlets, newspapers, TV series, plays, and musicals) are italicized or underscored. Titles of literary or artistic works without subdivisions (such as newspaper articles, magazine articles, poems, and episodes in a TV series) are placed in quotation marks.

Smith's *Easy World Wide Web—Worth Waiting For* (Book with preposition at end of title.)

Saturday Night Live (TV series.)

Clark and Clark's *HOW: A Handbook for Office Workers* (Book.)

"How to Get the Most From a Placement Service" (Magazine article.)

Gershwin's "An American in Paris" (Symphonic tone poem.)

"Career Development," a link at *Hoover's Online* (Link and Web site.)

Life Is Beautiful (Movie.)

Now complete the reinforcement exercises for Level II.

L e v e l   I I I

Additional Rules of Capitalization

Beginning Words

In addition to capitalizing the first word of a complete sentence, capitalize the first words in quoted sentences, independent phrases, enumerated items, and formal rules or principles following colons.

John F. Kennedy said, "Man is the most extraordinary computer of all." (Quoted sentence.)

No, not at the present time. (Independent phrase.)

Big utilities formed an alliance to sell the following:

1. Electricity

2. Natural gas

3. Energy management services (Enumerated items.)

Our office manager responded with his favorite rule: Follow the company stylebook for correct capitalization. (Rule following colon.)

Celestial Bodies

Capitalize the names of celestial bodies such as Jupiter, Saturn, and Neptune. Do not capitalize the terms *earth*, *sun*, or *moon* unless they are used as the names of specific bodies in the solar system.

Where on earth did you find that ancient typewriter?

Venus and Mars are the closest planets to Earth.

Ethnic References

Terms that relate to a particular culture, language, or race are capitalized.

In Hawaii, Asian and Western cultures merge.

Both English and Hebrew are spoken by Jews in Israel.

African Americans and Hispanics turned out to support their candidates.

Note: Hyphenate terms such as *African-American* and *French-Canadian* when they are used as adjectives (*African-American collection* or *French-Canadian citizens*). Do not hyphenate these terms when they are nouns.

Words Following *marked* and *stamped*

Capitalize words that follow the words *marked* and *stamped*.

For greater care in transport, the package was stamped "Fragile."

That bill was marked "Paid in Full" on September 15.

Special Uses of Personal Titles and Terms

Generally, titles are capitalized according to the specifications set forth earlier. However, when a title of an official appears in that organization's minutes, bylaws, or other official documents, it may be capitalized.

The Controller will have authority over college budgets. (Title appearing in bylaws.)

By vote of the stockholders, the President is empowered to implement a stock split. (Title appearing in annual report.)

When the terms *ex, elect, late*, and *former* are used with capitalized titles, they are not capitalized.

The projections of ex-Vice President Gore have proven accurate.

Mayor-elect Cortazzo addressed the city council.

Titles other than *sir, ladies*, and *gentlemen* are capitalized when used in direct address.

May I ask, Doctor, what the prognosis is for my mother?

You, ladies and gentlemen, are well aware of the gravity of the situation.

Now complete the reinforcement exercises for Level III.

HOTLINE QUERIES

Q: I don't know how to describe the copies made from our copy machine. Should I call them *Xerox* copies or something else?

A: They are *Xerox* copies only if made on a Xerox copier. Copies made on other machines may be called *xerographic* copies, *machine* copies, or *photocopies*.

Q: In the doctor's office where I work, I see the word *medicine* capitalized, as in *the field of Medicine*. Is this correct?

A: No. General references should not be capitalized. If it were part of a title, as in the Northwestern College of *Medicine*, it would be capitalized.

Q: I work for the National Therapy Association. When I talk about *the association* in a letter, should I capitalize it?

A: No. When a shortened form of an organization name is used alone, it is generally not capitalized. In formal or legal documents (contracts, bylaws, printed announcements), it may be capitalized.

Q: I work for a state agency, and I'm not sure what to capitalize or hyphenate in this sentence: *State agencies must make forms available to non-English speaking applicants.*

A: Words with the prefix *non* are usually not hyphenated (*nonexistent, nontoxic*). But when *non* is joined to a word that must be capitalized, it is followed by a hyphen. Because the word *speaking* combines with *English* to form a single-unit adjective, it should be hyphenated. Thus, the expression should be typed *non-English-speaking applicants*.

Q: When we use a person's title, such as *business manager*, in place of a person's name, shouldn't the title always be capitalized?

A: No. Business titles are capitalized only when they precede an individual's name, as in *Business Manager Smith*. Do not capitalize titles when they replace an individual's name: *Our business manager will direct the transaction*.

Q: How do you spell *marshal*, as used in *the Grand Marshal of the Rose Parade*?

A: The preferred spelling is with a single *l*: *marshal*. In addition to describing an individual who directs a ceremony, the noun *marshal* refers to a high military officer or a city law officer who carries out court orders (*the marshal served papers on the defendant*). As a verb, *marshal* means "to bring together" or "to order in an effective way" (*the attorney marshaled convincing arguments*). The similar-sounding word *martial* is an adjective and means "warlike" or "military" (*martial law was declared after the riot*).

Name _____

Level I

A. (Self-check) In the following sentences, use standard proofreading marks to correct errors you find in capitalization. Use three short lines (=) under a lowercase letter to indicate that it is to be changed to a capital letter. Draw a diagonal (/) through a capital letter you wish to change to a lowercase letter. Indicate at the right the total number of changes you have made in each sentence.

Example: The Bandit Henry McCarthy was also known as Billy the kid.   2

1. You are invited to the Company Picnic of Digital computer corporation in Magnolia park next week.   _____

2. Born in Dade county, Mr. nunez grew up in the state of florida.   5

3. All Ford Motor Company Cars and Light Trucks carry a Warranty.   _____

4. Isaac Bantu is studying spanish, accounting, Management, and Keyboarding.   5

5. Use India ink to make dark headings on the manila folders.   _____

6. Pelee island is located on the canadian side of lake erie.   4

7. Regulations of the Occupational Safety and health administration resulted in costly expenses for our Company.   _____

8. Salt lake city, in the State of Utah, was founded by Brigham Young and a small Party of Mormons in 1847.   4

9. All sales representatives of the Company met in the Kingston room of the sheridan royal inn.   _____

10. Both the Senate and the house recently passed consumer protection laws.   1

Check your answers below.

B. Use proofreading marks to correct any capitalization errors in these sentences. Indicate the total number of changes at the right. If no changes are needed, write *0*.

1. Although he majored in Marketing, Bryan also took Spanish, Management 102, and Finance 202.   _____

2. Representatives from the methodist, presbyterian, baptist, and catholic faiths will hold a Conference in San antonio, texas.   7

3. Ryan Anderson was sent to our Kansas city branch office for the Month of March, but he hopes to return in April.   _____

4. Newspaper articles indicate that Joe Fujimoto, ph.d., has joined your Company.   2

5. Expansion of the internet has seriously affected business at The Boeing Company. (The word *the* is part of the company name.)   _____

6. All company representatives gathered in atlantic city in the zenith room of the holiday inn for the spring sales meeting.   6

10. (1) House
Administration company   8. (4) Lake City state party   9. (5) company Room Sheridan Royal Inn
4. (3) Spanish management keyboarding   5. (1) India   6. (4) Island Canadian Lake Erie   7. (3) Health
ranty   1. (5) company picnic Computer Corporation Park   2. (3) County Nunez Florida   3. (4) cars light trucks war-

365

7. Work schedules will have to be adjusted in november for veterans day. _____

8. Last/Fall Ms. Adams took out a policy with the Prudential life insurance company. (The word *the* is part of the company name.) __5__

9. The windy city is attractive to many local Tourists as well as to european visitors. _____

10. Professor Solis employed the socratic method of questioning students to elicit answers about/Business/Management. __3__

11. After driving through New York state, we stayed in New York city and visited the Empire State building. _____

12. Members of the environmental protection agency observed conditions along the east bank of the maumee river. __5__

13. Dennis O'Rourke completed the requirements for a master's degree at the Massachusetts institute of technology. _____

14. The report contained some roman numerals and many greek symbols in the engineering equations. __2__

15. Last spring my political science class visited the tishman building in westwood village. _____

L e v e l   I I

A. **(Self-check)** Use proofreading marks to correct errors you find in capitalization. Indicate at the right the total number of changes you make.

Example: Project manager Peter Meggison was promoted to Vice President.   __3__

1. Nicolle Scott, a member of our marketing research department, will be our new Far East representative. _____

2. Please consult figure 52D in appendix B for instructions in computing the depreciation of equipment. __2__

3. We will ask sales manager Sperazza to be chairman of an investigation committee. _____

4. Both mother and aunt grace received Radio Shack/Cordless/Phones as Christmas gifts. __5__

5. The fishing industry in the Pacific northwest is affected by recent federal regulations. _____

6. Our business manager and our executive vice president attended an e-business seminar in southern Illinois. __C__

7. My Uncle recommended that I read the article entitled "how management is guided by research." _____

8. Address the envelope to Ms. Susan Sutkowski, director, employee services, Omega Corporation, 304 Hilyard Street, Eugene, Oregon. __3__

9. The president met with the secretary of state to discuss peace talks in the Middle East. _____

10. Centron Oil Company, with headquarters in western Texas, distributes its products throughout the entire northern hemisphere. __2__

Check your answers below.

B. Use proofreading marks to correct errors in the following sentences. Indicate the number of changes you make for each sentence.

1. Jasmine Lee, President of Lee and Associates, offered the position of Budget Director to Bill Venable. _____

2. My sister, my cousin, and I will fly to visit mother, father, and uncle Eduardo over the Spring holidays. ___4___

3. Because Brazil, Australia, and Argentina are located in the southern hemisphere, their Summers and Winters are the opposite of ours. _____

4. When the president, the secretary of state, and the secretary of labor traveled to the State of Minnesota, stringent security measures were effected. ___1___

5. To locate the exact amount of federal funding, look on line 7, page 6 of supplement no. 4. _____

6. The Sales Manager of Datacom hurried to gate 16 to catch flight 263 to newark. _____

7. I'm looking for the magazine article entitled "The 100 best american companies to work for." _____

8. The letter is addressed to Daniel Robles, director of research and development, blum corporation, p.o. box 58, gulfport, florida 33707. _____

9. Macy's advertisement featured Royal Manor Dishes and teflon-coated pans. _____

10. Overtime compensation for Carmen Corregas was referred to our employee relations department. ___3___

11. Kristen shopped for kleenex tissues and kodak film at her local wal-mart. _____

12. Franklin became an assistant to the administrator of the Governor Bacon Health center, which is operated by the department of health and social services of the State of Delaware. _____

13. Business Manager Connie Murphy devised a procedure for expediting Purchase Orders from Area D Offices. _____

14. For lunch Ahmal ordered a big mac, french fries, and a coca-cola. ___4___

15. A midwesterner who enjoys sunshine, Mr. Winkler travels south each Winter to vacation in Southern Georgia. _____

Level III

A. (Self-check) Use standard proofreading marks to indicate necessary changes. Write the total number of changes at the right.

Example: Mercury, venus, earth, and mars are dense and solid. **3**

1. Because the package was marked "fragile," we handled it carefully. _____

2. The guiding principle of capitalization is this: capitalize *specific* names and references, but do not capitalize *general* references. ___1___

3. Members of both hispanic and asian cultures participated in the city's celebration. _____

4. The Late President Theodore Roosevelt is remembered for his initiation of policies to conserve american natural resources. _____

5. Large tracts of the amazon tropical rain forest have been cleared for the following: _____
   1. cattle ranches
   2. lumber
   3. tax incentives

6. Spacecraft from earth have recently been sent to the planets Mars, Jupiter, and _____
   Venus.

7. Oversupply of american dollars causes the dollar's value to decline compared _____
   with the german mark, the swiss franc, the japanese yen, and the french franc.

8. The library of congress featured a collection of african-american writers. _____

9. You, Sir, are in danger of being held in contempt of court. _____

10. Our/Organization's bylaws state the following: "The Secretary of the Association _____
    will submit an agenda two weeks before each meeting."

Check your answers below.

B. Use proofreading marks to indicate necessary changes. Write the total number of
   changes at the right.

1. As the Sun beat down on the crowd, the Vice Chancellor continued his gradua- _____
   tion address.

2. Would you like a ride home? yes, thank you very much. _____

3. Our Advertising Agency operates according to this rule: you must spend money _____
   to make money.

4. Terry noticed that the english spoken by asians in hong kong sounded more _____
   british than american.

5. Please take the file marked "confidential" to our human resources department. _____

6. The Minutes of the last meeting show that the Vice President, acting, on behalf of _____
   the President, conducted the meeting despite the lack of a quorum.

7. Governor-Elect Hudson sat beside Ex-Mayor Benedict and senator Waller at the _____
   morning/Ceremony.

8. Tell me, doctor, how dangerous this procedure really is. _____

9. Some factors I am considering in seeking a job are the following: _____
   1. income
   2. geographical location
   3. job security

10. Benjamin Disraeli provided England with its/National motto when he said, _____
    "something will turn up."

C. *Review of Levels I, II, and III.* Select (a) or (b) to indicate correct capitalization.

1. (a) our marketing manager   (b) our Marketing Manager   _____

2. (a) the World Trade center   (b) the World Trade Center   _____

3. (a) awarded a Bachelor's degree   (b) awarded a bachelor's degree   _____

4. (a) courses in English and sociology   (b) courses in english and sociology   _____

9. (1) sir 10. (1) organization
6. (1) Earth 7. (5) American German Swiss Japanese French 8. (4) Library Congress African-American
1. (1) Fragile 2. (1) Capitalize 3. (2) Hispanic Asian 4. (2) late American 5. (4) Amazon Cattle Lumber Tax

368   **Chapter 19**   Capitalization

5. (a) the Pacific Room at the Marriott (b) the pacific room at the Marriott _____
6. (a) French fries and a pepsi-cola (b) french fries and a Pepsi-Cola _____
7. (a) a file marked "urgent" (b) a file marked "Urgent" _____
8. (a) avoid the sun's rays (b) avoid the Sun's rays _____
9. (a) the president's appeal to Congress (b) the President's appeal to Congress _____
10. (a) exit from highway 10 (b) exit from Highway 10 _____

D. **Writing Exercise.** On a separate sheet write one or two paragraphs summarizing an article from a local newspaper. Choose an article with as many capital letters as possible. Apply the rules of capitalization you learned in this chapter.

Editor's Challenge

The following letter report contains intentional errors representing spelling, proofreading, punctuation, capitalization, and language principles covered thus far. You should mark 45 changes. If you correct a misplaced modifier, it counts as one change.

HOLST BROTHERS CONSTRUCTION

2230 CULVER BOULEVARD
CULVER CITY, CA 92390

(310) 828-4493

January 4, 200x

Ms. Danielle M. Forrester
President, Interior Design Institute
455 Rodeo Drive
Beverly Hills, CA 90025

Dear Ms. Forrester:

Here is a brief report about our work with the cheviot hills residence being prepared as the showcase house for the interior design institute. The renovation and remodeling is progressing on schedule, and should be ready for the photographers from metropolitan home magazine june 1.

Past Progress

During the Fall the work crew completed the following tasks, removal of all wood shingles, repair of the plywood roof base and installation of a permawear tile roof. In december we replaced damaged window facings we also repaired the plumbing in two baths and the kitchen. As you requested we investigated italian marble for the entry and spanish tiles for the patio. A price sheet for those items are enclosed.

Current Progress

At present we are concentrating on the Living Room which required ceiling repair and electrical rewiring, see page 6 of your blueprints. The pyramid skylight has been installed in the library, however, we had to alter two bookcases in doing so. After consulting the President and General Manager of our company, a decision was made that we should absorb some of the extra costs involved, however, other off budget items will be your responsibility.

Future Schedule

In February we expect to complete all the interior finish work, the painters will apply two coats of anderson no. 343 wall primer. I believe that Ms. Chin and Mr. Darwin whom you suggested would be decorating the downstairs, could begin there work february 15. Just have them call my Supervisor or I to arrange the exact date.

Sincerely yours,

Rick Overmyer

Rick Overmyer

Enclosure

learning.web.ways

Goal: To improve your employment application letters.

You have written a super résumé, and now you want to write a terrific application letter to introduce your résumé. You know that many Web sites offer tips on writing cover letters.

1. With your Web browser on the screen, go to *Internweb.com* **<http://www.internweb.com/top7.asp>.**

2. Read "Top Seven Cover Letter Myths." Print a copy.

3. Using a search engine, locate another Web site with cover letter advice. Find three tips that you did not learn from the "Seven Myths" article. Make a note of them.

4. End your session. Submit your printouts and answers to the questions posed here.

P O S T T E S T

Underline any letter that should be capitalized.

1. Both the president and the personnel manager were fluent in spanish and english.

2. Blanca studied english literature, accounting, and psychology at pasadena city college.

3. The engineers will meet in the san marino room of the red lion inn next thursday.

4. Although we ordered a model 500 sony calculator, we received a model 400 calculator.

5. My mother, my father, and uncle michael will spend the easter holidays with us.

CHECKLIST OF BONUS LEARNING RESOURCES

The following additional learning resources are available to you. Your instructor will tell you which to complete.

- Web Editor's Challenge Exercise

- Web Interactive Chapter Review

- Web PowerPoint Slides

- Web Crossword Puzzle

- WebCheck Reinforcement Exercises 19.1, 19.2

- Self-Help Exercises

- Electronic Study Guide

chapter 20
Numbers

Objectives

When you have completed the materials in this chapter, you will be able to do the following:

Level I

- Correctly choose between figure and word forms to express general numbers, money, and numbers beginning sentences.
- Express dates, clock time, addresses, and telephone numbers appropriately.

Level II

- Use the correct form in writing related numbers, consecutive numbers, periods of time, and ages.
- Use the correct form in expressing numbers in conventional phrases, with abbreviations and symbols, and as round numbers.

Level III

- Express correctly weights, measures, and fractions.
- Use the correct form in expressing percentages, decimals, and ordinals.

Should word or figure form be used to express numbers in the following sentences? Underline any incorrect form and write an improved form. For example, *$10* or *ten dollars*?

1. On the fifth of September at five p.m., our 1st computer   _____
   left the assembly line.

2. When Robin reached 18 years of age, she assumed owner-   _____
   ship of over fifty acres of property in two states.

3. Please take sixteen dollars to pick up 50 thirty-two-cent   _____
   stamps at the post office.

4. Of the twenty VCRs we had in stock on May 2nd, we   _____
   have only four VCRs left today.

5. The art treasure measures only nine inches by twelve   _____
   inches, but it is said to be worth nearly two million
   dollars.

1. 5th 5 p.m. first   2. eighteen 50 acres   3. $16 fifty 32-cent   4. 20 VCRs May 2 4 VCRs
5. 9 by 12 inches $2 million

Just as capitalization is governed by convention, so is the expression of numbers. Usage and custom determine whether numbers are to be expressed in the form of a figure (for example, *5*) or in the form of a word (for example, *five*). Numbers expressed as figures are shorter and more easily comprehended, yet numbers used as words are necessary in certain instances. The following guidelines are observed in expressing numbers that appear in written *sentences*. Numbers that appear in business documents such as invoices, statements, and purchase orders are always expressed as figures.

Level I

Basic Guidelines for Expressing Numbers

General Rules

The numbers *one* through *ten* are generally written as words. Numbers above *ten* are written as figures.

Study Tip

To remember it better, some people call this the "Rule of Ten": Words for one through ten; figures for 11 and above.

> The jury consisted of *nine* regular members and *one* alternate.
>
> Gift taxes are imposed by *49* states.

Numbers that begin sentences are written as words. If a number involves more than two words, however, the sentence should be rewritten so that the number no longer falls at the beginning.

> *Twenty-three* investors provided capital for the down payment.
>
> A total of *320* distributors agreed to market the product. (Not *Three hundred twenty* distributors agreed to market the product.)

Money

Career Tip

If your company has a style manual, check it for number preferences. Larger companies may prescribe the figure or word form they prefer for often-used numbers.

Sums of money $1 or greater are expressed as figures. If a sum is a whole dollar amount, most business writers omit the decimal and zeros (even if the amount appears with fractional dollar amounts).

> Although he budgeted only *$50*, Mike spent *$94.50* for his cell phone.
>
> Our monthly statement showed purchases of *$7.13*, *$10*, *$43.50*, *$90*, and *$262.78*.

Sums less than $1 are written as figures that are followed by the word *cents*. If they are part of sums greater than $1, use a dollar sign and a decimal instead of the word *cents*.

> Lisa said she had only *65 cents* with her.
>
> Supplies for the project were listed at $1.35, *$.99*, $2.80, $1, and *$.40*.

Dates

In dates, numbers that appear after the name of the month are written in cardinal figures (*1, 2, 3*, etc.). Those that stand alone or appear before the name of a month are written in ordinal figures (*1st, 2nd, 3rd*, etc.*)

*Some writers today are using the more efficient *2d* and *3d* instead of *2nd* and *3rd*.

The meeting is scheduled for *October 5th* in our office.

On the *2nd* of January and again on the *18th*, we called for service.

Most American business communicators express dates in the following form: month, day, year. An alternative form, used primarily in military and international correspondence, begins with the day of the month. Some business organizations prefer the international date style for its clarity, since it separates the numerical date of the month from the year.

By *October 1, 2002*, all construction on the subway must be completed. (General date format.)

The contract was originally signed *25 June 2001*. (Military and international format.)

Clock Time

Figures are used when clock time is expressed with *a.m.* or *p.m.* Omit the colon and zeros with whole hours. When exact clock time is expressed with *o'clock*, either figures or words may be used. Note that phrases such as "in the afternoon" or "in the morning" may follow clock time expressed with *o'clock* but not with time expressed with *a.m.* and *p.m.*

The first shift starts at *8 a.m.*, and the second begins at *3:30 p.m.*

At *four* (or *4*) *o'clock* in the afternoon we'll announce the winner.

Addresses and Telephone Numbers

Except for the number *One*, house numbers are expressed as figures.

805 Riverside Drive	27321 Van Nuys Boulevard
One Peachtree Plaza	1762 Cone Street

Street names that involve the number *ten* or a lower number are written entirely as words. In street names involving numbers greater than *ten*, the numeral portion is written in figures. If no compass direction (*North, South, East, West*) separates a house number from a street number, the street number is expressed in ordinal form (*-st, -d, -th*).

503 Second Street

11901 Ninth Avenue

2320 West 11 Street

613 North 102 Avenue

327 39th Avenue (Use *th* when no compass direction separates house number and numerical portion of street name.)

Telephone and fax numbers are expressed with figures. When used, the area code is placed in parentheses preceding the telephone number. As an alternate form, you may separate the area code from the telephone number with a hyphen.

Please call us at *555-1101* for further information.

You may reach me at *(801) 643-3267, Ext. 244*, after 9:30 a.m.

Orders faxed to us at *(415) 392-2194* will be processed immediately.

Call our toll-free number at *800-340-3281* for the latest sports updates.

Now complete the reinforcement exercises for Level I.

Spot the Blooper

From *The Suburban & Wayne Times*: "Cases of Lyme disease, which is transmitted by deer-carrying ticks, are on the rise." (What unintended meaning resulted from the unneeded hyphen?)

Special Guidelines for Expressing Numbers

Related Numbers

Numbers used similarly in the same document are considered related and should be expressed as the largest number is expressed. Thus, if the largest number is greater than *ten*, all the numbers should be expressed as figures.

> Only *3* companies out of *147* failed to return the survey form.
>
> Of the *35* documents processed, *19* letters and *4* memoranda were urgent.
>
> Nearly 20 employees will be expected to share the 15 computers, 8 printers, and 3 fax machines. (Note that items appearing in a series are always considered to be related.)

Unrelated numbers within the same reference are written as words or figures according to the general guidelines presented earlier in this chapter.

> *Two* proposals covered *22* employees working in *three* branch offices.
>
> During the *four* peak traffic hours, *three* bridges carry at least *20,000* cars.

Study Tip

With consecutive numbers, remember that the second number is ALWAYS a figure. The first number is usually a word, unless it requires three or more words (*120 5-year-old* children.)

Consecutive Numbers

When two numbers appear consecutively and both modify a following noun (such as *ten 34-cent* stamps), generally express the first number in words and the second in figures. If, however, the first number cannot be expressed in *one or two words*, place it in figures also (*120 34-cent* stamps). Do not use commas to separate the figures.

> Historians divided the era into *four 25-year* periods. (Use word form for the first number and figure form for the second.)
>
> We ordered *ten 25-page* color brochures. (Use word form for the first number and figure form for the second.)
>
> Did you request *twenty 100-watt* bulbs? (Use word form for the first number and figure form for the second.)
>
> We'll need at least *150 100-watt* bulbs. (Use figure form for the first number since it requires more than two words.)

Periods of Time

Periods of time that can be expressed in one or two words are usually written in word form when used in a general way. Periods of time that cannot be expressed in one or two words are written in figure form.

> Congress has regulated minimum wages for over *forty-five years*. (Use word form for periods of time that can be expressed in one or two words.)
>
> We agreed to keep the book for only *fifteen days*.
>
> After a *183-day* strike, workers returned to their jobs. (Use figure form for a period of time that cannot be expressed in one or two words.)

Figures may be used to achieve special emphasis in expressing business concepts such as discount rates, interest rates, warranty periods, credit terms, loan periods, and payment terms.

> You earn a *2 percent* discount if your bill is paid within *10 days* of purchase.

> High interest rates are offered even on 6- and 9-month certificates of deposit.

> Your loan must be repaid within *60 days* in accordance with its terms.

Ages and Anniversaries

Ages and anniversaries that can be expressed in one or two words are generally written in word form. Those that require more than two words are written in figures. Figures are also used when an age (a) appears immediately after a name, (b) is expressed in exact years and months, or (c) is used in a legal or technical sense.

> When she was *thirty-one*, Victoria Baker became the company's president. (Use word form for age expressed in two or fewer words.)

> This year marks the *twenty-fifth* anniversary of the company's founding. (Use word form for anniversary expressed in two or fewer words.)

> Tom Siebold, *63*, plans to retire in two years. (Use figure form for age appearing immediately after name.)

> The child was adopted when he was *3 years* and *8 months* old. (Use figure form for age expressed in terms of exact years and months.)

> Although the legal voting age is *18*, young people must be *21* to purchase alcohol.

Numbers Used in Conventional Phrases, With Abbreviations, and With Symbols

Numbers used in conventional phrases are expressed as figures.

page 4	Policy 04-168315	Area Code 213
Room 14	Volume 5	Section 16
Option 3	Form 1040	Public Law 96-221

Numbers used with abbreviations are expressed as figures.

Apt. 16	Serial No. 265188440	Nos. 199 and 202
Ext. 280	Account No. 286-32-5891	Social Security No. 535-52-2016

Notice that the word *number* is capitalized and abbreviated when it precedes a number. Notice, too, that no commas are used in serial, account, and policy numbers.

Symbols (such as #, %, ¢) are usually avoided in contextual business writing (sentences). In other business documents where space is limited, however, symbols are frequently used. Numbers appearing with symbols are expressed as figures.

15%	44¢	#10 nails	2/10, n/60

Round Numbers

Round numbers are approximations. They may be expressed in word or figure form, although figure form is shorter and easier to comprehend.

Almost *400* (or *four hundred*) employees signed the petition.

At last count we had received about *20* (or *twenty*) reservations.

For ease of reading, round numbers in the millions or billions should be expressed with a combination of figures and words.*

The president asked for a budget cut of *$8 billion*.

Last year the domestic cat population rose to a record *68 million*, while the number of dogs declined to *56 million*.

Nearly *1.5 million* imported cars were sold this year.

Now complete the reinforcement exercises for Level II.

Level III

Additional Guidelines for Expressing Numbers

The following guidelines will help you use appropriate forms for weights and measurements, fractions, percentages, decimals, and ordinals.

Weights and Measurements

Weights and measurements are expressed as figures.

My new Sony cordless phone measures only *3 by 6 inches*.

Our specifications show the weight of the printer to be *7 pounds 9 ounces*.

The truck required *21 gallons* of gasoline and *2 quarts* of oil to travel *150 miles per hour*.

In sentences the nouns following weights and measurements should be spelled out (for example, *21 gallons* instead of *21 gal.*). In business forms or in statistical presentations, however, such nouns may be abbreviated.

9′ × 12′   #10   7 oz.   30 sq. yds.   2 lb.   12 qt.

Fractions

Simple fractions are expressed as words. If a fraction functions as a noun, no hyphen is used. If it functions as an adjective, a hyphen separates its parts.

Over *three fourths* of the students attended the lecture. (Fraction used as a noun.)

A *two-thirds* majority is needed to carry the measure. (Fraction used as an adjective.)

Complex fractions appearing in sentences may be written either as figures or as a combination of figures and words.

Study Tip

A fraction immediately followed by an *of* phrase usually functions as a noun (*one third of the cars*). Therefore, it is not hyphenated.

*Note that only when *one million* is used as an approximation is it generally written in word form; otherwise, it is written *1 million*.

The microcomputer will execute a command in *1 millionth* of a second. (Combination of words and figures is easier to comprehend.)

Flight records revealed that the emergency system was activated *13/200* of a second after the pilot was notified. (Figure form is easier to comprehend.)

Mixed fractions (whole numbers with fractions) are always expressed by figures.

Office desks are expected to be *35¼* inches long, not *35½* inches. (Notice that no space follows a whole number and a key fraction.)

Use the extended character set of your word processing program to insert fractions that are written in figures. Fractions written in figures that are not found in extended character sets of word processing programs are formed by using the diagonal to separate the two parts. When fractions that are constructed with diagonals appear with key fractions, be consistent by using the diagonal construction for all the fractions involved.

The envelope measured *3 5/8* inches by *6 1/2* inches. (Notice that fractions that must be constructed with diagonals are separated from their related whole numbers.)

Percentages and Decimals

Percentages are expressed with figures followed by the word *percent*. The percent sign (%) is used only on business forms or in statistical presentations.

Interest rates have been as low as *5½ percent* and as high as *19 percent*.

Union leaders report that *52 percent* of all workers joined the union.

Decimals are expressed with figures. If a decimal does not contain a whole number (an integer) and does not begin with a zero, a zero should be placed before the decimal.

Daryl Thomas set a record when he ran the race in *9.86* seconds. (Contains a whole number.)

Close examination revealed the settings to be *.005* inch off. (Begins with a zero.)

Less than *0.1* percent of the operating costs will be borne by taxpayers. (Zero placed before decimal that neither contains a whole number nor begins with a zero.)

Ordinals

Although ordinal numbers are generally expressed in word form (*first, second, third,* etc.), three exceptions should be noted: (a) figure form is used for dates appearing before a month or appearing alone, (b) figure form is used for street names involving numbers greater than *ten*, and (c) figure form is used when the ordinal would require more than two words.

- **Most ordinals**

  The company is celebrating its *fortieth anniversary*.

  Before the *eighteenth century*, spelling was not standardized.

  Of 237 sales representatives, Joanna ranked *second* in total sales.

  Paul Guerrero represents the *Twenty-ninth Congressional District*.

- **Dates**

  Your payment must be received by the *30th* to qualify for the cash discount.

  On the *2d* and the *18th* of June we experienced power outages.

- **Streets**

  Traffic lights installed on *Second Street* have improved pedestrian safety.

  Our Customer Service Division has moved to *35th Street*.

- **Larger ordinals.**

  First Federal Bank ranks *103d* in terms of capital investments.

  Now complete the reinforcement exercises for Level III.

HOTLINE QUERIES

Q: I recently saw the following format used by a business to publish its telephone number on its stationery and business cards: 512.582.0903. Is it now an option to use periods in telephone numbers?

A: To my knowledge, it's not an acceptable option. Yet, I've seen this format used, particularly in graphics design. It seems to be a stylistic affectation, perhaps reflecting European influences. To some, the style is upscale and chic; to others, it's just confusing. Telephone numbers written in the traditional formats are most readily recognized. That's why it's safe to stick with hyphens or parentheses: 512-582-0903 or (513) 582-0903.

Q: My manager is preparing an advertisement for a charity event. She has written this: *Donors who give $100 dollars or more receive plaques.* I know this is not right, but I can't exactly put my finger on the problem.

A: The problem is in *$100 dollars.* That is like saying *dollars dollars.* Drop the word *dollars* and use only the dollar sign: *Donors who give $100 or more . . . .*

Q: I'm never sure when to hyphenate numbers, such as *thirty-one.* Is there some rule to follow?

A: When written in word form, the numbers *twenty-one* through *ninety-nine* are hyphenated. Numbers are also hyphenated when they form compound adjectives and precede nouns (*ten-year-old* child, *16-story* building, *four-year* term, *30-day* lease).

Q: I've always been confused by *imply* and *infer.* Which is correct in this sentence: *We (imply or infer) from your letter that the goods are lost.*

A: In your sentence use *infer.* *Imply* means "to state indirectly." *Infer* means "to draw a conclusion" or "to make a deduction based on facts." A listener or reader *infers.* A speaker or writer *implies.*

Q: When fractions are written as words, why are they hyphenated sometimes and not hyphenated other times?

A: Most writers do not hyphenate a fraction when it functions as a noun (*one fourth of the letters*). When a fraction functions as an adjective, it is hyphenated (*a one-third gain in profits*).

Q: Should I put quotation marks around figures to emphasize them? For example, *Your account has a balance of "$2,136.18."*

A: Certainly not! Quotation marks are properly used to indicate an exact quotation, or they may be used to enclose the definition of a word. They should not be used as a mechanical device for added emphasis.

Q: I'm an engineer, and we have just had a discussion in our office concerning spelling. I have checked the dictionary, and it shows *usage*. Isn't this word ever spelled *useage*?

A: No. The only spelling of *usage* is without the internal *e*. You are probably thinking of the word *usable*, which does have a variant spelling—*useable*. Both forms are correct, but *usable* is recommended for its simplicity. Incidentally, if the word *usage* can be replaced by the word *use*, the latter is preferred (*the use* [not *usage*] *of ink pens is declining*).

Q: How should I spell the word *lose* in this sentence: *The employee tripped over a* (*lose* or *loose*) *cord*?

A: In your sentence use the adjective *loose*, which means "not fastened," "not tight," or "having freedom of movement." Perhaps you can remember it by thinking of the common expression *loose change*, which suggests unattached, free coins jingling in your pocket. If you *lose* (*mislay*) some of those coins, you have less money and fewer *o*'s.

Name _____

Level I

A. **(Self-check)** Choose (a) or (b) to complete the following sentences.

1. All (a) eleven, (b) 11 supermarkets refused to stock the tabloid. *B*

2. (a) 15, (b) Fifteen applicants responded to the advertisement. *B*

3. Fidelity Federal will reopen on the (a) 14th, (b) fourteenth of June. *A*

4. Duplicating this brochure will cost (a) 4 cents, (b) $.04 a page. *A*

5. Ellen has collected (a) $20.00, (b) $20 for the office gift. *B*

6. His address is listed as (a) Three, (b) 3 Meadowlark Drive. *B*

7. Financial institutions are clustered on (a) Seventh, (b) 7th Avenue. *A*

8. Send the letter to (a) 320 27th Street, (b) 320 27 Street. *A*

9. Please call our toll-free number at (a) 800.439.8799, (b) (800) 439-8700. *B*

10. We plan to meet again at (a) 9:00 a.m., (b) 9 a.m. Tuesday. *B*

Check your answers below.

B. Assume that the following phrases appear in business correspondence. Write the preferred forms in the spaces provided. If a phrase is correct as shown, write *C*.

Example: 8930 23 Avenue   **8930 23rd Avenue**

1. fourteen assistants   *14 Assistants*
2. Tenth Street   *C*
3. $.09 per issue   *9 cents per issue*
4. 7 e-mail messages   *Seven e-mail messages*
5. June ninth   *June 9th*
6. 5th Avenue   *Fifth Avenue*
7. $6.59, 98 cents, and $30.00   *$50.*
8. the eighteenth of September   *the 18th*
9. 9:00 p.m.   *9 p.m*
10. eight o'clock   *C*
11. thirty-three desks   *33 Desks*
12. January 22nd   *C Jan 22*
13. 12655 32nd Street   *C*
14. 12655 West 32nd Street   *32 Street*
15. two executives   *C*
16. twenty-four dollars   *$24*

17. 7 Hampton Square   _Seven_

18. 1 Hampton Square   _One_

19. sixty-six rooms   _66 rooms_

20. 7 o'clock   _Seven_

21. (military style) April 15, 2002   _15 April 2002_

22. 2742 8th Street   _Eighth_

23. six thirty p.m.   _6:30 p.m._

24. the fourth of May   _4th_

25. one hundred dollars   _$100_

26. ninety cents   _90 cents_

27. 18307 Eleventh Street   _11th_

28. 18307 North Eleventh Street   _North 11_

29. 50 states   _C_

30. 2 laptops   _Two_

C. Rewrite these sentences correcting any errors you note.

1. On February 15th Alicia submitted the following petty cash disbursements: $2.80, 95 cents, $5.00, and 25 cents.

2. Tonja James moved from seventeen sixteen Sunset Drive to one Bellingham Court.

3. 24 branch banks compose the Federal Reserve System.

4. On the 18 of March, I sent you 3 e-mail messages about restricting Internet use.

5. Although McDonald's advertised a sandwich that cost only fifty-five cents, most customers found that lunch cost between two dollars and two dollars and ninety-nine cents.

6. Regular work breaks are scheduled at 10:00 a.m. in the morning and again at 3:30 p.m. in the afternoon.

7. We want to continue operations through the thirtieth, but we may be forced to close by the twenty-second.

_____

_____

8. 259 contracts had been signed before the June 1st deadline

_____

_____

L e v e l   I I

A. **(Self-check)** Select (a) or (b) to complete each of the following sentences.

1. Visitors flocked to (a) two 100-room, (b) 2 100-room resort hotels in Orlando.   _A_

2. Laura Lozano has worked there for (a) twenty-seven, (b) 27 years.   _A_

3. A seminar on investing is being held in (a) Room Two, (b) Room 2.   _B_

4. Of the 650 envelopes sent, (a) nine, (b) 9 were returned.   _B_

5. Although she is only (a) 21, (b) twenty-one, Miss Love was appointed manager.   _B_

6. Judge Boni reduced the jury's award to (a) $2 million, (b) $2,000,000.   _A_

7. Have you completed your IRS Form (a) Ten Forty, (b) 1040?   _B_

8. Next week our company celebrates its (a) 25th, (b) twenty-fifth anniversary.   _B_

9. Your short-term loan covers a period of (a) 60, (b) sixty days.   _A_

10. The serial number on my monitor is (a) 85056170, (b) 85,056,170.   _A_

Check your answers below.

B. For the following sentences underscore any numbers or words that are expressed inappropriately and write the correct forms in the spaces provided. If a sentence is correct as written, write *C*.

Example: We need 10 34-cent stamps to complete the mailing.   _ten_

1. The advisory committee is composed of 17 members, of whom _five_ are supervisors, _three_ are consultants, and _nine_ are technicians.   _5, 3, 9_

2. To qualify for the federal grant, we submitted 3 100-page proposals.   _three_

3. Protected by steel armor, today's undersea telephone cables are expected to last 25 years.   _twenty-five_

4. Seven transatlantic cables can carry nearly 2,000,000 simultaneous phone calls.   _two million_

5. The following policy Nos. are listed for John Daley: No. 1355801 and No. 1355802.   _C_

1.a 2.a 3.b 4.b 5.b 6.a 7.b 8.b 9.a 10.a

6. Model 8,400 costs $10,000 and can be leased for $275 a month.

   8400

7. A revolutionary new lightbulb will reduce the demand for electricity by 8,000,000,000 kilowatt-hours per year.

   8 billion

8. Of the 65 typed pages, nine pages require minor revisions and six pages demand heavy revision.

   9, 6

9. John Edwards, forty-one, and Tanya Downing, thirty-three, were interviewed for the two executive positions.

   41, 33

10. On page twenty-one of Volume two, the total sales are listed at nearly $22 million.

    21, 2

11. All three electrical appliances have warranties limited to ninety days.

    90

12. The total book club membership of eight hundred thousand received the four bonus books.

    800,000, 4

13. Only 43 of the 57 staff members could attend the two training sessions.

    2

14. Approximately thirty positions will be reclassified before June 15.

    30

15. When the child was two years six months old, his parents established a trust fund for $1.6 million.

    2 years and six mo

16. Bill Gates' mansion on Lake Washington features a wall of twenty-four video screens, parking for twenty cars, and a reception hall for one hundred people.

    24, 20, 100

17. Taking 7 years to construct, the 40,000 square-foot home reportedly cost more than fifty million dollars.

    Seven

18. With 4 pickups daily, the delivery service serves two thousand employees in 45 departments.

    four, 2,000

C. Assume that the following phrases appear in business correspondence. Write the preferred forms in the spaces provided. If a phrase is correct as shown, write C.

   1. four rooms with eleven computers and fifteen desks

      11, 15

   2. three seventy-five pound weights

      three 75

   3. loan periods of sixty days

      60

   4. Martha Diamond, fifty-eight, and John Diamond, sixty-one

      58, 61

   5. Account No. 362,486,012

      362486012

   6. three point two billion dollars

      $3.2 billion

   7. Room Five

      Room 5

   8. seventeen years

      17 years C

   9. ninety-one books

      91 books

   10. about two hundred guests

       200

   11. four point four million people

       4.4 million

   12. Section three point two

       Section 3.2

   13. twenty-five four-bedroom homes

       twenty-five 4 bedroom

   14. warranty period of two years

       C

   15. insurance for 15 computers, 12 printers, and 3 VCRs

       C

L e v e l   I I I

A. (Self-check) Choose (a) or (b) to complete the following sentences.

1. Operators watch a screen that measures (a) 11″ × 11″, (b) 11 by 11 inches.   _B_

2. Over (a) four fifths, (b) 4/5 of the workers approved the pact.   _A_

3. Coca-Cola controls more than (a) 30 percent, (b) thirty percent of the total soft-drink market in Japan.   _A_

4. Senator Williams represents the (a) 26th, (b) Twenty-sixth Congressional District.   _b_

5. Surprising pollsters, Senator Williams received a (a) two-thirds, (b) two thirds majority.   _A_

6. Our company warehouses were transferred to (a) Sixty-second, (b) 62d Street.   _B_

7. We need a rug measuring (a) 9 by 12 feet, (b) nine by twelve feet.   _A_

8. Maintenance costs are only (a) 0.5, (b) .5 percent above last year's.   _A_

9. Did you remember to order (a) five, (b) 5 quarts of motor oil?   _B_

10. The elevator stops at the (a) 14th, (b) fourteenth floor.   _A_

Check your answers below.

B. Rewrite the following sentences with special attention to appropriate number usage.

1. "Superman the Escape," the world's fastest roller coaster, travels one hundred miles per hour and is forty-one stories high.

   _____

   _____

2. On May 15th nearly 1/3 of the visitors to Magic Mountain lined up for a high-speed joyride on two fifteen-passenger rail cars.

   _____

   _____

3. Swiss engineers used precise instruments to ensure that Superman's three thousand feet of steel track were within 0.05 inches of specifications.

   _____

   _____

4. Of the four hundred major North American roller coasters, Florida's "Hurricane Force" ranks one hundred fourth in speed comparisons.

   _____

   _____

5. To ride Superman, you must be at least fifty inches tall and weigh seventy-five pounds.

   _____

   _____

1.b 2.a 3.a 4.b 5.a 6.b 7.a 8.a 9.b 10.b

6. Only the Superman ride can reach speeds of one hundred mph in seven seconds, achieving a gravity force of four point five with 6.5 seconds of weightlessness at the top.

_____

_____

7. Located in the 19th Congressional District, Magic Mountain is thirty miles north of Los Angeles and attracts over eight hundred thousand visitors each summer.

_____

_____

8. Visitors who attend between the fifteenth and the thirtieth of March will receive a special discount of forty percent on all rides and concessions.

_____

_____

9. Maintenance costs of six thousand dollars each month are necessary for Superman's two four thousand-pound vehicles.

_____

_____

10. In 2,001 Magic Mountain plans three ten-day celebrations to commemorate the nation's two hundred twenty-fifth anniversary.

_____

_____

C. **Writing Exercise.** In your local newspaper find ten sentences with numbers. Write those sentences on a separate sheet. After each one, explain what usage rule the number style represents. Strive to find examples illustrating different rules.

Editor's Challenge

The following e-mail message contains intentional errors representing language principles covered thus far. Use proofreading marks to make 50 changes.

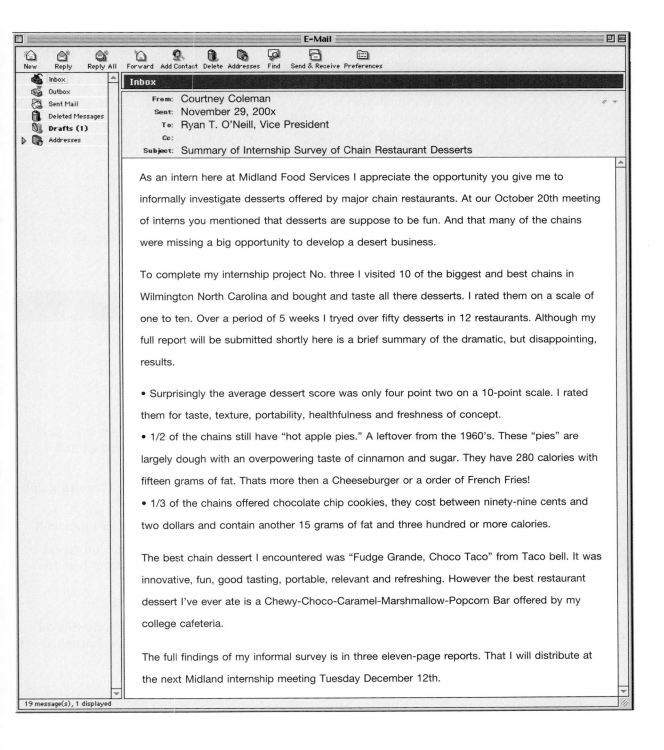

E-Mail

New   Reply   Reply All   Forward   Add Contact   Delete   Addresses   Find   Send & Receive   Preferences

Inbox
Outbox
Sent Mail
Deleted Messages
Drafts (1)
Addresses

Inbox

From: Courtney Coleman
Sent: November 29, 200x
To: Ryan T. O'Neill, Vice President
Cc:
Subject: Summary of Internship Survey of Chain Restaurant Desserts

As an intern here at Midland Food Services I appreciate the opportunity you give me to informally investigate desserts offered by major chain restaurants. At our October 20th meeting of interns you mentioned that desserts are suppose to be fun. And that many of the chains were missing a big opportunity to develop a desert business.

To complete my internship project No. three I visited 10 of the biggest and best chains in Wilmington North Carolina and bought and taste all there desserts. I rated them on a scale of one to ten. Over a period of 5 weeks I tried over fifty desserts in 12 restaurants. Although my full report will be submitted shortly here is a brief summary of the dramatic, but disappointing, results.

• Surprisingly the average dessert score was only four point two on a 10-point scale. I rated them for taste, texture, portability, healthfulness and freshness of concept.
• 1/2 of the chains still have "hot apple pies." A leftover from the 1960's. These "pies" are largely dough with an overpowering taste of cinnamon and sugar. They have 280 calories with fifteen grams of fat. Thats more then a Cheeseburger or a order of French Fries!
• 1/3 of the chains offered chocolate chip cookies, they cost between ninety-nine cents and two dollars and contain another 15 grams of fat and three hundred or more calories.

The best chain dessert I encountered was "Fudge Grande, Choco Taco" from Taco bell. It was innovative, fun, good tasting, portable, relevant and refreshing. However the best restaurant dessert I've ever ate is a Chewy-Choco-Caramel-Marshmallow-Popcorn Bar offered by my college cafeteria.

The full findings of my informal survey is in three eleven-page reports. That I will distribute at the next Midland internship meeting Tuesday December 12th.

19 message(s), 1 displayed

Underline numbers that are expressed inappropriately. Write corrected forms in the spaces provided.

1. It took the IRS seven years to collect the 750,000 dollars owed by the 2 companies. _____

2. Before the third of the month, we had received seventeen calls about the bicycle we advertised for twenty dollars. _____

3. The department had eighteen employees, and they shared four telephones, ten file cabinets, and seven computers. _____

4. Professor Yeoman reported that five hundred students enrolled, an increase of ten percent over last year. _____

5. We will need ten fifty-page booklets before December 1st. _____

learning.web.ways

Goal: To learn how to be more successful in employment interviewing.

You've sent out your résumés and landed a couple of promising interviews. But you'd like to learn more about what to expect and how to answer interview questions.

1. With your Web browser on the screen, go to the Guffey Student Web Site **<http://www.westwords.com/guffey/students.html>** and click **Job Search**.

2. Click **Job Interview Resources**. Then click **About's Career Planning: Job Interviews.**

3. Click on **Job Interviewing** and read about the various kinds of interviews.

4. Use the browser **Back** button to return to the home page. Click on **Great Answers to Tough Interview Questions.** Print two pages from this site. What are three typical interview questions?

5. Return to the home page and explore other articles on interviewing.

6. Return to the Guffey Web site and select another site with interviewing advice. Print one page from this site. What are three tips that you learned about interviewing from this site?

7. End your session. Submit your printouts and answers.

1. $750,000 two   2. 3d or 3rd 17 $20   3. 18   4. 500 10 percent
5. 50-page December 1

CHECKLIST OF BONUS LEARNING RESOURCES

The following additional learning resources are available to you. Your instructor will tell you which to complete.

- Web Editor's Challenge Exercise
- Web Interactive Chapter Review
- Web PowerPoint Slides
- Web Crossword Puzzle
- WebCheck Reinforcement Exercises 20.1, 20.2
- Self-Help Exercises
- Electronic Study Guide

Unit Review Chapters 19–20

Name _____

First, review Chapters 19–20. Then test your comprehension of those chapters by completing the exercises that follow. Compare your responses with those shown at the end of the book.

Level I

Select (a) or (b) to describe the group of words that is more acceptably expressed.

1. (a) courses in Business Law, Spanish, and Sociology
   (b) courses in business law, Spanish, and sociology _____

2. (a) living in Ventura county
   (b) living in Ventura County _____

3. (a) the State of Ohio
   (b) the state of Ohio _____

4. (a) during summer vacation
   (b) during Summer vacation _____

5. (a) a victorian home
   (b) a Victorian home _____

6. (a) the 22nd of June
   (b) the twenty-second of June _____

7. (a) twenty dollars
   (b) $20 _____

8. (a) on 11th Street
   (b) on Eleventh Street _____

9. (a) on December 15th
   (b) on December 15 _____

Use proofreading marks to correct any errors in capitalization or number usage in the following sentences. In the space at the right, indicate how many changes you made.

10. 20 Nokia Cell Phones will be discounted twenty-five dollars each until June 15. _____

11. At least 90 students enrolled in three sections of Marketing. _____

12. Over two thousand Microsoft employees were invited to the Fall picnic on October tenth. _____

Level II

Select (a) or (b) to describe the group of words that is more acceptably expressed.

13. (a) your Aunt and Uncle
    (b) your aunt and uncle _____

14. (a) travel east on Highway 10
    (b) travel East on Highway 10 _____

15. (a) our manager, Joe Lopez
    (b) our Manager, Joe Lopez _____

16. (a) their receiving department
    (b) their Receiving Department _____

17. (a) a message from Lisa Cantrell, Sales Director
    (b) a message from Lisa Cantrell, sales director _____

18. (a) a message from Sales Director Cook
    (b) a message from sales director Cook _____

19. (a) for the next two years
    (b) for the next 2 years _____

20. (a) 2 twenty-five page booklets
    (b) two 25-page booklets _____

21. (a) nine computers serving 14 offices   (b) 9 computers serving 14 offices   _____

Use proofreading marks to correct any errors in capitalization or number usage in the following sentences. In the space at the right, indicate how many changes you made.

22. His lunch of a big mac, french fries, and a coca-cola cost two dollars and seventy-five cents.   _____

23. The CEO, two Vice Presidents, three Managers, and 15 sales representatives attended the East coast conference.   _____

24. Sales manager Vorman had only fifty 100-page color brochures for the audience of 130 people.   _____

L e v e l   I I I

Select the correct group of words below and write its letter in the space provided.

25. (a) our chief executive officer, Mr. Spiros   (b) our Chief Executive Officer, Mr. Spiros   _____

26. (a) U.S. Vice President-Elect   (b) U.S. Vice President-elect   _____

27. (a) a package stamped "photographs"   (b) a package stamped "Photographs"   _____

28. (a) our 28th anniversary   (b) our twenty-eighth anniversary   _____

29. (a) less than 0.1 percent   (b) less than .1 percent   _____

30. (a) 4 quarts of ice cream   (b) four quarts of ice cream   _____

31. (a) a 10% return   (b) a 10 percent return   _____

32. (a) on his 20th birthday   (b) on his twentieth birthday   _____

33. (a) the bright moon   (b) the bright Moon   _____

34. (a) oriental and asian cultures   (b) Oriental and Asian cultures   _____

35. (a) 2/3 interest   (b) a two-thirds interest   _____

Hotline Review

Write the letter of the word or phrase that correctly completes each sentence.

36. May I _____ from your remark that you will be unable to attend the meeting?   _____
    a. imply   **b.** infer

37. The audience _____ from the speaker's remarks that the company would suffer a loss in profits.   _____
    a. implied   **b.** inferred

38. Workmen wore _____ clothing during the hot weather.   _____
    a. lose   **b.** loose

39. _____ everyone will be watching the series on TV.   _____
    a. Almost   **b.** Most

40. I know that you felt _____ about the error.   _____
    a. badly   **b.** bad

Name _____

Short Reports

Reports are a fact of life in the business world today. They are important because they convey needed information, and they help decision makers solve problems. Organizing information into a meaningful report is an important skill you will want to acquire if your field is business.

Characteristics of Reports

As an introduction to report writing, this workshop focuses on the most important characteristics of reports. You'll learn valuable tips about the format, data, headings, and writing plan for short business reports.

Format. How should a business report look? Three formats are commonly used. *Letter format* is appropriate for short reports prepared by one organization for another. A letter report, as illustrated in Figure 20.1, is like a letter except that it is more carefully organized. It includes side headings and lists where appropriate. *Memo format* is common for reports written within an organization. These internal reports look like memos—with the addition of side headings. *Report format* is used for longer, more formal reports. Printed on plain paper (instead of letterhead or memo forms), these reports begin with a title followed by carefully displayed headings and subheadings.

Data. Where do you find the data for a business report? Many business reports begin with personal observation and experience. If you were writing a report on implementing flextime for employees, you might begin by observing current work schedules and by asking what schedules employees preferred. Other sources of data for business reports include company records, surveys, questionnaires, and interviews. If you want to see how others have solved a problem or collect background data on a topic, you can consult magazines, journals, and books. Much information is available electronically through on-line library indexes or from searching databases and the Internet.

Headings. Good headings in a report highlight major ideas and categories. They guide the reader through a report. In longer reports they divide the text into inviting chunks, and they provide resting places for the eyes. Short reports often use *functional* heads (such as *Problem*, *Summary*, and *Recommendations*). Longer reports may employ *talking heads* (such as *Short-Term Parking Solutions*) because they provide more information to the reader. Whether your heads are functional or talking, be sure they are clear and parallel. For example, use *Visible Costs* and *Invisible Costs* rather than *Visible Costs* and *Costs That Don't Show*. Don't enclose headings in quotation marks, and avoid using headings as antecedents for pronouns. For example, if your heading is *Laser Printers*, don't begin the next sentence with *These produce high-quality output* . . . .

Figure 20.1
Short Report—Letter Format

Liberty Environmental, Inc.
2593 North Glebe Road
Arlington, VA 22207   (804) 356-1094

October 9, 200x

Ms. Sharon J. Goode
Richmond Realty, Inc.
3390 Chesterfield Avenue
Richmond, VA 22368

Dear Ms. Goode:

At the request of Richmond Realty, I have completed a preliminary investigation of its Mountain Park property listing. The following findings and recommendations are based on my physical inspection of the site, official records, and interviews with officials and persons knowledgeable about the site.

Findings and Analyses

My preliminary assessment of the Mountain Park listing and its immediate vicinity revealed rooms with damaged floor tiles on the first and second floors of 2539 Mountain View Drive. Apparently, in recent remodeling efforts, these tiles had been cracked and broken. Examination of the ceiling and attic revealed possible contamination from asbestos. The insulation material surrounding the hot-water storage tank was in poor condition.

Located on the property is Mountain Technology, a possible hazardous waste generator. Although I could not examine its interior, this company has the potential for producing hazardous material contamination. Moreover, several large dumpsters in the parking area collect trash and debris from surrounding businesses. Because these dumpsters were uncovered, they pose a risk to the general public.

Recommendations

To reduce its potential environmental liability, Richmond Realty should take the following steps in regard to its Mountain Park listing:

- Conduct an immediate asbestos survey at the site, including inspection of ceiling insulation material, floor tiles, and insulation around a gas-fired heater vent pipe at 2539 Mountain View Drive.

- Prepare an environmental audit of the generators of hazardous waste currently operating at the site, including Mountain Technology.

- Obtain lids for the dumpsters situated in the parking areas and ensure that the lids are kept closed.

If you would like to discuss the findings or recommendations in this report, please call me and I will be glad to answer your questions.

Sincerely,

Scott R. Evans

Scott R. Evans

Skill Check 6.1 Reviewing the Characteristics of Short Reports

Select a letter to indicate the best format for the report described.

(a) Memo format   (b) Letter format   (c) Report format

1. A short report to a company from an outside consultant _____

2. A short report from a product manager to her boss _____

3. A long report describing a company's diversity program _____

4. If you were writing a report to persuade management to purchase more computers, the best way to begin collecting data would be to
   a. observe current use
   b. consult books and journals
   c. search the Internet _____

5. Which combination of report headings is best?
   a. Delivery costs, Suppliers
   b. Reduction of delivery costs, Recommendations
   c. "Delivery costs," "Supply Costs"
   d. Reducing delivery costs, Finding new suppliers _____

Writing Plan for a Short Report

Short reports often have three parts: introduction, findings, and recommendations. If the report is purely informational, a summary may be made instead of recommendations.

Introduction. This part of a report may also be called *Background*. In this section, you'll want to explain why you are writing. You may also (a) describe what methods and sources were used to gather information and why they are credible, (b) provide any special background information that may be necessary, and (c) offer a preview of your findings.

Findings. This section may also be called *Observations, Facts, Results,* or *Discussion*. Important points to consider in this section are organization and display. You may wish to organize the findings (a) chronologically (for example, to describe the history of a problem), (b) alphabetically (if you were, for example, evaluating candidates for a position), (c) topically (for example, discussing sales by regions), or (d) from most to least important (such as listing criteria for evaluating equipment). To display the findings effectively, you could (a) use side headings, (b) number each finding, (c) underline or boldface the key words, or (d) merely indent the paragraphs.

Summary or Recommendations. Some reports just offer information. Such reports may conclude with an impartial summary. Other reports are more analytical, and they generally conclude with recommendations. These recommendations tell readers how to solve the problem and may even suggest ways to implement the necessary actions. To display recommendations, number each one and place it on a separate line.

Notice that the letter report in Figure 20.1 includes an introduction, findings and analyses, and recommendations.

Writing Application 6.1

Organize the following information into a short letter report. As Cynthia M. Chavez, president, Chavez and Associates, you have been hired as a consultant to advise the St. Petersburg, Florida, City Council. The City Council has asked you and your associates to investigate a problem with Pinellas Park Beachway.

In 1979 St. Petersburg constructed a 12-foot pathway, now called the Pinellas Park Beachway. It was meant originally for bicycle riders, but today it has become very popular for joggers, walkers, bikers, in-line skaters, skateboarders, sightseers, and animal owners walking their dogs. In fact, it's become so popular that it is dangerous. Last year the St. Petersburg Police Department reported an amazing 65 collisions in the area. And this does not count the close calls and minor accidents that no one reported. The City Council wants your organization to identify the problem and come up with some workable recommendations for improving safety.

As you look into the matter, you immediately decide that the council is right. A problem definitely exists! In addition to the many pedestrians and riders, you see that families with rented pedal-powered surreys clog the beachway. Sometimes they even operate these vehicles on the wrong side. Your investigation further reveals that bicyclists with rental bikes do not always have bells to alert walkers. And poor lighting makes nighttime use extremely dangerous. You've noticed that conditions seem to be worst on Sundays. This congestion results from nearby art and crafts fairs and sales, attracting even more people to the crowded area.

Your investigation confirms that the beachway is dangerous. But what to do about it? In a brainstorming session, your associates make a number of suggestions for reducing the dangers to users. By the way, the council is particularly interested in lessening the threat of liability to the city. One of your associates thinks that the beachway should be made at least 15 or more feet wide. Another suggests that the beachway be lighted at night. Someone thinks that a new path should be built, on the beach side of the existing beachway; this path would be for pedestrians only. Educating users about safety rules and etiquette would certainly be wise for everyone. One suggestion involves better striping or applying colors to designate different uses for the beachway. And why not require that all rental bicycles be equipped with bells? One of the best recommendations involved hiring uniformed "beach hosts" who would monitor the beachway, give advice, offer directions, and generally patrol the area.

In a short report, outline the problem and list your recommendations. Naturally, you would be happy to discuss your findings and recommendations with the St. Petersburg City Council.

Appendix A Developing Spelling Skills

Why Is English Spelling So Difficult?

No one would dispute the complaint that many English words are difficult to spell. Why is spelling in our language so perplexing? For one thing, our language has borrowed many of its words from other languages. English has a Germanic base on which a superstructure of words borrowed from French, Latin, Greek, and other languages of the world has been erected. For this reason, its words are not always formed by regular patterns of letter combinations. In addition, spelling is made difficult because the pronunciation of English words is constantly changing. Today's spelling was standardized nearly 300 years ago, but many words are pronounced differently today than they were then. Therefore, pronunciation often provides little help in spelling. Consider, for example, the words *sew* and *dough*.

What Can Be Done to Improve One's Spelling?

Spelling is a skill that can be developed, just as arithmetic, typing, and other skills can be developed. Because the ability to spell is a prerequisite for success in business and in most other activities, effort expended to acquire this skill is effort well spent.

Three traditional approaches to improving spelling have met with varying degrees of success.

1. Rules or Guidelines

The spelling of English words is consistent enough to justify the formulation of a few spelling rules, perhaps more appropriately called guidelines since the generalizations in question are not invariably applicable. Such guidelines are, in other words, helpful but not infallible.

2. Mnemonics

Another approach to improving one's ability to spell involves the use of mnemonics or memory devices. For example, the word *principle* might be associated with the word *rule*, to form in the mind of the speller a link between the meaning and the spelling of *principle*. To spell *capitol*, one might think of the *dome* of the capitol building and focus on the *o*'s in both words. The use of mnemonics can be an effective device for the improvement of spelling only if the speller makes a real effort to develop the necessary memory hooks.

3. Rote Learning

A third approach to the improvement of spelling centers on memorization. The word is studied by the speller until it can be readily reproduced in the mind's eye.

The 1-2-3 Spelling Plan

Proficiency in spelling is not attained without concentrated effort. Here's a plan to follow in mastering the 400 commonly misspelled words included in this appendix. For each word, try this 1-2-3 approach.

1. Is a spelling guideline applicable? If so, select the appropriate guideline and study the word in relation to that guideline.
2. If no guideline applies, can a memory device be created to aid in the recall of the word?
3. If neither a guideline nor a memory device will work, the word must be memorized. Look at the word carefully. Pronounce it. Write it or repeat it until you can visualize all its letters in your mind's eye.

Before you try the 1-2-3 plan, become familiar with the six spelling guidelines that follow. These spelling guidelines are not intended to represent all the possible spelling rules appearing in the various available spelling books. These six guidelines are, however, among the most effective and helpful of the recognized spelling rules.

Guideline 1: Words Containing *ie* or *ei*

Although there are exceptions to it, the following familiar rhyme can be helpful.

(a) Write *i* before *e*
(b) Except after *c*,
(c) Or when sounded like *a*
     As in *neighbor* and *weigh*.

Study these words illustrating the three parts of the rhyme.

(a) *i* Before *e*		(b) Except After *c*	(c) or When Sounded Like *a*
achieve	grief	ceiling	beige
belief	ingredient	conceive	eight
believe	mischief	deceive	freight
brief	niece	perceive	heir
cashier	piece	receipt	neighbor
chief	shield	receive	reign
convenient	sufficient		their
field	view		vein
friend	yield		weight

Exceptions: These exceptional *ei* and *ie* words must be learned by rote or with the use of a mnemonic device.

caffeine	height	seize
either	leisure	sheik
financier	neither	sleight
foreigner	protein	weird

Guideline 2: Words Ending in *e*

For most words ending in an *e*, the final *e* is dropped when the word is joined to a suffix beginning with a vowel (such as *ing, able,* or *al*). The final *e* is retained when a suffix beginning with a consonant (such as *ment, less, ly,* or *ful*) is joined to such a word.

Final *e* Dropped	Final *e* Retained
believe, believing	arrange, arrangement
care, caring	require, requirement
hope, hoping	hope, hopeless
receive, receiving	care, careless
desire, desirable	like, likely
cure, curable	approximate, approximately
move, movable	definite, definitely
value, valuable	sincere, sincerely
disperse, dispersal	use, useful
arrive, arrival	hope, hopeful

Exceptions: The few exceptions to this spelling guideline are among the most frequently misspelled words. As such, they deserve special attention. Notice that they all involve a dropped final *e*.

acknowledgment	ninth
argument	truly
judgment	wholly

Guideline 3: Words Ending in *ce* or *ge*

When *able* or *ous* is added to words ending in *ce* or *ge*, the final *e* is retained if the *c* or *g* is pronounced softly (as in *change* or *peace*).

advantage, advantageous	change, changeable
courage, courageous	service, serviceable
outrage, outrageous	manage, manageable

Guideline 4: Words Ending in *y*

Words ending in a *y* that is preceded by a consonant normally change the *y* to *i* before all suffixes except those beginning with an *i*.

Change *y* to *i* Because *y* Is Preceded by a Consonant	Do Not Change *y* to *i* Because *y* Is Preceded by a Vowel
accompany, accompaniment	employ, employer
study, studied, studious	annoy, annoying, annoyance
duty, dutiful	stay, staying, stayed
industry, industrious	attorney, attorneys
carry, carriage	valley, valleys
apply, appliance	**Do Not Change *y* to *i* When Adding *ing***
try, tried	
empty, emptiness	accompany, accompanying
forty, fortieth	apply, applying
secretary, secretaries	study, studying
company, companies	satisfy, satisfying
hurry, hurries	try, trying

Exceptions: day, daily; dry, dried; mislay, mislaid; pay, paid; shy, shyly; gay, gaily.

Guideline 5: Doubling a Final Consonant

If one-syllable words or two-syllable words accented on the second syllable end in a single consonant preceded by a single vowel, the final consonant is doubled before the addition of a suffix beginning with a vowel.

Although complex, this spelling guideline is extremely useful and therefore well worth mastering. Many spelling errors can be avoided by applying this guideline.

One-Syllable Words	Two-Syllable Words
can, canned	acquit, acquitting, acquittal
drop, dropped	admit, admitted, admitting
fit, fitted	begin, beginner, beginning
get, getting	commit, committed, committing
man, manned	control, controller, controlling
plan, planned	defer, deferred (but deference*)
run, running	excel, excelled, excelling
shut, shutting	occur, occurrence, occurring
slip, slipped	prefer, preferring (but preference*)
swim, swimming	recur, recurred, recurrence
ton, tonnage	refer, referring (but reference*)

*Because the accent shifts to the first syllable, the final consonant is not doubled.

Here is a summary of conditions necessary for application of this guideline.

1. The word must end in a single consonant.

2. The final consonant must be preceded by a single vowel.

3. The word must be accented on the second syllable (if it has two syllables).

Words derived from *cancel, offer, differ, equal, suffer,* and *benefit* are not governed by this guideline because they are accented on the first syllable.

Guideline 6: Prefixes and Suffixes

For words in which the letter that ends the prefix is the same as the letter that begins the main word (such as in *dissimilar*), both letters must be included. For words in which a suffix begins with the same letter that ends the main word (such as in *coolly*), both letters must also be included.

Prefix	Main Word	Main Word	Suffix
dis	satisfied	accidental	ly
ir	responsible	incidental	ly
il	literate	clean	ness
mis	spell	cool	ly
mis	state	even	ness
un	necessary	mean	ness

On the other hand, do not supply additional letters when adding prefixes to main words.

Prefix	Main Word
dis	appoint (*not* dissappoint)
dis	appearance
mis	take

Perhaps the most important guideline one can follow in spelling correctly is to use the dictionary whenever in doubt.

400 Most Frequently Misspelled Words* (Divided into 20 Lists of 20 Words Each)

List 1	List 2	List 3
1. absence	21. afraid	41. applying
2. acceptance	22. against	42. approaches
3. accessible	23. aggressive	43. appropriate
4. accidentally	24. all right	44. approximately
5. accommodate	25. almost	45. arguing
6. accompaniment	26. alphabetical	46. argument
7. accurately	27. already	47. arrangement
8. accustom	28. although	48. article
9. achievement	29. amateur	49. athlete

*Compiled from lists of words most frequently misspelled by students and businesspeople.

10. acknowledgment, acknowledgement	30. among	50. attack
11. acquaintance	31. amount	51. attendance, attendants
12. acquire	32. analysis	52. attitude
13. across	33. analyze	53. attorneys
14. actually	34. angel, angle	54. auxiliary
15. adequately	35. annoyance	55. basically
16. admitted	36. annual	56. beautiful
17. adolescence	37. answer	57. before
18. advantageous	38. apologized	58. beginning
19. advertising	39. apparent	59. believing
20. advice, advise	40. appliance	60. benefited

List 4	List 5	List 6
61. biggest	81. companies	101. description
62. breath, breathe	82. competition	102. desirable
63. brief	83. completely	103. destroy
64. business	84. conceive	104. development
65. calendar	85. conscience	105. difference
66. capital, capitol	86. conscientious	106. dining
67. career	87. conscious	107. disappearance
68. careless	88. considerably	108. disappoint
69. carrying	89. consistent	109. disastrous
70. cashier	90. continuous	110. discipline
71. ceiling	91. controlling	111. discussion
72. certain	92. controversial	112. disease
73. challenge	93. convenience	113. dissatisfied
74. changeable	94. council, counsel	114. distinction
75. chief	95. cylinder	115. divide
76. choose, chose	96. daily	116. doesn't
77. cloths, clothes	97. deceive	117. dominant
78. column	98. decision	118. dropped
79. coming	99. define	119. due
80. committee	100. dependent	120. during

List 7	List 8	List 9
121. efficient	141. February	161. happiness
122. eligible	142. fictitious	162. hear, here
123. embarrass	143. field	163. height

124. encourage	144. finally	164. heroes
125. enough	145. financially	165. hopeless
126. environment	146. foreigner	166. hoping
127. equipped	147. fortieth	167. huge
128. especially	148. forty, fourth	168. humorous
129. exaggerate	149. forward, foreword	169. hungry
130. excellence	150. freight	170. ignorance
131. except	151. friend	171. imaginary
132. exercise	152. fulfill	172. imagine
133. existence	153. fundamentally	173. immediately
134. experience	154. further	174. immense
135. explanation	155. generally	175. importance
136. extremely	156. government	176. incidentally
137. familiar	157. governor	177. independent
138. families	158. grammar	178. indispensable
139. fascinate	159. grateful	179. industrious
140. favorite	160. guard	180. inevitable

List 10	List 11	List 12
181. influential	201. leisurely	221. mechanics
182. ingredient	202. library	222. medicine
183. initiative	203. license	223. medieval
184. intelligence	204. likely	224. mere
185. interest	205. literature	225. miniature
186. interference	206. lives	226. minutes
187. interpretation	207. loneliness	227. mischief
188. interrupt	208. loose, lose	228. misspell
189. involve	209. losing	229. mistake
190. irrelevant	210. luxury	230. muscle
191. irresponsible	211. magazine	231. mysterious
192. island	212. magnificence	232. naturally
193. jealous	213. maintenance	233. necessary
194. judgment	214. manageable	234. neighbor
195. kindergarten	215. maneuver	235. neither
196. knowledge	216. manner	236. nervous
197. laboratory	217. manufacturer	237. nickel
198. laborer	218. marriage	238. niece

| 199. laid | 219. mathematics | 239. ninety |
| 200. led, lead | 220. meant | 240. ninth |

List 13	List 14	List 15
241. noticeable	261. passed, past	281. possible
242. numerous	262. pastime	282. practical
243. obstacle	263. peaceable	283. precede
244. occasionally	264. peculiar	284. preferred
245. occurrence	265. perceive	285. prejudice
246. off	266. performance	286. preparation
247. offered	267. permanent	287. prevalent
248. official	268. permitted	288. principal, principle
249. omitted	269. persistent	289. privilege
250. operate	270. personal, personnel	290. probably
251. opinion	271. persuading	291. proceed
252. opportunity	272. phase, faze	292. professor
253. opposite	273. philosophy	293. prominent
254. organization	274. physical	294. proving
255. origin	275. piece	295. psychology
256. original	276. planned	296. pursuing
257. paid	277. pleasant	297. quantity
258. pamphlet	278. poison	298. quiet, quite
259. parallel	279. political	299. really
260. particular	280. possession	300. receipt

List 16	List 17	List 18
301. receiving	321. satisfying	341. speak, speech
302. recognize	322. scenery	342. specimen
303. recommend	323. schedule	343. stationary, stationery
304. reference	324. science	344. stopped
305. referring	325. secretaries	345. stories
306. regard	326. seize	346. straight, strait
307. relative	327. sense, since	347. strenuous
308. relieving	328. sentence	348. stretch
309. religious	329. separation	349. strict
310. reminiscent	330. sergeant	350. studying
311. repetition	331. serviceable	351. substantial
312. representative	332. several	352. subtle

313. requirement	333. shining	353. succeed
314. resistance	334. shoulder	354. success
315. responsible	335. significance	355. sufficient
316. restaurant	336. similar	356. summary
317. rhythm	337. simply	357. suppose
318. ridiculous	338. sincerely	358. surprise
319. sacrifice	339. site, cite	359. suspense
320. safety	340. source	360. swimming

List 19	List 20
361. syllable	381. tremendous
362. symbol	382. tried
363. symmetrical	383. truly
364. synonymous	384. undoubtedly
365. technique	385. unnecessary
366. temperament	386. until
367. temperature	387. unusual
368. tendency	388. useful
369. than, then	389. using
370. their, there	390. vacuum
371. themselves	391. valuable
372. theories	392. varies
373. therefore	393. vegetable
374. thorough	394. view
375. though	395. weather, whether
376. through	396. weird
377. together	397. were, where
378. tomorrow	398. wholly, holy
379. tragedies	399. writing
380. transferred	400. yield

Appendix B Developing Vocabulary Skills

If you understand the meanings of many words, you can be said to have a "good vocabulary." Words are the basis of thought. We think with words, we understand with words, we communicate with words.

A large working vocabulary is a significant asset. It allows us to use precise words that say exactly what we intend. In addition, we understand more effectively what we hear and read. A large vocabulary also enables us to score well on employment and intelligence tests. Lewis M. Terman, who developed the Stanford-Binet IQ tests, believes that vocabulary is the best single indicator of intelligence.

In the business world, where precise communication is extremely important, surveys show a definite correlation between vocabulary size and job performance. Skilled workers, in the majority of cases, have larger vocabularies than unskilled workers. Supervisors know the meanings of more words than the workers they direct, and executives have larger vocabularies than employees working for them.

Having a good vocabulary at our command doesn't necessarily ensure our success in life, but it certainly gives us an advantage. Improving your vocabulary will help you expand your options in an increasingly complex world.

Vocabulary can be acquired in three ways: accidentally, incidentally, and intentionally. Setting out intentionally to expand your word power is, of course, the most efficient vocabulary-building method. One of the best means of increasing your vocabulary involves using 3-by-5 cards. When you encounter an unfamiliar word, write it on a card and put the definition of the word on the reverse side. Just five to ten minutes of practice each day with such cards can significantly increase your vocabulary.

Your campaign to increase your vocabulary can begin with the 20 lists of selected business terms and words of general interest included in this appendix. You may already know partial definitions for some of these words. Take this opportunity to develop more precise definitions for them. Follow these steps in using the word lists:

1. Record the word on a 3-by-5 card.
2. Look up the word in your dictionary. Compare the dictionary definitions of the word with the definition alternatives shown after the word in your copy of *Business English*. Select the correct definition, and write its letter in the space provided in your textbook. (The definitions provided in your textbook are quite concise but should help you remember the word's most common meaning.)

3. On the reverse side of your card, write the phonetic spelling of the word and the word's part of speech. Then write its definition using as much of the dictionary definition as you find helpful. Try also to add a phrase or sentence illustrating the word.

4. Study your 3-by-5 cards often.

5. Try to find ways to use your vocabulary words in your speech and writing.

List 1

1. adjacent	= (a) previous, (b) similar, (c) overdue, (d) nearby	_____
2. ambivalence	= having (a) uncertainty, (b) ambition, (c) compassion, (d) intelligence	_____
3. belligerent	= (a) overweight, (b) quarrelsome, (c) likable, (d) believable	_____
4. contingent	= (a) conditional, (b) allowable, (c) hopeless, (d) impractical	_____
5. decadent	= in a state of (a) repair, (b) happiness, (c) decline, (d) extreme patriotism	_____
6. entitlement	= (a) label, (b) tax refund, (c) screen credit, (d) legal right	_____
7. equivalent	= (a) subsequent, (b) identical, (c) self-controlled, (d) plentiful	_____
8. paramount	= (a) foremost, (b) high mountain, (c) film company, (d) insignificant	_____
9. plausible	= (a) quiet, (b) acceptable, (c) notorious, (d) negative	_____
10. unilateral	= (a) powerful, (b) harmonious, (c) one-sided, (d) indelible	_____

List 2

1. affluent	= (a) rich, (b) slippery, (c) persistent, (d) rebellious	_____
2. autocrat	= one who (a) owns many cars, (b) is self-centered, (c) has power, (d) collects signatures	_____
3. benevolent	= for the purpose of (a) religion, (b) doing good, (c) healing, (d) violence	_____
4. entrepreneur	= (a) business owner, (b) traveler, (c) salesperson, (d) gambler	_____
5. impertinent	= (a) stationary, (b) bound to happen, (c) obsolete, (d) rude and irreverent	_____
6. imprudent	= (a) unwise, (b) crude, (c) vulnerable, (d) lifeless	_____
7. mediator	= one who seeks (a) overseas trade, (b) profits, (c) safe investment, (d) peaceful settlement	_____
8. preponderance	= (a) thoughtful, (b) exclusive right, (c) superiority, (d) forethought	_____
9. recipient	= (a) receiver, (b) respondent, (c) voter, (d) giver	_____
10. reprehensible	= (a) obedient, (b) independent, (c) blameworthy, (d) following	_____

List 3

1. affable	= (a) cheap, (b) pleasant, (c) strange, (d) competent	_____
2. consensus	= (a) population count, (b) attendance, (c) tabulation, (d) agreement	_____
3. criterion	= (a) standard, (b) command, (c) pardon, (d) law	_____
4. diligent	= (a) gentle, (b) industrious, (c) prominent, (d) intelligent	_____

5. hydraulic = operated by means of (a) air, (b) gasoline, (c) liquid, (d) mechanical parts _____

6. hypothesis = (a) triangle, (b) promulgate, (c) highest point, (d) theory _____

7. phenomenon = (a) imagination, (b) rare event, (c) appointment, (d) clever saying _____

8. reticent = (a) silent, (b) strong-willed, (c) inflexible, (d) disagreeable _____

9. sanctuary = a place of (a) healing, (b) refuge, (c) rest, (d) learning _____

10. stimulus = something that causes (a) response, (b) light, (c) pain, (d) movement _____

List 4

1. beneficiary = one who (a) receives a license, (b) creates goodwill, (c) receives proceeds, (d) makes friends _____

2. constrain = (a) restrict, (b) filter, (c) use, (d) inform _____

3. corroborate = (a) contradict, (b) recall, (c) erode, (d) confirm _____

4. dun (n) = a demand for (a) legal action, (b) payment, (c) credit information, (d) dividends _____

5. equitable = (a) fair, (b) profitable, (c) similar, (d) clear _____

6. fluctuate = (a) rinse out, (b) magnetic field, (c) pricing schedule, (d) swing back and forth _____

7. indolent = (a) self-indulgent, (b) lazy, (c) pampered, (d) uncertain _____

8. nullify = (a) disappear, (b) imitate, (c) invalidate, (d) enhance _____

9. obsolete = (a) ugly, (b) outmoded, (c) audible, (d) scant _____

10. stabilize = to make (a) pleasant, (b) congenial, (c) traditional, (d) firm _____

List 5

1. arbitrate = (a) decide, (b) construct, (c) conquer, (d) ratify _____

2. coalition = (a) deliberation, (b) allegiance, (c) adherence, (d) alliance _____

3. collate = (a) assemble, (b) denounce, (c) supersede, (d) uninformed _____

4. conglomerate = combination of (a) executives, (b) companies, (c) investments, (d) countries _____

5. franchise = (a) fictitious reason, (b) right, (c) obligation, (d) official announcement _____

6. logistics = (a) speculations, (b) analytic philosophy, (c) reasonable outcome, (d) details of operation _____

7. proxy = authority to (a) act for another, (b) write checks, (c) submit nominations, (d) explain _____

8. subsidiary = (a) below expectations, (b) country dominated by another, (c) company controlled by another, (d) depressed financial condition _____

9. termination = (a) end, (b) inception, (c) identification, (d) evasive action _____

10. virtually = (a) absolutely, (b) precisely, (c) almost entirely, (d) strictly _____

List 6

1. affiliate	= (a) trust, (b) attract, (c) effect, (d) join	_____
2. alter	= (a) table for religious ceremony, (b) solitary, (c) attribute, (d) modify	_____
3. boisterous	= (a) vociferous, (b) masculine, (c) cheerful, (d) brusque	_____
4. configuration	= (a) stratagem, (b) foreign currency, (c) form, (d) comprehension	_____
5. conveyance	= (a) vehicle, (b) transformation, (c) baggage, (d) consortium	_____
6. infringe	= (a) ravel, (b) decorative border, (c) encroach, (d) frivolous	_____
7. jurisdiction	= (a) science of law, (b) enunciation, (c) justice, (d) authority	_____
8. nonpartisan	= (a) unbiased, (b) antisocial, (c) ineffective, (d) untenable	_____
9. parity	= (a) price index, (b) justice under law, (c) plenitude, (d) equality of purchasing power	_____
10. usury	= (a) method of operation, (b) implementation, (c) illegal interest, (d) customary	_____

List 7

1. anonymous	= (a) multiplex, (b) powerless, (c) vexing, (d) nameless	_____
2. cartel	= (a) combination to fix prices, (b) ammunition belt, (c) partnership to promote competition, (d) placard	_____
3. conjecture	= (a) coagulation, (b) gesticulation, (c) guesswork, (d) connection	_____
4. disparity	= (a) unlikeness, (b) separation, (c) lacking emotion, (d) repudiation	_____
5. environment	= (a) urban area, (b) zenith, (c) surroundings, (d) latitude	_____
6. impetus	= (a) oversight, (b) stimulus, (c) hindrance, (d) imminent	_____
7. portfolio	= a list of (a) books, (b) security analysts, (c) corporations, (d) investments	_____
8. quiescent	= (a) presumptuous, (b) latent, (c) immoderate, (d) volatile	_____
9. surrogate	= (a) substitute, (b) accused, (c) authenticate, (d) suspend	_____
10. tariff	= (a) marsupial, (b) announcement, (c) ship, (d) duty	_____

List 8

1. accrue	= (a) conform, (b) accumulate, (c) diminish, (d) multiply	_____
2. amortize	= (a) pay off, (b) reduce, (c) romance, (d) kill	_____
3. commensurate	= (a) infinitesimal, (b) erroneous, (c) reliable, (d) proportional	_____
4. consortium	= (a) configuration, (b) partnership or association, (c) royal offspring, (d) rental property	_____
5. discernible	= (a) perceptive, (b) pretentious, (c) recognizable, (d) dissident	_____
6. frugal	= (a) thrifty, (b) wasteful, (c) judicious, (d) profligate	_____
7. pecuniary	= (a) rudimentary, (b) eccentric, (c) financial, (d) distinctive	_____
8. retract	= (a) disavow, (b) reorganize, (c) reciprocate, (d) hide	_____

9. scrutinize	= (a) cheerfully admit, (b) baffle, (c) persist, (d) examine carefully	_____
10. tenacious	= (a) falling apart, (b) holding on, (c) immobile, (d) chagrined	_____

List 9

1. amiable	= (a) contumacious, (b) impetuous, (c) feasible, (d) congenial	_____
2. credible	= (a) plausible, (b) deceitful, (c) religious, (d) tolerant	_____
3. defendant	= one who (a) sues, (b) answers suit, (c) judges, (d) protects	_____
4. dissipate	= (a) accumulate, (b) partition, (c) liquify, (d) scatter or waste	_____
5. incentive	= (a) impediment, (b) support, (c) motive, (d) remuneration	_____
6. innocuous	= (a) harmless, (b) injection, (c) facetious, (d) frightening	_____
7. oust	= (a) install, (b) instigate, (c) shout, (d) expel	_____
8. pittance	= (a) tiny amount, (b) tithe, (c) abyss, (d) pestilence	_____
9. plaintiff	= one who (a) defends, (b) is sad, (c) sues, (d) responds	_____
10. superfluous	= (a) extraordinary, (b) very slippery, (c) shallow, (d) oversupplied	_____

List 10

1. adroit	= (a) ideal, (b) resilient, (c) witty, (d) skillful	_____
2. derogatory	= (a) minimal, (b) degrading, (c) originating from, (d) devious	_____
3. escrow	= (a) international treaty, (b) public registration, (c) licensed by state, (d) type of deposit	_____
4. facsimile	= (a) principle, (b) prototype, (c) exact copy, (d) counterfeit	_____
5. inordinate	= (a) unwholesome, (b) excessive, (c) unimportant, (d) treacherous	_____
6. logical	= (a) reasoned, (b) irrelevant, (c) lofty, (d) intricate	_____
7. malfeasance	= (a) prevaricate, (b) injurious, (c) superstitious, (d) misconduct	_____
8. noxious	= (a) pernicious, (b) unusual, (c) pleasant, (d) inconsequential	_____
9. résumé	= (a) budget report, (b) minutes of meeting, (c) photo album, (d) summary of qualifications	_____
10. spasmodic	= (a) paralyzing, (b) intermittent or fitful, (c) internal, (d) painful	_____

List 11

1. animosity	= (a) happiness, (b) deep sadness, (c) hatred, (d) study of animals	_____
2. caveat	= (a) headwear, (b) warning, (c) neckwear, (d) prerogative	_____
3. conscientious	= (a) meticulous, (b) productive, (c) cognizant, (d) sophisticated	_____
4. cosmopolitan	= (a) provincial, (b) multicolored, (c) heavenly, (d) worldly	_____
5. decipher	= (a) preclude, (b) decode, (c) demise, (d) reproach	_____
6. euphemism	= (a) religious discourse, (b) facial expression, (c) figurative speech, (d) inoffensive term	_____
7. fraudulent	= (a) loquacious, (b) candid, (c) deceitful, (d) despotic	_____

8. peripheral = (a) supplementary, (b) imaginary, (c) visionary, _____
   (d) supernatural

9. pungent = (a) knowledgeable, (b) wise religious man, (c) acrid, _____
   (d) vulnerable

10. requisite = (a) essential, (b) demand, (c) skillful, (d) discreet _____

List 12

1. ad valorem = (a) esteemed, (b) genuine, (c) recompense, (d) proportional _____

2. carte blanche = (a) white carriage, (b) credit terms, (c) full permission, _____
   (d) geographical expression

3. de facto = (a) prejudicial, (b) actual, (c) valid, (d) unlawful _____

4. esprit de corps = (a) group enthusiasm, (b) strong coffee, (c) central authority, _____
   (d) government overturn

5. modus operandi = (a) method of procedure, (b) practical compromise, _____
   (c) business transaction, (d) flexible arbitration

6. per capita = per unit of (a) income, (b) population, (c) birth, (d) household _____

7. per diem = (a) daily, (b) weekly, (c) yearly, (d) taxable _____

8. prima facie = (a) self-taught, (b) apparent, (c) principal, (d) artificial effect _____

9. status quo = (a) haughty demeanor, (b) steadfast opinion, (c) position of _____
   importance, (d) existing condition

10. tort = (a) rich cake, (b) extended dream, (c) wrongful act, (d) lawful _____
    remedy

List 13

1. acquit = (a) discharge, (b) pursue, (c) interfere, (d) impede _____

2. annuity = (a) yearly report, (b) insurance premium, (c) tuition refund, _____
   (d) annual payment

3. complacent = (a) appealing, (b) self-satisfied, (c) sympathetic, _____
   (d) scrupulous

4. contraband = (a) discrepancy, (b) opposing opinion, (c) smuggled goods, _____
   (d) ammunition

5. insolvent = (a) uncleanable, (b) unexplainable, (c) bankrupt, _____
   (d) unjustifiable

6. malicious = marked by (a) good humor, (b) ill will, (c) great pleasure, _____
   (d) injurious tumor

7. negligent = (a) careless, (b) fraudulent, (c) unlawful, (d) weak _____

8. nominal = (a) enumerated, (b) beneficial, (c) extravagant, _____
   (d) insignificant

9. rescind = (a) consign, (b) oppose, (c) repeal, (d) censure _____

10. stringent = (a) rigid, (b) expedient, (c) compliant, (d) resilient _____

List 14

1. affirm = (a) business organization, (b) validate, (c) elevate, (d) encircle _____

2. exonerate = (a) commend, (b) declare blameless, (c) banish, (d) emigrate _____

3. expedite = (a) elucidate, (b) get rid of, (c) amplify, (d) rush _____

4. hamper (v)   = (a) impede, (b) delineate, (c) release, (d) assuage   _____

5. implement (v)   = (a) suppress, (b) ameliorate, (c) carry out, (d) attribute   _____

6. induce   = (a) teach, (b) construe, (c) persuade, (d) copy   _____

7. obliterate   = (a) obstruct, (b) prevent, (c) minimize, (d) erase   _____

8. quandary   = a state of (a) doubt, (b) certainty, (c) depression,   _____
                     (d) apprehension

9. surmount   = (a) hike, (b) overcome, (c) interpret, (d) specify   _____

10. veracity   = (a) truthfulness, (b) swiftness, (c) efficiency, (d) persistence   _____

List 15

1. aggregate   = constituting (a) hostile crowd, (b) word combination, (c) total   _____
                     group, (d) sticky mass

2. ambiguous   = (a) peripatetic, (b) uncertain, (c) enterprising, (d) deceptive   _____

3. amend   = (a) alter, (b) pray, (c) praise, (d) utter   _____

4. apportion   = (a) sanction, (b) ratify, (c) estimate, (d) divide   _____

5. collaborate   = (a) scrutinize, (b) cooperate, (c) surrender, (d) accumulate   _____

6. ingenuity   = (a) innocence, (b) torpor, (c) cleverness, (d) self-composure   _____

7. irretrievable   = not capable of being (a) sold, (b) identified, (c) explained,   _____
                     (d) recovered

8. lenient   = (a) liberal, (b) crooked, (c) benevolent, (d) explicit   _____

9. retrench   = (a) dig repeatedly, (b) curtail, (c) reiterate, (d) enlighten   _____

10. trivial   = (a) composed of three parts, (b) momentous, (c) paltry,   _____
                     (d) economical

List 16

1. audit   = (a) examine, (b) speak, (c) exchange, (d) expunge   _____

2. arrears   = (a) old-fashioned, (b) gratuity, (c) overdue debt, (d) option   _____

3. curtail   = (a) obstruct, (b) restore, (c) rejuvenate, (d) shorten   _____

4. encumber   = (a) grow, (b) substantiate, (c) burden, (d) illustrate   _____

5. exemplify   = (a) segregate, (b) divulge, (c) illustrate, (d) condone   _____

6. extension   = (a) unusual request, (b) prolonged journey, (c) haphazard   _____
                     results, (d) extra time

7. fortuitous   = (a) accidental, (b) courageous, (c) radical, (d) assiduous   _____

8. innovation   = (a) reorganization, (b) occupancy, (c) introduction, (d) solution   _____

9. syndicate   = (a) union of writers, (b) council of lawmakers, (c) group of   _____
                     symptoms, (d) association of people

10. venture   = (a) speculative business transaction, (b) unsecured loan,   _____
                     (c) stock split, (d) gambling debt

List 17

1. acquiesce   = (a) gain possession of, (b) confront, (c) implore, (d) comply   _____

2. enumerate   = (a) articulate, (b) list, (c) enunciate, (d) see clearly   _____

3. erratic   = (a) pleasurable, (b) wandering, (c) exotic, (d) serene   _____

4. expedient = serving to promote (a) fellowship, (b) one's self-interests, (c) good of others, (d) speedy delivery _____

5. feasible = (a) auspicious, (b) profuse, (c) reasonable, (d) extraneous _____

6. literal = (a) exact, (b) devout, (c) apropos, (d) noticeable _____

7. lucrative = (a) providential, (b) swift, (c) pleasant, (d) profitable _____

8. negotiable = (a) essential, (b) adequate, (c) open to discussion, (d) economical _____

9. nonchalant = (a) dull, (b) cool, (c) unintelligent, (d) sagacious _____

10. reconcile = (a) resolve differences, (b) calculate, (c) modify, (d) remunerate _____

List 18

1. byte = (a) dental occlusion, (b) computer storage, (c) digits processed as a unit, (d) type font _____

2. disk = (a) magnetic storage medium, (b) print wheel, (c) computer belt, (d) program _____

3. execute = (a) eradicate, (b) inquire, (c) oppose, (d) carry out _____

4. memory = (a) printer logic, (b) computer storage, (c) automatic printout, (d) software _____

5. menu = list of (a) parts, (b) selections, (c) serial numbers, (d) vendors _____

6. microfiche = sheet of (a) computer printouts, (b) microimages, (c) reduced digits, (d) tiny cards _____

7. program = (a) alphabetical list, (b) computer log, (c) coded instructions, (d) microprocessor _____

8. prompt (n) = (a) reminder, (b) on time, (c) code, (d) format _____

9. retrieve = (a) acquiesce, (b) instruct, (c) remove code, (d) recover information _____

10. software = (a) equipment, (b) programs, (c) plastic component, (d) solid-state semiconductor _____

List 19

1. apprehensive = (a) knowledgeable, (b) fearful, (c) reticent, (d) autonomous _____

2. circumspect = (a) cautious, (b) uncertain, (c) cooperative, (d) frugal _____

3. collateral = (a) revenue, (b) secret agreement, (c) book value, (d) security for a loan _____

4. insinuation = (a) disagreeable proposal, (b) indirect suggestion, (c) elucidating glimpse, (d) flagrant insult _____

5. liaison = (a) legal obligation, (b) treaty, (c) connection between groups, (d) quarantine _____

6. procrastinate = (a) predict, (b) reproduce, (c) postpone, (d) advance _____

7. ratification = the act of (a) confirming, (b) reviewing, (c) evaluating, (d) inscribing _____

8. renovate = (a) renegotiate, (b) restore, (c) supply, (d) deliver _____

| 9. saturate | = to fill (a) slowly, (b) dangerously, (c) as expected, (d) to excess | _____ |
| 10. vendor | = (a) seller, (b) manufacturer, (c) tradesman, (d) coin collector | _____ |

List 20

1. abhorrent	= (a) disagreeable, (b) attractive, (c) valueless, (d) adducible	_____
2. appraisal	= (a) general information, (b) certification, (c) estimation, (d) approval	_____
3. collusion	= (a) secret agreement, (b) direct conflict, (c) partial exclusion, (d) original artwork	_____
4. commingle	= (a) socialize, (b) mix, (c) separate, (d) communicate	_____
5. dissolution	= (a) intemperance, (b) soluble, (c) unsolvable, (d) separation	_____
6. ensue	= (a) change subtly, (b) relinquish, (c) track down, (d) follow immediately	_____
7. rejuvenate	= to make (a) youthful, (b) slender, (c) sturdy, (d) impregnable	_____
8. stipulation	= (a) permission, (b) requirement, (c) rejection, (d) concurrence	_____
9. subsidy	= (a) scholarship, (b) financial assistance, (c) payment due, (d) unacknowledged payment	_____
10. tenuous	= (a) flimsy, (b) indecisive, (c) cautious, (d) firm	_____

Appendix C Reference Guide to Document Formats

Business documents carry two kinds of messages. Verbal messages are conveyed by the words chosen to express the writer's ideas. Nonverbal messages are conveyed largely by the appearance of a document. If you compare an assortment of letters and memos from various organizations, you will notice immediately that some look more attractive and more professional than others. The nonverbal message of professional-looking documents suggests that they were sent by people who are careful, informed, intelligent, and successful. Understandably, you're more likely to take seriously documents that use attractive stationery and professional formatting techniques.

Over the years certain practices and conventions have arisen regarding the appearance and formatting of business documents. Although these conventions offer some choices (such as letter and punctuation styles), most business letters follow standardized formats. To ensure that your documents carry favorable nonverbal messages about you and your organization, you'll want to give special attention to the appearance and formatting of your letters, envelopes, memos, and fax cover sheets.

Letter Parts

Professional-looking business letters are arranged in a conventional sequence with standard parts. Following is a discussion of how to use these letter parts properly. Figure C.1 illustrates the parts in a block-style letter.

Letterhead

Most business organizations use 8 1/2- by 11-inch paper printed with a letterhead displaying their official name, address, and telephone and fax numbers.

Dateline

On letterhead paper you should place the date two lines below the last line of the letterhead or 2 inches from the top edge of the paper (line 13). On plain paper place the date immediately below your return address. Since the date appears 2 inches from the top, start the return address an appropriate number of lines above it. The

island graphics
893 Dillingham Boulevard Honolulu, HI 96817-8817

Letterhead

↓ 2 inches or 1 blank line below letterhead

September 13, 200x

Dateline

↓ 1 to 9 blank lines

Mr. T. M. Wilson, President
Visual Concept Enterprises
1901 Kaumualii Highway
Lihue, HI 96766

Inside address

↓ 1 blank line

Dear Mr. Wilson

Salutation

↓ 1 blank line

SUBJECT: BLOCK LETTER STYLE

Subject line

↓ 1 blank line

This letter illustrates block letter style, about which you asked. All typed lines begin at the left margin. The date is usually placed two inches from the top edge of the paper or one blank line below the last line of the letterhead, whichever position is lower.

This letter also shows open punctuation. No colon follows the salutation, and no comma follows the complimentary close. Although this punctuation style is efficient, we find that most of our customers prefer to include punctuation after the salutation and the complimentary close.

Body

If a subject line is included, it appears two lines below the salutation. The word *SUBJECT* is optional. Most readers will recognize a statement in this position as the subject without an identifying label. The complimentary close appears one blank line below the end of the last paragraph.

↓ 1 blank line

Sincerely

Mark H. Wong

↓ 3 blank lines

Mark H. Wong
Graphics Designer

Complimentary
close and signature
block

↓ 1 blank line

MHW:pil

Block Style, Open Punctuation

Figure C.1
Letter and Punctuation Styles

Modified Block Style,
Mixed Punctuation

most common dateline format is as follows: *June 9, 2002.* Don't use *th* (or *rd*) when the date is written this way. For European or military correspondence, use the following dateline format: *9 June 2002.* Notice that no commas are used.

Addressee and Delivery Notations

Delivery notations such as *FAX TRANSMISSION, OVERNIGHT DELIVERY, CONFIDENTIAL,* or *CERTIFIED MAIL* are typed in all capital letters two line spaces above the inside address.

In block-style letters, as shown in Figure C.1, all lines begin at the left margin. In modified block-style letters, as shown at the right of Figure C.1, the date is centered or aligned with the complimentry close and signature block, which start at the center. The date may also be backspaced from the right margin. Paragraphs may be blocked or indented. Mixed punctuation includes a colon after the salutation and a comma after the complimentary close.

Inside Address

Type the inside address—that is, the address of the organization or person receiving the letter—single-spaced, starting at the left margin. The number of lines between the dateline and the inside address depends on the size of the letter body, the type size (point or pitch size), and the length of the typing lines. Generally, one to nine blank lines are appropriate.

Be careful to duplicate the exact wording and spelling of the recipient's name and address on your documents. Usually, you can copy this information from the letterhead of the correspondence you are answering. If, for example, you are responding to *Jackson & Perkins Company,* don't address your letter to *Jackson and Perkins Corp.*

Always be sure to include a courtesy title such as *Mr., Ms., Mrs., Dr.,* or *Professor* before a person's name in the inside address—for both the letter and the envelope.

Attention Line

An attention line allows you to send your message officially to an organization but to direct it to a specific individual, office, or department. However, if you know an individual's complete name, it's always better to use it as the first line of the inside address and avoid an attention line. Here are two common formats for attention lines:

MultiMedia Enterprises
931 Calkins Road
Rochester, NY 14301

ATTENTION MARKETING DIRECTOR

MultiMedia Enterprises
Attention: Marketing Director
931 Calkins Road
Rochester, NY 14301

Attention lines may be typed in all caps or with upper- and lowercase letters. The colon following *Attention* is optional. Notice that an attention line may be placed one blank line below the address block or printed as the second line of the inside address. You'll want to use the latter format if you're composing on a word processor because the address block may be copied to the envelope and the attention line will not interfere with the last-line placement of the zip code. (Mail can be sorted more easily if the zip code appears in the last line of a typed address.)

Whenever possible, use a person's name as the first line of an address instead of putting that name in an attention line. Some writers use an attention line because they fear that letters addressed to individuals at companies may be considered private. They worry that if the addressee is no longer with the company, the letter may be forwarded or not opened. Actually, unless a letter is marked "Personal" or "Confidential," it will very likely be opened as business mail.

Salutation

For most letter styles place the letter greeting, or salutation, one blank line below the last line of the inside address or the attention line (if used). If the letter is addressed to an individual, use that person's courtesy title and last name (*Dear Mr. Lanham*). Even if you are on a first-name basis (*Dear Leslie*), be sure to add a colon (not a comma or a semicolon) after the salutation. Do not use an individual's full name in the salutation (not *Dear Mr. Leslie Lanham*) unless you are unsure of gender (*Dear Leslie Lanham*).

For letters with attention lines or those addressed to organizations, the selection of an appropriate salutation has become more difficult. Formerly, *Gentlemen* was used generically for all organizations. With increasing numbers of women in business management today, however, *Gentlemen* is problematic. Because no universally acceptable salutation has emerged as yet, you'll probably be safest with *Ladies and Gentlemen* or *Gentlemen and Ladies*. Better yet, address your message to a specific person.

Subject and Reference Lines

Although experts suggest placing the subject line one blank line below the salutation, many businesses actually place it above the salutation. Use whatever style your organization prefers. Reference lines often show policy or file numbers; they generally appear one blank line above the salutation.

Body

Most business letters and memorandums are single-spaced, with double line spacing between paragraphs. Very short messages may be double-spaced with indented paragraphs.

Complimentary Close

Typed one blank line below the last line of the letter, the complimentary close may be formal (*Very truly yours*) or informal (*Sincerely yours* or *Cordially*). The simplified letter style omits a complimentary close.

Signature Block

In most letter styles the writer's typed name and optional identification appear two to three blank lines below the complimentary close. The combination of name, title, and organization information should be arranged to achieve a balanced look. The name and title may appear on the same line or on separate lines, depending on the length of each. Use commas to separate categories within the same line, but not to conclude a line. Women may choose to include *Ms., Mrs.,* or *Miss* before their names. Parentheses are optional. Men do not use *Mr.* before their names.

Sincerely yours,   Cordially yours,

Jeremy M. Wood, Manager   Casandra Baker-Murillo
Technical Sales and Services   Executive Vice President

Some organizations include their names in the signature block. In such cases the organization name appears in all caps one blank line below the complimentary close, as shown here:

Cordially,

LITTON COMPUTER SERVICES

Ms. Shelina A. Simpson
Executive Assistant

Reference Initials

If used, the initials of the typist and writer are typed one blank line below the writer's name and title. Generally, the writer's initials are capitalized and the typist's are lowercased, but this format varies.

Enclosure Notation

When an enclosure or attachment accompanies a document, a notation to that effect appears one blank line below the reference initials. This notation reminds the typist to insert the enclosure in the envelope, and it reminds the recipient to look for the enclosure or attachment. The notation may be spelled out (*Enclosure, Attachment*), or it may be abbreviated (*Enc., Att.*). It may indicate the number of enclosures or attachments, and it may also identify a specific enclosure (*Enclosure: Form 1099*).

Copy Notation

If you make copies of correspondence for other individuals, you may use *cc* to indicate courtesy copy or carbon copy, *pc* to indicate photocopy, or merely *c* for any kind of copy. A colon following the initial(s) is optional.

Second-Page Heading

When a letter extends beyond one page, use plain paper of the same quality and color as the first page. Identify the second and succeeding pages with a heading consisting of the name of the addressee, the page number, and the date. Use either of the following two formats:

Ms. Rachel Ruiz   2   May 3, 200x

Ms. Rachael Ruiz
Page 2
May 3, 200x

Both headings appear on line 7 (one inch from top edge) followed by two blank lines to separate them from the continuing text. Avoid using a second page if you have only one line or the complimentary close and signature block to fill that page.

Plain-Paper Return Address

If you prepare a personal or business letter on plain paper, place your address immediately above the date, as shown in Figure C.2. Do not include your name; you will type (and sign) your name at the end of your letter. If your return address contains two lines, begin typing it about 2 inches from the top edge of the paper. Avoid abbreviations except for a two-letter state abbreviation.

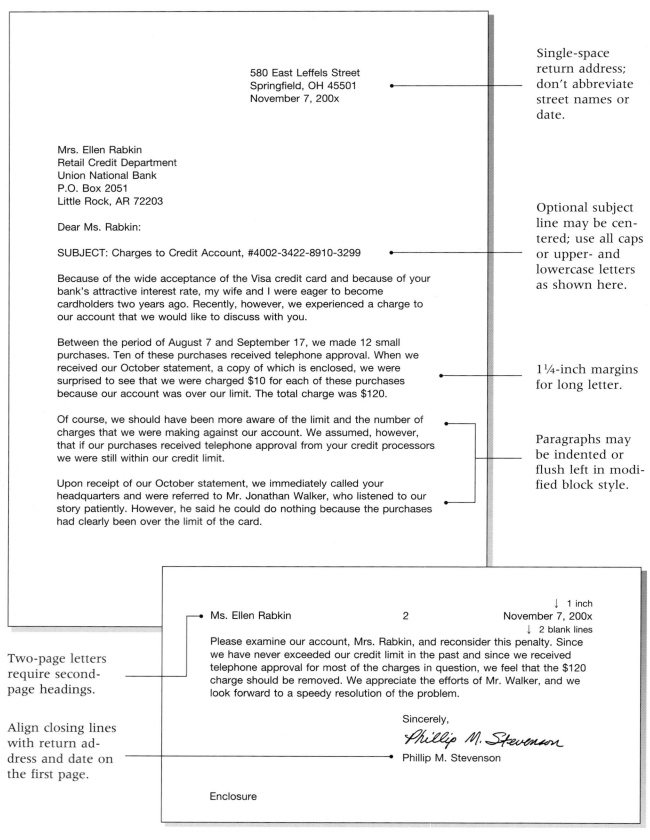

580 East Leffels Street
Springfield, OH 45501
November 7, 200x

Mrs. Ellen Rabkin
Retail Credit Department
Union National Bank
P.O. Box 2051
Little Rock, AR 72203

Dear Ms. Rabkin:

SUBJECT: Charges to Credit Account, #4002-3422-8910-3299

Because of the wide acceptance of the Visa credit card and because of your bank's attractive interest rate, my wife and I were eager to become cardholders two years ago. Recently, however, we experienced a charge to our account that we would like to discuss with you.

Between the period of August 7 and September 17, we made 12 small purchases. Ten of these purchases received telephone approval. When we received our October statement, a copy of which is enclosed, we were surprised to see that we were charged $10 for each of these purchases because our account was over our limit. The total charge was $120.

Of course, we should have been more aware of the limit and the number of charges that we were making against our account. We assumed, however, that if our purchases received telephone approval from your credit processors we were still within our credit limit.

Upon receipt of our October statement, we immediately called your headquarters and were referred to Mr. Jonathan Walker, who listened to our story patiently. However, he said he could do nothing because the purchases had clearly been over the limit of the card.

↓ 1 inch
Ms. Ellen Rabkin   2   November 7, 200x
                                                        ↓ 2 blank lines
Please examine our account, Mrs. Rabkin, and reconsider this penalty. Since we have never exceeded our credit limit in the past and since we received telephone approval for most of the charges in question, we feel that the $120 charge should be removed. We appreciate the efforts of Mr. Walker, and we look forward to a speedy resolution of the problem.

Sincerely,

Phillip M. Stevenson

Phillip M. Stevenson

Enclosure

Single-space return address; don't abbreviate street names or date.

Optional subject line may be centered; use all caps or upper- and lowercase letters as shown here.

1¼-inch margins for long letter.

Paragraphs may be indented or flush left in modified block style.

Two-page letters require second-page headings.

Align closing lines with return address and date on the first page.

Figure C.2
Letter on Plain Paper, Modified Block Style

For letters prepared in the block style, type the return address at the left margin. For modified block-style letters, start the return address at the center to align with the complimentary close.

Letter Styles

Business letters are generally prepared in one of three formats. The most popular is the block style, but the simplified style has much to recommend it.

Block Style

In the block style, shown in Figure C.1, all lines begin at the left margin. This style is a favorite because it is easy to format.

Modified Block Style

The modified block style differs from block style in that the date and closing lines appear in the center, as shown at the bottom of Figure C.1. The date may be (1) centered, (2) begun at the center of the page (to align with the closing lines), or (3) backspaced from the right margin. The signature block—including the complimentary close, writer's name and title, or organization identification—begins at the center. The first line of each paragraph may begin at the left margin or may be indented five or ten spaces. All other lines begin at the left margin.

Simplified Style

Introduced by the Administrative Management Society a number of years ago, the simplified letter style, shown in Figure C.3, requires little formatting. Like the block style, all lines begin at the left margin. A subject line appears in all caps two blank lines below the inside address and two blank lines above the first paragraph. The salutation and complimentary close are omitted. The signer's name and identification appear in all caps four blank lines below the last paragraph. This letter style is efficient and avoids the problem of appropriate salutations and courtesy titles.

Letter Placement

Business letters should be typed so that they are framed by white space. The most attractive placement results with side margins of 1 1/4 to 1 1/2 inches. However, some organizations prefer business writers to use standard margins of 1 inch (the defaults of many word processing programs). To balance a letter on the page, you can adjust the number of lines between the dateline and the address block (one to nine blank lines depending on the letter length).

Punctuation Styles

Two punctuation styles are commonly used for letters. *Open* punctuation, shown with the block-style letter in Figure C.1, contains no punctuation after the salutation or complimentary close. *Mixed* punctuation, shown with the modified block style letter in Figure C.1, requires a colon after the salutation and a comma after the complimentary close. Many business organizations prefer mixed punctuation, even in a block-style letter. If you choose mixed punctuation, be sure to use a colon—not a comma or semicolon—after the salutation. Even when the salutation is a first name, the colon is appropriate.

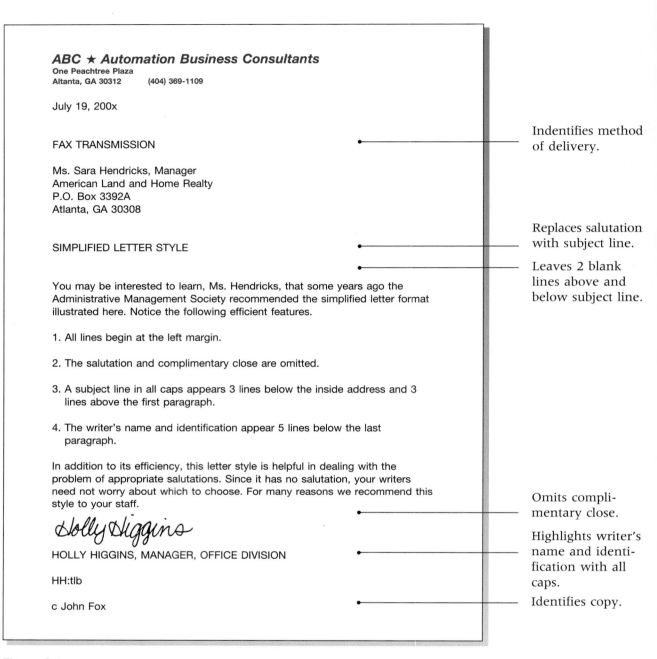

ABC ★ Automation Business Consultants
One Peachtree Plaza
Altanta, GA 30312   (404) 369-1109

July 19, 200x

FAX TRANSMISSION

Ms. Sara Hendricks, Manager
American Land and Home Realty
P.O. Box 3392A
Atlanta, GA 30308

SIMPLIFIED LETTER STYLE

You may be interested to learn, Ms. Hendricks, that some years ago the
Administrative Management Society recommended the simplified letter format
illustrated here. Notice the following efficient features.

1. All lines begin at the left margin.

2. The salutation and complimentary close are omitted.

3. A subject line in all caps appears 3 lines below the inside address and 3
   lines above the first paragraph.

4. The writer's name and identification appear 5 lines below the last
   paragraph.

In addition to its efficiency, this letter style is helpful in dealing with the
problem of appropriate salutations. Since it has no salutation, your writers
need not worry about which to choose. For many reasons we recommend this
style to your staff.

Holly Higgins

HOLLY HIGGINS, MANAGER, OFFICE DIVISION

HH:tlb

c John Fox

Callout annotations (right margin):
- Indentifies method of delivery.
- Replaces salutation with subject line.
- Leaves 2 blank lines above and below subject line.
- Omits complimentary close.
- Highlights writer's name and identification with all caps.
- Identifies copy.

Figure C.3
Simplified Letter Style

Envelopes

An envelope should be printed on the same quality and color of stationery as the letter it carries. Because the envelope introduces your message and makes the first impression, you need to be especially careful in addressing it. Moreover, how you fold the letter is important.

Return Address

The return address is usually printed in the upper left corner of an envelope, as shown in Figure C.4. In large companies some form of identification (the writer's initials, name, or location) may be typed above the company name and return address. This identification helps return the letter to the sender in case of nondelivery. On an envelope without a printed return address, single-space the return address in the upper left corner. Beginning 1/4 inch from the top and 1/2 inch from the left edge, type the writer's name, title, company, and mailing address.

Mailing Address

On legal-sized No. 10 envelopes (4 1/8 by 9 1/2 inches), begin the address 2 inches from the top and about 4 1/4 inches from the left edge, as shown in Figure C.4. For small envelopes (3 5/8 by 6 1/2 inches), begin typing about 2 1/2 inches from the left edge.

The U.S. Postal Service recommends that addresses be typed in all caps without any punctuation. This Postal Service style, shown in the small envelope in Figure C.4, was originally developed to facilitate scanning by optical character readers. Today's OCRs, however, are so sophisticated that they scan upper- and lowercase letters easily. Many companies today do not follow the Postal Service format because they prefer to use the same format for the envelope as for the inside address. If the same format is used, writers can take advantage of word processing programs to "copy" the inside address to the envelope, thus saving keystrokes and reducing

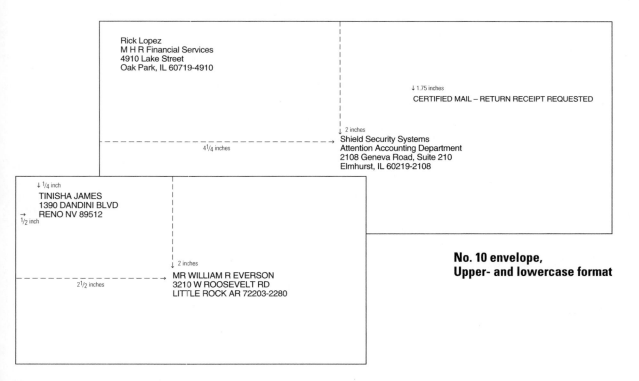

**No. 10 envelope,
Upper- and lowercase format**

No. 6¾ envelope, Postal Service uppercase format

Figure C.4
Envelope Formats

errors. Having the same format on both the inside address and the envelope also looks more professional and consistent. For these reasons you may choose to use the familiar upper- and lowercase combination format. But you will want to check with your organization to learn its preference.

Folding

The way a letter is folded and inserted into an envelope sends additional nonverbal messages about a writer's professionalism and carefulness. Most businesspeople follow the procedures shown here, which produce the least number of creases to distract readers.

For large No. 10 envelopes, begin with the letter face up. Fold slightly less than one third of the sheet toward the top, as shown below. Then fold down the top third to within 1/3 inch of the bottom fold. Insert the letter into the envelope with the last fold toward the bottom of the envelope.

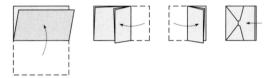

For small No. 6 3/4 envelopes, begin by folding the bottom up to within 1/3 inch of the top edge. Then fold the right third over to the left. Fold the left third to within 1/3 inch of the last fold. Insert the last fold into the envelope first.

Memorandums

Some offices use memo forms imprinted with the organization name and, optionally, the department or division names, as shown in Figure C.5. Although the design and arrangement of memo forms vary, they usually include the basic elements of *TO, FROM, DATE,* and *SUBJECT*. Large organizations may include other identifying headings, such as *FILE NUMBER, FLOOR, EXTENSION, LOCATION,* and *DISTRIBUTION*.

Because of the difficulty of aligning computer printers with preprinted forms, many business writers use a standardized memo template (sometimes called a "wizard"). This template automatically provides attractive headings with appropriate spacing and formatting. Other writers store their own preferred memo formats. Either method eliminates alignment problems.

If no printed or stored computer forms are available, memos may be typed on company letterhead or on plain paper, as shown in Figure C.6. On a full sheet of paper, start on line 13; on a half sheet, start on line 7. Double-space and type in all caps the guide words: *TO:, FROM:, DATE:, SUBJECT:*. Align all the fill-in information two spaces after the longest guide word (*SUBJECT:*). Leave three lines after

```
┌────────────────────────────────────────────────────────────────────┐
│                                                                      │
│  FIRST FEDERAL BANK                          Interoffice             │
│  Mortgage Department                         Memorandum              │
│                                                                      │
│     TO:                                                              │
│                                                                      │
│     FROM:                                                            │
│                                                                      │
│     DATE:                                                            │
│                                                                      │
│     SUBJECT:                                                         │
│                                                                      │
└────────────────────────────────────────────────────────────────────┘
```

```
┌────────────────────────────────────────────────────────────────────┐
│                          PYRAMID, INC.                               │
│                          Internal Memo                               │
│                                                                      │
│                                                                      │
│           TO:                        DATE:                           │
│                                                                      │
│          FROM:                       FILE:                           │
│                                                                      │
│        SUBJECT:                                                      │
│                                                                      │
│                                                                      │
└────────────────────────────────────────────────────────────────────┘
```

Figure C.5
Printed Memo Forms

```
┌────────────────────────────────────────────────────────────────────┐
│                                                                      │
│                            ↓ 2 inches                                │
│                              MEMO                                     │
│                                                                      │
│     TO:          Dawn Stewart, Manager  Ꮽᙢ   DATE: February 3, 200x  │
│                  Sales and Marketing                                 │
│                                                                      │
│     FROM:        Jay Murray, Vice President                          │
│                  Operations                                          │
│                                                                      │
│     SUBJECT:     TELEPHONE SERVICE REQUEST FORMS                     │
│                         ↓ 2 blank lines                              │
│                                                                      │
│  To speed telephone installation and improve service within the Bremerton │
│  facility, we are starting a new application procedure.              │
│                                                                      │
│  Service request forms will be available at various locations within the three │
│  buildings. When you require telephone service, obtain a request form at one of │
│  the locations that is convenient for you. Fill in the pertinent facts, obtain │
│  approval from your division head, and send the form to Brent White. Request │
│  forms are available at the following locations:                     │
│                                                                      │
```

Figure C.6
Memo on Plain Paper

the last line of the heading and begin typing the body of the memo. Like business letters, memos are single-spaced.

Memos are generally formatted with side margins of 1 1/4 inches, or they may conform to the printed memo form.

E-Mail Messages

Because e-mail is a developing communication medium, formatting and usage are still fluid. The following suggestions, illustrated in Figure C.7, may guide you in setting up the parts of an e-mail message, but always check with your organization to observe its practices.

To Line

Include the receiver's e-mail address after *To*. Some writers personalize the line somewhat by naming the receiver first, followed by that person's e-mail address in angle brackets, such as *Marilyn Lammers <mlammers@accountpro.com>*.

From Line

Most systems automatically include your name and e-mail address after *From*.

Cc

Insert the e-mail address of anyone who is to receive a copy of the message. *Cc* stands for *carbon copy* or *courtesy copy*. Don't be tempted, though, to send needless copies just because it's so easy.

Figure C.7
Typical E-Mail Message

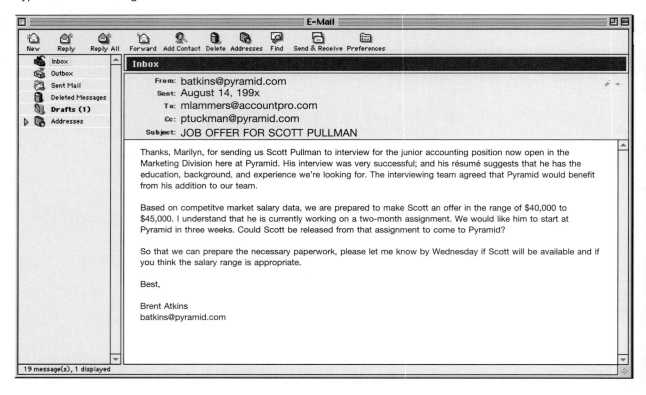

Bcc

Include here the e-mail address of anyone who is to receive a copy of the message without the receiver's knowledge. *Bcc* stands for *blind carbon copy*. Writers are also using the *bcc* line for mailing lists. When a message is being sent to a number of people and their e-mail addresses should not be revealed, the *bcc* line works well to conceal the names and addresses of all receivers.

Subject

Identify the subject of the memo briefly. Be sure to include enough information to be clear and compelling.

Fax Cover Sheet

Documents transmitted by fax are usually introduced by a cover sheet, such as that shown in Figure C.8. As with memos, the format varies considerably. Important items to include are (1) the name and fax number of the receiver, (2) the name and fax number of the sender, (3) the number of pages being sent, and (4) the name and telephone number of the person to notify in case of unsatisfactory transmission.

When the document being transmitted requires little explanation, you may prefer to attach an adhesive note (such as a Post-it™ fax transmittal form) instead of a full cover sheet. These notes carry essentially the same information as shown in our printed fax cover sheet. They are perfectly acceptable in most business organizations and can save considerable paper and transmission costs.

Figure C.8
Fax Cover Sheet

```
                          FAX TRANSMISSION

        DATE: _____     FAX
        TO:   _____     NUMBER:_____
              _____
              _____
                                          FAX
        FROM: _____     NUMBER:_____

        NUMBER OF PAGES TRANSMITTED INCLUDING THIS COVER SHEET:____

        MESSAGE:



```

```
        If any part of this fax transmission is missing or not clearly received, please call:

        NAME: _____

        PHONE:_____

```

Self-Help Exercises

Name _____

Nearly every student who takes business English says, "I wish I had more exercises to try my skills on." Because of the many requests, we provide this set of self-help exercises for extra reinforcement. Immediate feedback is an important ingredient in successful learning. Therefore, a key to these exercises begins on p. 502. Don't check the key, of course, until you complete each exercise.

Use a current dictionary to complete the following exercise.

1. *Amanuensis* originally meant   _____
   (a) deterioration of sight   (b) coarse herbs including pigweeds
   (c) a slave with secretarial duties   (d) a female warrior

2. An *autocrat* is one who enjoys   _____
   (a) owning many cars   (b) ruling by himself or herself
   (c) democratic relationships   (d) racing automobiles

3. The words *in so much as* should be written   _____
   (a) in so much as   (b) in somuchas
   (c) insomuch as   (d) in somuch as

4. The word *logistics* is   _____
   (a) plural but may be used with a   (b) plural and always requires a
       singular verb   plural verb
   (c) singular   (d) neither singular nor plural

5. The abbreviation *Mme.* stands for   _____
   (a) madame   (b) mademoiselle
   (c) master in mechanical engineering (d) monsieur

6. In grammar the word *neuter* means   _____
   (a) asexual   (b) neutral
   (c) neither feminine nor masculine   (d) both feminine and masculine

7. The word *(non)productive* should be written   _____
   (a) non-productive   (b) nonproductive
   (c) non productive   (d) non-Productive

8. When the word *notwithstanding* is used to mean "nevertheless," it functions as what   _____
   part of speech?
   (a) conjunction   (b) adverb
   (c) preposition   (d) adjective

9. The plural of the word *proxy* is   _____
   (a) proxies'   (b) proxys
   (c) proxy's   (d) proxies

10. In Sri Lanka a *rupee* is a monetary unit equal to   _____
    (a) 10 cents   (b) 100 cents
    (c) 50 cents   (d) $2

11. *Foggy Bottom* is the site of   _____
    (a) a cathedral in London   (b) the State Department
    (c) a famous Irish castle   (d) a San Francisco night club

Name _____

Worksheet 1

A. This exercise is designed to help you develop a better understanding of the parts of speech. Using Chapter 2, write a brief definition or description of the eight parts of speech listed here. Then list three words as examples of each part of speech.

	Brief Definition	**Three Examples**
1. noun	names person, place, thing, concept	Anthony paper truth
2. pronoun	_____	
3. verb	_____	
4. adjective	_____	
5. adverb	_____	
6. preposition	_____	
7. conjunction	_____	
8. interjection	_____	

B. Fill in the parts of speech for all the words in these sentences. Use a dictionary if necessary.

I immediately called Greg, and he waited for the manager with me.

1. I _____ **5.** and _____ **9.** the _____

2. immediately _____ **6.** he _____ **10.** manager _____

3. called _____ **7.** waited _____ **11.** with _____

4. Greg _____ **8.** for _____ **12.** me _____

Gosh, the computer and printer processed this lengthy report in twenty seconds.

13. Gosh _____ **17.** printer _____ **21.** report _____

14. the _____ **18.** processed _____ **22.** in _____

15. computer _____ **19.** this _____ **23.** twenty _____

16. and _____ **20.** lengthy _____ **24.** seconds _____

We arrived promptly, but the committee meeting started late.

25. We _____ **28.** but _____ **31.** meeting _____

26. arrived _____ **29.** the _____ **32.** started _____

27. promptly _____ **30.** committee _____ **33.** late _____

Worksheet 2

Fill in the parts of speech for all the words in these sentences. Use a dictionary if necessary.

I sold property in Fresno, but one transaction may not clear escrow.

1. I _____
2. sold _____
3. property _____
4. in _____

5. Fresno _____
6. but _____
7. one _____
8. transaction _____

9. may _____
10. not _____
11. clear _____
12. escrow _____

Oh, did Lee really think he could change that method of operation?

13. Oh _____
14. did _____
15. Lee _____
16. really _____

17. think _____
18. he _____
19. could _____
20. change _____

21. that _____
22. method _____
23. of _____
24. operation _____

The old accounting system was neither accurate nor efficient, but one company had used it faithfully for the past forty years.

25. The _____
26. old _____
27. accounting _____
28. system _____
29. was _____
30. neither _____
31. accurate _____

32. nor _____
33. efficient _____
34. but _____
35. one _____
36. company _____
37. had _____
38. used _____

39. it _____
40. faithfully _____
41. for _____
42. the _____
43. past _____
44. forty _____
45. years _____

Kerry quietly slipped into an empty seat during the long class film.

46. Kerry _____
47. quietly _____
48. slipped _____
49. into _____

50. an _____
51. empty _____
52. seat _____
53. during _____

54. the _____
55. long _____
56. class _____
57. film _____

Name _____

Worksheet 1

Locating Subjects and Verbs

Action verbs tell what the subject is doing or what is being done to the subject. For each of the following sentences, locate the action verb and underline it twice. Then locate the subject of the verb and underline it once.

To locate the subject, use the verb preceded by *who?* or *what?* In the example the verb is *answered*. To help you find the subject, ask, *who answered?*

Example: A group of applicants answered the advertisement.

1. One of our top salespeople sold $2 million worth of life insurance.

2. The speaker in the afternoon session made a dynamic presentation.

3. Our telephones rang constantly during the sales campaign.

4. In the winter we will hire four new workers for this department.

5. Our management team built a strong program of sales and service.

6. The most successful salespeople received trips to Hawaii.

7. In the meantime, our personnel manager will send you an application form.

8. Last week we released our new line of office supplies.

9. One of the vice presidents was given a promotion recently.

10. Today's computers require managers to think with new clarity and precision.

Linking verbs (such as *am, is, are, was, were, be, being,* and *been*) often join to the sentence words that describe or rename the subject. In the following sentences, underline the linking verbs twice and the subjects once.

Examples: E. J. Todd was president of the organization last year.
In the morning the air is cool.

11. Mr. Thomas is the office manager for Ryerson Metals Corporation.

12. The new copiers are very dependable.

13. Mrs. Seymour is the person for the job.

14. Mr. Torres has been office manager for nine years.

15. Our new offices are much brighter than our previous ones.

Worksheet 2

Sentence Patterns

Finish the sentences below in the patterns indicated.

Subject–Verb

Example: Birds <u>sing.</u>

1. The audience _____.

2. Rain _____.

3. Car horns _____.

4. The burglar alarm _____.

5. In 1945 World War II _____.

6. Last year's sales _____.

Subject–Action Verb–Object

Example: The sales director made <u>a call.</u>

7. Our salesperson sold a _____.

8. The secretary typed a _____.

9. Ricky mailed the _____.

10. I telephoned _____.

11. Someone locked _____.

12. The clerk filed all the _____.

Subject–Linking Verb–Complement

Examples: She is very <u>friendly.</u>
Bill could have been the <u>manager.</u>

13. Sales have been _____.

14. Susan is the new _____.

15. Last year the owner was _____.

16. I am _____.

17. The writer could have been _____.

18. The caller was _____.

Compose original sentences in the following patterns.

19. (Subject–verb) _____

20. (Subject–verb) _____

21. (Subject–action verb–object) _____

22. (Subject–action verb–object) _____

23. (Subject–linking verb–complement) _____

Worksheet 3

Sentence Types

From the list below select the letter that accurately describes each of the following groups of words. If the groups of words need end punctuation marks, add them.

a = fragment   d = question
b = statement   e = exclamation
c = command

1. The management of a multinational corporation with branch offices in several cities _____

2. Send me a brochure describing your latest workout equipment _____

3. Will you be working next weekend or during the week _____

4. The work schedule is usually posted late in the week _____

5. Wow, he ran 98 yards for a touchdown _____

6. If you have an opportunity to be promoted to a managerial position _____

7. For a generous return on your funds, invest in second trust deeds _____

8. In all levels of business, written and spoken English is extremely important in achieving success _____

9. Because it is difficult to improve your language skills on your own _____

Sentence Faults

From the list below select the letter that accurately describes each of the following groups of words.

a = correctly punctuated sentence   c = comma splice
b = fragment   d = run-on sentence

10. I'll have the answer soon, first I must make a telephone call. _____

11. If you consider all the pros and cons before you make a decision. _____

12. We have no idea what to order only Mrs. Sanchez can do that. _____

13. Your entire department is entitled to overtime compensation. _____

14. You check the current address list, and I'll check the old one. _____

15. You check the current address list, I'll check the old one. _____

16. You check the current address list I'll check the old one. _____

17. Although we have complete confidence in our products and prices. _____

18. When you return from the conference, please submit a brief report describing the information you learned. _____

19. We must focus our charitable contributions on areas that directly relate to our business, therefore we are unable to send a check this year. _____

20. If you agree that this memo accurately reflects our conversation. _____

Name _____

L e v e l   I

Write the preferred plural forms of the nouns shown below. Use a dictionary if necessary.

1. giraffe _____
2. foot _____
3. switch _____
4. Bush _____
5. box _____
6. language _____
7. fax _____
8. sandwich _____
9. income tax _____
10. child _____
11. success _____
12. value _____
13. dress _____
14. branch _____
15. recommendation _____
16. woman _____
17. mismatch _____
18. taxi _____
19. loaf (of bread) _____
20. annex _____
21. belief _____
22. Ross _____
23. storm _____
24. ranch _____
25. Jones _____
26. Chavez _____
27. letter _____
28. business _____
29. computer _____
30. wish _____

Write the preferred plural forms of the nouns shown below. Use a dictionary if necessary.

1. wharf _____

2. chief of police _____

3. 1990 _____

4. Wolf _____

5. embargo _____

6. L.V.N. _____

7. size 10 _____

8. amt. _____

9. faculty _____

10. by-product _____

11. entry _____

12. looker-on _____

13. company _____

14. knife _____

15. court-martial _____

16. A _____

17. Sherman _____

18. memo _____

19. valley _____

20. zero _____

21. life _____

22. yr. _____

23. Murphy _____

24. runner-up _____

25. oz. _____

26. journey _____

27. M.B.A. _____

28. wolf _____

29. Kelly _____

30. minority _____

Write the preferred plural forms of the nouns shown below. Use a dictionary if necessary.

1. datum _____

2. thesis _____

3. bacterium _____

4. Chinese _____

5. parenthesis _____

6. Miss Bundy (informal) _____

7. alumna _____

8. Mr. West and Mr. Turner (formal) _____

9. genus _____

10. news _____

11. p. (page) _____

12. f. (and following pages) _____

13. larva _____

14. Mrs. Smythe and Mrs. Webb (formal) _____

15. memorandum _____

Select the correct word in parentheses and complete the sentences in your own words.

16. The goods produced in that factory (is, are) _____

_____

17. Politics in Washington (is, are) _____

_____

18. Several (formula, formulas) _____

_____

19. Four separate (analysis, analyses) _____

_____

20. In the business curriculum Economics I (is, are) _____

_____

Name _____

Level I

Worksheet 1

Before you begin this exercise, review the five-step plan for placing apostrophes:

1. Look for possessive construction. (Usually two nouns appear together.)

2. Reverse the nouns. (Use a prepositional phrase, such as *interest of three years*.)

3. Examine ownership word. (Does it end in an *s* sound?)

4. If ownership word does *not* end in an *s* sound, add an apostrophe and *s*.

5. If ownership word does end in an *s* sound, usually add just an apostrophe.

Using apostrophes, change the following prepositional phrases into possessive constructions.

Example: interest of three years   **three years' interest**

1. books of all students — *students' books*
2. office of this company — *company's office*
3. toys of the children — *children's toys*
4. rent of two months — *two months' rent*
5. mansion of the movie star — *movie star's mansion*
6. feelings of all the neighbors — *neighbors' feelings*
7. the landing of the pilot — *pilot's landing*
8. agreement of both partners — *both partners' agreement*
9. notebook of Jeffrey — *Jeffrey's notebook*
10. strengths of the department — *department's strengths*
11. time of two years — *two years' time*
12. customs of those people — *people's customs*
13. merger of last week — *last week's merger*
14. credit from the bank — *bank's credit*
15. savings of citizens — *citizens' savings*
16. mountains of Canada — *Canada's mountains*
17. requirements of the employer — *employer's requirements*
18. résumés of all candidates — *candidates' résumés*
19. policies of the government — *government's policies*
20. fees of both attorneys — *both attorneys' fees*

Worksheet 2

Write the correct possessive form of the word in parentheses in the space provided.

1. Applicants will have at least a (year) wait for an apartment. — *year's*

2. Several (drivers) inquiries prompted the posting of a better sign. — *drivers'*

3. We found the (carpenter) tools after he left the building. — *carpenter's*

4. The electronics store installed a hidden video camera to observe a suspected (thief) activities. — *thief's*

5. The (day) news is summarized every hour on WABC. — *day's*

6. Our new (employees) cafeteria is busy from 11 a.m. to 1 p.m. — *employees'*

7. Only the (CEO) car may be parked in the special zone. — *CEO's*

8. Most (readers) letters supported the magazine's editorial position. — *readers'*

9. Where is the (caller) message? — *caller's*

10. All (authors) rights are protected by copyright law. — *authors'*

Correct any errors in the following sentences by underlining the errors and writing the correct forms in spaces provided. If a sentence is correct as written, write C.

11. Many of the <u>secretaries'</u> desks had dictionaries and reference manuals on them. — *secretaries'*

X 12. The names of these <u>customers'</u> are not alphabetized. Correct — *customers'*

13. Some of the <u>country's</u> biggest manufacturers are being investigated. — *country's*

14. This account has been credited with four <u>months'</u> interest. — *months'*

15. Certainly your <u>organization's</u> voice mail system is excellent. — *organization's*

16. The vice <u>president's</u> resignation left a vital position unfilled. — *president's*

17. Are you researching your <u>family's</u> genealogy? — *family's*

18. I am prepared to protest the bill of my attorney, William Glass. — *C*

19. In three <u>years'</u> time the software paid for itself. — *years'*

20. Not a single <u>farmer's</u> crop was undamaged by the storm. — *farmer's*

21. A <u>citizens'</u> committee was formed to address parking problems. — *citizens'*

22. One <u>year's</u> interest on the account amounted to $120. — *year's*

23. Each <u>customer's</u> complimentary game tickets were mailed today. — *customer's*

24. <u>Children's</u> clothing is on the first floor. — *children's*

25. The announcement of new benefits for employees was made in the <u>supervisor's</u> memo. — *supervisor's*

L e v e l   I I

Correct any errors in the following sentences by underlining the errors and writing the correct form in the spaces provided. If the sentence is correct as written, write C.

1. The document required the notary <u>public's</u> signature and his seal. — *public's*

2. At least one <u>companies'</u> records are computerized. — *company's*

3. After school Juan stopped at the stationers for supplies.

4. My <u>uncle's lawyer's suggestions</u> in this matter were excellent.

5. The <u>desk's top</u> had to be refinished by a skilled woodworker.

6. We borrowed my aunt's and uncle's motor home.

7. All R.N.s' uniforms must now be identical.

8. This month's expenses are somewhat less than last months.

9. Debbie's and Julie's stereo sets had excellent fidelity.

10. The <u>president's secretary's telephone number</u> has been changed.

11. Have you called the new sales' representative?

12. My two brothers-in-law's beards are neat and well trimmed.

13. Three birds nests fell to the ground during the windstorm.

14. I'm going over to Ricks to pick him up.

15. We spent our vacation enjoying New Englands' historical towns.

16. CBS's report on the vote was better than any other station's.

17. Clark's and Clark's reference manual is outstanding.

18. The Los Angeles' symphony planned an evening of Beethoven.

19. The two architects licenses were issued together.

20. Our sales this year are greater than last years.

21. All FBI agents must pass rigorous security investigations.

22. Diana's and Jason's marriage license was lost.

23. The first lady answered all the reporters questions carefully.

24. Workers said they expected a days pay for an honest days work.

25. Robin and John's new car came with a five-year warranty.

Handwritten answers in right margin: & Stationer's; Suggestions of my uncle's lawyer; desktop's; aunt and uncle's; C; month; C; C (item 21)

L e v e l   I I I

Write the correct form of the words shown in parentheses.

Example: The (Stivers) cat is missing. ...... Stiverses'

1. I see that (someone else) books got wet also.

2. Lee (Ross) office is on the south side of the campus.

3. Both (class) test results were misplaced.

4. Beth (Saunders) home is farther away than anyone else's.

5. The bank is reconsidering the (Rodriguez) loan application.

6. I have no idea where (Les) car is parked.

7. Only my (boss) desk is cluttered.

8. The other (boss) desks are rather neat.

9. Did you hear that the (Horowitz) are moving?

10. Several (actress) costumes were so valuable that insurance policies were taken out to insure them.   _____

11. I think that was Mr. (Harris) parking spot you just took.   _____

12. Mrs. (Burns) history class met outside on that balmy day.   _____

13. Who is (James) partner for the laboratory experiment?   _____

14. That (waitress) station consists of four tables.   _____

15. None of the (Garvey) belongings were missing.   _____

16. Have you visited the (Morris) vacation home?   _____

17. Only Mrs. (Betz) car remained in the parking lot.   _____

18. It looks as if the (Walker) home is getting a new roof.   _____

19. Mr. (Simons) new Internet connection provided instant access.   _____

20. Mr. (Jones) property is on Kelton Avenue.   _____

21. Professor (White) lecture was well organized and informative.   _____

22. Have you seen the (Williams) four-room tent that they took camping last weekend?   _____

23. We heard that the (Kimball) may be moving.   _____

Name _____

Level I

Worksheet 1

List seven pronouns that could be used as subjects of verbs.

1. _____ 3. _____ 5. _____ 7. _____

2. _____ 4. _____ 6. _____

List seven pronouns that could be used as objects of verbs or objects of prepositions.

8. _____ 10. _____ 12. _____ 14. _____

9. _____ 11. _____ 13. _____

Pronouns as Subjects

Select the correct pronoun to complete each sentence below. All the omitted pronouns function as subjects of verbs.

15. Mrs. Georges and (I, me) submitted purchase requisitions.   _____

16. We thought that the manager and (she, her) would attend.   _____

17. Will you and (he, him) be going to the sales meeting?   _____

18. Mr. North and (they, them) expect to see you Saturday.   _____

19. It is difficult to explain why Bob and (her, she) decided to move.   _____

20. Of all the applicants only (we, us) agreed to be tested now.   _____

21. We believe that Ramon and (she, her) deserve raises.   _____

22. After Ms. Cortez and (he, him) had returned, customers were handled more rapidly.   _____

23. Only you and (her, she) will participate in the demonstration.   _____

24. Did you hear that the sales manager and (he, him) will be promoted?   _____

25. Professor Smith suggested that you and (I, me) work together on a report.   _____

Worksheet 2

Personal Pronouns as Objects

Select the correct pronoun to complete each sentence below. All the omitted pronouns function as objects of verbs or prepositions. Prepositions have been underlined to help you identify them.

1. Just between you and (I, me), our branch won the sales trophy.   _____

2. Michelle said that she had seen you and (he, him) at the airport.   _____

3. We hope to show (they, them) the billing procedure this afternoon.   _____

4. Everybody <u>but</u> (I, me) is ready to leave. _____

5. Have you talked <u>with</u> Brad and (her, she) about this change? _____

6. We need more workers <u>like</u> Maria and (him, he) to finish the job. _____

7. All supervisors <u>except</u> Mrs. Young and (her, she) approved the plan. _____

8. This insurance program provides you and (they, them) with equal benefits. _____

9. Terms of the settlement were satisfactory <u>to</u> (we, us). _____

10. Every operator <u>but</u> Molly and (I, me) had an opportunity for overtime. _____

Possessive Case Pronouns

Remember that possessive case pronouns (*yours, his, hers, its, whose,* and *theirs*) do not contain apostrophes. Do not confuse these pronouns with the following contractions: *it's* (it is), *there's* (there is), *who's* (who is), and *you're* (you are). In the following sentences, select the correct word.

11. Do you think (its, it's) necessary for us to sign in? _____

12. Is (theirs, their's) the white house at the end of the street? _____

13. The contract and all (its, it's) provisions must be examined. _____

14. (There's, Theirs) a set of guidelines for us to follow. _____

15. Jack's car and (hers, her's) are the only ones left in the lot. _____

16. The check is good only if (its, it's) signed. _____

17. I was told that Sue's and (yours, your's) were the best departments. _____

18. (Who's, Whose) umbrella is that lying in the corner? _____

19. Most car registrations were sent April 1, but (our's, ours) was delayed. _____

20. (You're, Your) taking Courtney's place, aren't you? _____

Level II

Select the correct pronoun to complete these sentences.

1. Do you expect Mr. Jefferson and (they, them) to meet you? _____

2. No one could regret the error more than (I, me, myself). _____

3. These photocopies were prepared by Charles and (she, her). _____

4. (We, Us) policyholders are entitled to group discounts. _____

5. Procrastination disturbs Steven as much as (I, me, myself). _____

6. For the summer only, Universal Parcel is hiring James and (I, me, myself). _____

7. Have you corresponded with the authors, Dr. Lee and (she, her)? _____

8. On that project no one works as hard as (he, him, himself). _____

9. Everyone but Mr. Foster and (he, him) can help customers if necessary. _____

10. Do you know if Gary and (I, me, myself) signed it? _____

11. Only Erik (himself, hisself) knows what is best for him. _____

12. We asked two women, Denise and (she, her), to come along. _____

13. The proceeds are to be divided among Mr. Shelby, Mrs. Huerra, and (she, her). _____

14. Miss Greerson thinks that Mr. Cardillo is a better salesperson than (she, her). _____

15. All property claims must be submitted to my lawyer or (I, me, myself) before April 15. _____

16. The result was acceptable to both management and (us, we). _____

17. At a keyboard no one is more accurate than (she, her). _____

18. The best time for you and (he, him) to enroll is in January. _____

19. The president and (I, me, myself) will inspect the facility. _____

20. Everyone except Kevin and (I, me, myself) was able to join the program. _____

21. Send an application to Human Resources or (I, me, myself) immediately. _____

22. (She and I, Her and me, Her and I) are among the best-qualified candidates. _____

23. Have you invited Jon and (she, her, herself) to our picnic? _____

Level III

Worksheet 1

Remember that pronouns that rename the subject and that follow linking verbs must be in the nominative case: (*It was he who placed the order*). When the infinitive *to be* has no subject (and that subject must immediately precede the infinitive *to be*), the pronoun that follows must be in the nominative case (*My sister is often taken to be I*). *No* subject = *no*minative.

In the following sentences, select the correct word.

1. It must have been (her, she) who called this morning. _____

2. I certainly would not like to be (he, him). _____

3. Do you think that it was (they, them) who complained? _____

4. Tram answered the telephone by saying, "This is (her, she)." _____

5. Mrs. Richards thought the salesperson to be (he, him). _____

6. If you were (she, her), would you take the job? _____

7. Cecile is sometimes taken to be (her, she). _____

8. Jim said that yesterday's driver could have been (he, him). _____

9. Miss Soriano asked Frank and (I, me) to help her. _____

10. Was it (they, them) who made the contribution? _____

11. The most accurate proofreader seems to be (he, him). _____

12. Producer Edwards would not allow me to be (he, him) in the production. _____

13. Mr. Fox wants to assign you and (her, she) the project. _____

14. Are you sure it was (I, me) who was called to the phone? _____

15. The visitor was thought to be (she, her). _____

16. If it had not been (she, her) who made the announcement, I would not have believed it. _____

17. How could anyone have thought that Margaret was (I, me)? _____

18. I do not wish to discourage either you or (he, him). _____

19. If anyone is disappointed, it will be (I, me). _____

20. What makes Joan wish to be (she, her)? _____

21. Do you think it was (he, him) who made the large contribution? _____

22. Mr. Rivera selected you and (he, him) because of his confidence in your abilities. _____

23. If it had been (she, her), we would have recognized her immediately. _____

24. Everyone thought the new manager would be (she, her). _____

25. Because the president is to be (he, him), Mr. Thomas will act as CEO. _____

Worksheet 2

Select the correct word to complete the following sentences.

1. Only the president and (he, him) can grant leaves of absence. _____

2. The manager mistook Danielle to be (I, me). _____

3. The body of the manuscript is followed by (its, it's) endnotes. _____

4. Our staff agreed that you and (she, her) should represent us. _____

5. How can you believe (us, we) to be guilty? _____

6. I'm not sure (their's, there's) enough time left. _____

7. Everyone thought the new manager would be (he, him). _____

8. My friend and (I, me) looked for jobs together. _____

9. This matter will be kept strictly between you and (I, me). _____

10. Good students like you and (she, her) are always prepared. _____

11. Judge Waxman is fully supported by (we, us) consumers. _____

12. We agree that (your, you're) the best person for the job. _____

13. Send the announcement to Ms. Nguyen and (she, her) today. _____

14. All employees except Kim and (he, him) will be evaluated. _____

15. Many locker combinations are listed, but (your's, yours) is missing. _____

16. Apparently the message was intended for you and (I, me, myself). _____

17. Was it (he, him, himself) who sent the mystery e-mail message? _____

18. The bank is closed, but (it's, its) ATM is open. _____

19. Please submit the report to (him or me, he or I) before May 1. _____

20. (There's, Theirs) only one path for us to follow. _____

21. For you and (he, him), I would suggest careers in marketing. _____

22. These personnel changes affect you and (I, me, myself) directly. _____

23. My friend and (I, me, myself) are thinking of a trip to Hawaii. _____

24. Only two branches plan to expand (they're, their) display rooms. _____

25. The operator thought it was (she, her) calling for assistance. _____

26. Because you are a member of the audit review team, you have a better overall picture of the operations than (I, me, myself). _____

27. Though you may not agree with our decision, I hope you'll support Todd and (I, me) in our effort to get the job done. _____

28. Some of the recent decisions made by (us, we) supervisors will be reviewed by the management council when it meets in January. _____

29. I wonder if it was (she, her) who sent the anonymous e-mail message about additional company downsizing. _____

30. Do you think (theirs, their's, there's) any real reason to change our computer passwords every month? _____

Name _____

L e v e l   I

Pronouns must agree with the words for which they substitute. Don't let words and phrases that come between a pronoun and its antecedent confuse you.

Examples: **Every one of the women had *her* forms ready. (Not *their*.)**
The supervisor, along with four assistants, offered *his* support. (Not *their*.)

Select the correct word(s) to complete these sentences.

1. Mrs. Kennedy, in addition to many other members of the staff, sent (her, their) best wishes. _____

2. Every employee must have (his, her, his or her, their) physical examination completed by December 31. _____

3. After a job well done, everyone appreciates (his, her, his or her, their) share of credit. _____

4. Several office workers, along with the manager, announced (his or her, their) intention to vote for the settlement. _____

5. Individuals like Mr. Herndon can always be depended on to do (her, his, his or her, their) best in all assignments. _____

6. If a policyholder has a legitimate claim, (he, she, he or she, they) should contact us immediately. _____

7. Every one of the employees brought (her or his lunch, their lunches) to the outdoor event. _____

8. When a customer walks into our store, treat (him, her, him or her, them) as you would an honored guest in your home. _____

9. Carolyn Davis, along with several other company representatives, volunteered to demonstrate (her, his, his or her, their) equipment. _____

10. A few of the members of the touring group, in addition to their guide, wanted (his or her picture, their pictures) taken. _____

11. Any female member of the project could arrange (her, their) own accommodations if desired. _____

12. Every player on the men's ball team complained about (his, their) uniform. _____

Rewrite this sentence to avoid the use of a common-gender pronoun. Show three versions.

Every employee must obtain his parking permit in the personnel office.

13. _____

14. _____

15. _____

Underline any pronoun–antecedent errors in the following sentences. Then write a corrected form in the space provided. If a sentence is correct, write *C*.

1. Either Miss Monahan or Miss Chavez left their machine on Friday. _____

2. The Federal Drug Administration has not yet granted it's approval for the drug. _____

3. Every clerk, every manager, and every executive will be expected to do their part in making the carpooling program a success. _____

4. Somebody left his book on the chair. _____

5. Neither one of the men wanted to have their remarks quoted. _____

6. Every one of the delegates to the women's conference was wearing their name tag. _____

7. The vice president and the marketing director had already made their reservations. _____

8. Each of the pieces of equipment came with their own software. _____

9. The firm of Higgins, Thomas & Keene, Inc., is moving their offices to Warner Plaza. _____

10. Every manager expects the employees who report to them to be willing to earn their salaries. _____

11. Neither of the women had her driver's license in the car. _____

12. We hoped that someone in the office could find their copy of the program. _____

13. Either the first telephone caller or the second one did not leave their number. _____

14. If everybody will please take their seats, we can get started. _____

15. The faculty agreed to publicize their position on budget cuts. _____

16. We saw that HomeCo reduced their prices on lawn mowers. _____

17. Few of the laser printers had the sale price marked on it. _____

18. Every one of the male employees immediately agreed to a small cut in their contract. _____

19. Each bridesmaid will pay for their own gown. _____

20. All managers and employees know that she or he must boost productivity. _____

Worksheet 1

In selecting *who* or *whom* to complete the sentences below, follow these five steps:

> **Example:** We do not know (who, whom) the contract names.
>
>   **1.** Isolate the *who* clause: *(who, whom)* the contract names
>
>   **2.** Invert to normal subject–verb order: the contract names *(who, whom)*
>
>   **3.** Substitute pronouns: the contract names *him*
>
>   **4.** Equate: the contract names *whom*
>
>   **5.** Complete: We do not know *whom* the contract names.

  1. (Who, Whom) will you invite to your party?   _____

  2. Rick Nash is the student (who, whom) the teacher asked to make an   _____
  oral report.

  3. Do you know (who, whom) will be taking your place?   _____

  4. To (who, whom) did she refer in her letter?   _____

  5. Did Mr. Glade say (who, whom) he wanted to see?   _____

  6. Dr. Truong is a man (who, whom) everyone respects.   _____

  7. (Who, Whom) was president of your organization last year?   _____

  8. (Who, Whom) do you want to work with?   _____

  9. (Who, Whom) has the best chance to be elected?   _____

  10. I know of no one else (who, whom) plays so well.   _____

In choosing *who* or *whom* to complete these sentences, ignore parenthetical phrases such as *I think, we know, you feel,* and *I believe*.

  11. Julie is a person (who, whom) I know will be successful on the job.   _____

  12. The personnel director hired an individual (who, whom) he thought   _____
  would be the best performer.

  13. Is Ms. Hastings the dealer (who, whom) you think I should call?   _____

  14. Major Kirby, (who, whom) I think will be elected, is running in the   _____
  next election.

  15. (Who, Whom) do you believe will be given the job?   _____

Worksheet 2

In the following sentences, selecting *who, whom, whoever,* or *whomever* first requires isolating the clause within which the pronoun appears. Then, *within the clause,* determine whether a nominative or objective case pronoun is required.

> **Example:** Give the package to (whoever, whomever) opens the door.
>   (*He* or *she* opens the door = *whoever* opens the door.)

  1. A bonus will be given to (whoever, whomever) sells over $100,000.   _____

  2. Discuss the problem with (whoever, whomever) is in charge of the   _____
  program.

3. We will interview (whoever, whomever) you recommend. _____

4. You may give the tickets to (whoever, whomever) you wish. _____

5. Johnson said to give the parking pass to (whoever, whomever) asked for it. _____

6. The committee members have promised to cooperate with (whoever, whomever) is selected to chair the committee. _____

7. Please call (whoever, whomever) you believe can repair the machine. _____

8. (Whoever, Whomever) is nominated for the position must be approved by the full membership. _____

9. Reservations have been made for (whoever, whomever) requested them in advance. _____

10. (Whoever, Whomever) is chosen to lead the delegation will command attention at the caucus. _____

In choosing *who* or *whom* to complete these sentences, be especially alert to pronouns following the linking verbs. Remember that the nominative *who* is required as a subject complement.

Example: Was it (who, whom) I thought it was? (It was *he* = *who*.)

11. (Who, Whom) is the customer who wanted a replacement? _____

12. The visitor who asked for me was (who, whom)? _____

13. Was the new CEO (who, whom) we thought it would be? _____

14. The winner will be (whoever, whomever) is tops in sales. _____

15. For (who, whom) was this new printer ordered? _____

Worksheet 3

In the following sentences, select the correct word.

1. (Who, Whom) did you call for assistance? _____

2. Mr. Lincoln, (who, whom) we thought would never be hired, did well in his first assignment. _____

3. By (who, whom) are you currently employed? _____

4. You should hire (whoever, whomever) you feel has the best qualifications. _____

5. Did the caller say (who, whom) he wanted to see? _____

6. The man (who, whom) I saw yesterday walked by today. _____

7. (Whoever, Whomever) is first on the list will be called next. _____

8. The secretary sent notices to customers (who, whom) she felt should be notified. _____

9. Is the manager (who, whom) we thought it would be? _____

10. The manager praised the clerk (who, whom) worked late. _____

11. She is the one (who, whom) Kevin helped yesterday. _____

12. Many of us thought Mr. Alison was a nice person with (who, whom) to work. _____

13. (Who, Whom) is Stacy often mistaken to be? _____

14. (Who, Whom) did you say to call for reservations? _____

15. Please make an appointment with (whoever, whomever) you consider to be the best internist. _____

16. Here is a list of satisfied customers (who, whom) you may wish to contact. _____

17. (Whoever, Whomever) is suggested by Mr. Arthur must be interviewed. _____

18. The candidate (who, whom) the party supports will win. _____

19. Marcia is one on (who, whom) I have come to depend. _____

20. For (who, whom) are these contracts? _____

21. To (who, whom) did you say I should address this letter? _____

22. Do you know (who, whom) their sales representative is? _____

23. Bonus checks go to (whoever, whomever) increases sales by 25 percent. _____

24. Rodney Wilson, (who, whom) was our first choice, was appointed. _____

Name _____

Level I

Fill in the answers below with information found in your text.

1. What kind of action verbs direct action toward a person or thing? _____

2. What kind of action verbs do not require an object to complete their action? _____

3. What kind of verbs link to the subject words that rename or describe the subject? _____

4. What do we call the nouns, pronouns, and adjectives that complete the meaning of a sentence by renaming or describing the subject? _____

In each of the following sentences, indicate whether the underlined verb is transitive (*T*), intransitive (*I*), or linking (*L*). In addition, if the verb is transitive, write its object. If the verb is linking, write its complement. The first two sentences are followed by explanations to assist you.

5. Jeff <u>ran</u> along the dirt path back to his home. (The verb *ran* is intransitive. It has no object to complete its meaning. The phrase *along the dirt path* tells where Jeff ran; it does not receive the action of the verb.) _____

6. It <u>might have been</u> Fran who called yesterday. (The verb phrase ends with the linking verb *been*. The complement is *Fran*, which renames the subject *it*.) _____

7. Juan <u>filed</u> the address cards of our most recent customers. _____

8. Customers <u>crowded</u> into the store at the beginning of the sale. _____

9. Sherry <u>was</u> a lifeguard at the pool last summer. _____

10. Levi Strauss first <u>sold</u> pants to miners in San Francisco in the 1800s. _____

11. The bank <u>sent</u> your canceled checks last week. _____

12. Chocolate fudge ice cream <u>tastes</u> better than chocolate mint. _____

13. Do you think it <u>was</u> he who suggested the improvement? _____

14. We <u>walked</u> around the shopping mall on our lunch hour. _____

15. Our company recruiter <u>asks</u> the same questions of every candidate. _____

16. Many corporations <u>give</u> gifts to important foreign clients. _____

17. This dictionary <u>is</u> the best on the market for office workers. _____

18. All employees <u>listened</u> intently as the CEO discussed annual profits. _____

19. Ellen <u>feels</u> justified in asking for a raise. _____

20. Customers <u>have</u> high expectations from most advertised products. _____

Worksheet 1

Transitive verbs that direct action toward an object are in the active voice. Transitive verbs that direct action toward a subject are in the passive voice. Writing that incorporates active voice verbs is more vigorous and more efficient than writing that contains many passive voice verbs. To convert a passive voice verb to the active voice, look for the doer of the action. (Generally the agent of the action is contained in a *by* phrase.) In the active voice the agent becomes the subject.

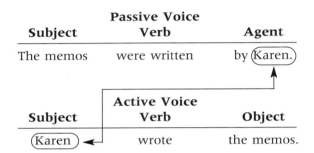

For each of the following sentences, underline the agent (doer of the action). Write that word in the space provided. Then rewrite the sentence changing the passive voice verbs to active voice. Your rewritten version should begin with the word (and its modifiers) that you identified as the agent.

Agent

1. The mail was not picked up by our mailcarrier yesterday. _____

_____

_____

2. Our order was shipped last week by Mattel. _____

_____

_____

3. Withdrawals must be authorized by Mrs. Bradford beginning next week. _____

_____

_____

4. Bill was asked by Mr. Stern to be responsible for turning out the lights when he left. _____

_____

_____

5. Employees who travel a great deal were forced by management to surrender their frequent-flier mileage awards. _____

_____

_____

Worksheet 2

Some sentences with passive voice verbs do not identify the doer of the action. Before these sentences can be converted, a subject must be provided. Use your imagination to supply subjects.

Passive: Interest will be paid on all deposits. (*By whom?* By First Federal.)

Active: First Federal will pay interest on all deposits.

By whom?

1. The letters must be completed before 5 p.m. _____
   _____
   _____

2. Checks were written on an account with insufficient funds. _____
   _____
   _____

3. Our computer was programmed to total account balances. _____
   _____
   _____

4. Decisions were made in the courts that affected the daily lives of all Americans. _____
   _____
   _____

5. When home video games were first introduced, it was thought that they were too expensive to sell in mass quantities. _____
   _____
   _____

6. Cash discounts are given only when orders are paid immediately with cash. _____
   _____
   _____

7. Employees working with computers were warned to change their passwords frequently. _____
   _____
   _____

8. For shipments sent in our packaging materials, the value is limited to $500. _____
   _____
   _____

Write the correct answers in the spaces provided.

1. If I (was, were) you, I would complete my degree first. _____

2. The personnel director recommended that Jeff (be, is) hired with the condition that he continue college courses at night. _____

3. If Mr. Greer (was, were) in the office yesterday, he did not sign the checks. _____

4. One of the stockholders moved that a committee (be, is) constituted to study the problem immediately. _____

5. If the manager were here, he (will, would) sign the work order and we could proceed. _____

6. The civil defense chief suggested that all homes (are, be) stocked with an emergency supply of food and water. _____

7. Joyce said that if she (was, were) the travel agent, she would have planned the trip differently. _____

8. It has been moved and seconded that funds (are, be) allocated for repairs. _____

9. Dr. Washington suggested that the patient (rest, rests) for the next two days. _____

10. Angela wished that she (was, were) able to fly to Phoenix to visit her sister. _____

11. If Mrs. Balfour (was, were) in my position, she probably would have done the same thing. _____

12. Hendricks suggested that the cafeteria (is, be) opened earlier so that swing-shift employees could use it. _____

13. Under the circumstances, even if the voter registration drive (was, were) successful, we might lose the election. _____

14. The professor recommended that everyone (meet, meets) in the parking lot before the field trip. _____

15. He acts as though he (was, were) the only employee who wants the weekend off. _____

16. After consulting management, our manager suggested that all employees (are, be) given three-week vacations. _____

17. If the fax machine (was, were) working, you could have had the figures immediately. _____

18. If Rick (was, were) at the sales meeting, I missed him. _____

19. Laurie uses credit cards as if she (was, were) an heiress. _____

20. It has been moved and seconded that the meeting (is, be) adjourned. _____

Name _____

L e v e l   I

Select the correct verb.

1. Did you tell me that the caller's name (is, was) Martin?   _____

2. The accident (occured, occurred) late last evening.   _____

3. Mr. Anderson said that the car you are driving (is, was) red.   _____

4. Are you sure that her maiden name (is, was) Spitnale?   _____

5. We were taught that an ounce of prevention (is, was) worth a pound of cure.   _____

In the space provided, write the verb form indicated in parentheses.

Example: Joan (carry) the heavy books every day. (present tense)   **carries** _____

6. American firms (plan) to expand their markets abroad. (present tense)   _____

7. A Kentucky Fried Chicken franchise (sell) American-style fast food in Japan. (future)   _____

8. The giant Mitsubishi conglomerate (supply) the Colonel with chicken in Japan. (past)   _____

9. The marketing director (study) possible sales sites in foreign countries. (present)   _____

10. We (analyze) such factors as real estate, construction costs, and local attitudes toward fast food. (future)   _____

11. Management (apply) a complex formula to forecast the profitability of the new business. (past)   _____

12. We (consider) the vast differences between the two cultures. (past tense)   _____

13. A local franchise (vary) the side dishes to accommodate cultural preferences. (present)   _____

14. Kentucky Fried Chicken (insist) on retaining its original recipe in foreign stores. (present)   _____

15. It (appeal) to the average customer in Japan. (future)   _____

16. Doing business in Japan (require) appreciation of rituals and formalities. (present)   _____

17. In East Asia the presentation of business cards (demand) special attention to ceremony. (future)   _____

Worksheet 1

Select the correct verb.

1. The condition of the streets has (became, become) intolerable. _____

2. Ice (froze, freezed) in the pipes last night. _____

3. Before leaving on her vacation, Mrs. Stanton (hid, hide) her silver and other valuables. _____

4. Have you (chose, chosen) a location for the new equipment? _____

5. Three new homes were recently (builded, built) on Fairfax Avenue. _____

6. After he had (drank, drunk) two glasses of milk, he asked for more. _____

7. We must have (forget, forgotten) the keys. _____

8. Are you sure you have (gave, given) him the correct combination? _____

9. Andre and the others had (went, gone) on the hike earlier. _____

10. The smaller dog was (bit, bitten) by a larger neighborhood dog. _____

Underline any errors in the following sentences. Write the correct form in the space provided. Write *C* if the sentence is correct as written. Do not add helping verbs.

Example: After we <u>run</u> out of food, we had to return to camp headquarters. **ran**_____

11. We had ate a small snack before we ordered dinner. _____

12. Yesterday the birds sung sweetly. _____

13. Mr. Jefferson was stricken just as he left the witness stand. _____

14. Hundreds of mushrooms sprung up after the rain. _____

15. Many people were shook by the minor earthquake yesterday. _____

16. Tracy had wore her new boots only twice. _____

17. He had wrote a large portion of his report before leaving. _____

18. Their car was stole from its parking place overnight. _____

19. Because of a threatening storm, she should have took a cab. _____

20. If we had went to the movie premier, we would have seen the stars. _____

Worksheet 2

Lie–Lay

Use the chart below to help you select the correct form of *lie* or *lay* in these sentences.

Present	Present Participle	Past	Past Participle
lie (rest)	lying (resting)	lay (rested)	lain (have, has, or had rested)
lay (place)	laying (placing)	laid (placed)	laid (have, has, or had placed)

Example: This afternoon I must (rest) down before dinner.   lie _____

1. I am sure that I (placed) the book on the desk yesterday.   _____

2. Andrea angrily told her dog to (rest) down.   _____

3. This month's bills have been (resting) in the drawer for weeks.   _____

4. Bill has (placed) his books on the desk near the entrance.   _____

5. The worker was (placing) concrete blocks for the foundation.   _____

6. This evening I must (rest) down before we leave.   _____

7. Yesterday I (rested) in my room worrying about today's exam.   _____

8. (Place) the papers in a stack over there.   _____

9. The candy has (rested) on the shelf for several weeks.   _____

10. Let the fabric (rest) there for several hours until it dries.   _____

Now try these sentences to test your skill in using the forms of *lie* and *lay*.

11. Will you be able to (lie, lay) down before dinner?   _____

12. How long have these papers been (laying, lying) here?   _____

13. Please tell your very friendly dog to (lay, lie) down.   _____

14. Will the mason (lay, lie) bricks over the concrete patio?   _____

15. The contract has (laid, lain) in our file for over two months.   _____

16. Yesterday I (laid, lay) down in the afternoon.   _____

17. Mothers complain about clothes that are left (laying, lying) around.   _____

18. Returned books (lie, lay) in a pile at the library until the staff can return them to the stacks.   _____

19. I'm sure I (laid, layed, lied) my keys on this counter.   _____

20. When you were (lying, laying) the groceries down, did you see my keys?   _____

L e v e l   I I I

Keep your textbook handy so that you can look up the verb tenses required in the following sentences.

Example: By June 1 you (employ) here one full year. (future perfect, passive)   **will have been employed** _____

1. McDonald's (open) many restaurants in foreign countries. (present perfect)   _____

2. McDonald's (plan) to start a franchise. (present progressive)   _____

3. We (call) for service at least three times before a repairperson arrived. (past perfect)   _____

4. She (work) on that project for the past six months. (present perfect)   _____

5. We (see) the very first screening of the documentary. (past progressive)   _____

6. The mayor (sign) the proclamation at this afternoon's public ceremony. (future progressive)   _____

7. The water main (broke) by the bulldozer working on street repairs. (past perfect, passive)   _____

8. I (see) two good movies recently. (present perfect) _____

9. We (consider) the installation of a new e-mail system. (present progressive) _____

10. The president's message (hear) across the country by Americans in four time zones. (past progressive, passive) _____

The next sentences review Level II.

11. The alarm had (rang, rung) three times before we responded. _____

12. Yesterday we (drank, drunk) two quarts of milk. _____

13. You must (chose, choose) new stationery for the office. _____

14. The car has been (drove, driven) many miles. _____

15. Steve claims he (saw, seen) the report yesterday. _____

16. If Rasheed had (went, gone) earlier, he would have told us. _____

17. Sue said she (seen, saw) an accident on her way to work. _____

18. The tour guide checked to see if everyone had (ate, eaten). _____

19. Dr. White had (wrote, written) four letters about his new car. _____

20. The price of our stocks (raised, rose) again yesterday. _____

Name _____

L e v e l   I

Worksheet 1

For each of the following sentences, cross out any phrase that comes between a verb and its subject. Then select the correct verb and write it in the space provided.

Example: One ~~of the most interesting books on all the lists~~ (is, are)   **is** _____
          Becoming a Millionaire at 21.

1. Many Internet sites on the government's prohibited list (provide, provides) games or amusement that employees may not access. _____

2. The supervisor, together with two technicians, (is, are) working on the faulty circuit. _____

3. This company's supply of raw materials (come, comes) from South America. _____

4. A good many workers in addition to Martha (think, thinks) the work shifts should be rearranged. _____

5. Everyone except you and John (is, are) to repeat the test. _____

6. The table as well as two chairs (was, were) damaged. _____

7. A list with all the customers' names and addresses (is, are) being sent. _____

8. Other equipment, such as our terminals and printers, (need, needs) to be reevaluated. _____

9. One of the local newspapers (has, have) a bargain box. _____

10. Several copies of the report (is, are) being prepared for distribution. _____

11. The furniture, as well as all the equipment including computers, (is, are) for sale. _____

12. Effects of the disease (is, are) not known immediately. _____

13. Three salespeople, in addition to their district sales manager, (has, have) voiced the same suggestion. _____

14. Profits from his home business (is, are) surprising. _____

15. Every one of the potential businesses that you mention (sounds, sound) good. _____

16. A shipment of 8,000 drill sets (was, were) sent to four warehouses. _____

17. Everyone except the evening employees (is, are) coming. _____

18. We learned that two subsidiaries of the corporation (is, are) successful. _____

19. Officials in several levels of government (has, have) to be consulted. _____

20. A letter together with several enclosures (was, were) mailed yesterday. _____

Worksheet 2

For each of the following sentences, underline the subject. Then select the correct verb and write it in the space provided.

Example: Here (is, are) a <u>copy</u> of the findings for your files.   **is** _____

Suggestion: If you know that a subject is singular, temporarily substitute *he, she,* or *it* to help you select the proper verb. If you know that a subject is plural, temporarily substitute *they* for the subject.

1. The flow of industrial goods (travel, travels) through different distribution channels from the flow of consumer goods.   _____

2. Here (is, are) the newspaper and magazines you ordered.   _____

3. Coleman, Harris & Juarez, Inc., one of the leading management consultant firms, (is, are) able to accept our business.   _____

4. The books on the open shelves of our company's library (is, are) available to all employees.   _____

5. There (appear, appears) to be many significant points omitted from the report.   _____

6. The various stages in the life cycle of a product (is, are) instrumental in determining profits for that product.   _____

7. No one except the Cunninghams (was, were) able to volunteer.   _____

8. A member of the organization of painters and plasterers (is, are) unhappy about the recent settlement.   _____

9. The size and design of its container (is, are) influential in the appeal of a product.   _____

10. Just one governmental unit from the local, state, or national levels (is, are) all we need to initiate the project.   _____

11. American Airlines (has, have) been able to increase service while cutting costs.   _____

12. Only two seasons of the year (provide, provides) weather that is suitable for gliding.   _____

13. (Has, Have) the moving van of the Wongs arrived yet?   _____

14. At present the condition of the company's finances (is, are) extremely strong as a result of the recent bond sale.   _____

15. Incoming mail from three flights (is, are) now being sorted.   _____

16. The salary of Maria Chavez, along with the earnings of several other employees, (has, have) been increased.   _____

17. One of the best designs (appear, appears) to have been submitted by your student.   _____

For each of the following sentences, underline the subject. Then select the correct word and write it in the space provided.

1. Most of the salary compensation to which he referred (is, are) beyond basic pay schedules.

_____

2. The Committee on Youth Activities (has, have) enlisted the aid of several well-known athletes.

_____

3. Each young man and young woman (deserve, deserves) an opportunity to participate in local athletics.

_____

4. Either your company or one of your two competitors (is, are) going to win the government contract.

_____

5. All the work for our Special Products Division (is, are) yet to be assigned.

_____

6. Either of the two small businesses (is, are) able to secure a loan.

_____

7. City council members (was, were) sharply divided along partisan lines.

_____

8. Neither the packing list nor the two invoices (mention, mentions) the missing ottoman.

_____

9. Every one of your suggestions (merit, merits) consideration.

_____

10. Our survey shows that (everyone, every one) of the owner-managed businesses was turning a profit.

_____

11. Either Steven or you (is, are) expected to return the call.

_____

12. Each of the machines (has, have) capabilities that are suitable for our needs.

_____

13. Mrs. Roberts said that most of the credit for our increased sales (belong, belongs) to you.

_____

14. First on the program (is, are) the group of Indo-European folk dancers.

_____

15. Some of the enthusiasm (is, are) due to the coming holiday.

_____

16. After 10 p.m. the staff (has, have) to use the front entrance only.

_____

17. (Was, Were) any of the supervisors absent after the holiday?

_____

18. Many a young clerk and secretary (has, have) been helped by our in-service training programs.

_____

19. We were informed that neither management nor the employees (has, have) special privileges.

_____

20. Most of the work that was delivered to us four days ago (is, are) completed.

_____

In the following sentences, select the correct word.

1. Reed says that 75 feet of plastic pipe (has, have) been ordered.

_____

2. The number of women in the labor force (is, are) steadily increasing.

_____

3. Phillip said that he is one of those individuals who (enjoy, enjoys) a real challenge. _____

4. Over two thirds of the stock issue (was, were) sold immediately after it was released. _____

5. Gerald is the only one of the four applicants who (was, were) prepared to complete the application form during the interview. _____

6. That most offices are closed on weekends (is, are) a factor that totally escaped Mr. Brotherton. _____

7. The majority of the employees (favor, favors) the reorganization plan. _____

8. Telephones (is, are) one item that we must install immediately. _____

9. At least four fifths of the women in the audience (is, are) willing to participate in the show. _____

10. How could it be I who (am, is) responsible, when I had no knowledge of the agreement until yesterday? _____

11. Let it be recorded that on the second vote the number of members in favor of the proposal (is, are) less than on the first vote. _____

12. Only half of the box of disks (is, are) left in the supply cabinet. _____

13. Are you one of those people who (like, likes) to sleep late? _____

14. I'm sure that it is you who (is, are) next on the list. _____

15. It looks as if 20 inches of extra cord (is, are) what we need. _____

16. Our office manager reports that a number of printers (need, needs) repair. _____

17. At least one third of the desserts purchased for the party (was, were) uneaten. _____

18. Hiking in Europe and sailing to Scandinavia (is, are) what I plan for my future vacations. _____

19. Sherry Lansing is one of our e-mail users who (complain, complains) about the system. _____

20. Whoever submitted an application earliest (has, have) the right to be interviewed first. _____

Name _____

A verb form ending in *ing* and used as a noun is a gerund.

> *Passing* the examination is important. (Gerund used as subject.)

A noun or pronoun modifying a gerund should be possessive.

> *Your* passing the examination is important.

Don't confuse verbals acting as nouns with those acting as adjectives.

> The man *passing* the test received his license. (*Passing* functions as an adjective describing *man*.)

> The man's *passing* the test is important. (Verbal noun *passing* functions as the subject of the verb *is*.)

In the following sentences, underline any gerunds and write their modifiers in the space provided. If a sentence contains no gerund, write *None*.

> **Example:** It is your <u>smoking</u> that disturbs the others.　　**your** _____

1. This job offer is contingent on your passing our physical examination. _____

2. Our office certainly did not approve of his investing in high-risk securities. _____

3. It was Mr. Cortina's gambling that caused him to lose his job. _____

4. The increase in sales is directly related to our placing the staff on a commission basis. _____

Some of the remaining sentences contain gerunds. If any error appears in the modifier, underline the error and write the correct form in the space provided. If the sentence is correct, write *C*.

> **Example:** Mrs. Salazar was instrumental in <u>us</u> acquiring the Collins' account.　　**our** _____

5. His recent award is directly related to Mr. Frank receiving a promotion. _____

6. The individual receiving the award could not be present to accept it. _____

7. Do you think you criticizing the manager had anything to do with your transfer? _____

8. We deeply appreciate you calling us to give us this news. _____

9. Is it Mr. Davidson writing that makes the message illegible? _____

10. It appears that us faxing the company is the only logical action to take at this time. _____

11. An employee taking a message must write clearly. _____

12. Mrs. Fackler said that me working overtime was unnecessary this weekend. _____

13. The employees working overtime this week will receive their overtime salary in next month's checks. _____

A verbal form used as an adjective (to describe or modify nouns and pronouns) is called a participle. When a participle, either as a separate word or as part of a phrase, introduces an independent clause, the participle or its phrase should be followed by a comma. When a phrase containing a participle interrupts the flow of a sentence with nonessential information, it should be set off with commas. The following sentences are punctuated correctly. Underline the participles and participial phrases.

1. While preparing the report, Isabelle verified all calculations.

2. Surrounded, the enemy troops raised a white flag.

3. Mr. Wilson, seeing his opportunity, brought up the subject of employee fringe benefits.

4. Our new records management system, installed just two months ago, is saving us money.

5. Miss Strawn, rereading the article several times, could not believe her eyes.

6. Opening a new account, Mr. and Mrs. Sams both filled out signature cards.

7. Irritated, the manager raised his voice.

8. A person opening a new account is required to have a valid signature card on file.

For each of the following sentences, add any commas necessary to punctuate verbal forms or phrases. In the space provided, write the comma(s) and preceding words. If a sentence is correct, write C.

Example: Comptroller Duffy restricted by federal guidelines revised many budget procedures.   **Duffy, guidelines,**

9. After choosing a model we placed our equipment order.   _____

10. Mr. Dallas consulting his local stockbroker opened an account.   _____

11. Reading a stock market ticker tape requires some training.   _____

12. Displaying security transactions large ticker-tape screens may be found in most brokerage houses.   _____

13. An executive representing a local brokerage firm called me.   _____

14. Terry Sanderson representing a local brokerage firm called me.   _____

15. Acting on her own behalf Miss Delgado placed an order for 100 shares of stock.   _____

From the sets of sentences that follow, select the sentence that is the more logically stated. Write its letter in the space provided.

1. (a) Hurriedly proofreading the report, three errors were found by Amy.
   (b) Hurriedly proofreading the report, Amy found three errors.   _____

2. (a) To get to the meeting quickly, a shortcut was taken by Mike.
   (b) To get to the meeting quickly, Mike took a shortcut.   _____

3. (a) In investing money in the stock market, one must expect risks.
   (b) In investing money in the stock market, risks must be expected.   _____

Name _____

Underline any errors in the following sentences. Then write the correct form. If the sentence is correct as written, write C.

1. You should of seen the looks on their faces! _____

2. No one except Mr. Levine and he had access to supplies. _____

3. We plan to attend the lecture too. _____

4. Just between you and I, this engine has never run more smoothly. _____

5. Some of the magazines we borrowed off of Mrs. Kelsey. _____

6. If you will address your inquiry too our Customer Relations Department, you will surely receive a response. _____

7. The personnel director, along with the office manager and she, is planning to improve our hiring procedures. _____

8. You could of done something about the error. _____

9. Because we have to many machines, we are planning a sale. _____

10. All salespeople except Ms. Berk and he were reassigned. _____

11. Did you obtain your copy of the newspaper off him? _____

12. Please get your passes from either Mrs. Bowman or he. _____

13. See if you can get some change for the machine off of her. _____

14. Both the project coordinator and he should have verified the totals before submitting the bid. _____

15. The commission for the sale has to be divided between Ms. Carpenter and he. _____

16. Because to few spaces are available, additional parking must be found on nearby streets. _____

17. If you and he could of come yesterday, we might have been able to help you. _____

18. So that we may better evaluate your application, please supply references too. _____

19. You could of had complimentary tickets if you had called her. _____

20. The marketing manager assigned too many customers to Ann and I. _____

For each of the following sentences, underline any errors in the use of prepositions. Then write a correct form. Mark C if the sentence is correct as written.

1. We think that beside salary the major issue is working conditions. _____

2. Your support and participation in this new Web program are greatly appreciated. _____

3. The warranty period was over with two months ago. _____

4. Please come into see me when you are ready for employment. _____

5. Just inside of the office entrance is the receptionist. _____

6. Old Mr. Wiggins left $3 million to be divided between three heirs. _____

7. Will you be able to deliver the goods like you said you would? _____

8. For most of us very few opportunities like this ever arise. _____

9. Exactly what type software did you have in mind? _____

10. Some of the trucks were moved in to the garage at dusk. _____

11. When can we accept delivery of the electrical components ordered from Hellman, Inc.? _____

12. Because of your concern and involvement in our community action campaign, we have received thousands of dollars in contributions. _____

13. I know the time and date of our next committee meeting, but I do not know where it is at. _____

14. If you were willing to accept further responsibility, I would assign you the committee chairmanship. _____

15. Joanna could not help from laughing when she saw her e-mail. _____

16. Please hurry up so that we may submit our proposal quickly. _____

17. What style furniture is most functional for the waiting room? _____

18. After going into meet the supervisor, Carla was hired. _____

19. All parking lots opposite to the corporate headquarters will be cleaned. _____

20. Immediately after Kathy graduated high school, she started college. _____

Level III

In the following sentences, select the correct word.

1. Mrs. Skelton found that her voice was rising as she became more and more angry (a) at, (b) with the caller. _____

2. We know of no one who is more expert (a) in, (b) with cell phone technology than Dr. France. _____

3. If you concur (a) with, (b) in this action, please notify your representative. _____

4. After corresponding (a) to, (b) with their home office, I was able to clear up the error in my account. _____

5. The houses in that subdivision are identical (a) to, (b) with each other. _____

6. If you (a) plan to attend, (b) plan on attending the summer session, you'd better register immediately. _____

7. A few of the provisions are retroactive (a) for, (b) to January 1. _____

8. Jeff talked (a) to, (b) with his dog in a stern voice. _____

9. Standing (a) on, (b) in line is not my favorite activity. _____

10. She made every effort to reason (a) to, (b) with the unhappy customer. _____

11. Apparently the letters on the screen do not sufficiently contrast (a) with, (b) to the background. _____

12. The courses, faculty, and students in this school are certainly different (a) from, (b) than those at other schools. _____

13. Do you dare to disagree (a) to, (b) with him? _____

14. We want a bond paper similar (a) with, (b) to this 20-pound paper. _____

15. I am angry (a) at, (b) with the proposal that we share the equipment. _____

16. The president insisted that he was completely independent (a) of, (b) from his campaign contributors. _____

17. He went on working oblivious (a) from, (b) to the surrounding chaos. _____

18. The figures on the balance sheet could not be reconciled (a) to, (b) with the actual account totals. _____

19. A number of individuals agreed (a) to, (b) with the plan. _____

20. If you are desirous (a) about, (b) of taking a June vacation, you had better speak to the office manager soon. _____

Name _____

L e v e l   I

Name four coordinating conjunctions:

1. _____ 2. _____ 3. _____ 4. _____

When coordinating conjunctions connect independent clauses (groups of words that could stand alone as sentences), the conjunctions are preceded by commas. The two independent clauses form a compound sentence.

Compound Sentence: We hope to increase sales in the South, *but* we need additional sales personnel.

Use a comma only if the sentence is compound. When the words preceding or following the coordinating conjunction do not form an independent clause, no comma is used.

Simple Sentence: The bank will include the check with your monthly statement *or* will send the check to you immediately.

In the following sentences, selected coordinating conjunctions have been underlined. Mark (a) or (b) for each sentence.

a = No punctuation needed   b = Insert a comma before the under-
                                        lined conjunction

5. Mr. Green is a specialist in information systems and he will be responsible for advising and assisting all our divisions.   _____

6. Mr. Green is a specialist in information systems and will be responsible for advising and assisting all our divisions.   _____

7. This is a sales meeting but other topics of interest may also be discussed.   _____

8. I have studied the plan you are developing and feel that it has real merit.   _____

9. We seek the reaction of the council and of others who have studied the plan.   _____

10. Our executive vice president will make the presentation in New York or he will unveil the plan in London.   _____

11. I think that the plan will be effective and that it will save us time and money.   _____

12. This new benefit plan will cost the employee more money but the expanded benefits will more than offset the increased costs.   _____

13. We are taking over a portion of the fourteenth floor but we will not be moving into that area until March.   _____

14. Send me your latest price list for all camera equipment and place my name on your mailing list for future mailings.   _____

15. Our international telephone costs are very high and may become even more exorbitant if we don't use e-mail more extensively.   _____

1. Name five conjunctive adverbs:

   (a) _____   (c) _____   (e) _____

   (b) _____   (d) _____

2. When a conjunctive adverb joins independent clauses, what punctuation
   mark precedes the conjunctive adverb?   _____

3. Many words that serve as conjunctive adverbs can also function as parenthetical adverbs. When used parenthetically, adverbs are set off by   _____
   what punctuation marks?

In the following sentences words acting as conjunctive or parenthetical adverbs are underlined. Add necessary commas and semicolons to punctuate the sentences.

4. The company is planning <u>nevertheless</u> to proceed with its expansion.

5. The price of the tour is contingent upon double occupancy <u>that is</u> two people must
   share accommodations.

6. This organization <u>on the other hand</u> is quite small in the industry.

7. Our bank is extending its teller service until 6 p.m. <u>hence</u> we are better able to accommodate your banking needs.

8. Stationery and supplies are stored on open shelves <u>however</u> printed forms are kept
   in filing cabinets.

9. Our group will travel first to New York <u>then</u> we will proceed to Paris.

10. The manager has <u>consequently</u> requested a leave of absence.

11. We have few summer jobs available in our organization <u>consequently</u> we have to tell
    young people to look elsewhere.

12. When they graduate <u>on the other hand</u> these same young people will find a different
    employment picture with our organization.

13. We are <u>nevertheless</u> sending you samples of our principal products.

14. Profits were poor last year <u>on the other hand</u> profits this year are much better.

15. Today's job market is very competitive <u>however</u> recent graduates can find jobs if
    they are well trained and persistent.

16. Job candidates <u>consequently</u> often prepare different résumés for each opening.

17. Most recruiters prefer chronological résumés <u>consequently</u> we advise our graduates
    to follow the traditional résumé format.

18. Personnel professionals spend little time reading a cover letter <u>hence</u> keep your letter
    short.

19. A résumé emphasizes what you have done <u>however</u> a cover letter stresses what you
    can do for an employer.

20. During an employment interview recruiters try to uncover negative information
    <u>however</u> job candidates try to minimize faults and weaknesses.

The correlative conjunctions *both . . . and, either . . . or, neither . . . nor,* and *not only . . . but (also)* should be used in parallel constructions. That is, the words these conjunctions join should be similarly patterned. Compare the words that *follow* the conjunctions. For example, if a verb follows *either,* a verb should follow *or.* If the active voice is used with *neither,* then the active voice should be used with *nor.* Study the following examples.

Parallel: Vicki is *either* typing the Collins' report *or* proofreading it. (Both conjunctions are followed by verbs.)

Not Parallel: *Either* Vicki is typing the Collins' report *or* proofreading it. (The subject follows *either* and a verb follows *or.*)

Parallel: I have *neither* pumped the gas *nor* checked the oil.

Not Parallel: *Neither* have I pumped the gas *nor* was the oil checked. (An active voice construction follows *neither* while a passive voice construction follows *nor.*)

In the following, write the letters of the sentences that are constructed in parallel form.

1. (a) We have neither the energy to pursue this litigation nor do we have the finances.   _____
    (b) To pursue this litigation, we have neither the energy nor the finances.

2. (a) You may either write a research report or a book report can be made.   _____
    (b) You may either write a research report or make a book report.

3. (a) He is not only clever but also witty.   _____
    (b) Not only is he clever but he is also witty.

4. (a) The booklet contains both information and it has an application blank.   _____
    (b) The booklet contains both information and an application blank.

Revise the following sentences so that the correlative conjunctions are used in parallel construction.

5. Either you can fax him your response or you can send him an e-mail message. _____

    _____

    _____

6. Our goals are both to educate motorists and also lives may be saved. _____

    _____

    _____

7. Neither does Tony have a job offer nor does he even have an interview lined up. _____

    _____

    _____

8. We knew either that we had to raise more money or begin selling stock. _____

    _____

    _____

Name _____

L e v e l   I

Use *T* or *F* to indicate whether the following statements are true or false.

1. A phrase is a group of related words *without* a subject and a verb. _____

2. A clause is a group of related words containing a subject and a verb. _____

3. An independent clause has a subject and a verb and makes sense by itself. _____

4. A dependent clause contains a subject and a verb but depends for its meaning on an-other clause. _____

5. Words such as *after*, *if*, and *when* are used preceding independent clauses. _____

Indicate whether the following groups of words are phrases (*P*), independent clauses (*I*), or dependent clauses (*D*). If you indicate that a group of words is an independent clause, capitalize the first word (use ≡) and place a period at the end of the group of words.

Example: he stood in a very long line.   I _____

6. in the past year _____

7. although she came to every meeting _____

8. she came to every meeting _____

9. during the period from spring to fall _____

10. if sales continue to climb as they have for the past four months _____

11. the director asked for additional personnel _____

12. as soon as we can increase our production _____

13. we can increase our production _____

14. because your organization has financial strength _____

15. in the future _____

16. faster telephone service is now available _____

17. in order that we may improve service to our customers _____

18. we will compute your average monthly gas consumption _____

19. when he returns to the office _____

20. fill out and mail the enclosed card _____

21. by next fall _____

22. we are reworking our original plans _____

23. since a good résumé has five essential parts _____

24. because your old résumé listed your work history and then went on to describe previous jobs in grim and boring detail disregarding their current relevance _____

25. a good résumé is a breath of fresh air to an employer _____

Add necessary commas to the following sentences. If a sentence requires no punctuation, write *C* next to it.

1. If you follow my suggestions you will help to improve the efficiency of our department.

2. You will if you follow my suggestions help to improve the efficiency of our department.

3. You will help to improve the efficiency of our department if you will follow my suggestions.

4. When completed the renovation should make the seventh floor much more attractive.

5. Let's discuss the problem when Mrs. Gardner returns.

6. The motorist who parked his car in the restricted area is in danger of being ticketed.

7. Our latest company safety booklet which was submitted over six weeks ago is finally ready for distribution.

8. As you may know we have paid dividends regularly for over seventy years.

9. These payments provided there is no interruption in profits should continue for many years to come.

10. If necessary you may charge this purchase to your credit card.

11. Any employee who wishes to participate may contact our Human Resources Department.

12. James Gilroy who volunteered to head the program will be organizing our campaign.

13. I assure you that you will hear from Ms. Higgins as soon as she returns.

14. Before you send in the order may I see the catalog?

15. May I see the catalog before you send in the order?

16. The additional premium you were charged which amounted to $176.12 was issued because of your recent accident.

17. As expected the proposal should help us more clearly define long-term objectives.

18. We will submit the proposal within four working days if that schedule meets with your approval.

19. Before we sign any contract we must make site visits and verify all information.

20. In this proposal I have outlined a seven-step purchasing program that meets all the objectives you indicated were important to you.

Use the information provided within parentheses to construct dependent clauses for the following sentences. Add subordinating conjunctions such as *who, which, although,* and *since.*

Example: Dr. Cushman recently moved his practice to Whittier. (Dr. Cushman specializes in pediatrics.)

Dr. Cushman, who specializes in pediatrics, recently moved his practice to Whittier.

1. The original agreement was drawn between Mr. Hightower and Columbia Communications. (The agreement was never properly signed.) _____ _____ _____

2. Atlantic Insurance Company serves not only individuals but also communities. (Atlantic Insurance Company is a company of people rather than statistics.) _____ _____ _____

3. Thank you for informing us that your credit card is missing. (This credit card has an expiration date of April 30.) _____ _____ _____

Combine the following clauses into single sentences.

4. (Your account is four months past due.) We will be forced to take legal action. We must hear from you within seven days. _____ _____ _____

5. Sally Horton won an award as this month's outstanding employee. (She works in the Quality Control Department.) Ms. Horton is secretary to the manager in that department. _____ _____ _____

6. (The Federal National Mortgage Association does not make loans directly to consumers.) It does, however, help supply money to the home mortgage industry. _____ _____ _____

7. We are sending you four poster advertisements. They will appear in advertisements in magazines in April. (April marks the beginning of a national campaign featuring our sports clothes.) _____ _____ _____

8. Mr. Girard plans to retire at the end of this year. (Mr. Girard has worked at Rocketwell for 37 years.) After he retires, Mr. Girard plans to spend more time with his orchid collection._____ _____ _____

Name _____

Level I

Add necessary commas to the following sentences. For each sentence indicate the number of commas that you added. If a sentence is correct, write *C*.

1. Your present insurance Mr. Nelson does not cover the care and custody of property belonging to others. _____

2. By the way have you updated the fire insurance coverage on your home and its contents? _____

3. When the matter is resolved however we hope to continue our mutually profitable business relationship. _____

4. Debbie is from Ames Iowa and is now working in Des Moines. _____

5. I believe that Cole's sister Samantha will be accompanying us. _____

6. The alternate plan on the other hand will not improve employee profit-sharing benefits. _____

7. Send the shipment to Data Products 750 Grant Road Tucson Arizona 85703 as soon as possible. _____

8. It appears sir that an error has been made in your billing. _____

9. You have until Friday April 30 to make complete payment on your past-due account. _____

10. Mr. Franklin T. Molloy who is an advertising executive has been elected chairman of the council. _____

11. Anyone who is interested in applying for the job should see Mrs. Sheridan. _____

12. I hope that your brother Gary will be able to join us. _____

13. You will in addition receive a free brochure outlining our software programs. _____

14. Our new line of umbrellas pens and attaché cases will be available soon. _____

15. All things considered the company will be obligated to pay only those expenses directly related to the conference. _____

16. Only Mr. Hudson who is a specialist in information systems is qualified to write that report. _____

17. You can avoid patent trademark and copyright problems by working with an attorney. _____

18. We are convinced incidentally that our attorney's fees are most reasonable. _____

19. Mr. Van Alstyne developed the policy Ms. Thorson worked on the budget and Mr. Seibert handled compensation issues. _____

20. With your help our team can meet its goal by November or December of this year. _____

Add necessary commas to the following sentences. For each sentence indicate the number of commas that you added. If a sentence is correct, write C.

1. We must find a practical permanent solution to our Internet access problems. _____

2. For a period of about six months it will be necessary to reduce all expenditures. _____

3. Melissa Meyer speaking on behalf of all classified employees gave a welcoming address. _____

4. We held a marketing meeting last week and we included representatives from all divisions. _____

5. I am looking forward to getting together with you when you are again in Rochester. _____

6. We do appreciate as I have told you often your continuing efforts to increase our sales. _____

7. Consumer patterns for the past five years are being studied carefully by our marketing experts. _____

8. For some time we have been studying the growth in the number of working women. _____

9. After you have examined my calculations please send the report to Bill Thompson. _____

10. Please send the report to Bill Thompson after you have examined my calculations. _____

11. Would you please after examining my calculations send the report to Bill Thompson. _____

12. Our personnel director is looking for intelligent articulate young people who desire an opportunity to grow with a young company. _____

13. Call me as soon as you return or drop me a card within the next week. _____

14. Beginning on the 15th of June Delco is slashing prices on house paints. _____

15. I mentioned to him at that time that we could not locate the monitor. _____

16. As soon as I can check the inventory we will place an order. _____

17. On October 25 the president and I visited Sandra Goodell who is president of Sandra Goodell Public Relations. _____

18. You may at your convenience submit a report describing when where and how we should proceed. _____

19. To begin the purchase process we will need your request by Thursday June 1 at the latest. _____

20. Any student who has not signed up for a team by this time must see the instructor. _____

Add necessary commas to the following sentences. For each sentence indicate the number of commas that you added. If a sentence is correct, write C.

1. Michael Ferrari Ph.D. has written another book on consumer buying. _____

2. In 2001 our company expanded its marketing to include the United Kingdom. _____

3. By 2002 12 of our competitors were also selling in Great Britain. _____

4. In 1998 our staff numbered 87; in 2002 103. _____

5. It was a large manila envelope not a white folder in which the contract was placed. _____

6. Long before our president conducted his own research into marketing trends among youthful consumers. (Tricky!) _____

7. "We prefer not to include your name" said the auditor "when we publish the list of inactive accounts." _____

8. You may sign your name at the bottom of this sheet and return it to us as acknowledgment of this letter. _____

9. The provisions of your Policy No. 85000611 should be reviewed every five years. _____

10. Irving Feinstein M.D. will be the speaker at our next meeting. _____

11. Dr. Feinstein received both an M.D. and a Ph.D. from Northwestern University. _____

12. Ever since we have been very careful to count the number of boxes in each shipment. _____

13. Mrs. Birdsall said "Charges are payable whether or not we installed the instrument." _____

14. Did you say it was Mr. Samuels not Mrs. Lambert who made the sale? _____

15. Ten computers were sold in January; nine in February. _____

16. Our figures show that 17365000 separate rental units were occupied in September. _____

17. "The function of a supervisor" remarked Sid Stern "is to analyze results not to try to control how the job is done." _____

18. By the way it was the president not the vice president who ordered the cutback. _____

19. "A diamond" said the therapist "is a chunk of coal that made good under pressure." _____

20. Whoever signs signs at her own risk. _____

Name _____

Level I

Punctuate the following groups of words as single sentences. Add commas and semicolons. Do not add words or periods to create new sentences.

Example: Come in to see our new branch office, meet our friendly tellers and manager.

1. Our principal function is to help management make profits however we can offer advice on personnel problems as well.

2. Delegates came from as far as Brownsville Texas Seattle Washington and Bangor Maine.

3. Jerry looked up names Andrea addressed envelopes and Janelle stuffed the envelopes.

4. Thank you for your order it will be filled immediately.

5. Employees often complain about lack of parking space on the other hand little interest was shown in a proposed carpooling program.

6. Computers are remarkable however they are only as accurate as the people who program them.

7. This sale is not open to the general public we are opening the store to preferred customers only.

8. Some of the employees being promoted are Jill Roberts secretary Legal Department Lea Lim clerk Human Resources and Mark Cameron dispatcher Transportation Department.

9. We will be happy to cooperate with you and your lawyers in settling the estate however several matters must be reviewed.

10. In the morning I am free at 10 a.m. in the afternoon I have already scheduled an appointment.

11. The book was recently selected for a national award thus its sales are soaring.

12. Look over our catalog fill out your order and send it in the enclosed envelope.

13. We hope that we will not have to sell the property but that may be our only option.

14. The film that you requested is now being shown to law students in Michigan it will be shown during June in California and it will be used during July and August in the states of Florida and North Carolina.

15. We do not sell airline seats we sell customer service.

16. Our convention committee is considering the Hyatt Regency Hotel Columbus Ohio Plaza of the Americas Hotel Dallas Texas and the Brown Palace Hotel Denver Colorado.

17. As requested the committee will meet Thursday May 4 however it is unable to meet Friday May 5.

18. Market research involves the systematic gathering recording and analyzing of data.

Add colons, semicolons, or commas to the following sentences. Do not add words or periods. Write *C* after the sentence if it is correct.

1. Three phases of our business operation must be scrutinized purchasing, production, and shipping.

2. The candidates being considered for supervisor are Ned Bingham, Sean Davis, and Anna Donato.

3. George Steinbrenner, New York Yankees owner, said "I want this team to win. I'm obsessed with winning, with discipline, with achieving. That's what this country's all about."

4. Following are four dates reserved for counseling. Sign up soon.

   September 28   January 4

   September 30   January 6

5. At its next meeting the board of directors must make a critical decision should the chief executive officer be retained or replaced?

6. This year's seminar has been organized to give delegates an opportunity to exchange ideas, plans, techniques, and goals.

7. The three Cs of credit are the following character, capacity, and capital.

8. Our Boston tour package included visits to these interesting historical sites the House of Seven Gables, Bunker Hill, the Boston Tea Party Ship and Museum, and Paul Revere's home.

9. I recommend that you take at least three courses to develop your language arts skills Business English 31, Business Communication 32, and Report Writing 35.

10. The speaker said that "membership is voluntary" but that contributions would be greatly appreciated.

11. Several of the tax specialists on the panel were concerned with the same thought government spending continues to rise while taxes are being reduced.

12. For each individual the credit bureau keeps the following information on file income, housing status, employment record, and estimate of character.

13. Scholarships will be awarded to Jill Hofer Jeremy Stone and Carolena Garay.

14. Our favorite Colorado resort is noted for fly fishing, mountain biking, tennis, and hiking.

15. Our favorite Colorado resort is noted for the following fly-fishing, mountain biking, and hiking.

Add colons, semicolons, dashes, or commas as needed. If a word following a colon should not be capitalized, use a proofreading mark (/) to indicate lowercase. Show words to be capitalized with (═). Mark *C* if a sentence is correct as it stands.

1. There are three ways to make a credit check namely in person, by mail, or by telephone.

2. Please order the following supplies Cartridges, paper, and labels.

3. Although we are expanding our services we continue to do business according to our original philosophy that is we want to provide you with flexible and professional investment services on a highly personal basis.

4. Word processing specialists are taught this rule Never turn the power off at a work-station unless a document has been stored.

5. Dr. Ruglio's plane departed at 2 15 and should arrive at 6 45.

6. We invited Jeff, Kevin, Tony, and Tom but Tony was unable to come.

7. Three of our top executives namely Mr. Thomas, Mr. Wright, and Mrs. Stranahan are being transferred to the Milwaukee office.

8. On our list of recommended reading is *Investment an Introduction to Analysis*.

9. The library, as you are already aware, needs space for additional books, particularly in the nonfiction field and even greater space will be required within the next five years.

10. Our airline is improving service in several vital areas for example baggage handling, food service, and weather forecasts.

11. Julie Schumacher was hired by a brokerage house and given the title of "registered representative" that is she is able to buy and sell securities.

12. Professor Wilson listed five types of advertising Product, institutional, national, local, and corrective.

13. We considered only one location for our fall convention namely San Francisco.

14. Many important questions are yet to be asked concerning our program for instance how can we meet our competitor's low prices in the Southwest?

15. If possible, call him as soon as you return to the office but I doubt that he is still at his desk.

Name _____

Add any necessary punctuation to the following sentences. If a sentence is correct, write *C*.

1. Will you please send this c o d shipment as soon as possible

2. You did say the meeting is at 10 a m didn't you

3. Mr. Kephart is a C P A working for Berman, Inc

4. Do you know if Donald L Cullens Jr applied for the job

5. Help The door is jammed

6. Will you please Miss Juarez send your card today for your free gift

7. What a day this has been

8. Although most candidates had A A degrees two applicants had B A degrees

9. Our C E O and C F O normally make all budget decisions

10. Cynthia asked if invitations had been sent to Miss Tan Mr Roe and Ms Rich

11. All calls made before 9 a m E S T are billed at a reduced rate

12. Alan Bennett M D and Gina Caracas Ph D were our keynote speakers

13. Because Susanne typed 80 w p m she was hired as a word processing specialist for the EPA

14. We're expanding marketing efforts in Germany France and the U K

15. The C P U of this computer is made entirely of parts from the U S A

16. The sales representative did say that the price of the car was f o b Detroit didn't he

17. Would you please check Policy Nos 44657001 and 44657002 to see if each includes $50000 comprehensive coverage

18. Did you say the order was received at 5 p m P S T

19. Wow How much was the lottery prize

20. Do we need Z I P codes for packages sent to S A

Write *T* (true) or *F* (false) after the following statements.

1. In typewritten or simple word processing–generated material, a dash is formed by typing two successive underscores. _____

2. Parentheses are often used to enclose explanations, references, and directions. _____

3. Dashes must be avoided in business writing since they have no legitimate uses. _____

4. Question marks and exclamation points may be used to punctuate parenthetical statements (enclosed within parentheses) within other sentences. _____

5. If a comma falls at the same point where words enclosed by parentheses appear, the comma should follow the final parenthesis. _____

Write the letter of the correctly punctuated sentence in the blank provided.

6. (a) I am busy on all those dates—oh, perhaps October 18 is free. _____
   (b) I am busy on all those dates: oh, perhaps October 18 is free.
   (c) I am busy on all those dates, oh, perhaps October 18 is free.

7. (Deemphasize) _____
   (a) Directions for assembly, see page 15, are quite simple.
   (b) Directions for assembly—see page 15—are quite simple.
   (c) Directions for assembly (see page 15) are quite simple.

8. (a) Eat, sleep, and read: that's what I plan to do on my vacation. _____
   (b) Eat, sleep, and read—that's what I plan to do on my vacation.
   (c) Eat, sleep, and read, that's what I plan to do on my vacation.

9. (a) If the others can attend (May 21), could you make your report? _____
   (b) If the others can attend, (May 21) could you make your report?
   (c) If the others can attend (May 21) could you make your report?

10. (Normal emphasis) _____
    (a) Mrs. Hemphill (who is an excellent manager) may be promoted.
    (b) Mrs. Hemphill, who is an excellent manager, may be promoted.
    (c) Mrs. Hemphill—who is an excellent manager—may be promoted.

11. (a) "What is needed for learning is a humble mind." (Confucius) _____
    (b) "What is needed for learning is a humble mind.": Confucius
    (c) "What is needed for learning is a humble mind."—Confucius

12. (a) The due date is past (July 1;) however, your payment is welcome. _____
    (b) The due date is past; (July 1) however, your payment is welcome.
    (c) The due date is past (July 1); however, your payment is welcome.

13. (a) Only one person knows my password—Denise Powell, and I have confidence in _____
       her.
    (b) Only one person knows my password (Denise Powell), and I have confidence in
       her.
    (c) Only one person knows my password; Denise Powell, and I have confidence in
       her.

14. (Emphasize) _____
    (a) Our current mortgage rates: see page 10 of the enclosed booklet—are the lowest
       in years.
    (b) Our current mortgage rates (see page 10 of the enclosed booklet) are the lowest
       in years.
    (c) Our current mortgage rates—see page 10 of the enclosed booklet—are the lowest
       in years.

L e v e l   I I I

Write *T* (true) or *F* (false) for each of the following statements.

1. When the exact words of a speaker are repeated, double quotation marks are used to _____
   enclose the words.

2. To indicate a quotation within another quotation, single quotation marks (apostrophes _____
   on most keyboards) are used.

3. When a word is defined, its definition should be underscored. _____

4. The titles of books, magazines, newspapers, and other complete works published _____
   separately may be underscored or italicized.

5. The titles of chapters of books and magazine articles may be underscored or enclosed in quotation marks. _____

6. Periods and commas are always placed inside closing quotation marks. _____

7. Brackets are used when a writer inserts his or her own remarks inside a quotation. _____

8. The Latin word *sic* may be used to call attention to an error in quoted material. _____

9. Semicolons and colons are always placed outside closing quotation marks. _____

10. Question marks and exclamation points may be placed inside or outside closing quotation marks. _____

Write the letter of the correctly punctuated statement.

11. (a) "Jobs," said Mr. Steele, "will be plentiful this summer." _____
    (b) "Jobs, said Mr. Steele, will be plentiful this summer."
    (c) "Jobs", said Mr. Steele, "will be plentiful this summer."

12. (a) The manager said, "This memo is clearly marked Confidential." _____
    (b) The manager said, "This memo is clearly marked 'Confidential'."
    (c) The manager said, "This memo is clearly marked 'Confidential.'"

13. (a) A *chattel* is defined as a "piece of movable property." _____
    (b) A "chattel" is defined as a *piece of movable property*.
    (c) A "chattel" is defined as a "piece of movable property."

14. (a) Do you know who it was who said, "Forewarned is forearmed." _____
    (b) Do you know who it was who said, "Forewarned is forearmed"?
    (c) Do you know who it was who said, "Forewarned is forearmed."?

15. (a) "We warn all e-mail users to avoid messages that are 'flaming,'" said the CEO. _____
    (b) "We warn all e-mail users to avoid messages that are "flaming," said the CEO.
    (c) "We warn all e-mail users to avoid messages that are 'flaming'", said the CEO.

Complete Punctuation Review

Insert all necessary punctuation in the following sentences. Correct any incorrect punctuation. Do not break any sentences into two sentences.

1. Did you see the article entitled Soaring Salaries of C E O s that appeared in The New York Times

2. This years budget costs are much higher than last years, therefore I will approve overtime only on a case by case basis.

3. The S.E.C. has three new members Dr. Carla Chang Professor Mark Rousso and Robert Price Esq

4. Needless to say all contract bids must be received before 5 pm E S T

5. We formerly depended on fixed-rate not variable rate mortgages.

6. The following representatives have been invited Christine Lenski DataCom Industries, Mark Grant LaserPro, Inc., and Ivan Weiner Image Builders.

7. Last year we moved corporate headquarters to Orlando Florida but maintained production facilities in Atlanta.

8. (Quotation) Did Dr. Tran say We will have no class Friday.

9. Graduation ceremonies for BA candidates are at 11 am, graduation ceremonies for MBA candidates are at 2 pm.

10. As we previously discussed the reorganization will take effect on Monday August 8.

11. We feel however that the cars electrical system should be fully warranted for five years.

12. Will you please send copies of our annual report to Anna Golan and D A Rusterholz?

13. Although he had prepared carefully Mitchell feared that his presentation would bomb.

14. In the event of inclement weather we will close the base and notify the following radio stations KJOW KLOB and KOB-TV.

15. (Emphasize) Three excellent employees Gregorio Morales, Dawna Capps, and DaVonne Williams will be honored at a ceremony Friday June 5.

16. (Quotation) "Your attitude not your aptitude will determine your altitude, said Zig Ziglar.

17. By May 15 our goal is to sell 15 cars, by June 15 20 additional cars.

18. The full impact of the E P A ruling is being studied you will receive information as it becomes available.

19. If the fax comes in before 9 pm we can still meet our June 1 deadline.

20. Send the contract to Ms Courtney Worthy Administrative Assistant Globex Industries 7600 Normandale Boulevard Milwaukee WI 53202 as soon as possible.

21. (Deemphasize) Please return the amended budget proposal see page 2 for a summary of the report to the presidents office by Friday March 4.

22. Prospective entrepreneurs were told to read a Success magazine article entitled A Venture Expert's Advice.

23. Larry Zuckerman our former manager now has a similar position with I B M.

24. Employees are concerned primarily with three job issues namely wages, security, and working conditions.

25. As expected this years expenses have been heavy, consequently we may have to freeze hiring for the next six months.

Name _____

Level I

Write the letter of the group of words that is correctly capitalized.

1. (a) a case of german measles   (b) a case of German measles   _____
2. (a) in the field of marketing   (b) in the field of Marketing   _____
3. (a) the Hancock Building   (b) the Hancock building   _____
4. (a) for all Catholics and Protestants   (b) for all catholics and protestants   _____
5. (a) an order for china and crystal   (b) an order for China and crystal   _____
6. (a) both Master's and Doctor's degrees   (b) both master's and doctor's degrees   _____
7. (a) Oklahoma State   (b) Oklahoma state   _____
8. (a) a class in conversational French   (b) a class in Conversational French   _____
9. (a) a memo from our Sacramento Office   (b) a memo from our Sacramento office   _____
10. (a) a salad with French dressing   (b) a salad with french dressing   _____
11. (a) an irish setter   (b) an Irish setter   _____
12. (a) traffic in the big apple   (b) traffic in the Big Apple   _____
13. (a) the King Edward room   (b) the King Edward Room   _____
14. (a) a holiday on Memorial Day   (b) a holiday on Memorial day   _____
15. (a) the waters of Delaware bay   (b) the waters of Delaware Bay   _____

Use proofreading marks to capitalize (≡) or to show lowercase (/) letters in the following sentences.

16. Bob's Chevron Station is located on Speedway Avenue in the next County.

17. Many employees of the Meredith Corporation plan to participate in the Company's profit-sharing plan.

18. The federal trade commission has approved ITT's request for service to 21 Cities.

19. During the Winter I will enroll in management, business english, and accounting.

20. The American Association Of Nurses will open its annual meeting in the Pacific ballroom of the Regency hotel in San Francisco.

21. Our persian cat and russian wolfhound cohabit quite peacefully.

22. Last Summer my family and I visited epcot center in orlando.

23. The two companies signed a stipulation of interest agreement last april.

24. Interior designers recommended italian marble for the entry and spanish tiles for the patio.

25. A limousine will take guests from kansas city international airport directly to the alameda plaza hotel.

Write the letter of the group of words that is correctly capitalized.

1. (a) my uncle and my aunt   (b) my Uncle and my Aunt   _____

2. (a) Very sincerely yours,   (b) Very sincerely Yours,   _____

3. (a) Send it to Vice President Lee   (b) Send it to vice president Lee   _____

4. (a) Volume II, Page 37   (b) Volume II, page 37   _____

5. (a) located in western Indiana   (b) located in Western Indiana   _____

6. (a) stored in building 44   (b) stored in Building 44   _____

7. (a) within our Human Resources Department   (b) within our human resources department   _____

8. (a) the Federal Communications Commission   (b) the federal communications commission   _____

9. (a) in appendix III   (b) in Appendix III   _____

10. (a) heading South on Highway 5   (b) heading south on Highway 5   _____

11. (a) the book *Love and Will*   (b) the book *Love And Will*   _____

12. (a) both federal and state laws   (b) both Federal and State laws   _____

13. (a) Q-tips and kleenexes   (b) Q-Tips and Kleenexes   _____

14. (a) orders from Sales Director Ali   (b) orders from sales director Ali   _____

15. (a) a trip to the east coast   (b) a trip to the East Coast   _____

Use proofreading marks to capitalize (≡) or to show lowercase letters (/) in the following sentences.

16. We have a directive from Ruth Jones, Supervisor, Administrative Services Division.

17. The President of our Company gave an address entitled "Leadership: What Effective Managers do and how They do it."

18. Gina Schmidt, customer service representative, attended a convention in the east.

19. To reach my home, proceed north on highway 10 until you reach exit 7.

20. Mayor Bruno visited the governor in an attempt to increase the city's share of State funding.

21. The best article is "Does your training measure up?" by Leslie Brokaw.

22. John placed his ray-ban sunglasses on the formica counter.

23. Sue's Mother and Father were scheduled to leave on flight 37 from gate 6 at phoenix sky harbor international airport.

24. In April our data entry and data verification departments will be merged into the technical services division.

25. Taxicab, Bus, and Limousine service are available from the airport to the ritz-carlton hotel.

Write the letter of the group of words that is correctly capitalized.

1. (a) photographs sent from
       Venus to Earth
   (b) photographs sent from
       Venus to earth   _____

2. (a) a room marked "private"
   (b) a room marked "Private"   _____

3. (a) the Egyptian Room and the
       Sahara Room
   (b) the Egyptian room and the
       Sahara room   _____

4. (a) the finest production on earth
   (b) the finest production on Earth   _____

5. (a) from Senator-Elect Ross
   (b) from Senator-elect Ross   _____

6. (a) When, sir, are you free?
   (b) When, Sir, are you free?   _____

7. (a) some asian cultures
   (b) some Asian cultures   _____

8. (a) an envelope stamped"
       "confidential
   (b) an envelope stamped
       "Confidential"   _____

9. (a) our sales director, Joe Hines
   (b) our Sales Director, Joe Hines   _____

10. (a) to ex-President Bush
    (b) to Ex-President Bush   _____

Use proofreading marks to capitalize (≡) or to show lowercase (/) letters in the following sentences.

11. The check that was returned was stamped "Insufficient funds."

12. A paddleboat traveled south down the Mississippi river.

13. No one recognized ex-senator Thurston when he toured Napa valley.

14. We wonder, professor, if the gravity of Mars might be similar to that of earth.

15. The Organization's bylaws state: "On the third Monday of every month the Club's Treasurer will prepare the financial report."

16. The President of our Company has traveled to Pacific Rim Countries to expand foreign markets.

17. The secretary of state met with the president to discuss this country's National policy toward african nations.

18. Have you any sheets of bond paper left? only a few.

19. In malaysia we soon learned that moslems do not eat pork and that buddhists and hindus do not eat beef.

20. Although he was known as a "banker's banker," Mr. Lee specialized in Mortgage Financing.

Name _____

L e v e l   I

In the space provided, write the letter of the correctly expressed group of words.

1. (a) for 24 employees   (b) for twenty-four employees   _____
2. (a) only 9 pens left   (b) only nine pens left   _____
3. (a) twenty-five dollars   (b) $25   _____
4. (a) on the thirtieth of May   (b) on the 30th of May   _____
5. (a) it cost 20 cents   (b) it cost twenty cents   _____
6. (a) (military style) 5 April 2002   (b) April 5, 2002   _____
7. (a) $2.05, 85¢, and $5.00   (b) $2.05, $.85, and $5   _____
8. (a) we started at 9 a.m.   (b) we started at nine a.m.   _____
9. (a) 2 Highland Avenue   (b) Two Highland Avenue   _____
10. (a) 226 Sixth Street   (b) 226 6th Street   _____

Underline any errors in the expression of numbers in the following sentences. Write the correct forms.

11. 194 representatives were sent the price lists December 1st.   _____

12. 2 companies have moved their corporate offices to twenty-fifth avenue.   _____

13. Three of the least expensive items were priced at $5.00, $3.29, and 99 cents.   _____

14. If your payment of $100.00 is received before the 2 of the month, you will receive a discount.   _____

15. On February 1st the guidelines for all fifteen departments went into effect.   _____

16. Our office, formerly located at Two Ford Place, is now located at One Kent Avenue.   _____

17. Please call me at 815 611-9292, Ext. Three, before 4 p.m.   _____

18. On May 15th 2 performances will be given at two p.m. and eight p.m.   _____

19. 3 of our employees start at 8:00 a.m., and 5 start at 8:30 a.m.   _____

20. If reservations are made before the fifteenth of the month, the fare will be 204 dollars.   _____

21. Grossmont College offers a fifteen-hour training course that costs one hundred twenty-five dollars.   _____

22. Classes meet Monday through Thursday from 11:45 a.m. until one p.m.   _____

23. The Werners moved from 1762 Milburn Avenue to 140 East 14th Street.   _____

24. Lisa had only $.25 left after she purchased supplies for forty-four dollars.   _____

25. On the third of January and again on the 18th, our machine needed service.   _____

Write the letter of the correctly expressed group of words.

1. (a) for 82 students in 3 classes   (b) for 82 students in three classes   _____

2. (a) an interest period of ninety days   (b) an interest period of 90 days   _____

3. (a) over the past thirty years   (b) over the past 30 years   _____

4. (a) two 35-day contracts   (b) 2 35-day contracts   _____

5. (a) he is 45 years old   (b) he is forty-five years old   _____

6. (a) line three   (b) line 3   _____

7. (a) nearly 2.6 billion   (b) nearly 2,600,000,000   _____

8. (a) fifty 10-page pamphlets   (b) 50 10-page pamphlets   _____

9. (a) Lois Lamb, 65, and John Lamb, 66   (b) Lois Lamb, sixty-five, and John Lamb, sixty-six   _____

10. (a) exactly two years and seven months ago   (b) exactly 2 years and 7 months ago   _____

Underline any errors in the expression of numbers in the following sentences. Write the corrected form.

11. We have received 50 reservations over the past 14 days. _____

12. Tour guests will be transported in three thirty-five-passenger air-conditioned motor coaches throughout the fifteen-day excursion. _____

13. 53 of the corporations had operating budgets that exceeded one million dollars. _____

14. Only 10 telephones are available for the forty-eight employees in 5 offices. _____

15. Chapter eight in Volume two provides at least three references to pumps. _____

16. About 100 chairs are stored in Room Four, and another eight chairs are in Room 14. _____

17. We ordered two thirty-inch desks and three chairs. _____

18. Of the twenty requests we received, five were acted on immediately and three had to be tabled. _____

19. The 2 loans must be repaid within 90 days. _____

20. When she was 24 years old, Mrs. Markham supervised over 120 employees. _____

21. Only two of the 125 letters in the mass mailing were undeliverable. _____

22. Frank Morris, sixty-four, plans to retire in one year. _____

23. Linda Hannan and her fifteen-person company signed a three million dollar contract. _____

24. She purchased new equipment to beam fifty-two World Cup games from nine locations to forty million avid soccer fans in Pacific Rim countries. _____

25. The thirty-year mortgage carries an interest rate of eight percent. _____

Assume all the following phrases appear in complete sentences. Write the letter of the phrase that is appropriately expressed.

1. (a) the tank holds just 9 gallons   (b) the tank holds just nine gallons   _____

2. (a) only a three percent gain   (b) only a 3 percent gain   _____

3. (a) 4/5 of the voters   (b) four fifths of the voters   _____

4. (a) a 50% markup   (b) a 50 percent markup   _____

5. (a) a one-half share   (b) a one half share   _____

6. (a) a decline of .5 percent   (b) a decline of 0.5 percent   _____

7. (a) he placed 3d in the state   (b) he placed third in the state   _____

8. (a) in the nineteenth century   (b) in the 19th century   _____

9. (a) a 5-pound box of candy   (b) a five-pound box of candy   _____

10. (a) at least 95% of the stockholders   (b) at least 95 percent of the stockholders   _____

Underline any errors in the expression of numbers. Write the corrected form.

11. A No. Ten envelope actually measures four and a half by nine and a half inches.   _____

12. The two candidates in the 33d Congressional District waged hard-hitting campaigns.   _____

13. Tests show that the driver responded in less than seven two hundredths of a second.   _____

14. Great strides in communication technology have been made in the 20th century.   _____

15. The desk top measured thirty and three-fourths inches by sixty and a half inches.   _____

16. Payment must be received by the thirtieth to qualify for a three percent discount.   _____

17. Our office was moved about fifty blocks from 7th Street to 58th Street.   _____

18. Place the date of a business letter on line 13, which is two inches from the top edge of the paper.   _____

19. The computer weighs thirty-one pounds and is seventeen and a half inches wide.   _____

20. Appropriation measures must be passed by a 2/3 majority.   _____

21. She ordered a nine by twelve rug to cover two-thirds of the floor.   _____

22. After completing Form Ten Forty, the accountant submitted his bill for 800 dollars.   _____

23. By the year 2,005, women will represent forty-eight percent of the workforce.   _____

24. Nine different airlines carry over one hundred thousand passengers daily.   _____

25. The company car was filled with fifteen gallons of gasoline and one quart of oil.   _____

Chapter 1 Self-Help Answers

1. c 2. b 3. c 4. a 5. a 6. c 7. b 8. b 9. d 10. b 11. b

Chapter 2 Self-Help Answers

Worksheet 1

A. 2. substitutes for a noun *he she it* 3. shows action or joins words that describe the subject *jumps works is* 4. describes nouns or pronouns *tall soft five* 5. modifies verbs, adjectives, or other adverbs *hurriedly very nicely* 6. joins nouns and pronouns to the sentence *to for at* 7. connects words or groups of words *and but or* 8. shows strong feelings *Wow! Gosh! No!*
B. 1. pronoun 2. adv 3. verb 4. noun 5. conj 6. pronoun 7. verb 8. prep 9. adj 10. noun 11. prep 12. pronoun 13. interj 14. adj 15. noun 16. conj 17. noun 18. verb 19. adj 20. adj 21. noun 22. prep 23. adj 24. noun 25. pronoun 26. verb 27. adverb 28. conj 29. adj 30. adj 31. noun 32. verb 33. adv

Worksheet 2

1. pronoun 2. verb 3. noun 4. prep 5. noun 6. conj 7. adj 8. noun 9. verb 10. adv 11. verb 12. noun 13. interj. 14. verb 15. noun 16. adv 17. verb 18. pronoun 19. verb 20. verb 21. adj 22. noun 23. prep 24. noun 25. adj 26. adj 27. adj 28. noun 29. verb 30. conj 31. adj 32. conj 33. adj 34. conj 35. adj 36. noun 37. verb 38. verb 39. pronoun 40. adv 41. prep 42. adj 43. adj 44. adj 45. noun 46. noun 47. adv 48. verb 49. prep 50. adj 51. adj 52. noun 53. prep 54. adj 55. adj 56. adj. 57. noun

Chapter 3 Self-Help Answers

Worksheet 1

1. (S) one (V) sold 2. (S) speaker (V) made 3. (S) telephones (V) rang 4. (S) we (V) will hire 5. (S) team (V) built 6. (S) salespeople (V) received 7. (S) manager (V) will send. 8. (S) we (V) released 9. (S) one (V) was given 10. (S) computers (V) require 11. (S) Mr. Thomas (V) is 12. (S) copiers (V) are 13. (S) Mrs. Seymour (V) is 14. (S) Mr. Torres (V) has been 15. (S) offices (V) are

Worksheet 2

Answers will vary. 1. applauded 2. fell 3. honked 4. rang 5. ended 6. dropped 7. policy 8. letter 9. letter 10. him 11. the door 12. letters 13. good 14. manager 15. Mr. Jones 16. Mary 17. Mr. Smith 18. John 19–23. *Answers will vary.*

Worksheet 3

1. a 2. c 3. d 4. b 5. e 6. a 7. c 8. b 9. a 10. c 11. b 12. d 13. a 14. a 15. c 16. d 17. b 18. a 19. c 20. b

Chapter 4 Self-Help Answers

Level I

1. giraffes 2. feet 3. switches 4. Bushes 5. boxes 6. languages 7. faxes 8. sandwiches 9. income taxes 10. children 11. successes 12. values 13. dresses 14. branches 15. recommendations 16. women 17. mismatches 18. taxis 19. loaves 20. annexes 21. beliefs 22. Rosses 23. storms 24. ranches 25. Joneses 26. Chavezes 27. letters 28. businesses 29. computers 30. wishes

Level II

1. wharves 2. chiefs of police 3. 1980s 4. Wolfs 5. embargoes 6. L.V.N.s 7. size 10s 8. amts. 9. faculties 10. by-products 11. entries 12. lookers-on 13. companies 14. knives 15. courts-martial 16. A's 17. Shermans 18. memos 19. valleys 20. zeros 21. lives 22. yrs. 23. Murphys 24. runners-up 25. oz. 26. journeys 27. M.B.A.s 28. wolves 29. Kellys 30. minorities

Level III

1. data 2. theses 3. bacteria 4. Chinese 5. parentheses 6. the Miss Bundys 7. alumnae 8. Messrs. West and Turner 9. genera 10. news 11. pp. 12. ff. 13. larvae 14. Mmes. Smythe and Webb 15. memoranda or memorandums 16. are 17. is or are 18. formulas 19. analyses 20. is

Chapter 5 Self-Help Answers

Level I

Worksheet 1

1. students' books 2. company's office 3. children's toys 4. two months' rent 5. movie star's mansion 6. neighbors' feelings 7. pilot's landing 8. partners' agreement 9. Jeffrey's notebook 10. department's strengths 11. two years' time 12. people's customs 13. week's merger 14. bank's credit 15. citizens' savings 16. Canada's mountains 17. employer's requirements 18. all candidates' résumés 19. government's policies 20. both attorneys' fees

Worksheet 2

1. year's 2. drivers' 3. carpenter's 4. thief's 5. day's 6. employees' 7. CEO's 8. readers' 9. caller's 10. authors' 11. secretaries' 12. C 13. country's 14. months' 15. organization's 16. president's 17. family's 18. C 19. years' 20. farmer's 21. citizens' 22. year's 23. customer's 24. Children's 25. supervisor's

Level II

1. public's 2. company's 3. stationer's 4. The suggestions of my uncle's lawyer 5. desk top or top of the desk 6. aunt and uncle's 7. C 8. last month's 9. C 10. telephone number of the president's secretary 11. sales 12. C or beards of my two brothers-in-law 13. birds' 14. Rick's 15. England's 16. C 17. Clark and Clark's 18. Angeles 19. architects' 20. last year's 21. C 22. Diana and Jason's 23. reporters' 24. day's day's 25. C

Level III

1. someone else's 2. Ross' or Ross's 3. classes' 4. Saunders' or Saunders's 5. Rodriguezes' 6. Les' or Les's 7. boss's 8. bosses' 9. Horowitzes 10. actresses' 11. Harris' or Harris's

12. Burns' or Burns's 13. James' or James's 14. waitress's
15. Garveys' 16. Morrises' 17. Betz' or Betz's 18. Walkers'
19. Simons' or Simons's 20. Jones' or Jones's 21. White's
22. Williamses' 23. Kimballs

Chapter 6 Self-Help Answers

Level I

Worksheet 1

1–14. *Order of answers may vary.* 1–7. I, you, he, she, it, we,
they 8–14. me, you, him, her, it, us, them 15. I 16. she
17. he 18. they 19. she 20. we 21. she 22. he 23. she
24. he 25. I

Worksheet 2

1. me 2. him 3. them 4. me 5. her 6. him 7. her 8. them
9. us 10. me 11. it's 12. theirs 13. its 14. There's 15. hers
16. it's 17. yours 18. Whose 19. ours 20. You're

Level II

1. them 2. I 3. her 4. We 5. me 6. me 7. her 8. he 9. him
10. I 11. himself 12. her 13. her 14. she 15. me 16. us
17. she 18. him 19. I 20. me 21. me 22. She and I 23. her

Level III

Worksheet 1

1. she 2. he 3. they 4. she 5. him 6. she 7. she 8. he
9. me 10. they 11. he 12. him 13. her 14. I 15. she
16. she 17. I 18. him 19. I 20. she 21. he 22. him 23. she
24. she 25. he

Worksheet 2

1. he 2. me 3. its 4. she 5. us 6. there's 7. he 8. I 9. me
10. her 11. us 12. you're 13. her 14. him 15. yours 16. me
17. he 18. its 19. him or me 20. There's 21. him 22. me
23. I 24. their 25. she 26. I 27. me 28. us 29. she 30. there's

Chapter 7 Self-Help Answers

Level I

1. her 2. his or her 3. his or her 4. their 5. their 6. he or
she 7. his or her lunch 8. him or her 9. her 10. their pictures 11. her 12. his 13. Every employee must obtain his or
her . . . 14. Every employee must obtain a parking permit
. . . 15. All employees must obtain their parking permits. . . .

Level II

1. use *her* instead of *their* 2. *its* instead of *it's* 3. *his* or *her* instead of *their* 4. *his* or *her* for *his* 5. *his* for *their* 6. *her* for *their*
7. C 8. *its* for *their* 9. *its* for *their* 10. *him* or *her* for *them*
11. C 12. *his* or *her* for *their* 13. *his* or *her* for *their* 14. *his* or
her seat for *their seats.* 15. *its* for *their* 16. *its* for *their* 17. *them*
for *it* 18. *his* for *their* 19. *her* for *their* 20. *they* for *she* or *he*

Level III

Worksheet 1

1. Whom 2. whom 3. who 4. whom 5. whom 6. whom
7. Who 8. Whom 9. Who 10. who 11. who 12. who 13.
whom 14. who 15. Who

Worksheet 2

1. whoever 2. whoever 3. whomever 4. whomever 5. whoever 6. whoever 7. whoever 8. Whoever 9. whoever 10.
Whoever 11. Who 12. who 13. who 14. whoever 15.
whom

Worksheet 3

1. Whom 2. who 3. whom 4. whoever 5. whom 6. whom
7. Whoever 8. who 9. who 10. who 11. whom 12. whom
13. Who 14. Whom 15. whomever 16. whom 17. Whoever
18. whom 19. whom 20. whom 21. whom 22. who 23.
whoever 24. who

Chapter 8 Self-Help Answers

Level I

1. transitive 2. intransitive 3. linking 4. complements 5. I
6. L—Fran 7. T—cards 8. I 9. L—lifeguard 10. T—pants
11. T—checks 12. L—better 13. L—he 14. I 15. T—questions 16. T—gifts 17. L—best 18. I 19. L—justified 20. T—
expectations

Level II

Worksheet 1

1. mail carrier 2. Mattel 3. Mrs. Bradford 4. Mr. Stern
5. management

Worksheet 2

Answers may vary. 1. clerks 2. Mr. Smith 3. John 4. judges
5. manufacturers 6. we 7. management 8. we

LEVEL III

1. were 2. be 3. was 4. be 5. would 6. be 7. were 8. be
9. rest 10. were 11. were 12. be 13. was 14. meet 15. were
16. be 17. were 18. was 19. were 20. be

Chapter 9 Self-Help Answers

LEVEL I

1. is 2. occurred 3. is 4. is 5. is 6. plan 7. will sell 8. supplied 9. studies 10. will analyze 11. applied 12. considered
13. varies 14. insists 15. will appeal 16. requires 17. will demand

Level II

Worksheet 1

1. become 2. froze 3. hid 4. chosen 5. built 6. drunk 7. forgotten or forgot 8. given 9. gone 10. bitten 11. eaten
12. sang 13. C or struck 14. sprang 15. shaken 16. worn
17. written 18. stolen 19. taken 20. gone

Worksheet 2

1. laid 2. lie 3. lying 4. laid 5. laying 6. lie 7. lay 8. Lay
9. lain 10. lie 11. lie 12. lying 13. lie 14. lay 15. lain
16. lay 17. lying 18. lie 19. laid 20. laying

Level III

1. has opened 2. is planning 3. had called 4. has worked
5. were seeing 6. will be signing 7. had been broken

8. have seen **9.** are considering **10.** was being heard **11.** rung **12.** drank **13.** choose **14.** driven **15.** saw **16.** gone **17.** saw **18.** eaten **19.** written **20.** rose

Chapter 10 Self-Help Answers

Level I

Worksheet 1

1. provide **2.** is **3.** comes **4.** think **5.** is **6.** was **7.** is **8.** needs **9.** has **10.** are **11.** is **12.** are **13.** have **14.** are **15.** sounds **16.** was **17.** is **18.** are **19.** have **20.** was

Worksheet 2

1. travels **2.** are **3.** is **4.** are **5.** appear **6.** are **7.** was **8.** is **9.** are **10.** is **11.** has **12.** provide **13.** Has **14.** is **15.** is **16.** has **17.** appears.

Level II

1. is **2.** has **3.** deserves **4.** is **5.** is **6.** is **7.** were **8.** mention **9.** merits **10.** every one **11.** are **12.** has **13.** belongs **14.** is **15.** is **16.** has **17.** Were **18.** has **19.** have **20.** is

Level III

1. has **2.** is **3.** enjoy **4.** was **5.** was **6.** is **7.** favor **8.** are **9.** are **10.** am **11.** is **12.** is **13.** like **14.** are **15.** is **16.** need **17.** were **18.** are **19.** complain **20.** has

Chapter 11 Self-Help Answers

Level I

1. your **2.** his **3.** Mr. Cortina's **4.** our **5.** Mr. Frank's **6.** C **7.** your criticizing **8.** your calling **9.** Mr. Davidson's **10.** our faxing **11.** C **12.** my working **13.** C

Level II

1. While preparing the report **2.** Surrounded **3.** seeing his opportunity **4.** installed just two months ago **5.** rereading the article several times **6.** Opening a new account **7.** Irritated **8.** opening a new account **9.** model, **10.** Dallas, stockbroker, **11.** C **12.** transactions, **13.** C **14.** Sanderson, firm, **15.** behalf,

Level III

1. b **2.** b **3.** a **4.** b **5.** b **6.** a **7.** b
8. Completing the examination in only 20 minutes, Maria earned a perfect score.
9. To locate the members' names and addresses, we used a current directory.
10. Driving through the desert, we thought the highway seemed endless.
11. To stay in touch with customers, sales representatives made telephone contacts.
12. Addressing an audience for the first time, I felt my knees shake and my voice wobble.

Chapter 12 Self-Help Answers

Level I

1. more effective **2.** worst **3.** friendlier or more friendly **4.** least certain **5.** more beautiful **6.** fastest **7.** better **8.** noisiest **9.** quieter **10.** most sincere **11.** most skilled **12.** least

13. slower or more slowly **14.** more likely **15.** most unusual **16.** fewer **17.** better **18.** more credible **19.** worst **20.** least

Level II

1. loudly **2.** C **3.** C **4.** Fewer **5.** more quietly **6.** bad **7.** conflict-of-interest **8.** C **9.** C **10.** latter **11.** well **12.** satisfactorily **13.** house to house **14.** C **15.** surely **16.** quietly **17.** really **18.** charge account **19.** not-too-distant **20.** fewer

Level III

1. b **2.** b **3.** a **4.** b **5.** a **6.** a **7.** a **8.** a **9.** neatly **10.** well (for *good*) **11.** C **12.** recently enacted **13.** worst (for *worse*) **14.** an (for *a*) **15.** had hardly **16.** round-the-world **17.** bad (for *badly*) **18.** fewer people **19.** said only **20.** an 840-acre

Chapter 13 Self-Help Answers

Level I

1. should have (for *should of*) **2.** him (for *he*) **3.** C **4.** me (for *I*) **5.** from (for *off of*) **6.** to (for *too*) **7.** her (for *she*) **8.** could have (for *could of*) **9.** too (for *to*) **10.** him (for *he*) **11.** from (for *off*) **12.** him (for *he*) **13.** from (for *off of*) **14.** C **15.** him (for *he*) **16.** too (for *to*) **17.** could have (for *could of*) **18.** C **19.** could have (for *could of*) **20.** me (for *I*)

Level II

1. besides (for *beside*) **2.** support of **3.** omit *with* **4.** in to (for *into*) **5.** inside the office **6.** among (for *between*) **7.** as (for *like*) **8.** C **9.** type of software **10.** into (for *in to*) **11.** C **12.** concern for **13.** omit *at* **14.** C **15.** omit *from* **16.** omit *up* **17.** style *of* **18.** going *in to* meet **19.** omit *to* **20.** graduated *from*

Level III

1. b **2.** a **3.** b **4.** b **5.** b **6.** a **7.** b **8.** a **9.** b **10.** b **11.** a **12.** a **13.** b **14.** b **15.** a **16.** a **17.** b **18.** b **19.** a **20.** b

Chapter 14 Self-Help Answers

Level I

The order of Answers 1–4 may vary. **1.** and **2.** or **3.** nor **4.** but **5.** b **6.** a **7.** b **8.** a **9.** a **10.** b **11.** a **12.** b **13.** b **14.** b **15.** a

Level II

Answers may vary. **1.** therefore, however, consequently, moreover, then, hence **2.** semicolon **3.** commas **4.** planning, nevertheless, **5.** occupancy; that is, **6.** organization, on the other hand, **7.** 6 p.m.; hence **8.** shelves; however, **9.** York; then **10.** has, consequently, **11.** organization; consequently, **12.** graduate, on the other hand, **13.** are, nevertheless, **14.** year; on the other hand, **15.** competitive; however, **16.** candidates, consequently, **17.** résumés; consequently, **18.** letter; hence **19.** done; however, **20.** information; however,

Level III

1. b **2.** b **3.** a **4.** b
5. You can either fax your response or send an e-mail message.
6. Our goals are both to educate motorists and also to save their lives.
7. Tony has neither a job interview nor even an interview lined up.
8. We knew that we had to either raise more money or begin selling stock.

Chapter 15 Self-Help Answers

Level I

1. T **2.** T **3.** T **4.** T **5.** F **6.** P **7.** D **8.** I **9.** P **10.** D **11.** I
12. D **13.** I **14.** D **15.** P **16.** I **17.** D **18.** I **19.** D **20.** I **21.** P
22. I **23.** D **24.** D **25.** I

Level II

1. suggestions, **2.** will, if you follow my suggestions, **3.** C
4. completed, **5.** C **6.** C **7.** booklet, which was submitted
over six weeks ago, **8.** know, **9.** payments, provided there is
no interruption in profits, **10.** necessary, **11.** C **12.** Gilroy,
who volunteered to head the program, **13.** C **14.** order,
15. C **16.** charged, which amounted to $176.12, **17.** expected,
18. days, **19.** contract, **20.** C

Level III

1. Although never signed, the original agreement was drawn
between Mr. Hightower and Columbia Communications.
2. Atlantic Insurance Company, which is a company of people
rather than statistics, serves not only individuals but also
communities.
3. Thank you for informing us that your credit card, which
has an expiration date of April 30, is missing.
4. Because your account is four months past due, we will be
forced to take legal action unless we hear from you within
seven days.
5. Sally, who works as secretary to the manager in the
Quality Control Department, won an award as this month's
outstanding employee.
6. Although the Federal National Mortgage Association does
not make loans directly to consumers, it helps supply money
to the home mortgage industry.
7. We are sending you four poster advertisements that will
appear in magazines in April, which marks the beginning of a
national campaign featuring our sports clothes.
8. Mr. Girard, who has worked at Rocketwell for 37 years,
plans to retire at the end of this year and spend more time
with his orchid collection.

Chapter 16 Self-Help Answers

Level I

1. (2) insurance, Mr. Nelson, **2.** (1) By the way, **3.** (2) resolved, however, **4.** (2) Ames, Iowa, **5.** C **6.** (2) plan, on the
other hand, **7.** (4) Data Products, 750 Grant Road, Tucson,
Arizona 85703, **8.** (2) appears, sir, **9.** (2) Friday, April 30,
10. (2) Molloy, who is an advertising executive, **11.** C **12.** C
13. (2) will, in addition, **14.** (2) umbrellas, pens, **15.** (1) considered, **16.** (2) Hudson, who is a specialist in information
systems, **17.** (2) patent, trademark, **18.** (2) convinced, incidentally, **19.** (2) policy, budget, **20.** C

Level II

1. (1) practical, **2.** (1) months, **3.** (2) Meyer, employees,
4. (1) week, **5.** C **6.** (2) appreciate, often, **7.** C **8.** C **9.** (1)
calculations, **10.** C **11.** (2) please, calculations, **12.** (1) intelligent, **13.** (1) return, **14.** (1) June, **15.** C **16.** (1) inventory,
17. (1) Goodell, **18.** (2) when, where, **19.** (3) process,
Thursday, June 1, **20.** C

Level III

1. (2) Ferrari, Ph.D., **2.** C **3.** (1) 1997, **4.** (1) 2002, **5.** (2)
envelope, not a white folder, **6.** (1) before, **7.** (2) name," said
the auditor, **8.** C **9.** C **10.** (2) Feinstein, M.D., **11.** C **12.** (1)
since, **13.** (1) said, **14.** (2) Samuels, not Mrs. Lambert,
15. (1) nine, **16.** (2) 17, 365,000 **17.** (3) supervisor," remarked Sid Stern, results, **18.** (3) way, president, vice president, **19.** (2) diamond," said the therapist, **20.** (1) signs, signs

Chapter 17 Self-Help Answers

Level I

1. profits; however, **2.** Brownsville, Texas; Seattle,
Washington; and Bangor, **3.** names, envelopes, **4.** order;
5. space; on the other hand, **6.** remarkable; however, **7.** public; **8.** Roberts, secretary, Legal Department; Lea Lim, clerk,
Human Resources; and Mark Cameron, dispatcher, **9.** estate;
however, **10.** 10 a.m.; **11.** award; **12.** catalog, order,
13. property, **14.** Michigan; California; **15.** seats; **16.** Hyatt
Regency Hotel, Columbus, Ohio; Plaza of the Americas Hotel,
Dallas, Texas; and the Brown Palace Hotel, Denver, Colorado
17. requested, Thursday, May 4; however, Friday, **18.** gathering, recording,

Level II

1. scrutinized: **2.** C **3.** said: **4.** C **5.** decision: **6.** C **7.** following: **8.** sites: **9.** skills: **10.** C **11.** thought: **12.** file: **13.** Hofer,
Stone, **14.** C **15.** following:

Level III

1. check; namely, **2.** supplies: cartridges **3.** services, philosophy; that is, **4.** rule: **5.** 2:15 6:45 **6.** Tom; **7.** executives—
namely, Mr. Thomas, Mr. Wright, and Mrs. Stranahan—
8. Investment: An **9.** field; **10.** areas; for example, **11.** representative"; that is, **12.** advertising: product **13.** convention,
namely, **14.** program; for instance, **15.** office;

Chapter 18 Self-Help Answers

Level I

1. c.o.d. possible. **2.** 10 a.m., didn't you? **3.** CPA Inc.
4. Donald L. Cullens Jr. job? **5.** Help! jammed! **6.** please,
Miss Juarez, gift. **7.** been! **8.** A.A. degrees, B.A. degrees.
9. CEO and CFO decisions. **10.** Tan, Mr. Roe, and Ms. Rich.
11. 9 a.m. EST rate. **12.** Bennett, M.D., Caracas, Ph.D., speakers. **13.** 80 wpm, EPA. **14.** Germany, France, and the U.K.
15. CPU U.S.A. **16.** f.o.b. Detroit, didn't he? **17.** Nos. $50,000
coverage. **18.** 5 p.m. PST? **19.** Wow! prize? **20.** ZIP S.A.?

Level II

1. F (use two hyphens) **2.** T **3.** F **4.** T **5.** T **6.** a **7.** c **8.** b
9. a **10.** b **11.** c **12.** c **13.** b **14.** c

Level III

1. T **2.** T **3.** F **4.** T. **5.** F **6.** T **7.** T **8.** T **9.** T **10.** T **11.** a
12. c **13.** a **14.** b **15.** a

Complete Punctuation Review

1. "Soaring Salaries of CEOs" The New York Times? **2.** This
year's last year's; therefore, case-by-case **3.** SEC members: Dr.
Carla Chang, Professor Mark Rousso, and Robert Price, Esq.

4. say, 5 p.m. EST. 5. fixed-rate, not variable-rate, 6. invited: Christine Lenski, DataCom Industries; Mark Grant, LaserPro, Inc.; and Ivan Weiner, 7. Orlando, Florida, 8. say, "We Friday"? 9. B.A. 11 a.m.; M.B.A. 2 p.m. 10. discussed, Monday, August 8. 11. feel, however, car's 12. D. A. Rusterholz. 13. carefully, "bomb." 14. weather, stations: KJOW, KLOB, and KOB-TV. 15. employees—Gregorio Williams— Friday, June 5. 16. attitude, aptitude, altitude," 17. cars; by June 15, 18. EPA studied; 19. 9 p.m., 20. Ms. Courtney Worthy, Administrative Assistant, Globex Industries, 7600 Normandale Boulevard, Milwaukee, WI 53202, 21. (see page 2 for a summary of the report) to the president's Friday, 22. Success "A Venture Expert's Advice." 23. Zuckerman, our former manager, IBM. 24. issues; namely, 25. expected, this year's heavy; consequently,

Chapter 19 Self-Help Answers

Level I

1. b 2. a 3. a 4. a 5. a 6. b 7. a 8. a 9. b 10. a 11. b 12. b 13. b 14. a 15. b 16. station county 17. company's 18. Federal Trade Commission cities 19. winter English 20. of Ballroom Hotel 21. Persian Russian 22. summer Epcot Center Orlando 23. Stipulation of Interest Agreement April 24. Italian Spanish 25. Kansas City International Airport Alameda Plaza Hotel

Level II

1. a 2. a 3. a 4. b 5. a 6. b 7. a 8. a 9. b 10. b 11. a 12. a 13. b 14. a 15. b 16. supervisor 17. president company Do How Do It 18. East 19. Highway Exit 20. Governor state 21. "Does Your Training Measure Up?" 22. Ray-Ban Formica 23. mother and father Flight 37 Gate 6 Phoenix Sky Harbor International Airport 24. Data Entry and Data Verification Departments Technical Services Division 25. bus limousine Ritz-Carlton Hotel

Level III

1. a 2. b 3. a 4. a 5. b 6. a 7. b 8. b 9. a 10. a 11. Funds 12. River 13. Senator Valley 14. Professor Earth 15. organization's 16. president company countries 17. national African 18. Only 19. Malaysia Moslems Buddhists Hindus 20. mortgage financing

Chapter 20 Self-Help Answers

Level I

1. a 2. b 3. b 4. b 5. a 6. a 7. b 8. a 9. a 10. a 11. A total of 194 December 1 12. Two 25th Avenue 13. $5 $.99 14. $100 2d 15. February 1 15 departments. 16. 2 Ford Place 17. (815) 611-9292, Ext. 3 or 805-611-9292, Ext. 3 18. May 15 two 2 p.m. 8 p.m. 19. Three 8 a.m. five 20. 15th $204 21. 15-hour $125 22. 1 p.m. 23. 14 24. 25 cents $44 25. 3d

Level II

1. b 2. b (preferred) 3. a 4. a 5. b 6. b 7. a 8. a 9. a 10. b 11. fourteen 12. three 35-passenger 13. Fifty-three $1 million 14. ten 48 five 15. Chapter 8 Volume 2 16. Room 4

8 chairs 17. 30-inch 18. 20 requests 5 3 19. two loans 20. twenty-four years 21. Only 2 22. 64 23. 15-person $3 million 24. 52 40 million 25. thirty-year or 30-year 8 percent

Level III

1. a 2. b 3. b 4. b 5. a 6. b 7. b 8. a 9. a 10. b 11. No. 10 4 1/2 by 9 1/2 inches 12. Thirty-third 13. 7/200 14. twentieth 15. 30 3/4 inches by 60 1/2 inches 16. 30th 3 percent 17. 50 blocks Seventh 18. 2 inches 19. 31 pounds 17 1/2 inches 20. two-thirds 21. 9 by 12 two thirds 22. Form 1040 $800 23. 2005 48 percent 24. 100,000 25. 15 gallons 1 quart

Answers to Unit Reviews

Unit 1 Review (Chapters 1–3)

1. F 2. T 3. F 4. F 5. T 6. F 7. T 8. F 9. T 10. T 11. b 12. c 13. d 14. b 15. a 16. c 17. b 18. a 19. c 20. a 21. b 22. c 23. a 24. b 25. d 26. c 27. a or b 28. e 29. b 30. c 31. a or b 32. d 33. e 34. b 35. a or b 36. c 37. a 38. b 39. b 40. c

Unit 2 Review (Chapters 4–7)

1. a 2. b 3.b 4. c 5. a 6. b 7. b 8. a 9. b 10. d 11. c 12. a 13. c 14. b 15. a 16. b 17. a 18. b 19. a 20. b 21. c 22. b 23. b 24. b 25. d 26. b 27. a or b 28. a 29. b 30. b 31. a 32. a 33. b 34. b 35. b 36. b 37. a 38. a 39. b 40. b

Unit 3 Review (Chapters 8–11)

1. c 2. c 3. a 4. b 5. a 6. a 7. b 8. a 9. a 10. a 11. a 12. b 13. a 14. b 15. b 16. a 17. b 18. b 19. b 20. a 21. a 22. 2 23. 0 24. 1 25. b 26. a 27. a 28. b 29. b 30. a 31. b 32. b 33. b 34. a 35. a 36. b 37. a 38. b 39. b 40. b

Unit 4 Review (Chapters 12–15)

1. a 2. b 3. b 4. a 5. b 6. a 7. b 8. c 9. (0) 10. (1) office, 11. (0) 12. (1) résumé, 13. a 14. a 15. b 16. a 17. a 18. a 19. (2) success; consequently, 20. (1) search, 21. (0) 22. (1) Caracas, 23. (1) reported, 24. (2) believes, however, 25. a 26. b 27. a 28. b 29. a 30. (1) impression, 31. (1) week, 32. (0) 33. (2) markedly; moreover, 34. (1) bodyguards, 35. (2) earth; however, 36. b 37. a 38. b 39. a 40. b

Unit 5 Review (Chapters 16–18)

1. (2) service, Ms. Chitwood, 2. C 3. (2) recruiting, hiring, 4. C 5. (2) feels, on the other hand, 6. C 7. c 8. b 9. a 10. a 11. b 12. a 13. c 14. a 15. a 16. b 17. a 18. c 19. a 20. c 21. c 22. a 23. b 24. b 25. b 26. c 27. b 28. c 29. c 30. b 31. b 32. b 33. a 34. a 35. b

Unit 6 Review (Chapters 19–20)

1. b 2. b 3. b 4. a 5. b 6. a 7. b 8. a 9. b 10. (3) Twenty stereos $25 11. (1) marketing 12. (3) 2,000 fall October 10 13. b 14. a 15. a 16. a 17. b 18. a 19. a 20. b 21. a 22. (5) Big Mac Coca-Cola $2. 75 23. (6) 2 vice presidents 3 managers Coast 24. (1) Manager 25. a 26. b 27. b 28. b 29. a 30. a 31. b 32. b 33. a 34. b 35. b 36. b 37. b 38. b 39. a 40. b

Index

Hyphenation
  compound adjectives and, 214
  of fractions, 378
  of *non-*, 269, 364
  of numbers, 380
  prefixes and, 269
  reference manuals and, 9
  of telephone numbers, 375
  of *thank you*, 35
  trends in, 131
  troublesome, 217

I

Idioms, 233
i.e., e.g., 187
if and *wish* clauses, and subjunctive verb
  forms, 130
impact, 56
Imperative mood. *See* Verbs/moods
imply, infer, 380
in, into, 231
Inclusive language, 169
Indefinite adjectives, 295
Indefinite pronouns, 88, 103–104
Independent clauses. *See also* Clauses, in-
  dependent and dependent
  use of semicolon with, 312, 315
  using commas with, 296
Indicative mood. *See* Verbs, moods
Infinitives, 87, 182–183
Inflected forms, 6
Inside address, 421
Interjections, 20
Internet, dictionaries on, 7–8. *See also* Hot
  links
Interrogatives. *See* Questions
Intransitive verbs. *See* Verbs,
  Intransitive/Transitive
Introductory clauses
  dependent, 264
  using commas with, 296
Introductory verbal phrases
  and avoiding misplaced modifiers,
    185–186
  using commas with, 296
Italics (underscores), 333, 335
its, it's, 150

K

Key words, 204

L

Labels, in dictionary entries, 6
later, latter, 269
less, fewer, 108
Lettered items, capitalization of, 361
Letterhead, 419
Letters. *See* Business letters
lie, lay, 127, 146–147, 150, 269
life-style, 235
like, 232, 336
Linking verbs, 30, 128–129
Lists
  punctuation in, 317

use of colon with, 313
lose, loose, 381

M

Management and Technology Dictionary
  (online), 7
many a, 105
marshal, martial, 268
maybe, may be, 250
may/can, 131
Measures, 167
Memos, 283–285, 428–430
Merriam Webster Online (CD-ROM), 4, 7
*Merriam-Webster's Collegiate Dictionary,
  Tenth Edition,* 4
*Merriam-Webster's New International
  Dictionary,* 4
Merriam Webster's word of the day hot
  link, 5
Microsoft Encarta World English
  Dictionary (CD-ROM), 7
Mnemonics, 399–400
Modern Language Association Style Manual,
  71
Modifiers
  absolute, 216
  adjectives as articles, 212
  adverbs and double negatives,
    212–213
  misplaced, 185–186
  this/that, these/those, 213
Money, expressing in numbers, 374, 380
Moods. *See* Verbs, moods
Motions, and subjunctive verb forms,
  · 130
Ms., 250

N

Namers. *See* Nouns
Names, line-ending decisions and,
  250
Nominative case, 84, 86–87, 88, 107
non-, 269, 364
none, 169
Nonessential clauses
  using commas with, 297
  using parentheses with, 331–332
Noun markers, 18
Nouns, 18. *See also* Proper nouns
  animate *vs.* inanimate, 69
  collective, 105, 167
  common and proper, 51
  compound, 70
  concrete and abstract, 51
  descriptive *vs.* possessive, 70
  plurals, 52–56
  possessive, 67–82
  Purdue University Online Writing Lab
    hot link, 31
Number
  agreement and, 102–103
  for personal pronouns, 84, 102
Numbers
  a vs. the and, 167
  capitalization of numbered items, 361

and reference manuals, 9, 374–380
  use of period in, 329
  using commas with, 297–298

O

Objective case, 84, 230
Omission of words, using commas with,
  298
OneLook Dictionaries (online), 7
online, on-line, 21
On-Line English Grammar hot link
  (verbs), 149
Online writing labs (OWLs), 26
or, nor, 104, 166
Ordinals, expressing in figures, 379–380
Organization names, capitalization of,
  358–359, 361
Oxford English Dictionary, 4
Oxford English Dictionary, 2nd ed. (CD-
  ROM), 4

P

Paragraphs, writing effective, 203
Parallel construction, 206, 248–249
Parentheses
  use of dashes with parenthetical ex-
    pressions, 315, 330–331
  uses for, 331–332
  using commas with parenthetical ex-
    pressions, 294
Participles. *See* Tense, present and past
  participles
Parts of speech, 18–20. *See* individual
  parts
Passive voice. *See* Verbs, active/passive
  voice
Past tense, 142–143, 149
Percents
  expressing in figures, 379
  use of hyphen in, 217
Perfect tense, 148–149
Period
  placement of, 334, 335
  uses for, 328–329
Person, 84
personal, personnel, 235
Personal pronouns
  appositives, 86
  comparatives, 86
  compound subjects and objects, 85
  nominative case, 84, 86–87, 88
  objective case, 84–85, 88
  possessive case, 85, 88
  reflexives, 86
Phrases
  distinguishing from clauses, 246
  positioning, 185–186
  prepositional, 128
  as subjects, 168
Plurals. *See* Nouns, plurals
Pocket dictionary, 4
Portions, verb-subject agreement with,
  167–168, 169
Possessive constructions
  apostrophes and, 68–69

Time, expressing in numbers, 375, 376–377
Titles
  literary and artistic, 362
  of people, 359–361, 363, 364
  and subtitles, 316
  use of quotation marks with, 333
to, too, 89, 231
to be, 87
to line, on e-mail message, 430
Topic sentences, 203–204
toward, towards, 22
Transitional expressions, 205, 247
Transitive verbs. *See* Verbs, transitive/intransitive

U

Unabridged dictionary, 4
under, hyphenation of, 73
Underscores, 333, 335
usage, 381
Usage labels, in dictionaries, 6
Utah Valley State College On-line Writing Lab hot link, 105

V

Verbals
  gerunds, 182
  infinitives, 182–183
  misplaced modifiers and, 185–186
  participles, 183–184
  punctuation of, 184–185
Verbs
  action, 18
  active/passive voice, 129
  helping (auxiliary), 143
  irregular, 144–148
  linking, 128–129
  moods, 130
  On-Line English Grammar hot link, 149
  and subject and verb agreement, 163–169
  tense (*See* Tense)
  transitive/intransitive, 127–128
  University of Ottawa hot link, 127
Vocabulary skills, developing, 409–417
Voice. *See* Verbs, active and passive voice
Voice of tact, 129

W

Weights, expressing in figures, 378
who, which, that, 265, 266
who, whom, 106–107, 108
who clauses, 168
whoever, whomever, 107, 317
-wide, 235
-wise, 35
Wordiness, avoiding, 120–122

X

Xerox, 364

Y

yet, 249